The Self

McGraw-Hill Series in Social Psychology

CONSULTING EDITOR, Philip G. Zimbardo

The Self

Jonathon D. Brown
University of Washington

Boston, Massachusetts   Burr Ridge, Illinois   Dubuque, Iowa
Madison, Wisconsin   New York, New York   San Francisco, California   St. Louis, Missouri

McGraw-Hill

A Division of The **McGraw·Hill** Companies

THE SELF

Copyright © 1998 by The McGraw-Hill Companies, Inc. All rights reserved.
Printed in the United States of America. Except as permitted under the United
States Copyright Act of 1976, no part of this publication may be reproduced or
distributed in any form or by any means, or stored in a data base or retrieval
system, without the prior written permission of the publisher.

This book is printed on acid-free paper.

2 3 4 5 7 8 9 0 QF/QF 9 0 9 8

ISBN 0-07-008306-1

Editorial director: *Jane Vaicunas*
Sponsoring editor: *Mickey Cox*
Editorial coordinator: *Ralph Adams*
Marketing manager: *Jim Rosa*
Project manager: *Jim Labeots*
Production supervisor: *Heather D. Burbridge*
Designer: *Michael Warrell*
Compositor: *Shepherd Inc.*
Typeface: *10/12 Palatino*
Printer: *Quebecor Printing Book Group/Fairfield*

Library of Congress Cataloging-in-Publication Data

Brown, Jonathon D.
  The self / Jonathon D. Brown.
    p. cm.
  Includes bibliographical references and index.
  ISBN 0-07-008306-1 (alk. paper)
    1. Self.   2. Self psychology.   I. Title.
  BF697.B758   1998
  155.2—dc21   97-1298

http://www.mhcollege.com

To Sheri, Jacob, and Adam, for sharing yourselves with me.
May you stay forever young.
—Bob Dylan
Forever Young, published by Ram's Horn Music (1973, 1985)

About the Author

JONATHON D. BROWN is Associate Professor of Psychology at the University of Washington. He received his Ph.D. from UCLA in 1986. He has written and published numerous articles and chapters on the self, and is the recipient of a Presidential Young Investigator Award from the National Science Foundation. He is currently interested in understanding how self-esteem influences people's responses to success and failure. In his spare time, he aggravates himself playing tennis.

Preface

Few topics engage our attention more completely than the way we think and feel about ourselves. For centuries, people have wondered how these thoughts and feelings develop, what role they play in guiding behavior, and how or even if they can be changed to yield greater happiness and satisfaction.

Many psychology students are also interested in issues of this nature. Unfortunately, their curiosity is not always satisfied by the courses they take. Instead of learning about themselves, they learn rather isolated bits and pieces of a person in various classes. They are left to their own devices when it comes to assembling these pieces into a unified whole.

This book attempts to address (and redress) this gap. Its topic is the psychological study of the self, defined as the study of the way people think and feel about themselves. It is, I think, a unique book. Specialty books on the self have been written, but no textbook on the topic currently exists. This omission is lamentable, because the self appeals to a wide range of scholars. Personality and social psychologists are especially interested in the self, but developmental, cognitive, motivational, and clinical psychologists also research this topic. The self is also a vibrant topic of study within the fields of sociology, philosophy, and anthropology. This text reviews these various perspectives, integrating them within a single volume.

This book is primarily intended for upper-level undergraduate classes and graduate courses in psychology, sociology, and related fields. In writing this book, I have sought to be comprehensive without being encyclopedic; accessible without being simplistic. The book can be used as a supplemental text (e.g., as a reader in a social psychology course) or as the primary text in a class devoted entirely to the study of the self.

For the last eight years, I have taught a course on the self at the University of Washington. It is my hope that many teachers will be inspired to develop such a course now that a suitable textbook is available. Finally, this book should also prove useful as a sourcebook to my colleagues who are interested in the study of the self.

Jonathon D. Brown

Acknowledgments

Writing a book on "The Self" sounds like a solitary endeavor, but many people contributed their time and talents to making this book a reality. First, I would like to thank Richard Felson, Rich Gonzales, David Kenny, Michael Kernis, Shawn McNulty, James Shepperd, and Bill Swann for sharing research findings and ideas with me. Connie Hammen, Darrin Lehman, Barry Schlenker, Shelley Taylor, and Bernard Weiner also read and commented on various chapters of this book, and I am grateful for their input. This book also benefited greatly from the thoughtful comments of several anonymous reviewers. Many students also helped me write this book. I am especially grateful to Sandra Barnat, Kathleen Cook, Keith Dutton, and Margaret Marshall for helping me track down and digest countless articles and books, or by helping me clarify what I had written.

I would also like to thank the staff at McGraw-Hill for their help and support. I have particularly appreciated the efforts of Ralph Adams, Susan Elia, Jim Labeots, and Brian McKean.

Finally, I thank my mother; and my late father, who often asked "But do you *make* anything?" Here you go, Dad, I made a book.

Foreword

There are few topics or concepts in psychology that have been on a more bumpy, circuitous ride over the past century than that of The Self. At first, William James invited it to have a seat up front with him. Then it moved to the back seat as other more easily manipulated or experimentally modifiable concepts were explored. But then it got dumped out of psychology's vehicle altogether when the Behaviorists disowned any connection with such fuzzy stuff that was not grounded in readily observable responses. Personality psychologists picked up this tireless hitchhiker and let it ride along with clinically-related passengers. But paradoxically, it remained for a new driver, Social Psychology, to invite The Self back up front to where the action is. Although social psychology has been traditionally focused on interpersonal relationships—from dyads to groups—the cognitive revolution in psychology has had the effect of refocusing some social psychology on intrapsychic processes. And what is both more individual and central to interpersonal relationships than The Self?

So in recent years, The Self has been brought right up front again, in fact, this time in the driver's seat, in some new and innovative theorizing by social psychologists. Their investigations are illuminating issues such as self-regulation, self-esteem, self-monitoring, self-centered biased thinking, stereotypes, dissonance, and even the role of cultural forces in shaping conceptions of The Self.

This book carefully documents these changing conceptions and the value accorded The Self in psychology over time. But it then goes much further in outlining the many alternative conceptions of this increasingly central domain in social psychological thinking. New research and conceptions are juxtaposed with the classic and traditional. Relationships between self-conceptions and a host of interesting phenomena are illuminated through well-chosen research investigations and a broad-based scholarship that spans many domains of knowledge. The author has created a text that has something vital for readers with quite varied backgrounds and levels of expertise.

More advanced readers and psychologists generally familiar with the field of research that forms the domain of "Self research," will be pleased to discover that many of Jonathon Brown's topics and treatments of core material that we often find dry, and sometimes even dull, in their original formulation, come to life and become intellectually stimulating in his skilled hands. Indeed, many professional reviewers of this text have been so inspired by the exciting and innovative ways the author has organized and presented traditional material, that they now plan to develop new courses around this book.

Students of social psychology and of personality psychology who come to this book fresh, without that prior bias of knowing too much of the previous Self literature, will be intrigued to find out that many of the basic questions they have about human nature are answered here. Among the primary motivations for students to take psychology courses is their curiosity about who they are, how they have come to think and react as they do to other people and their environments. They want to know how to best "know thyself," and how to regulate their emotions and behavior to achieve desired goals. They ask questions of psychology such as, why are some people pessimistic and depressed, while others are optimistic and resilient in the face of stress or even failure, what is self-esteem, and why do other people see the world so differently than I do? These concerns are addressed by the author in a style that lays out complex ideas in a "reader friendly," accessible style that is long on interest and short on jargon.

But all readers can depend upon getting a unique blend of ideas about The Self from philosophy, sociology, and psychology, freshly prepared, rigorously researched, and captivatingly presented. Jonathon Brown's gift to us can be used as a supplement to social psychology or personality psychology courses, as well as the core text in a full course on The Self. In both cases, readers will come away from the table satisfied that they have had a feast that was "worth the detour," as Michelin restaurant guides say of only the best.

The **McGraw-Hill Series in Social Psychology** has been designed to celebrate the significant contributions being made by researchers, theorists, and practitioners of social psychology in understanding the social nature of the Human Condition. Their body of work holds the potential of enriching the quality of our lives through wise applications of their knowledge. This series of texts has become a showcase for presenting new theories, original syntheses, creative analyses, and current methodologies by some of the most distinguished scholars in our field. Our authors reveal a common commitment to sharing their vision and expertise with a broad audience ranging from their colleagues to graduate students, and especially to undergraduates with an interest in social psychology. Each of our authors has been guided by the objective of conveying the essential lessons and principles of his or her area of expertise in an interesting style, one that informs without resorting to technical jargon, and that inspires others to utilize these ideas at conceptual or practical levels. This book clearly achieves both objectives. It is the best current statement about the nature of The Self based on a deep understanding of basic social psychological processes, and its clearly delivered message will be appreciated by scholars and students alike.

Although each text in our series is created to stand alone as the best representative of its domain of scholarship, taken as a whole, they represent the core of social psychology. Teachers may elect to use any of these texts as "in-depth" supplements to a general textbook, or ideally, paired with the briefer overview of social psychology found in David Myers' text, **Exploring Social Psychology,** eloquently written text for our series. Some teachers have organized their social psychology course entirely around a judicious selection of these monographs, thereby providing students with a richer background that they integrate through their lectures. In either case, Jonathon Brown's original contribution to our understanding of this most basic aspect of human nature is the book for you.

Philip G. Zimbardo, Series Editor
Stanford University

Contents

CHAPTER 1

Introduction

By the slimmest of margins, the citizens of Quebec voted recently not to secede from Canada. Although the referendum failed, over 60 percent of French-speaking Quebeckers voted for separation, despite evidence that secession would bring economic, political, and social instability. What fuels such intense devotion to ethnic identity? Why would people be willing to risk so much for the chance of establishing a separate French-speaking country?

Naturally, there are many answers to these questions, including years of anger at the British stemming from the battles on the Plains of Abraham. But there is a more psychological issue involved as well. Many French Canadians are concerned that their French identity is being compromised by the dominant Anglo culture they see encroaching upon them. They want to retain their identity, even if doing so entails sacrifice and strife. In short, they want to think of themselves as French.

In a general sense, this book is concerned with understanding issues of this sort. It is concerned with understanding how people think and feel about themselves, how they *want* to think and feel about themselves, and how these thoughts and feelings develop and guide behavior. Questions like these are among the most interesting and important ones we can ask in our struggle to understand who we are. Questions like these form the heart of a psychological analysis of the self.

Chapter 1 is designed to acquaint you with the way psychologists study the self. In the first section of the chapter, we will define our terms and examine how the study of the self fits in with other areas of psychology.

The second section of this chapter places the study of self in a historical context. Here we will see that most American psychologists ignored the study of the self for many years. This neglect occurred because the behaviorist movement (which ruled American psychology) believed that people's thoughts and feelings about themselves were too subjective and too unimportant to study. Ultimately, various developments led psychologists to reconsider their opposition to the study of the self, and the self returned as an important topic of psychological inquiry.

1

The final section of this chapter previews the rest of this book, highlighting the many areas of psychology that now include a consideration of the self. Of course, psychologists are not the only ones who study the self. Philosophers, theologians, cultural anthropologists, and sociologists also consider such matters. Poets and novelists, too, explore the essence of selfhood, and numerous works on the topic can be found in libraries and bookstores. Although we will draw on many of these perspectives throughout this book, our emphasis will be on theoretically derived and empirically tested ideas regarding the nature of the self. Particular attention will be paid to the work of personality and social psychologists, as these researchers have actively studied the self in recent years.

WHAT PSYCHOLOGISTS MEAN BY SELF

> . . . self-awareness is . . . most illusive. You . . . find yourself as between the two mirrors of a barber-shop, with each image viewing each other one, so that as the self takes a look at itself taking a look at itself, it soon gets all confused as to the self that is doing the looking and the self which is being looked at. (Hilgard, 1949, p. 377)

The I and the ME

We'll begin by noting that the self has a unique quality, a quality we will refer to as a *reflexive* property. Consider the statement "I see Pat." The self is implicated in this statement by the use of the personal pronoun *I*. *I* am doing the seeing. Now consider the statement "I see me." Here, the self is implicated in two ways. I am still the one doing the seeing, and the thing I am seeing is *ME*. In more formal terms, we can say that people are able to take themselves as an object of their own attention. They look back on themselves, much as when they see their reflection in a mirror (hence the use of the word *reflexive*).

William James (1890) was one of the first psychologists to recognize this duality. He recommended using different terms, the *I* and the *ME*, as a means of distinguishing between these two aspects of the self. Following his suggestion, we will use the term *I* to refer to that aspect of self that is actively perceiving, thinking, or in our example above, seeing. We will use the term *ME* to refer to that aspect of self that is an object of our attention, thought, or perception. When I say "I see Pat," only the *I* is implicated. When I say "I see me," both uses of the term are implicated. I am doing the seeing, and what I see is me.

Defined in this manner, it might seem as if the *I* is synonymous with all basic psychological processes (e.g., perception, sensation, thought). This is not really so. It is not these processes, per se, but our subjective awareness of them that comprises the *I*. The *I* refers to our *awareness* that we are thinking or our *awareness* that we are perceiving, rather than to the physical or psychical processes themselves.

The *ME* is also very much a subjective, psychological phenomenon. As we use the term, the *ME* refers to people's ideas about who they are and what they are like. For example, I think I am athletic and I think I am impatient. Psychologists call these beliefs *self-referent thoughts.* Self-referent thoughts are simply thoughts that refer to oneself. They are people's ideas about what they are like. A variety of terms have been used to refer to these beliefs, including self-views, self-images, identities, and self-conceptions. For our purposes, these terms are interchangeable; they all refer to people's ideas about who they are or what they are like.

In addition to having thoughts about themselves, people also have feelings toward themselves. I may like myself as a person or feel bad about my perceived impatience. These are both examples of self-referent feelings— feelings that refer to oneself.

Psychologists generally use different terms to refer to these two aspects of the *ME.* The term *self-concept* refers to the way people characteristically *think* about themselves; the term *self-esteem* refers to the way people characteristically *feel* about themselves. The term *self* is used more broadly. It refers not only to how we think and feel about ourselves but also to processes we earlier identified as being aspects of the *I* (e.g., our awareness of our thinking and perceiving).

Although the *I* and the *ME* are both important aspects of the self, psychologists are most concerned with understanding the nature of the *ME.* They focus on how people think and feel *about themselves,* and how these thoughts and feelings develop and affect other aspects of psychological life. Philosophers, on the other hand, tend to be more concerned with understanding the nature of the *I.* They have sought to understand that aspect of self that seems to directly experience the world. We will have an opportunity to consider both approaches in this book, but we will devote most of our attention to understanding the nature of the *ME.*

Self-Psychology and Personality

A focus on the way people think and feel about themselves distinguishes self-psychology from other areas of psychology. One of these areas is personality psychology. Self-psychology is concerned with subjective experience (with what people *think* they are like); personality psychology is more concerned with objective experience (with what people are *actually* like).

To illustrate this distinction, let's reconsider my belief that I'm athletic. This is a self-referent thought—a belief I hold about what I am like. Whether or not I am athletic is an entirely different matter. Unfortunately, thinking I'm athletic doesn't necessarily make it so. If you saw me on a tennis court, you might not agree. The larger point here is that self-psychology is concerned with our *picture* of the self—our ideas about what we are like (Rosenberg, 1979). But our pictures may not be entirely accurate; they may not capture what we are really like.

In this book, we will think of personality psychology as the study of what people are *actually* like. Rather than focusing on people's ideas about themselves—which is the domain of self-psychology—personality psychology is concerned with what people are really like. It would not be uncommon, for example, to hear someone say "Jack *is* an extrovert" or "Jill *is* conscientious." These phrases suggest that we are referring to what the person is truly like, not simply to what the person thinks he or she is like.

Having said this, it should be noted that the distinction between self-psychology and personality psychology blurs. There are at least four reasons for this (McCrae & Costa, 1988).

1. **What we really are influences how we *think* about ourselves.** First, aspects of personality affect our *thoughts* about ourselves. In theory, people are free to think whatever they want about themselves. But in reality, people's ideas about what they are like are usually at least loosely tied to objective criteria. People with low intelligence—a personality characteristic—are unlikely to regard themselves as brilliant. It can happen, but it's unlikely. Similarly, people who are seven feet tall are unlikely to think of themselves as short. Again, it can happen, but it's unlikely. These examples show that although no one is born with a conception of the self as unintelligent or tall, people are born with certain physical and psychological characteristics that influence how they think about themselves.

    This is not to say that our thoughts about ourselves are identical with what we are actually like. All of us know people who think they are smarter than they are (or at least smarter than we think they are). We've also met people who strike us as obnoxious yet regard themselves as the greatest thing since sliced bread. Throughout this book we will see that although people's views of themselves are influenced by what they are really like, they are not faithful representations of their true characteristics. Most people think of themselves in overly positive terms—as somewhat better than what they are really like.

2. **What we really are influences how we *feel* about ourselves.** Another way in which self-psychology and personality are related is that personality affects how we *feel* about ourselves. Some important aspects of personality are inherited. For example, temperament refers to a person's general activity level and usual mood. This is an inheritable characteristic: From the moment they are born, some infants are more emotionally distressed than are other infants (Kagan, 1989). This personality variable influences self-esteem. People who are prone to experience negative emotions tend to feel more negatively about themselves (Watson & Clark, 1984). After all, it's hard to feel good about yourself when you're agitated or sad all the time. In this manner, a personality variable, temperament, can influence self-esteem.

3. **Self is one aspect of personality.** A third intersection between self-psychology and personality is that people's thoughts and feelings about themselves are one aspect of their personality. For example, some people think of themselves as attractive; other people think of themselves as unattractive. Although these thoughts don't tell us whether these people really are attractive or not, it is still the case that the people differ with respect to what they think they are like. These individual differences can be treated as personality variables.

We can also distinguish people according to how they feel about themselves. This is self-esteem research. Self-esteem research divides people into two categories: Those who feel good about themselves are designated as having high self-esteem; those who do not feel as good about themselves are designated as having low self-esteem. In this manner, individual differences in how people feel about themselves are treated as personality variables.

When we treat self-referent thoughts and feelings as individual difference variables, we are treating the self as one aspect of personality. In this sense, personality is a broader term that refers to the entire psychological nature of the individual (McCrae & Costa, 1988). Self-referent thoughts and feelings are a subset of personality.

4. **Self-report is often used to measure personality.** A fourth way in which self-psychology and personality are related is that personality researchers often use self-report to assess personality. Many personality tests ask people to indicate what they think they are like. For example, a test of extraversion might ask people "How sociable are you?" or "How shy are you?" Strictly speaking, tests like these are measuring people's ideas about what they are like, not what they are actually like.

To summarize, self-psychology and personality represent distinct, though related, approaches. Self-psychology is concerned with what people think they are like; personality psychology is concerned with what people are really or actually like. But the line between these two perspectives is often blurred.

When comparing self-psychology and personality, then, the question is really one of emphasis. Self-theorists believe that the psychological action resides at the level of the self, particularly when it comes to predicting freely chosen behavior. The individual who thinks she has a great wit and a keen sense of humor will be the one at the party telling story after story; this will be the case even though others may not be the least bit enamored with her repartee. As another example, consider the bright individual who, for whatever reason, doubts his ability. Despite the fact that the person is smart by some objective criteria, he may fail to excel in school because of the self-defeating belief that he lacks ability. The larger point is that people's beliefs about themselves sometimes clash with what they are really like. When this occurs, self-theorists believe that people's thoughts and feelings about themselves determine their behavior.

Self-Psychology and Phenomenology

In addition to considering the overlap between self-psychology and personality psychology, we can also examine the relation between self-psychology and a philosophical school of thought known as phenomenology (Schutz, 1972). The word *phenomenology* has its origins in the Greek word *phainesthai*, which means "to appear so" (Burns, 1979). Phenomenology is concerned with people's perception of reality, with the way the world appears to the individual. Phenomenology holds that it is these subjective perceptions, rather than the objective world itself, that govern our psychological lives.

The phenomenological approach is represented within Gestalt theories of perception. The Gestalt psychologists argued that the psychological world of the individual is not the same as the physical world (Wertheimer, 1912). To illustrate this point, let's examine an optical illusion you've probably seen before. Consider these two lines. Which is longer?

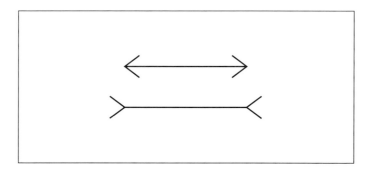

In actuality, the lines are the same length. But the second line appears longer. Now imagine that these are two chocolate bars and you ask children which one they prefer. The chances are good that even though the two lines *are* the same, the children will prefer the line that *appears* longer. What if the two lines are lines of broccoli? Now which one will most children prefer?

This is what phenomenology is all about. It says two things: (1) what we perceive is not necessarily the same as what exists in the external world, and (2) our behavior depends more on the world as it appears than on the world as it actually exists. Kurt Lewin, an influential motivational and social psychologist, framed the issue as follows:

> If an individual sits in a room trusting that the ceiling will not come down, should only his "subjective probability" be taken into account for predicting behavior or should we also consider the "objective probability" of the ceiling's coming down as determined by the engineers? To my mind, only the first has to be taken into account. (Lewin, 1951, p. 58)

Lewin's point is not that the objective world is unimportant. The objective world is important, but only insofar as it influences people's subjective perceptions. This is the essence of the phenomenological perspective. Phenomenologists emphasize that behavior depends on the perceived world—the world as it appears, rather than the world as it actually is.

An emphasis on how things seem rather than on what they are is reminiscent of the distinction we have drawn between self-psychology and personality. Self-psychology is phenomenological. It is concerned with people's perceptions or beliefs about what they are like, more than with what they are actually like. For the self-theorist, behavior often depends more on your beliefs about yourself than on what you really are like.

As a final, albeit extreme, illustration of this point, consider anorexia. The anorexic believes she is overweight and starves herself in an effort to lose weight. Even though by objective criteria she is thin, she acts as if she is fat because that's how she sees herself.

THE STUDY OF SELF IN AMERICAN PSYCHOLOGY

> One of the oddest events in the history of modern psychology is the manner in which the ego (or self) became sidetracked and lost to view. (Allport, 1943, p. 451)

Considering how important people's thoughts and feelings about themselves are in psychological life, you might think that the field of psychology has always been interested in the self. This is not so. Although William James gave the topic extended treatment in a landmark textbook written at the end of the nineteenth century (James, 1890), most American psychologists completely ignored the study of self during psychology's formative years. Only in the second half of this century has the self been restored to legitimacy as an object of scientific and psychological inquiry.

The Behaviorist Movement in American Psychology

To understand this state of affairs, we need to become familiar with the behaviorist movement in American psychology. For nearly 40 years (roughly 1915–1955), American psychology was ruled by behaviorism. The movement was founded by the American psychologist John Watson. Watson (1913) had become dissatisfied with the subjective nature of turn-of-the-century American psychology. Introspectionism was the dominant school of psychology at that time. The hallmark of the introspectionist movement was a systematic analysis of consciousness. The introspectionists would expose individuals to various stimuli (e.g., beeswax) and have them describe, in as small detail as possible, their subjective experience. The introspectionists would then take these reports and attempt to distill the basic elements of sensation. For example, Wundt, a founder of the introspectionist movement, concluded on the basis of his research that there were four elementary taste sensations: sweet, sour, bitter, and salty. All other tastes were regarded as combinations of these. In a similar manner, four elementary skin sensations were discovered: warmth, cold, pain, and pressure. All other sensations of touch were regarded as blends of these four (Woodworth, 1948).

Watson objected to this emphasis on private, subjective perception. He noted that people disagree on what they see, hear, smell, taste, and feel, and there is no way to resolve these disagreements. Watson argued that in order for psychology to take its place as an independent science, it must abandon the study of private, mental phenomena, and focus instead on the study of overt behavior. Writing with the conviction of a zealot, Watson (1913) spelled out his vision of psychology:

> Psychology, as the behaviorist views it, (a) is a purely objective experimental branch of natural science; (b) its theoretical goal is the prediction and control

of behavior; (c) introspection forms no essential part of its methods; and (d) it recognizes no dividing line between man and brute. (Watson, 1913, p. 158)

Two Central Assumptions of the Behaviorist Movement: Positivism and Mechanism

Ultimately, the behaviorist movement received its most influential and articulate treatment from two other American psychologists, B. F. Skinner and Clark Hull. The behaviorism of these psychologists was guided by two central assumptions. The first assumption is known as the doctrine of *positivism*. This is a methodological doctrine that maintains that only phenomena that can be concretely measured and verified by impartial observers are suitable for scientific analysis. The term comes from Auguste Comte (1798–1857). For Comte, positive meant observable and undebatable, not inferential or speculative (Boring, 1957).

The behaviorist movement also adopted the doctrine of *mechanism*. Mechanism is an assumption about the nature of psychological life. It asserts that thoughts play no role in directing behavior. Instead, behavior is assumed to be the function of simple stimulus–response bonds.[1] To illustrate, we might train a pigeon to peck at a particular pattern by giving the pigeon food whenever it pecks in the presence of the pattern. Over time, the pigeon comes to emit the behavior with greater and greater frequency when the stimulus is presented. According to the behaviorist, this occurs because the food (the reinforcer) strengthens the associative bonds between the pattern (the stimulus) and the pecking behavior (the response).

Mechanists view the relation between stimuli and responses as direct and immediate. Mental processes, except those pertaining to noticing or registering the stimulus itself, are regarded as entirely superfluous to understanding behavior. Another way of saying this is that these theorists believe behavior can be fully understood without considering mental processes. Pigeons (and people) behave as they do simply because certain responses have become attached or conditioned to certain environmental stimuli.

Positivism, Mechanism, and Self-Psychology

The positivistic and mechanistic leanings of the behaviorist movement led its advocates to disregard the study of the self. Let's look first at how the doctrine of positivism fits with the study of self. As applied to psychology, positivism holds that only concrete phenomena that can be objectively verified are admissible for psychological study. This rules out the self. The self cannot be directly observed; it is not a physical entity like an arm or a leg or a brain. It is by definition mental, and its measurement is inherently subjective. Subjectivity was anathema to the positivists. Anything that did not have a physical basis was not to be studied. This excluded the self; it also excluded the study of emotions, fantasies, dreams, and other important psychological phenomena.

---

[1]The term *mechanism* derives from the characterization of behavior as being rather machine-like or mechanical in nature.

The second problem the behaviorists had with the study of the self was even more fundamental than the measurement issue. This issue pertained to the explanatory value of the self. The behaviorists argued that even if the self could be objectively measured, it would be of only limited value to psychology. This is because the behaviorists were mechanists; they believed that environmental stimuli directly evoke behavioral responses. Intervening mental processes, like people's thoughts about themselves, were regarded as unnecessary to predict and understand behavior.

This is not to say that these thoughts didn't occur. As people, behaviorists realized they had thoughts (and feelings) about themselves. But they did not believe these thoughts and feelings influenced their behavior. They regarded these thoughts and feelings as epiphenomenal (epiphenomenal means "above the phenomena," or not directly part of the phenomena). From this perspective, even if we could objectively assess people's thoughts and feelings about themselves, there wouldn't be any point in doing so. It would not improve our understanding or prediction of behavior.

The doctrine of mechanism contrasts most sharply with what is known as a purposive or goal-directed analysis of behavior. According to a purposive model, behaviors are undertaken in order to achieve some goal (that is, they are undertaken for a purpose). An organism wants some object or end-state and takes steps to secure or attain it. This emphasis on goal-directed (or purposive) behavior is completely absent in mechanistic accounts of behavior.

To illustrate these differences, consider a person who thinks, "I'm hungry. I want something to eat," and then walks to the refrigerator and takes out some food. A purposive analysis of behavior would maintain that the thoughts "I'm hungry" and "I want something to eat" led the person to walk toward the refrigerator to get food. The behaviorists would disagree. They would contend that these thoughts did not initiate the behavior (i.e., that the thoughts were epiphenomenal). The person walked to the refrigerator simply because that is where the person has found food when hunger arose in the past.

Mechanism and Darwin's Theory of Natural Selection

Mechanism closely parallels Darwin's theory of natural selection. The process of natural selection is not a purposive one. Random variations occur among individual members of species. Some of these variations prove adaptive: They help the organism to survive and reproduce, and so they are selected for and endure. Thus, although natural selection is an active process, it is not one that is goal directed. The amphibians didn't think, "Gee, if only I could figure out how to lay eggs on land, I could become a reptile!" Instead, through random variation, some amphibians laid eggs with tougher shells. As the earth gradually warmed and became drier, these eggs had a selective advantage. Ultimately, these animals evolved into reptiles. The entire process is one of blind chance, not purposive. In the words of Solomon Asch (1952) "natural selection . . . produces without purpose the same result that would have been produced had a purposive agent been at work" (p. 97).

The mechanistic view of behavior is very similar to the process of natural selection (Skinner, 1990). Just as the theory of natural selection maintains that *physical characteristics* are shaped by their adaptive consequences, mechanism holds that *behavior* is shaped by its adaptive consequences. Behaviors that meet with reinforcement are strengthened or repeated; those that do not meet with reinforcement are weakened and extinguished. Just as laying eggs on land might prove adaptive, be selected for, and endure, so, too, do some behaviors prove adaptive and come to be part of the animals' repertoire.

Mechanism and Thorndike's Law of Effect

The application of this principle in psychology is best illustrated in Thorndike's (1911) analysis of instrumental learning. Working in the basement of William James's house, Thorndike placed various animals, usually cats or chicks, in an enclosed box. Food was placed outside the box. When the animal made a response that Thorndike had arbitrarily designated to be the correct one, the animal was allowed to escape the box and consume the food.

At first, Thorndike notes, the animal engages in relatively random behavior (these random movements are conceptually akin to the random mutations or variations that occur within members of species). At some point, the animal happens to make the response arbitrarily chosen by Thorndike to be the correct one. The door to the puzzle box is then opened and the animal is allowed to leave the box and consume the food. When the animal is later returned to the box, it tends to emit the *correct* response sooner than in the initial trial. After many such trials, the animal comes to emit the response immediately upon being placed in the box.

The behaviorist analyzes this behavior in terms of stimulus–response bonds. The reinforcing properties of the food cause the behavior (the response) to become associated with or attached to the puzzle box (the stimulus). When the animal is returned to the box, it emits whatever behavior has been most closely associated with the cues in the environment. In this case, this response is the one Thorndike had earlier labeled as the correct response.

It is important to note that, according to the behaviorist, the animal never makes the correct movements *in order* to get out of the box or *in order* to get the food. That would be too goal oriented or purposive. Instead, the animal makes the correct response simply because that behavior, more than all others, has come to be most firmly connected to the stimuli in the box via the reinforcing properties of the food. Thorndike (1911) described the process this way:

> The process involved in the learning was evidently a process of selection. The animal is confronted by a state of affairs or, as we may call it, a "situation." He reacts in the way that he is moved by innate nature or previous training to do, by a number of acts. These acts include the particular act that is appropriate and he succeeds. In later trials the impulse to this one act is more and more stamped in. . . . The profitless acts are stamped out. . . . So the animal finally performs in that situation only the fitting act. Here we have the simplest and at the same time the most widespread sort of intellect or learning in the world. There is no reasoning, no process of inference or comparison; there is

no thinking about things, no putting two and two together; there are no ideas—the animal does not think of the box or of the food or of the act he is to perform. (Thorndike, 1991, pp. 283–284)

Formally, this process of learning is known as the *law of effect*. According to the law of effect, behavior is ruled by the past—the effect it has had or the reinforcement it has met with in the past. It is not governed or even influenced by what is expected to happen in the future. That is why this is a nonpurposive view of behavior.

The behaviorists applied these principles to a wide range of behaviors, extending far beyond relatively simple acts like escaping a puzzle box. Through processes of association, stimulus–response bonds were presumed to govern very complex behaviors. By way of example, imagine that a person is just about to graduate from high school and thinks to herself, "I think it's important to be an educated person." She then sends out applications for admission to college. According to the behaviorist, her decision to attend college has nothing whatsoever to do with her beliefs about the person she wants to be, or even her ideas about the importance of a college education. She undertakes the behavior simply because she has been reinforced for this (or other highly similar) behaviors in the past. Her behavior is merely a learned response to a stimulus; her beliefs about herself, entirely epiphenomenal.

It is important to fully appreciate the impact these assumptions hold for a psychology of the self. Mechanism represents a far more fundamental aspect of behaviorism than does positivism. It argues that even if thoughts could be adequately measured, even if we could develop methodologies that would allow us to quantify mental experience in such a way that objective observers could agree on what is occurring, in short, even if thoughts could be admissible as scientific constructs, nothing important would be gained. Thoughts do not influence behavior, so they are superfluous. These assumptions ruled American psychology for more than half a century and led American psychologists to treat the self as a *persona non grata*.

> In face-to-face contact with another person, references to an initiating self are unavoidable. There is a "you" and there is an "I." I see what "you" do and hear what "you" say and you see what "I" do and hear what "I" say. We do not see the histories of selection responsible for what is done and therefore infer an internal origination, but the successful use of vernacular in the practice of psychology offers no support for its use in a science. In a scientific analysis, histories of variation and selection play the role of the initiator. There is no place in a scientific analysis of behavior for a mind or self. (Skinner, 1990, p. 1209)

The Decline of Behaviorism and the Return of the Self

Theorists Who Kept the Study of Self Alive

Despite behaviorism's dominance, not all theorists ignored the self during the first half of the twentieth century. Two American sociologists, Cooley (1902) and Mead (1934), undertook theoretical analyses of the self, including the important role it plays in the socialization process. We will cover their theories in Chapters 3 and 4.

Other psychologists, operating somewhat out of the orthodoxy of academic psychology, also retained an interest in the self. Some (e.g., Allport, 1943; Goldstein, 1940; Lecky, 1945; Rogers, 1951; Snygg & Combs, 1949) objected to the passive and disjointed portrait behaviorism painted of the individual. They argued that human behavior is not mechanically driven by the past but is actively oriented toward the future. People seek growth and challenge; their psychological lives exhibit activity and coherence and are governed by a unifying principle. They referred to this principle as self-actualization—a desire for a person to "become everything that one is capable of becoming" (Maslow, 1970, p. 46).

Self-relevant phenomena were also studied by a group of clinical psychologists. These theorists (e.g., Erikson, 1956; Sullivan, 1953) had become disenchanted with their training in psychoanalytic (Freudian) theory. Classical Freudian theory gave only passing attention to the self. Although the term *ego* is often used interchangeably with the self, this is not really warranted. For Freud, the ego consists of a set of mental processes (e.g., thinking, remembering, reasoning) that function to mediate between the inexorable demands of the id and the uncompromising rectitude of the superego. People's thoughts and feelings about themselves are only one aspect of the ego.

Ego processes did, however, play a role in the study of self. Their entry occurred with respect to the so-called ego-defense mechanisms or mechanisms of defense. Freud and his followers identified a set of psychological processes (e.g., rationalization, projection, identification, reaction formation) that function to insulate the individual from psychological pain. Oftentimes, these processes shield people from acknowledging unflattering truths about themselves. For example, people use rationalization to avoid thinking of themselves as someone who behaved in a negative manner or brought about a negative outcome. The use of this mechanism implies a self-image one is attempting to defend or protect (Hilgard, 1949).

Experimental Findings

In addition to these theoretical statements, several experimental findings highlighted the important role of mental processes, including ones that implicated the self. The most notable of these for our purposes was research on level of aspiration. This work was carried out by Kurt Lewin and his colleagues during the 1940s (Lewin, Dembo, Festinger, & Sears, 1944). Level of aspiration refers to a standard of performance people set for themselves when undertaking an achievement-oriented activity.

A ring toss provides a suitable example. Imagine that you are a participant in a typical experiment. Your task is to toss a ring over a peg. You are first given 10 practice trials to familiarize yourself with the task. Afterward, you are asked to indicate how many of the 10 rings you think you will throw over the peg on the next block of trials. You also decide how far away to stand from the peg; the farther the distance, the greater the difficulty. These judgments comprise your level of aspiration. This procedure is repeated after each block of 10 trials, allowing you to periodically adjust your aspiration level.

Imagine that on the first trial you anticipate tossing six rings over the peg from a distance of three feet. And in fact, that's just what you do. Now what will you do? If you are like most people, you will raise your aspiration level by making the game more difficult for yourself, either by increasing the number of tosses you expect to make ("this time I'll try for seven") or by moving back a step or two.

This sort of behavior is difficult to explain with reference only to mechanistic principles. Application of the law of effect suggests that you should merely repeat your prior performance; it has met with success (i.e., has been reinforced), so it should be repeated. Yet most people are not content to simply repeat their prior performance. Instead, they make the task increasingly more difficult for themselves until they reach a distance that is just far enough away to make the game challenging but not so far away as to make it impossible. The tendency for people to *avoid* repeating behaviors that have met with prior reinforcement runs counter to the law of effect and is therefore inconsistent with a mechanistic analysis of behavior. It suggests instead that people's behavior is purposive, guided by a desire to think favorably about their abilities and to experience feelings of pride.

> The law of effect would be truer if it held that a *person*, being rewarded, employs his past successes in whatever way he thinks is likely to bring him satisfaction in the future. . . . An individual's past performances often mean little or nothing to him. Only if the [self] would be served thereby, does he engage in a repetition of the successful act. (Allport, 1943, p. 468)

These and other findings led Allport (1943) to propose that there were two motivational systems. One, passively ruled by habit, instinct, and reflex; the other, actively guided by purpose, foresight, and volition.

> . . . [self]-involvement, or its absence, makes a critical difference in human behavior. When a person reacts in a neutral, impersonal, routine atmosphere, his behavior is one thing. But when he is behaving personally, perhaps excitedly, seriously committed to a task, he behaves quite differently. In the first condition his [self] is not engaged; in the second condition it is. (Allport, 1943, p. 122)

The Cognitive Revolution and the Study of Self

Twenty years after Allport offered his analysis, the grip of the behaviorist movement began to loosen. A new movement, known as the cognitive revolution, arose to take its place. The cognitive movement is diverse and has influenced every area of psychology. Its central assumption is that people (as well as lower animals) are not passive creatures who blindly respond to environmental stimuli. Instead, they are active organisms, capable of planning and initiating behaviors in order to achieve desired end-states. The emphasis is not solely on the past, as it is with behaviorism; it is on the present and the future.[2]

---

[2]This depiction of the cognitive movement does not mean that human behavior is always purposive and goal-directed. It is clear that people sometimes act out of habit and impulse. The cognitive revolution emphasizes only that behavior is *sometimes* thoughtful and goal-directed, not that it is always so.

The cognitive movement pays close attention to the internal, mental processes of the behaving organism. For this reason, it is quite compatible with the study of self. Self-relevant thoughts and feelings are one class of internal, mental processes that are relevant to a psychological analysis of behavior.

A willingness to treat the self as a legitimate topic of study led theorists to identify various functions of the self. Although there is not perfect agreement on the matter, six important functions of the self have been discussed. Three of these functions refer to an awareness of our own existence (i.e., the *I*); the other three refer to our ideas about what we are like (i.e., the *ME*).

The Functions of the *I*

First, our concept of self serves to differentiate or distinguish us from other objects and people. When we hit the table with a hammer we feel no pain; when we hit our thumb with a hammer it is quite a different matter. This distinction is an important one to master! As we will see in Chapter 4, making this distinction is a first step in forming a concept of self.

A concept of self also serves a motivational or volitional function. The realization that one is separate from other things and people is accompanied by the realization that one has control over some things but not others. We realize that we can't will the table to get up and move, but we can will ourselves to get up and move. Understanding what we can control and what we can't control is another important developmental milestone we will discuss in Chapter 4.

Finally, a concept of self also provides us with a sense of continuity and unity. I know I am the same person who sat here a few days ago because I possess a concept of self. Without such a concept, I would experience myself anew each day. I would awaken and ask myself: "Who is this guy?" In a similar vein, our concept of self provides unity to our psychological life. We perceive our various thoughts and perceptions as joined rather than fragmented. It is our sense of self that ties these experiences together. We will consider this function of the *I* at length in Chapter 2.

The Functions of the *ME*

In addition to considering three functions of the *I*, we can also consider three functions of the *ME*. Here we are referring to people's ideas about what they are like.

First, people's thoughts about themselves serve an important cognitive function (Epstein, 1973; Kelly, 1963; Markus, 1977). They influence the way people process and interpret information. For example, people are especially apt to notice information that fits the way they think about themselves, and to process this information rapidly and efficiently (Markus, 1977). People also show better memory for information they relate to themselves (Rogers, Kuiper, & Kirker, 1977), particularly information that matches the way they characteristically think about themselves (Markus, 1977).

Second, people's ideas about themselves guide their behavior. A person who thinks of herself as artistic engages in artistic pursuits; a person who regards herself as stylish wears the latest fashions. In more general terms, we can say that many of the activities people pursue and the lifestyle decisions they make are affected by what they think about themselves (Niedenthal, Cantor, & Kihlstrom, 1985; Snyder, 1979; Swann, 1990).

Finally, self-conceptions serve a motivational function. Because people can project their identities across time, into the future, they can strive to think of themselves as becoming a certain person (Markus & Ruvolo, 1989). A student can enroll in graduate school with an eye toward becoming a professor. If the student didn't possess a concept of self, she wouldn't possess a concept of "me as a professor."

OVERVIEW OF TEXT

Self-relevant phenomena are currently implicated in virtually all areas of psychology; they are also of interest to sociologists, anthropologists, and philosophers as well. Take a moment to skim the chapters in this book, and you will see what I mean.

Chapter Previews

In Chapter 2 we examine the nature of the self. Here we will be concerned with understanding what people think of when they think of *ME*. In exploring this issue, we will draw on many areas of psychology (e.g., cognitive, social), as well as on the fields of sociology. We will also consider the nature of the *I* in the context of an ancient philosophical problem known as the problem of personal identity.

In Chapter 3 we will consider how people come to know who they are and what they are like. Many forces shape the acquisition of self-knowledge, including a desire to know what we are really like, a desire to feel good about who we are, and a need to maintain consistent and stable views of ourselves. Our discussion here will draw most heavily on research in contemporary social psychology and personality.

In Chapter 4 we explore how the self develops. The questions we will pose here include: How do people come to develop a conception of themselves, and how do people's thoughts about themselves change over time? Our discussion here draws on the fields of developmental psychology, sociology, and social psychology.

In Chapter 5 we will examine the self from a cognitive perspective. Here we will examine (1) how self-knowledge is represented in memory; (2) what factors determine which of our many self-views is active at any given time; and (3) how self-knowledge influences the way people process information.

In Chapter 6 we will approach the self from the perspective of motivational psychology. Here we will explore how self-relevant processes initiate and guide behavior. We will also examine how self-relevant processes can sometimes interfere with effective behavioral regulation.

In Chapter 7 we will investigate the self from a social psychological perspective. Here we will ask: How do people present themselves to others, and what effect do these presentations have on people's private thoughts and feelings?

Chapter 8 examines the self from the perspective of personality psychology. Our focus here will be on understanding the nature and functions of self-esteem. We will ask: What is the essence of self-esteem? How does it develop and what consequences does self-esteem have for psychological life?

In Chapter 9 we focus on clinical psychology, exploring the role self-relevant processes play in depression. We will examine how people think and feel about themselves when they are depressed and explore how self-relevant processes affect the development of depression and recovery from depression.

In Chapter 10 we will consider the relation between self-relevant processes and psychological and physical health. A key issue here will be the question of whether it's best to know what we are really like, or whether we are better served by thinking of ourselves in ways that are a bit better than what we are really like.

What Won't Be Covered

The preceding section previewed some of the many issues we will be covering in this book. I want to conclude this chapter by noting what won't be covered in this text. First, we will not study the self from a spiritual or mystical perspective. Many religions, particularly Eastern religions, emphasize self-awareness or the need to get *outside* of the self. These perspectives lie beyond the scope of contemporary psychology. This doesn't mean that they are unimportant, only that they are not part of the psychology of the self.

Our analysis will also focus on modern approaches to understanding the self, as viewed through the lens of a Western cultural background. People's ideas about themselves very much depend on when they are born and where they live. These ideas have changed enormously over the centuries, ranging from a concern with the supernatural to a preoccupation with distinctive psychological qualities (Baumeister, 1986; Cushman, 1990; Gergen, 1985; Sampson, 1985). Our review will emphasize the way people think about themselves in modern times. We will also concentrate on a view of the self that dominates in contemporary Western cultures, although we will have occasion to document cross-cultural differences when data permit.

CHAPTER SUMMARY

This chapter introduced you to a psychological analysis of the self. We began by distinguishing two ways in which the term *self* is used (the *I* and the *ME*). We then examined the fit between self-psychology and personality psychology, and the overlap between self-psychology and the phenomenological perspective.

Following this, we placed the study of self in a historical context. Behaviorism was the dominant movement during psychology's formative years. It was governed by two assumptions (positivism and mechanism) that led psychologists to ignore the study of the self for nearly 50 years. Ultimately, the behaviorist movement waned and the self was restored to legitimacy within the field of psychology, with virtually all areas of psychology currently interested in self-relevant phenomena.

We ended the chapter by indicating what the book will cover and by noting several topics that will be omitted.

- This book presents a psychological analysis of the self. Psychologists study how people think and feel about themselves, how they *want* to think and feel about themselves, and how these thoughts and feelings develop and guide behavior.
- The self is comprised of two, correlated, aspects: the *I* and the *ME*. The *I* refers to that aspect of self that is actively experiencing the world (e.g., perceiving, thinking, or feeling). The *ME* refers to that aspect of self that is an object of our attention, thought, or perception. The *I* is implicated in (virtually) everything we do; it is nearly always present in consciousness. The *ME* is not always part of our experience; we very often take other people and things as the object of our attention.
- The term *self-concept* refers to the way people characteristically *think* about themselves; the term *self-esteem* refers to the way people characteristically *feel* about themselves.
- Self-psychology is concerned with subjective experience (with what people *think* they are like); personality psychology is more concerned with objective experience (with what people are *actually* like). Despite these differences, self-psychology and personality share many similarities. This occurs because what people are really like influences how they think and feel about themselves, and because people's thoughts and feelings about themselves represent one aspect of their personality.
- Phenomenology is a school of thought that emphasizes that behavior is guided by the world "as it appears," rather than by the world "as it really is." Self-psychology is phenomenological. It emphasizes that behavior is often guided by people's ideas about what they are like, rather than by what they are really like. Anorexia provides a dramatic example. Although the anorexic is actually thin, she perceives herself as being overweight and starves herself in an attempt to lose weight.
- The self was an important part of American psychology in the late nineteenth century, but the rise of the behaviorist movement in the early part of the twentieth century led most psychologists to ignore the self. The behaviorist movement was guided by two central assumptions: positivism and mechanism. Positivism is a methodological doctrine that holds that only concrete phenomena that can be objectively measured by neutral observers are suitable for scientific study. This emphasis on objectivity excluded the study of the self, as the self is inherently a subjective, psychological phenomenon. Mechanism is a doctrine about the nature of psychological life. It holds that thoughts play no role whatsoever in guiding behavior. This assumption also excluded the study of the self, as it maintained that people's thoughts and feelings about themselves do not guide their behavior.
- The mechanistic position of the behaviorist movement contrasts most sharply with a purposive or goal-directed analysis of behavior. According to a purposive model, behaviors are undertaken for a purpose. An organism wants or desires some object or end-state and takes steps to secure it. This emphasis on goal-directed behavior or purposive behavior is absent in mechanistic accounts of behavior.
- Not all theorists ignored the self during the era when behaviorism reigned. Sociologists and numerous clinical psychologists maintained that people's self-referent thoughts and feelings were an important topic for psychological study. Several experimental findings also cast doubt on a strictly mechanistic analysis of behavior.

These developments allowed the self to be restored as a legitimate topic of psychological study.

- Several functions of the self were identified. The *I* refers to our awareness that we are a distinct and unified entity, continuous over time, and capable of willful action. The *ME* influences the processing of information, and guides present and future behavior.

For Further Reading

ALLPORT, G. W. (1943). The ego in contemporary psychology. *Psychological Review, 50,* 451–478.

BORING, E. G. (1951). *A history of experimental psychology.* New York: Appleton, Century, Crofts.

WOODWORTH, R. S. (1948). *Contemporary schools of psychology* (2nd ed.). New York: Ronald Press.

CHAPTER 2

The Nature of the Self

Former President Lyndon Johnson once described himself as "a free man, an American, a United States Senator, a Democrat, a liberal, a conservative, a Texan, a taxpayer, a rancher, and not as young as I used to be nor as old as I expect to be" (cited in Gergen, 1971). Although not everyone thinks of themselves in such varied terms, everyone has a wealth of self-knowledge. They have ideas about their physical qualities and abilities; their social roles; their opinions, talents, and personality traits; and more.

In this chapter, we will examine the nature of the self. Our analysis will rely heavily on the work of William James, who wrote extensively on the topic in chapter 10 of his 1890 publication *The Principles of Psychology*. James was a philosopher as well as a psychologist, and his work represents a stunning blend of conceptual synthesis, metaphorical analysis, and penetrating observation. More than a century after its appearance, this work stands as the premier publication in American psychology. All serious students of the self must begin by studying James; accordingly, that is where our analysis begins.

The first section of this chapter explores the nature of the *ME*. Here we will be concerned with understanding what people think of when they answer the question "Who am I?" We will see that many of the ideas William James discussed over 100 years ago still apply today. At the same time, we will see that recent research has extended and refined many of James's ideas.

The second section of this chapter examines the affective and motivational aspects of the self. James devoted considerable attention to understanding the nature of self-feelings and the behaviors these feelings evoke. We will discuss his ideas and also examine recent research that has looked at the relation between various self-views (e.g., who you think you *should* be) and self-feelings.

The final section of this chapter examines the nature of the *I*. For centuries philosophers have pondered a philosophical question known as the problem of personal identity. The key question here is whether there is some aspect of self that accounts for the perceived unity of psychological life. William James also addressed this issue, and we will examine his proposed solution. We will also review the solutions offered by two earlier philosophers, John Locke and David Hume, as their attempts to solve the problem of personal identity set the stage for James's analysis.

THE NATURE OF THE ME

We will begin by considering the nature of the *ME*. As indicated in Chapter 1, we use this term to refer to people's ideas about who they are and what they are like. Before reading further, take a moment to reflect on how you think about yourself by completing the questionnaire shown in Table 2.1.

TABLE 2.1. Self-Exercise #1

Imagine you want someone to know what you are really like. You can tell this person 20 things about yourself. These can include aspects of your personality, background, physical characteristics, hobbies, things you own, people you are close to, and so forth—in short, anything that helps the person know what you are really like. What would you tell them?

1._____

2._____

3._____

4._____

5._____

6._____

7._____

8._____

9._____

10._____

11._____

12._____

13._____

14._____

15._____

16._____

17._____

18._____

19._____

20._____

Three Components of the Empirical Self

William James used the term "the empirical self" to refer to all of the various ways people think about themselves. His analysis is very broad.[1]

> The Empirical Self of each of us is all that he is tempted to call by the name of *me*. But it is clear that between what a man calls *me* and what he simply calls *mine* the line is difficult to draw. We feel and act about certain things that are ours very much as we feel and act about ourselves. Our fame, our children, the work of our hands, may be as dear to us as our bodies are, and arouse the same feelings and the same acts of reprisal if attacked. And our bodies themselves, are they simply ours, or are they *us?* (p. 291)

James went on to group the various components of the empirical self into three subcategories: (1) the material self, (2) the social self, and (3) the spiritual self.

Material Self

The material self refers to tangible objects, people, or places that carry the designation *my* or *mine*. Two subclasses of the material self can be distinguished. These are the bodily self and the extracorporeal (beyond the body) self. Rosenberg (1979) has referred to the extracorporeal self as the extended self, and we will adopt this terminology throughout the book.

The bodily component of the material self requires little explanation. A person speaks of *my arms* or *my legs*. These entities are clearly an intimate part of who we are. But our sense of self is not limited to our bodies. It extends to include other people (my children), pets (my dog), possessions (my car), places (my hometown), and the products of our labors (my painting).

It is not the physical entities themselves, however, that comprise the material self. Rather, it is our psychological ownership of them (Scheibe, 1985). For example, a person may have a favorite chair she likes to sit in. The chair itself is not part of the self. Instead, it is the sense of appropriation represented by the phrase "my favorite chair." This is what we mean when we talk about the extended self. It includes all of the people, places, and things that are *psychologically* part of who we are.

It is interesting to consider why James argued for such a sweeping definition of self. Prior to the time he wrote his book, psychological research on self was restricted to the physical self. Recall from Chapter 1 that the introspectionists had people report what they were thinking and feeling when exposed to various stimuli. Some of these reports concerned an awareness of one's bodily states. For example, a person might report that "my arms feel heavy" or "my skin feels warm." These are aspects of self. But James wanted to expand the study of self to include nonphysical aspects of the person. He believed that the self was fluid and encompassed more than our physical bodies.

---

[1] I will quote liberally from James throughout this chapter. It should be noted, however, that James always uses the male personal pronoun "he," a practice inconsistent with contemporary standards. In this instance, I judged fidelity to be more important than political correctness and have reproduced his words without editing them.

Given this fluidity, how can we tell whether an entity is part of the self? James believed we could make this determination by examining our emotional investment in the entity. If we respond in an emotional way when the entity is praised or attacked, the entity is likely to be part of the self.

> *In its widest possible sense, . . . a man's Self is the sum total of all that he CAN call his*, not only his body and his psychic powers, but his clothes and his house, his wife and children, his ancestors and friends, his reputation and works, his lands and horses, and yacht and bank-account. All these things give him the same emotions. If they wax and prosper, he feels triumphant; if they dwindle and die away, he feels cast down—not necessarily in the same degree for each thing, but in much the same way for all. (pp. 291–292)

Another way to determine whether something is part of the extended self is to see how we act toward it. If we lavish attention on the entity and labor to enhance or maintain it, we can infer that the entity is part of the self.

> [All of the components of the material self] are the objects of instinctive prefer-ences coupled with the most important practical interests of life. We all have a blind impulse to watch over our body, to deck it with clothing of an ornamen-tal sort, to cherish parents, wife and babes, and to find for ourselves a home of our own which we may live in and "improve."
>
> An equally instinctive impulse drives us to collect property; and the col-lections thus made become, with different degrees of intimacy, parts of our empirical selves. The parts of our wealth most intimately ours are those which are saturated with our labor. . . . and although it is true that a part of our de-pression at the loss of possessions is due to our feeling that we must now go without certain goods that we expected the possessions to bring in their train, yet in every case there remains, over and above this, a sense of the shrinkage of our personality, a partial conversion of ourselves to nothingness, which is a psychological phenomenon by itself. (p. 293)

In addition to underscoring the important role motivation plays in iden-tifying what is self from what is not, James also made an interesting point here about the nature of things that become part of the self. These posses-sions, James argued, are not simply valued for what they provide; they are also prized because they become part of us. "Not only the people but the places and things I know enlarge my Self in a sort of metaphoric way," James wrote (p. 308).

A good deal of research supports James's intuitions regarding the close connection between possessions and the self (see Belk, 1988). First, people spontaneously mention their possessions when asked to describe themselves (Gordon, 1968). People also amass possessions. Young children, for example, are avid collectors. They have bottle-cap collections, rock collections, shell col-lections, and so forth. These collections are not simply treasured for their mate-rial value (which is often negligible); instead, they represent important aspects of self. The tendency to treat possessions as part of the self continues through-out life, perhaps explaining why so many people have difficulty discarding old clothes or other possessions that have long outlived their usefulness.

There seem to be several reasons for this. First, possessions serve a symbolic function; they help people define themselves. The clothes we wear, the cars we drive, and the manner in which we adorn our homes and offices signal to ourselves (and others) who we think we are and how we wish to be regarded. People may be particularly apt to acquire and exhibit such signs and symbols when their identities are tenuously held or threatened (Wicklund & Gollwitzer, 1982). A recent Ph.D., for example, may prominently display his diploma in an attempt to convince himself (and others) that he is the erudite scholar he aspires to be. These functions support Sartre's (1958) claim that people accumulate possessions to enlarge their sense of self.

Possessions also extend the self in time. Most people take steps to ensure that their letters, photographs, possessions, and mementos are distributed to others at the time of their death. Although some of this distribution reflects a desire to allow others to enjoy the utilitarian value of these artifacts, Unruh (1983, cited in Belk, 1988) has argued that this dispersal also has a symbolic function. People seek immortality by passing their possessions on to the next generation.

People's emotional responses to their possessions also attest to their importance to the self. A person who loses a wallet often feels greater anguish over a lost photograph than over any money that is missing. Similarly, many car owners react with extreme anger (and often rage) when their cars are damaged, even when the damage is only slight in physical terms. Finally, many people who lose possessions in a natural disaster go through a grieving process similar to the process people go through when they lose a person they love (McLeod, 1984, cited in Belk, 1988).

Further evidence that possessions become part of the extended self comes from a series of investigations by Beggan (1992). In an initial study, participants were shown a variety of inexpensive objects (e.g., a key ring, plastic comb, playing cards). They were then given one object and told it was theirs to keep. Later, participants evaluated *their* object more favorably than the objects they didn't receive. A follow-up investigation found that this tendency was especially pronounced after participants had previously failed at an unrelated experimental test. There are several explanations for this "mere ownership effect," but one possibility is that once possessions become part of the self, we imbue them with value and use them to promote positive feelings of self worth.

Finally, the tendency to value self-relevant objects and entities even extends to letters of the alphabet. When asked to judge the pleasantness of various letters, people show enhanced liking for the letters that make up their own name, particularly their own initials (Greenwald & Banaji, 1995; Nuttin, 1985, 1987). This "name letter effect" provides further support for James's assertion that our sense of self extends far beyond our physical bodies to include those objects and entities we call *ours*.

Social Self

James called the second category of the empirical self the social self. The social self refers to how we are regarded and recognized by others. (I will refer to these aspects of self as a person's *social identities*.) As before, James's analysis was very broad.

> . . . *a man has as many social selves as there are individuals who recognize him* and carry an image of him in their mind. . . . But as the individuals who carry the images fall naturally into classes, we may practically say that he has as many different social selves as there are distinct *groups* of persons about whose opinion he cares. (p. 294)

Deaux, Reid, Mizrahi, and Ethier (1995) distinguished five types of social identities: personal relationships (e.g., husband, wife), ethnic/religious (e.g., African-American, Muslim), political affiliation (e.g., Democrat, pacifist), stigmatized groups (e.g., alcoholic, criminal), and vocation/avocation (e.g., professor, artist). Some of these identities are ascribed identities (ones we are born with, such as son or daughter) and others are attained identities (ones we acquire in life, such as professor or student).

Each of these identities is accompanied by a specific set of expectations and behaviors. We act differently in the role of "father" than in the role of "professor." Sometimes these differences are minor and unimportant; other times they are considerable and consequential.

> Many a youth who is demure enough before his parents and teachers, swears and swaggers like a pirate among his "tough" young friends. We do not show ourselves to our children as to our club-companions, to our customers as to the laborers we employ, to our own masters and employers as to our intimate friends. From this there results what practically is a division of the man into several selves; and this may be a discordant splitting, as where one is afraid to let one set of acquaintances know him as he is elsewhere; or it may be a perfectly harmonious division of labor, as where one tender to his children is stern to the soldiers or prisoners under his command. (p. 294)

The larger point James made here is a critical one. To a great extent, how we think of ourselves depends on the social roles we are playing (Roberts & Donahue, 1994). We are different *selves* in different social situations. This can cause difficulties when we are confronted with situations in which two or more social selves are relevant. Anyone who has simultaneously been both a parent and a child at a family reunion can attest to the difficulties such situations create. We are also surprised to encounter people we typically see in only one role or situation outside of that usual setting. Students, for example, are often flustered when they see their teachers outside of the classroom (e.g., at a movie, restaurant, or sporting event). They aren't used to seeing their teachers dressed so casually and acting so informally.

The tendency for people to show different sides of themselves in different social settings raises an important question: Is there a stable, core sense of self that transcends these various social roles? Some theorists have answered this question with an emphatic "no." They have maintained that the self is comprised entirely of our various social roles, and that there is no real, true, or genuine self that exists apart from these social roles (Gergen, 1982; Sorokin, 1947). Many (if not most) other theorists reject this position as too extreme.

While acknowledging that people behave differently in different social settings, these theorists also contend that there is a common sense of self that runs through these various social identities. William James was one adherent of this position. James believed that our social roles are one important aspect of self, but they are by no means the sole aspect of self nor the most important.

James went on to make an additional point about these social selves. He posited an instinctive drive to be noticed and recognized by others. We affiliate, James argued, not simply because we like company, but because we crave recognition and status.

> *A man's Social Self* is the recognition which he gets from his mates. We are not only gregarious animals, liking to be in sight of our fellows, but we have an innate propensity to get ourselves noticed, and noticed favorably, by our kind. No more fiendish punishment could be devised, were such a thing physically possible, than that one should be turned loose in society and remain absolutely unnoticed by all the members thereof. (p. 293)

To summarize, the social self includes the various social positions we occupy and the social roles we play. But it is not simply these identities, per se. It is more importantly the way we think we are regarded and recognized by others. It is how we think others *evaluate* us. These perceptions will figure prominently in our discussion of the reflected appraisal process in Chapter 3.

Spiritual Self

The third category in James's scheme is the spiritual self. The spiritual self is our *inner* self or our *psychological* self. It is comprised of everything we call *my* or *mine* that is not a tangible object, person, or place, or a social role. Our perceived abilities, attitudes, emotions, interests, motives, opinions, traits, and wishes are all part of the spiritual self. (I will refer to these aspects of the spiritual self as our *personal identities*.) In short, the spiritual self refers to our perceived inner psychological qualities. It represents our subjective experience of ourselves—how it feels to be us.

> By the spiritual self . . . I mean a man's inner or subjective being, his psychic faculties or dispositions. . . . These psychic dispositions are the most enduring and intimate part of the self, that which we most verily seem to be. We take a purer self-satisfaction when we think of our ability to argue and discriminate, of our moral sensibility and conscience, of our indomitable will, than when we survey any of our other possessions. (p. 296)

James proposed two different ways of thinking about the spiritual self. One way (which he called the abstract way) is to consider each attribute in isolation, as distinct from the others. The other way (which he called the concrete way) is to consider the attributes as united in a constant stream.

> . . . this spiritual self may be considered in various ways. We may divide it into faculties, . . . isolating them one from another, and identifying ourselves with either in turn. This is an abstract way of dealing with consciousness . . . ; or we may insist on a concrete view, and then the spiritual self in us will be either the entire stream of our personal consciousness, or the present

"segment" or "section" of that stream. . . . But whether we take it abstractly or concretely, our understanding the spiritual self at all is a reflective process, . . . the result of our abandoning the outward-looking point of view, and . . . [coming] *to think ourselves as thinkers.* (p. 296)

Later in this chapter we will see how James used this distinction to address an ancient philosophical debate, known as the problem of personal identity.

Finally, it's of interest to note the close connection between our possessions (which are aspects of the material self) and our emotions, attitudes, and beliefs (which are components of the spiritual self). As Abelson (1986) observed, this similarity is captured in our language. A person is said to *have* a belief, from the time the belief is first *acquired,* to the time it is *discarded* or *lost.* We also say things like "I *inherited* a view" or "I can't *buy* that!" Finally, we speak of people who have *abandoned* their convictions or *disowned* an earlier position. These terms imply that possessions and attitudes share an underlying conceptual property: They are both owned by the self (see Gilovich, 1991; Heider, 1956 for an elaboration of this view).

Tests and Refinements of James's Ideas

Does James's classification scheme describe the way you think about yourself? To answer this question, try to match the responses you gave to the questionnaire you completed earlier with James's analysis. I have used this questionnaire in my classes at the University of Washington, and I have found that students' answers do reliably fall into one of these three categories. The only trick is deciding which of the three categories is applicable. One way to make this determination is to consider whether the response is a noun or an adjective. Rosenberg (1979) notes that social identities are generally expressed as nouns and serve to place us in a broader social context (e.g., I am an American; I am a Democrat). In contrast, personal identities (aspects of what James called the spiritual self) are usually expressed as adjectives and serve to distinguish us from others (e.g., I am moody; I am responsible).

Gordon (1968) elaborated on James's scheme and produced a coding procedure with 8 major categories and 30 subcategories. This scheme is described in Table 2.2, and it is illustrated with a sample (composite) questionnaire in Table 2.3. You can compare the responses you gave with the ones shown there.

The Collective Self

James wrote at a time when psychology was the exclusive province of highly educated (and, by extension, well-to-do) males of European descent. His analysis is therefore somewhat parochial and narrow in scope. This limitation is apparent in the lack of attention James gave to people's ethnic, religious, and racial identities. These identities (termed the collective self by modern researchers) are of great significance to people, particularly those who occupy a minority status. For example, people place great importance on being "Irish," "Jewish," "an African-American," and so forth.

TABLE 2.2. Gordon's (1968) Identity Classification Scheme

A. Ascribed Identities
   1. Age
   2. Sex
   3. Name
   4. Race/Ethnicity
   5. Religion

B. Roles and Memberships
   6. Kinship (family—son, daughter, brother, sister)
   7. Occupation
   8. Student
   9. Political affiliation
   10. Social status (part of the middle class; an aristocrat)
   11. Territoriality/Citizenship (from Minneapolis; an American)
   12. Actual group memberships (Boy Scout; Shriner)

C. Abstract
   13. Existential (me; an individual)
   14. Abstract (a person; a human)
   15. Ideological and belief references (liberal; environmentalist)

D. Interests and Activities
   16. Judgments, tastes, likes (a jazz fan)
   17. Intellectual concerns (interested in literature)
   18. Artistic activities (a dancer; a painter)
   19. Other activities (a stamp collector)

E. Material Possessions
   20. Possessions
   21. Physical body

F. Major Senses of Self
   22. Competence (intelligent; talented; creative)
   23. Self-determination (ambitious; hardworking)
   24. Unity (mixed up; together)
   25. Moral worth (trustworthy; honest)

G. Personal Characteristics
   26. Interpersonal style (friendly; fair; nice; shy)
   27. Psychic style (happy; sad; curious; calm)

H. External References
   28. Judgments imputed to others (admired; well-liked)
   29. Immediate situation (hungry; bored)
   30. Uncodable

Source: Copyright 1965 John Wiley & Sons, Inc. Reprinted by permission of John Wiley & Sons, Inc.

Two related issues regarding these collective identities have received attention. One line of research has focused on how people evaluate these specific identities. Historically, minority status has carried a negative connotation. Minorities have been stigmatized and subject to discrimination. This state of affairs led some minority group members to resent, disavow, or even turn against their ethnic identity (Lewin, 1948).

TABLE 2.3. Sample Response to "What Would You Tell Them" Questionnaire

Response	James	Gordon
1. smart	spiritual	competence
2. brown hair, brown eyes	material	physical body
3. friendly	spiritual	interpersonal style
4. the daughter of Italian immigrants	material	kinship
5. am a junior at the UW	social	student
6. like psychology	spiritual	interests and activities
7. am Catholic	social	religion
8. work at a daycare	social	occupation
9. love theater	spiritual	interests and activities
10. own a red Honda Accord	material	possessions
11. a member of Greenpeace	social	actual group
12. plan to become a school teacher	social (future)	occupation
13. am 22	material	age
14. am an only child	social	kinship
15. love laughing and smiling	spiritual	judgments, tastes, likes
16. responsible	spiritual	self-determination
17. a dancer	social	artistic activities
18. trustworthy	spiritual	moral worth
19. moody	spiritual	psychic style; personality
20. petite	material	physical body

Recent years have seen a shift in these tendencies. Beginning with the Black Pride movement in the 1960s, minority groups have worked to improve the way their members evaluate their minority status. Rather than viewing their minority status as a stigma, group members are encouraged to celebrate their heritage and view their minority status as a source of pride. These efforts appear to be meeting with success. Most minority group members now evaluate their ethnic identity in positive terms (Crocker, Luhtanen, Blaine, & Broadnax, 1994; Phinney, 1990).

A second line of research has looked at how people maintain their ethnic identities when exposed to a dominant majority culture. Consider children of Latin-American descent who live in the United States today. Their Latin identity is apt to be paramount during their early (pre-school) years, as a result of housing and friendship patterns. Later, when they begin to attend school, they come into contact with the broader American culture. What happens to their ethnic identity then?

Table 2.4 describes four possible outcomes based on the strength of the children's identification with the majority and minority group (Phinney, 1990). Children who adopt the identity of the dominant culture, while still retaining a strong identification with their cultural background, are said to be acculturated, integrated, or bicultural. Those who abandon their ethnic identity for an American identity are said to be assimilated. Separation occurs among those who refuse to identify with the dominant culture, and those who lose their ties to both cultural groups are said to be marginalized.

TABLE 2.4. Four Identity Orientations Based on Degree of Identification with One's Ethnic Group and the Majority Group

| | | Identification with Ethnic Group | |
		Strong	Weak
Identification with Majority Group	Strong	Acculturated Integrated Bicultural	Assimilated
	Weak	Separated Dissociated	Marginalized

Source: Adapted from Phinney, 1990, *Psychological Bulletin, 108*, 499–514. Copyright 1990. Adapted by permission of The American Psychology Association.

Assimilation was the desired outcome for many turn-of-the century immigrants. These newly arrived Americans sought to completely immerse themselves in American culture and shed their ethnic identity. In so doing, many changed their names, tried to lose their accents, and studiously adopted the customs and mores of American culture.

The situation today is quite different. Cultural diversity and pluralism are celebrated, and many minority group members strive to become acculturated, not assimilated. Phinney (1990) describes several behaviors that facilitate this goal, including participation in ethnic activities, continued use of one's native language, and the forging of friendship patterns with other minority group members. Ethier and Deaux (1994) found that behaviors of this sort helped Hispanic students retain their ethnic identity during their first year in predominantly Anglo universities.

Cultural Differences in Identity Importance

Cultural differences in the importance people attach to their various identities have also been the subject of research. James argued that personal identities (aspects of the spiritual self) are more important to people than are their social identities (aspects of the social self).

> . . . men have arranged the various selves . . . in an hierarchical scale according to their worth. (p. 314) . . . with the bodily Self at the bottom, the spiritual Self at top, and the extracorporeal material selves and the various social selves between. (p. 313)

This hierarchical scheme varies across cultures (Markus & Kitayama, 1991; Triandis, 1989). Western countries (e.g., United States, Canada, and Western European countries) are very individualistic. They are competitive in orientation and emphasize ways in which people are different from one another. This emphasis leads citizens of these countries to place great importance on their personal identities. Eastern cultures (e.g., Japan, China, India), in contrast, tend to be more cooperative, collective, and interdependent. Instead of emphasizing the ways people are different from one another, these cultures emphasize ways in which people are linked together. Accordingly, people raised in these cultures emphasize their social identities.

An investigation by Cousins (1989) documents these tendencies. In this investigation, American and Japanese college students completed a questionnaire similar to the one you filled out earlier, and then placed a check mark next to the five responses they regarded as most self-descriptive. Researchers then classified each of the five responses according to whether it referred to a personal identity (a perceived trait, ability, or disposition), a social identity (a social role or relationship), or something else (e.g., physical characteristic).

Figure 2.1 presents the results of this investigation. The figure shows that the American students listed personal identities (e.g., I am honest; I am smart) 59 percent of the time, but Japanese students did so only 19 percent of the time. In contrast, Japanese students listed social identities (e.g., I am a student; I am a daughter) 27 percent of the time, but American students did so only 9 percent of the time. These findings document cross-cultural differences in the way people think about themselves (see also Trafimow, Triandis, & Goto, 1991).

Cousins (1989) documented another important cultural difference. People from Western cultures think of themselves as having psychological attributes that transcend particular situations. For example, when asked to describe herself, a person from a Western culture might say "I'm polite." People from Eastern cultures tend to think of themselves in relation to specific others and in specific situations; when asked to describe herself, a person from an Eastern culture might say "I'm polite at school," or "I'm polite with my father." The

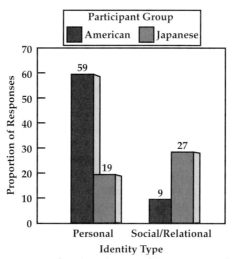

FIGURE 2.1. Identity statements by American and Japanese students in response to a "Who am I?" questionnaire. The data show that American students were more likely than Japanese students to describe themselves in terms of their personal attributes, whereas Japanese students were more likely than American students to describe themselves in terms of their social attributes. These findings document cross-cultural differences in the self-concept.

(Adapted from Cousins, 1989, *Journal of Personality and Social Psychology, 56,* 124–131. Copyright 1989. Adapted by permission of The American Psychological Association.)

key difference is that the response of the person from a Western cultural background is unbounded by the situation, but the response of the person from an Eastern cultural background specifies the relational or situational context.

Individual Differences in Identity Importance

Even within cultures, people differ in the importance they attach to their various identities (Cheek, 1989; Dollinger, Preston, O'Brien, & Dilalla, 1996). Before reading further, take a moment to complete the questionnaire shown in Table 2.5. This questionnaire, adapted from one designed by Cheek, Tropp, Chen, and Underwood (1994), measures the weight people give to their various identities. The scale distinguishes three types of identities: personal identities (our perceived inner or psychological qualities), social identities (the way we think we are regarded and recognized by others), and collective identities (our sense of belonging to a larger social group such as our race, ethnic heritage, and religion).

To determine your score, average your responses to the four items that refer to personal identities (items 1, 4, 7, and 10), the four items that refer to social

TABLE 2.5. Identity Questionnaire

These items describe different aspects of identity. Please read each item carefully and consider how it applies to you. Fill in the blank next to each item by choosing a number from the scale below:

> 1 = Not important to my sense of who I am
> 2 = Slightly important to my sense of who I am
> 3 = Somewhat important to my sense of who I am
> 4 = Very important to my sense of who I am
> 5 = Extremely important to my sense of who I am

1. _____ My dreams and imagination.

2. _____ My attractiveness to other people.

3. _____ Being a part of the many generations of my family.

4. _____ My emotions and feelings.

5. _____ My popularity with other people.

6. _____ My race or ethnic background.

7. _____ My personal self-evaluations; the private opinion I have of myself.

8. _____ My reputation; what others think of me.

9. _____ My religion.

10. _____ My personal values and moral standards.

11. _____ The ways in which other people react to what I say and do.

12. _____ My feeling of belonging to my community.

Source: Adapted from Cheek, Tropp, Chen, & Underwood, 1994. Paper presented at the 102nd Annual Convention of The American Psychological Association, Los Angeles. Reprinted by permission of Jonathan M. Cheek.

identities (items 2, 5, 8, and 11), and the four items that measure collective identities (items 3, 6, 9, and 12). Most American college students score highest on the
personal identity items, but not all do. Moreover, Asian-American students
place more importance on their collective identities than do European-American
students, further demonstrating how cultures shape the way people think about
themselves. Finally, there is evidence that, across cultures, the tendency to see
oneself in relational terms (which is a component of collectivism in this scale) is
more characteristic of women than of men (Kashima et al., 1995; Markus & Oyserman, 1989).

The Personal Narrative

One more issue regarding the nature of the *ME* merits consideration. To
this point, we have discussed the *ME* as if it consists of a haphazard collection
of perceived possessions, social roles, and traits. This is rarely the case. Most
(if not all) individuals organize the various aspects of their empirical self into a
coherent pattern.

McAdams (1996) has argued that this organization is generally accomplished in the context of a personal narrative. A personal narrative is a story a
person (implicitly) constructs about her life. The narrative includes the ways
the person thinks of herself, as well as the person's memories, feelings, and experiences. This ongoing story contains many of the literary devices that characterize works of fiction (e.g., plots and subplots, character descriptions).
Many stories also feature a critical turning point or self-defining juncture (e.g.,
to really know me, you need to know why I abandoned a lucrative career as a
taxi driver in favor of getting a Ph.D. in psychology). In short, a personal narrative unifies and makes sense of the various aspects of a person's life, including aspects of the empirical self.

SELF-FEELING, SELF-SEEKING, AND SELF-PRESERVATION

In addition to discussing the nature of the self, William James discussed self-
feelings and the motivational aspects of the self (which he called self-seeking
and self-preservation). As concerns self-feelings, James believed there are certain emotions that always involve the self as a point of reference. James called
these emotions self-complacency and self-dissatisfaction, and he distinguished
them from more general emotions, such as happiness and sadness. These self-
relevant emotions include:

> . . . pride, conceit, vanity, self-esteem, arrogance [and] vainglory, on the one
> hand; and on the other modesty, humility, confusion, diffidence, shame, mor-
> tification, contrition, the sense of obloquy, and personal despair. (p. 306)

James viewed these emotions as instinctive in nature, as

> . . . direct and elementary endowments of our nature . . . each as worthy to
> be classed as a primitive emotional species as are, for example, rage or pain.
> (pp. 306–307)

Finally, James believed that people have an innate drive to experience these positive feelings and to avoid experiencing these negative feelings.

> We know how little it matters to us whether *some* man, a man taken at large and in the abstract, proves a failure or succeeds in life—he may be hanged for aught we care—but we know the utter momentousness and terribleness of the alternative when the man is the one whose names we ourselves bear. *I* must not be a failure, is the very loudest of the voices that clamor in each of our breasts: let fail who may, *I* at least must succeed. . . . each of us is animated by *a direct feeling of regard for his own pure principle of individual existence. . . .* Whatever is me is precious; this is me; therefore this is precious; whatever is mine must not fail; this is mine; therefore this must not fail, etc. (p. 318)

What Determines Self-Feelings?

Having distinguished various self-relevant emotions, James considers how these feelings arise. In an oft-quoted passage, he offers the following formula

> Our self-feeling in this world depends entirely on what we *back* ourselves to be and do. It is determined by the ratio of our actualities to our supposed potentialities; a fraction of which our pretensions are the denominator and the numerator our successes; thus, Self-esteem = Success/Pretensions. (p. 310)

In Chapter 8 of this book we will spend a great deal of time discussing self-esteem. At that point, we will have the opportunity to examine the merits of James's formula. For now, let's simply be clear on what he is saying.

Pretensions as Values

James uses the term *pretensions* in two distinct ways. Sometimes he uses the term to refer to domains of personal importance.

> I who for the time have staked my all on being a psychologist, am mortified if others know much more psychology than I. But I am contented to wallow in the grossest ignorance of Greek. My deficiencies there give me no sense of personal humiliation at all. Had I "pretensions" to be a linguist, it would have been just the reverse. (p. 310)

Here James is saying that his performance as a psychologist evokes a stronger emotional reaction in him than does his performance as a linguist. In more general terms, he is arguing that outcomes in domains of high personal importance produce greater emotional reactions than do outcomes in domains of low personal importance. This treats pretensions in terms of values, in terms of what is important to the person.

To illustrate, imagine you are taking two classes. One is an elective that you are taking just for fun; the other class is in your major area of study. James's formula suggests that your performance in the latter class (the one that is more important) will evoke a stronger emotional reaction than will your performance in the former class (the one that is unimportant).

Pretensions as Aspirations

In addition to using the term pretensions to refer to what is important to a person, James also uses the term to refer to a person's aspiration level, a minimum level of performance with which a person would be satisfied.

> So we have the paradox of a man shamed to death because he is only the second pugilist or the second oarsman in the world. That he is able to beat the whole population of the globe minus one is nothing; he has pitted himself to beat that one; and as long as he doesn't do that nothing else counts. Yonder puny fellow, however, whom every one can beat, suffers no chagrin about it, for he has long ago abandoned the attempt to "carry that line" as the merchants say, of self at all. (pp. 310–311)

This passage treats pretensions in terms of one's level of aspiration. It says that how people feel about an attained outcome is not simply a function of the outcome itself—it depends on the standards people use for gauging success and failure.

By way of illustration, consider two students who both get Bs in a course. One student may be dissatisfied because he expected or wanted an A; the other student may be thrilled because he would have been satisfied with a C. Even though the objective outcome is the same, the two students have completely different emotional reactions. Why? Because as the phenomenological approach tells us, people's reactions to events are determined not simply by the event themselves but also by the meaning people give to the event. This point was recognized by Shakespeare over 400 years ago. In *Hamlet*, Shakespeare wrote, "There is nothing either good or bad, but thinking makes it so" (act II, scene 2, line 259). Whether we are elated or dejected to receive a grade of "B" depends on the meaning we attach to that grade. Does it represent a personal success or a personal failure? It is this perception, rather than the grade itself that guides our emotional life.

This analysis suggests that there are two routes to feeling good about your performance in some domain. You can either raise your level of accomplishment or lower your level of aspiration. According to James, either one will suffice to make you feel better.

> [Self-esteem] may be increased as well by diminishing the denominator as by increasing the numerator. To give up pretensions is as blessed a relief as to get them gratified. . . . Everything added to the Self is a burden as well as a pride. . . . our self-feeling is in our power. As Caryle says: "Make they claim of wages a zero, then hast thou the world under thy feet." (pp. 310–311)

Medvec, Madey, and Gilovich (1995) recently documented a related tendency. These investigators studied the emotional reactions of medalists at the 1992 Summer Olympics. The critical question of interest was whether silver medalists (who came in second) felt better than did bronze medalists (who came in third). Logically, silver medalists should feel better than bronze medalists, because they performed better. But Medvec et al. hypothesized that silver medalists would actually feel worse than bronze medalists because the

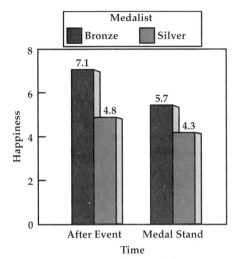

FIGURE 2.2. Happiness ratings immediately after an athletic event and on the medal stand among Olympic athletes. The data show that silver medalists (who came in second) were less happy than were bronze medalists (who came in third). These findings underscore that our emotional reactions to outcomes do not depend simply on the objective outcome itself, but also on our ideas about what might have been.
(Adapted from Medvec, Madey, & Gilovich, 1995, *Journal of Personality and Social Psychology, 69*, 603–610. Copyright 1995. Adapted by permission of The American Psychological Association.)

silver medalists would be thinking how they might have won the gold medal if only they had made a slight change in strategy or tried a little bit harder.

To test their ideas, Medvec et al. had neutral observers rate the emotional reactions (as revealed in facial expressions) of the two medalists immediately after their athletic competition had ended and later on the medal stand. In accordance with predictions, the data displayed in Figure 2.2 show that, at both time periods, athletes who came in second and won a silver medal exhibited less happiness than did those who came in third and won a bronze medal. These results are of interest because they underscore that emotional reactions to performance outcomes do not simply depend on the objective outcome itself.

Shame versus Guilt

In addition to exploring the manner in which people's achievements influence their self-feelings, researchers have extended James's ideas about the nature of negative self-relevant emotions (for a review, see Tangney & Fischer, 1995). One issue that has received attention is the difference between shame and guilt. Some theorists (e.g., Buss, 1980) have suggested that these emotions differ in terms of their public versus private nature. Whereas shame is a public emotion that follows from public disapproval or opprobrium, guilt represents a more private response to the perception that one has failed to live up to one's personal standards and ideals.

Other theorists (e.g., Barrett, 1995; Lewis, 1971; Lazarus, 1991; Niedenthal, Tangney, & Gavanski, 1994) have suggested that shame is a more encompassing emotion than is guilt. The focus of guilt is behavior: People feel guilty when they believe they have *done* something they shouldn't have done. In contrast, shame is a more undifferentiated perception that arises from the perception that one is a bad person or is wholly inadequate. In short, guilt involves a focus on particular misdeeds, whereas shame involves a sense that the entire self is bad (Barrett, 1995).

Finally, shame and guilt differ in terms of their behavioral tendencies (Lazarus, 1991; Roseman, Wiest, & Swartz, 1994). Guilt gives rise to a tendency to atone for one's (perceived) transgressions and to make reparations. In contrast, shame leads people to want to hide from others, to conceal one's (perceived) deficiencies and shortcomings.

Self-Feelings and Hypothetical Self-Views

The distinction between shame and guilt highlights that self-feelings are often influenced by our ideas about who we could be, should be, or ought to be. Generally speaking, these *hypothetical* self-views fall into four categories.

The Attainable Self

Some of these self-views are realistic. A person may wish to be "a better golfer," "more understanding," or "less competitive." These self-views, which are aspects of what Rosenberg (1979) calls the *committed self*, and Markus and her colleagues (Markus & Nurius, 1986; Markus & Ruvolo, 1989) call the *possible self*, are attainable. They represent the kind of person one wants to be and can be. This seems to be what James had in mind when he discussed pretensions as level of aspiration. His analysis also suggests that the closer our present self-view comes to these attainable selves, the better we feel about ourselves.

The Ideal Self

People also entertain more idealized or gloried views of themselves. They dream about being a "famous rock and roll star," "a millionaire," or "a Nobel laureate." Everyone entertains such views of themselves, but most people do not confuse these *idealized* self-images with the attainable self-image. They recognize that these ideal self-images are largely flights of fancy.

Not everyone makes this distinction, however. Horney (1945) believed that a rigid, idealized self characterizes the neurotic personality. The neurotic, she argued, cannot tolerate feelings of inferiority and so constructs an ideal self-image to hide behind. Such a person has an insatiable need to be the best at everything and to be liked, admired, and approved by everyone. It is impossible, of course, to live up to such rigid expectations, dooming the neurotic to disappointment and frustration.

It is important to note that it is not the possession of idealized self-images, per se, that distinguishes the neurotic from the normal personality. Everyone, to one extent or another, fantasizes about being something they are not. The problem arises when this idealized self becomes a *must* self: It is when we *must* be the "perfect husband," when we *must* be "a straight-A student," or when we *must* be the "most popular person in school" that the idealized self-image becomes a source of psychological distress (Blatt, 1985).

The Ought Self

Another, related type of belief concerns our ideas about what we should be or ought to be. A child, for example, may believe he has a duty to be "a loyal son who follows in the family business"; a married woman may feel that she has an obligation to be "a productive provider and a nurturant mother." Higgins (1987) has referred to these beliefs as elements of our *ought* selves, and has provided evidence that people are prone to feelings of guilt and anxiety when their perceptions of who they are now do not coincide with their ideas about who they think they ought to be.

The Undesired Self

Finally, people also think of themselves in terms of what they are afraid of becoming or do not want to become. One fears being "a failure at business," "an over-the-hill actor," or "dependent on one's children." Ogilvie (1987) refers to these images as aspects of the *undesired self* and has suggested that they play an important role in how happy and satisfied people are in their lives. The greater the psychological distance between how we think of ourselves now and what we fear becoming (i.e., the less like these negative self-images we are), the happier we are in life. These potential negative self-images can also serve an important motivational function. If not too extreme, they can function as incentives. They can force people to work hard in an attempt to avoid these negative identities (Oyserman & Markus, 1990).

Self-Feelings and Social Relationships

Social relationships constitute another important source of self-feelings. Recall that James believed that the material self includes not only our physical characteristics and possessions but also other members of the social world, such as our family, friends, and loved ones. In support of this assertion, people refer to others when describing themselves (e.g., "I am Hillary's husband") (Kuhn & McPartland, 1954; see also, Dollinger & Clancy, 1993), and include a representation of others in their self-concept (Aron, Aron, Tudor, & Nelson, 1991; Davis, Conklin, Smith, & Luce, 1996; Smith & Henry, 1996).

Basking in Reflected Glory

Being part of the self-concept, other people also evoke self-feelings. This tendency is most apparent with our loved ones (e.g., parents take great pride in the accomplishments of their children), but the effect also extends to less intimate relationships. Consider, for example, the wave of emotion that can overcome fans at a sporting event. After an important victory, it is not uncommon to see fans spilling onto the field chanting, "We're number one." The use of the personal pronoun "we" implies that the victory is experienced in a very personal way and that the feelings of euphoria are of a self-relevant nature (for relevant research, see Cialdini et al., 1986; Hirt, Zillmann, Erickson, & Kennedy, 1995).

Social Identity Theory

The link between social relationships and self-feelings is also thought to have motivational significance. This insight lies at the heart of social identity theory (Tajfel & Turner, 1986). Social identity theory asserts (1) that social relationships are an important component of the self-concept; (2) that people are motivated to feel good about themselves; and (3) that people feel better about themselves when they believe the groups they belong to are somehow better than the groups to which they do not belong.

Tests of the theory have taken many forms. Research using the minimal intergroup paradigm is of especial interest. In these studies, participants are divided into groups on the basis of relatively meaningless criteria. For example, participants might be shown two paintings and then be divided into groups based on which painting they liked best. Participants are then asked to apportion monetary rewards between the two groups. Reliably, people discriminate in favor of their own group, and doing so makes people feel better about themselves (Lemyre & Smith, 1985; Maass, Ceccarelli, & Rudin, 1996; Oakes & Turner, 1980). This tendency, which is known as ingroup favoritism, supports the claim that even trivial associations with others can have powerful effects on the way people feel about themselves.

Summary and Synthesis

Table 2.6 summarizes many of the ideas we've been discussing. The table builds on theoretical work by Brewer and Gardner (1996; see also, Greenwald & Breckler, 1985; Prentice, Miller, & Lightdale, 1994), and presents a four-fold classification of the empirical self. The first row describes the personal or individual self. Here, identity consists of those aspects of self that tend to distinguish us from others. The second row describes the social self. This aspect of self includes our social roles and our reputation in the minds of other people. The third row describes the relational self, which includes specific individuals who are part of our self-concept. The final row describes the collective self. This aspect of self consists of social categories to which we belong, including our racial, religious, and ethnic identities.

THE NATURE OF THE I

In Chapter 1 we distinguished between two aspects of self: the *I* (that aspect of self that actively experiences the world) and the *ME* (that aspect of self that is the object of one's own attention). So far we've been concerned only with un-

TABLE 2.6. Four-Fold Classification of the Empirical Self

Self-Concept Label	Description	Example	Relation to James's Analysis	Basis of Self-Feelings
Personal	Perceived physical characteristics, traits and abilities, and one's possessions.	I am blonde; I am shy; I own a Lexus	Aspects of the material self (excluding other people), and the spiritual self.	Personal achievements; correspondence between present self-views and various hypothetical self-views.
Social	Social roles and reputation in the minds of other people.	I am an accountant	Social self	Public recognition, fame; praise from others.
Relational	Other people with whom we have direct, personal contact.	I am Sheri's husband	Aspects of the material self.	Pride in the accomplishments of particular others with whom we are joined.
Collective	Social categories to which we belong.	I am Irish	Not discussed explicitly by James.	Ethnic pride; pride in the various groups of which we are members.

Source: Adapted from Brewer & Gardner, 1996, *Journal of Personality and Social Psychology, 71,* 83–93. Copyright 1996. Adapted by permission of The American Psychological Association

derstanding the nature of the *ME.* We have examined how people think and feel about themselves.

James also devoted considerable attention to understanding the nature of the *I.* His treatment of this issue takes place in the context of a philosophical puzzle known as *the problem of personal identity.* In the sections that follow, we will (1) describe the problem of personal identity, (2) consider how various philosophers preceding James attempted to solve the puzzle, and (3) then consider James's solution.

The Problem of Personal Identity

The problem of personal identity refers to the question of whether there is something that binds together our myriad perceptions and thoughts. Our mental lives are a kaleidoscope of shifting perceptions and sensations (we see, we hear, we think, we remember). These various perceptions seem tied together, and we use the term *I* to refer to this connection. It is *I* who heard the sound of thunder; it is *I* who thought about you yesterday. What is the nature of this *I* that appears to unite these perceptions? This is the problem of personal identity.

A deceptively simple answer is that the term refers to some aspect of our physical bodies. But what aspect? If you lost an arm or a leg, would you still refer to yourself with the personal pronoun *I*? Most people, it seems fair to say, would. Perhaps the appendages are not intimate enough to negate your identity; perhaps there is some other part of you that, if lost, would lead you to no longer refer to yourself with the personal pronoun *I*. But if so, what is it? Before answering, consider the following ancient puzzle of the ship of Theseus.

> The planks of a ship are removed one by one over intervals of time, and as each plank is removed it is replaced by a new plank. The removal of one plank and its replacement by another does not make the ship a different ship than before; it is the same ship with one plank different. Over time, each and every plank might be removed and replaced, but if this occurs gradually, the ship still will be the same ship. . . . [Thus], the identity of something over time does not require it to keep all the very same parts. (Nozick, 1981, p. 33)

The point of this story is that the physical properties of an entity are neither sufficient nor necessary to establish its identity. The Greek philosopher Aristotle recognized this point when he distinguished between the substance of an object and its form. The substance of an object is its matter—the material of which it is made. Its form is abstract and immaterial. Consider, for example, a bronze statue. The substance of the object (its matter) is bronze; statue is its form. If we melted the bronze and made some other object with it (say a poker for the fireplace), we would no longer have the same object, even though the substance of the object is still bronze.

The same is true, Aristotle argued, for a person. The essence of a person is not the person's physical substance, but the person's form, which Aristotle referred to as the person's Soul. For Aristotle (and many other theorists), the Soul is an immaterial (noncorporeal) entity that unites our various perceptions and establishes our identity. Although highly unlikely, it is possible that the same molecules and atoms that were once the body of Person X could come to comprise the body of another human being (Person Y). But even if this were to happen, Person X wouldn't be Person Y (any more than the melted bronze would be a statue). This is because the essence of a person is form, not substance.

The Substantialist School: The Soul Is the Tie That Binds

Aristotle's view of the Soul as an immaterial entity that unites the person's various perceptions and sensations held sway for over 2,000 years after his death. It was adopted by the Scholastic philosophers of the Middle Ages (e.g., Augustine, Aquinas), and by Descartes and his followers during the Age of Reason. To be sure, each philosopher amended the doctrine and emphasized different aspects and functions of the soul. But all believed that something *substantial* provided the unity behind our myriad perceptions. For this reason, adherents of this view are known as *substantialists*.

In more modern times (from the mid-1600s to the present day), numerous philosophers have tackled the problem of personal identity. In the remainder of this chapter, we will consider three such attempts, as they have been particularly influential to a psychology of the self.

Locke: Identity Is Memory

One philosopher who addressed this issue was the British philosopher John Locke (1632–1704). Locke wrote on a wide range of topics and is generally regarded as the father of modern democracy. His claim that people enter the world a blank slate (*tabula rasa*) undercut the notion that some people, by virtue of their birth, are privileged and destined to rule. Thomas Jefferson and other American colonists adopted Locke's position when writing the Declaration of Independence, asserting that "all men are created equal."

Locke also wrote about matters of moral responsibility. He wondered when people could be held accountable for their actions, a question akin to what today we would call the "insanity defense." He began by distinguishing two terms: man and person. Man refers to the physical aspects of existence, to our bodies. Person refers to our personal identity. In his major work, *An Essay Concerning Human Understanding,* Locke (1690/1979) defined a person as

> a thinking intelligent being that has reason and reflection and can consider itself as itself, . . . as the same thinking thing in different times and places. Further, as this consciousness can be extended backwards to any past action or thought, so far reaches the identity of that person.

Three aspects of Locke's analysis are particularly noteworthy for our purposes. First, Locke emphasized the *reflexive* nature of the human mind, the ability people have to take themselves as the object of their own attention. Along with earlier philosophers, Locke believed this ability was uniquely human (we will examine this proposition in Chapter 4). Second, his distinction between man and person is reminiscent of Aristotle's distinction between substance and form. Man is substance; person is form. Finally, Locke's reference to thought "across time and place" establishes that the criterion for *personhood* is an ability to remember our various perceptions in the prior situations of our lives. For Locke, then, the identity of the person is tied to memory; it extends as far back in time as the person has memories.

As applied to matters of moral responsibility, Locke argued that only a *person* can be held accountable for his actions. If a man commits a crime but has no memory for the act, then he was not acting as a "person" and is not responsible for his crimes.

By treating identity in terms of memory, Locke moved the study of self from the spiritual to the empirical. At the same time, his departure from the substantialist tradition was incomplete. Locke could not bring himself to believe that a person's perceptions were not united in some fashion. He concluded that our memories are suspended in, or inhere in, an immaterial substance. Although he believed we could never know what this immaterial substance or substratum was like, he was sure it existed.

Hume: Identity Is a Fiction

Locke's ideas were subsequently extended and modified by David Hume (1711–1776). Hume was a Scottish philosopher who applied a healthy skepticism to all matters. He is best known for his attack on the principle of causality. Hume argued that the true causes of events are never known directly, but are always inferred. Imagine, for example, we see someone roll Ball A at a stationary ball (Ball B). When Ball A strikes Ball B, Ball B begins to move. It is tempting under these circumstances to conclude that the first ball (or at least the force applied to it) caused the second ball to move. Hume cautioned that this is always an inference subject to error. Some other force may have caused the ball to move. The only thing we experience directly is the temporal succession of one ball coming into contact with another. Our conclusion that the first ball *caused* the second to move is entirely an inference; it is not a direct perception.

Hume applied these ideas to the study of the self in a chapter on personal identity in his *Treatise on Human Nature* (1739–1740). As had Locke, Hume assumed that the subjective unity of the self derives from memory: We remember having particular perceptions and thus perceive a unified entity as having those perceptions. Hume disagreed with Locke, however, as to whether these perceptions were joined in any fashion other than a subjective, psychological one. He did not believe they were. He did not believe there was an immaterial substance that was the bearer of this unity. Instead, he believed that all that existed were isolated perceptions. We perceive them as joined, but this perception is a fiction; the isolated perceptions themselves are not joined in any real fashion.

Hume's basis for reaching this conclusion is that he cannot find any such substance or unity in himself.

> There are some philosophers, who imagine we are every moment intimately conscious of what we call our SELF; that we feel its existence and its continuance in existence; and are certain, beyond the evidence of demonstration, both of its perfect identity and simplicity. . . . These philosophers are the curious reasoners concerning the material or immaterial substances in which they suppose our perceptions inhere. In order to put a stop to these endless cavils on both sides, I know no better method than to ask these philosophers in a few words, *What they mean by substance and inhesion?* . . . I desire those philosophers who pretend that we have an idea of the substance of our minds to point out the impression that produces it, and tell distinctly after what manner that impression operates, and from what object it is derived. Is it an impression of sensation or of reflection? Is it pleasant, or painful, or indifferent? Does it attend us at all times, or does it only return at intervals?
>
> For my part, when I enter most intimately into what I call *myself*, I always stumble on some particular perception or other of heat or cold, light or shade, love or hatred, pain or pleasure. I never can catch *myself* at any time without a perception. When my perceptions are removed for any time, as by sound sleep, . . . [I] may truly be said not to exist. . . . If anyone, upon serious and unprejudiced reflection, thinks he has a different notion of *himself*, I must con-

fess I can reason no longer with him. All I can allow him is, that he may be in the right as well as I, and that we are essentially different in this particular. He may, perhaps, perceive something simple and continued which he calls *himself*; though I am certain there is no such principle in me.

Hume goes on to say that our notions of personal identity derive from the fact that our thoughts follow one another so rapidly that we confuse temporal contiguity with unity.

> The mind is a kind of theatre, where several perceptions successively make their appearance. . . . [But] the comparison of the theatre must not mislead us. [It is only] the successive perceptions . . . that constitute the mind; [we haven't] the most distant notion of the place where these scenes are represented, or of the materials of which it is composed. . . . personal identity is nothing but a bundle or collection of different perceptions which succeed each other in an inconceivable rapidity.

To summarize, in agreement with Locke, Hume believed that thoughts and perceptions make up our sense of personal identity. Unlike Locke, however, Hume sees no unity to these perceptions. For Hume, "The identity which we ascribe to the mind of man is only a fictitious one." All we experience are thoughts and perceptions in rapid succession. The rapidity with which these thoughts appear gives rise to an illusion of unity. We perceive them to be joined and unified, but in fact, they are isolated and separate. For Hume, any view of self other than the mere succession of perceptions is a fiction.[2]

James: Identity Is a Continuous Feeling

With these theorists providing the background, William James tackled the problem of personal identity. He introduces the issue by noting that the nature of personal identity is one of the most formidable problems in the field of psychology.

> Ever since Hume's time, [the nature of personal identity] has been justly regarded as the most puzzling puzzle with which psychology has to deal; and whatever view one may espouse, one has to hold his position against heavy odds. If, with the Spiritualists, one contends for a substantial soul . . . one can give no positive account of what that may be. And, if with the Humians, one deny such a principle and say that the stream of passing thoughts is all, one runs against an entire commonsense of mankind, of which the belief in a distinct principle of selfhood seems an integral part. (p. 330)

James attempts to solve this enigma by staking out a middle ground between these various positions. He disagrees with those who postulate the existence of

---

[2]Having delivered his assertion that the self is nothing but a fiction, Hume proceeds to have misgivings in the appendix of his book. He writes: "Upon a more strict review of the section concerning *personal identity*, I find myself involved in such a labyrinth that, I must confess, I neither know how to correct my former opinions, [nor] how to make them consistent."

an immaterial substance in which our perceptions inhere; but he also disagrees with those who claim there is no tie binding these perceptions. Instead, James's position is that there is a unity to the self, provided by the thoughts and perceptions themselves and the feelings associated with them.

Let's look at how James developed his argument. He began by noting that everyone is familiar with an aspect of existence that seems peculiarly one's own.

> . . . all men must single out from the rest of what they call themselves some central principle. . . . Some would say that it is a simple active substance, the soul, of which they are thus conscious; others, that it is nothing but a fiction, the imaginary being denoted by the pronoun *I*, and between those two extremes of opinion all sorts of intermediaries would be found. . . . [But setting aside for the moment just what this central principle *is*,] let us try to settle for ourselves as definitely as we can, just how this central nucleus of the Self may *feel*. [For] whether it be a spiritual substance or only a delusive word . . . this central part of the Self is *felt*. [It is not] cognized only in an intellectual way . . . when it is found it is *felt*. (pp. 298–299)

James goes on to claim that this central nucleus of the self (the *I* as we have called it) is a component of the spiritual self. Earlier we noted that James believed the spiritual self could be conceptualized in two ways. The abstract way involved looking at each separate aspect of the spiritual self in isolation; the concrete way involved treating the spiritual self as a seamless flow of uninterrupted perceptions.

The solution he proposes to understanding personal identity is that personal identity is to be found in the concrete way of treating the spiritual self. Each perception flows by, but these perceptions are not isolated and distinct, joined only in an illusory manner by virtue of their close contiguity, as Hume had claimed. Instead, they are joined because they are part of the same stream (of consciousness). Moreover, it is the feelings associated with each perception that provide the tie that binds them. Each perception carries a distinctive feeling that we recognize as ours and ours alone.

> Each thought, out of a multitude of other thoughts of which it may think, is able to distinguish those which belong to its own [Self] from those which do not. The former have a warmth and intimacy about them of which the later are completely devoid. . . . (p. 330)

But how does each thought recognize this warmth and intimacy? James attempted to answer this question by invoking an analogy to a title that is bequeathed. If, at the very moment the recipient of the title comes into existence the bequestor dies, the bequeathed would come to own all previous thoughts as a condition of its birth. The present thought would be the owner of all previous thoughts.

> Each Thought dies away and is replaced by another. The other, among the things it knows, knows it own predecessor, and finding it "warm" in the way we have described, greets it saying: "Thou art *mine*, and part of the same self with me." Each later Thought knowing and including thus the Thoughts

which went before, is the final receptacle—and appropriating them is the final owner—of all that they contain and own. Each Thought is thus born an owner, and dies owned, transmitting whatever it realized as its Self to its own later proprietor. (p. 339)

Summary and Critique

To summarize, James's position is that the unity of the self can be explained entirely in psychological terms. Each successive thought is joined with previous thoughts by virtue of the feeling they share. There is no immaterial substance, but neither is identity a fiction. Personal identity is our uninterrupted memory for prior perceptions and our memory of the affect associated with them. Much as the ancient ship Theseus retained its identity when each plank was gradually replaced, so, too, does our identity remain intact as each idea, perception, or sensation fades and is immediately replaced by another that carries the same distinctive feeling.

> A uniform feeling of "warmth" . . . pervades [our various selves] and this is what gives them a *generic* unity, and what makes them the same *kind*. . . . where the resemblance and the continuity are no longer felt, the sense of personal identity goes too. (p. 335)

James's analysis is admittedly speculative, and not everyone has accepted his contention that the passing thought is the thinker (see, for example, Gergen, 1971). As it is doubtful whether such matters will ever yield to a definitive resolution, readers of this book are free to draw their own conclusions regarding the cogency of James's solution.

What is important to understand from the standpoint of this book is the attempt James made to understand the nature of the *I* within a psychology of the self. Many commentators on his chapter have claimed that James believed the nature of the *I* was not a suitable topic for psychological analysis (e.g., Allport, 1943). This is not entirely so. It is certainly the case that James believed psychology needn't concern itself with a soul substance, which he referred to as an "illusory term" and "a complete superfluity" (p. 348). But he also believed that the *I* (as it refers to our sense of personal identity) was a bona fide psychological phenomena worthy of investigation.

The close connection James saw between self and emotion is also of particular importance. This emphasis surfaced in his discussion of our memory for childhood events.

> We hear from our parents various anecdotes about our infant years, but we do not appropriate them as we do our own memories. Those breaches of decorum awaken no blush, those bright sayings no self-complacency. That child is a foreign creature with which our present self is no more identified in feeling than it is with some stranger's live child today. Why? Partly because great time-gaps break up all those early years—we cannot ascend to them by continuous memories; and partly because no representation of how the child *felt* comes up with the story. We know what he said and did; but no sentiment of his little body, of his emotions, of his psychic strivings as they felt to

him, comes up to contribute an element of warmth and intimacy to the narrative we hear, and the main bond of union with our present self thus disap-
pears. (p. 335)

This quote is noteworthy for several reasons. The first is the role of continuity. One reason we do not identify with our infancy is because of the gap.
We simply cannot remember being the child our parents describe. More interesting is the emphasis on affect, warmth, and intimacy. We do not relate to our
infancy because we cannot recapture the way we *felt* then. The implication is
that even if we could remember the incidents themselves, we would not identify with our infancy unless we also could remember what it felt like to be *us*.
For James, it is the continuity of warmth and intimacy that underlies personal
identity.

It is interesting to compare James's analysis to Locke's distinction between
man and person. Locke contended only someone who can remember committing an action can be held accountable for his or her behavior. James takes this
analysis one step further. It is not enough to simply remember committing an
act, James claims. One must also be able to access the feelings the act occa-
sioned. Imagine that someone accused of a crime says "I remember committing the act, but only in a cold detached way, with no connection to the feelings that were present, as if I were watching a film of some other person
committing the act." Would we be inclined to hold this person accountable for
his actions? James's analysis of the problem of personal identity says "no."
Personal identity requires more than memory; it requires an ability to recapture the feelings associated with the experience.

In more general terms, we began this section by asking whether there is
something we could lose that would negate our identity, that would lead us to
no longer refer to ourselves with the personal pronoun *I*. James's answer is
that this something is the way it feels to be us.

> If a man wakes up some fine day unable to recall any of his past experiences,
> so that he has to learn his biography afresh, *or if he only recalls the facts of it in a
> cold abstract way* . . . he feels, and he says that he is a changed person. (p. 336;
> emphasis added)

CHAPTER SUMMARY

In this chapter we have examined the nature of the self. We began by exploring the nature of the *ME*. William James divided the *ME* into three subcategories: the material
self (our bodies and extended selves), the social self (the various roles we play in social
life and the way we are recognized and regarded by others), and the spiritual self (our
inner or psychological self, including our ideas about our traits and abilities, values
and habits, and the way it feels to be us). We then looked at contemporary research
that has tested and extended James's scheme.

We then considered the nature of self-feelings. James identified a class of emotions
that directly implicate how people feel about themselves. These self-relevant emotions
include feelings of pride, guilt, shame, and humiliation. James believed these emotions

were instinctive in nature, and that people were motivated to experience the positive emotions and avoid the negative ones. Subsequent researchers have examined the nature of these emotions and the manner in which they are influenced by various self-views (e.g., our ideas about who we *ought* to be).

Finally, we considered the nature of the *I*. Ancient philosophers had postulated the existence of a soul substance, something substantial that comprises a person's essence and unites the person's perceptions. The British philosopher, John Locke, modified this position, asserting that identity is comprised of perceptions, sensations, and memories that reside in an immaterial substance. Another British philosopher, David Hume, further challenged this claim, arguing that perceptions, sensations, and memories are not joined in any fashion other than an illusory one. William James staked out a middle ground, arguing that there is no soul substance but that the perceptions are joined by virtue of the feelings they share.

Throughout our discussion of these issues, we have given particular attention to the views of William James. This emphasis is entirely commensurate with the influence he has had on the field. James wrote on a range of topics, and the insights he provided over 100 years ago have given subsequent researchers a wealth of testable hypotheses. We will have occasion to revisit many of these issues throughout the remainder of this text. Despite the breadth of his coverage, one idea runs like a leitmotif through James's analysis. This is the notion that whatever is self is laden with emotion. For James, emotion is the defining feature of that which is self.

- William James distinguished three components of the empirical self (or *ME*). These were (1) the material self (tangible objects, people, or places that carry the designation *my* or *mine*); (2) the social self (our social roles and the way we are recognized and regarded by others); and (3) the spiritual self (our inner or psychological self, including our perceived traits, abilities, emotions, and beliefs).
- Contemporary researchers have refined and expanded James's scheme to include the *collective* self and the *relational* self. The collective self refers to social categories to which we belong, including our racial, religious, and ethnic identities. The *relational* self includes specific individuals who are part of our self-concept (e.g., my children; my wife).
- People differ in the importance they attach to their various identities. People in Western cultures emphasize the ways in which they are different from others, and place great importance on their personal identities. People from Eastern cultures emphasize the ways in which they are similar to or are related to others, and they place more importance on their collective and relational identities. Individuals also differ within each culture.
- William James identified a class of emotions that always involves the self as a point of reference. He called the positive emotions self-complacency and the negative emotions self-dissatisfaction. James believed that these emotions were instinctive in nature and that people are motivated to experience the positive emotions and avoid experiencing the negative emotions. Subsequent researchers have built on James's analysis by (1) making finer distinctions among these emotions (e.g., by distinguishing between shame and guilt), and (2) exploring how these emotions are influenced by people's beliefs about who they could be, want to be, or ought to be.
- Other people can be an important source of self-feelings. People can bask in the reflected glory of other people's accomplishment (e.g., sports fans experience pride and euphoria when their team wins). People also derive feelings of self-worth from

the social groups to which they belong, and they feel better about themselves when they appraise their group in more positive terms than they evaluate other groups.

- For centuries, philosophers have pondered a puzzle known as the problem of personal identity. The problem centers around whether there is something that unites our various perceptions and sensations. Early philosophers (from Aristotle to Descartes) maintained that people possess a soul that unites these aspects of psychological life. John Locke, a British philosopher, tied personal identity to memory, arguing that the unity we experience is provided by our memories. David Hume, a Scottish philosopher, took issue with this claim and asserted that personal identity is entirely an illusion. William James built on these claims and argued that identity involves continuous memory for how it feels to be us.

For Further Reading

BREWER, M. B., & GARDNER, W. (1996). Who is this "we"? Levels of collective identity and self-representations. *Journal of Personality and Social Psychology, 71,* 83–93.

JAMES, W. (1890). *The principles of psychology* (Vol. 1). New York: Holt.

LYON, A. J. (1988). Problems of personal identity. In G. Parkinson (Ed.), *An encyclopedia of philosophy* (pp. 441–462). London: Rutledge.

MARKUS, H. R., & KITAYAMA, S. (1991). Culture and the self: Implications for cognition, emotion, and motivation. *Psychological Review, 98,* 224–253.

CHAPTER 3

The Search for Self-Knowledge

Make it thy business to know thyself, which is the most difficult lesson in the world.

—Cervantes (*Don Quixote*, Part ii, Chapter 42)

I have a friend who thinks he's creative, sensitive, shy, and warm. Another friend of mine thinks she's independent, self-motivated, competitive, and ambitious. Where do these ideas come from? Why do people think of themselves as they do, and to what extent do these views represent what people are really like?

Chapter 3 will explore questions of this nature. In investigating these issues, we will focus on people's ideas about their personality traits and abilities. We will be particularly concerned with traits and abilities that are socially valued and desirable, such as people's ideas about how intelligent, kind, loyal, and attractive they think they are. These are all aspects of what James (1890) called the spiritual self.

We will begin by considering when and why people search for self-knowledge. We will pay particular attention here to understanding what people *want* to think about themselves. This issue is important because a desire to think of ourselves in a particular way influences the way we seek self-knowledge.

In the second section of the chapter, we will examine important sources of self-knowledge. These sources include (1) the physical world, (2) the social world, and (3) the inner (psychological) world of thoughts and feelings. We will see that each of these sources of self-knowledge yields important information about what we are like, but none is unambiguous or free of distortion.

The third section of this chapter examines how people evaluate themselves. Here we will see that most people appraise themselves in very positive terms, and that these self-views are not always accurate or realistic. Finally, we note how biases in the way people seek self-knowledge promote these positive self-views.

BEGINNING THE SEARCH FOR SELF-KNOWLEDGE

Cultural factors provide the first signposts on the road to self-knowledge. To a great extent, who we are—and who we think we are—are determined by the time and place we are raised and live (Baumeister, 1986). If we are raised in a traditional agrarian society, we are unlikely to think of ourselves as a budding entrepreneur. It could happen, but it is unlikely.

The role of culture is most clearly seen with respect to how it shapes our social identities. Countries that have caste systems, such as India, virtually dictate people's social identities. But cultural factors also influence our personal identities. To regard oneself as a competitive person, for example, requires that we live in a culture that supplies the term and gives us the opportunity to act competitively. One can conceive of a society that stresses cooperation and doesn't even have a concept of competitiveness. If the concept isn't part of the culture, it isn't apt to be part of the self.

Cultural *expectations* also influence people's self-views. This point was illustrated in a study by Rubin, Provenzano, and Luria (1974). These investigators interviewed the mothers and fathers of one-day-old infants. They found that the parents were more apt to use words like "beautiful," "cute," and "pretty" when describing their newborn daughters than when describing their newborn sons. Pervasive cultural expectations like these inevitably influence the way people think about themselves.

Situations That Initiate a Search for Self-Knowledge

Cultural factors represent a passive form of self-knowledge acquisition, in that people gain self-knowledge without actively seeking it. This is not the only way people acquire self-knowledge, however. Sometimes, people deliberately set out to learn what they are like.

An active search for self-knowledge is particularly apt to occur when people make important changes in life. To illustrate, Deutsch, Ruble, Fleming, Brooks-Gunn, and Stangor (1988) studied women who were planning to get pregnant or were expecting the birth of a first child. They found that these women actively sought information about motherhood and incorporated this information into their self-concept. Moreover, doing so provided important benefits: Women who had clearly established an identity as a mother during pregnancy showed better postpartum adjustment and were more satisfied with their lives than were women who had difficulty establishing this identity (Oakley, 1980). These findings suggest that an active search for self-knowledge is especially likely (and especially beneficial) when people confront important life changes.

Motives That Guide the Search for Self-Knowledge

When people actively seek knowledge of themselves, they do not do so in a dispassionate, disinterested way. Instead, people have particular goals in mind, and these goals lead them to selectively seek, notice, and interpret information about themselves. This selectivity occurs as a result of three forces.

The Self-Enhancement Motive

The first of these forces is known as the self-enhancement motive. In Chapter 2, we noted that William James (1890) identified a class of self-relevant emotional states. Feeling proud or pleased with ourselves (on the positive side) and feeling humiliated or ashamed of ourselves (on the negative side) are examples of what James had in mind. The self-enhancement motive refers to the fact that people are motivated to experience these positive emotional states and to avoid experiencing these negative emotional states. People are motivated to *feel* good about themselves, to maximize their feelings of self-worth.

This emphasis on feelings differs a bit from how other theorists have defined self-enhancement needs. Other theorists have taken the term to mean that people are motivated to *think* of themselves in highly favorable terms (e.g., Rosenberg, 1979; Shrauger, 1975; Swann, 1990). It is certainly the case that in many situations and in many cultures, feelings of self-worth are promoted by thinking of oneself as highly capable or somehow *better* than one's peers. But this is not invariably so. In some situations and in some cultures, feelings of self-worth are promoted by thinking of oneself as ordinary or average, or even *worse* than others (parents, for example, may take pride in thinking their children are smarter and more talented than they themselves are). These sorts of differences mask an underlying similarity. In both cases, thoughts about the self serve to enhance feelings of self-worth. The universal need (which McDougall [1923] called the "master sentiment") is not a need to *think* of oneself in any specific way but a need to maximize feelings of self-worth. This is what we mean when we speak of a self-enhancement motive.

That being said, it is the case that in many cultures, particularly contemporary Western societies (e.g., United States, Canada, and Western Europe), feelings of self-worth are promoted by thinking of oneself in favorable terms—as exceptionally kind, likable, intelligent, and attractive, for example. In this case, self-enhancement needs lead people to seek information about themselves in such a way that they are apt to conclude that they possess these qualities.

The Accuracy Motive

Accuracy needs also influence the manner in which people seek knowledge of themselves. Sometimes people want to know the truth about themselves, without regard to whether they learn something good or bad (Trope, 1986). Three considerations are thought to underlie this need (Brown, 1991). First, sometimes people simply want to reduce uncertainty; they want to know what they are like for the sheer intrinsic pleasure of knowing what they are like.

People may also believe that they have a moral obligation to know what they are really like. This admonition is prominent in theological and philosophical thought. The existentialist philosophers, for example, held that people have an ethical obligation to uncover their true nature. People who evade self-understanding were considered to be weak, cowardly, and living a depraved or purposeless existence.

Finally, we seek accurate information about ourselves because knowing what we are really like can sometimes help us achieve other goals. One of these goals is survival. Let's imagine, just as an example, that I think of myself as incredibly fleet of foot when I am actually slower than a snail. If all I'm doing is running around a track by myself, my inaccurate beliefs about myself are probably doing me no harm. But if I intend to taunt a wild beast to see if I can outrun it when it gets mad and turns on me, it probably would be helpful for me to know how fast I really am; otherwise, I will die! The point here is that accurate self-knowledge is sometimes adaptive; sometimes, it is important for us to know what we are really like (Festinger, 1954).

Accurate self-knowledge can also be instrumental to maximizing feelings of self-worth (Sedikides & Strube, in press). Success is one of the things that makes people feel good about themselves. Knowing what you are really like can sometimes makes success more likely. For example, a person who is "all thumbs in the wood shop" is apt to experience repeated failure as a carpenter. It might be good for this person to know that his talents in this domain are somewhat limited, before he decides whether or not to pursue a career in woodworking. This is another reason why it is important to emphasize that self-enhancement refers to emotion—the desire to maximize feelings of self-worth, not the desire to think of oneself as good at everything. Self-enhancement needs can sometimes be met by knowing what we can't do well.

The Consistency Motive

A final force to consider is known as the consistency motive. In Chapter 1 we saw that our ideas about ourselves serve several important functions: They influence the way we process information, they guide our behavior, and they serve as end-states toward which our future behavior is oriented. Many theorists believe these functions give rise to a motive to protect the self-concept against change (e.g., Epstein, 1980; Lecky, 1945; Rosenberg, 1979; Swann, 1990). This motive leads people to seek and embrace information that is consistent with what they think they are like, and to avoid and reject information that is inconsistent with what they think they are like. Prescott Lecky (1945) was an early proponent of this position.

> According to self-consistency, the mind is a unit, an organized system of ideas. All of the ideas which belong to the system must seem to be consistent with one another. The center or nucleus of the mind is the individual's idea or conception of himself. If a new idea seems to be consistent with the . . . individual's conception of himself, it is accepted and assimilated easily. If it seems to be inconsistent, however, it meets with resistance and is likely to be rejected. (p. 246)

Not everyone endorses a self-consistency motive (Steele & Spencer, 1992), but it has played an important role in several influential theories. For example, cognitive dissonance theory (Festinger, 1957) maintains that the holding of two inconsistent cognitions produces an aversive state of arousal that people are motivated to avoid and reduce. Aronson (1968) subsequently amended this formulation, contending that one of the cognitions must involve people's beliefs about themselves. What produces dissonance, Aronson argued, is not the realization that "I did *X* when I believe *Y*," it is the recognition that "I'm not a hypocritical person but I just said or did something I don't believe in." We will have more to say about dissonance theory in Chapter 5.

The self-consistency motive also plays an important role in Swann's (1990, 1996) self-verification theory. Self-verification theory contends that once people develop ideas about what they are like, they strive to verify these self-views. Consider, for example, a person who thinks of herself as highly intelligent. According to Swann, this person is motivated to verify this view of herself. To do so, she can (1) engage in activities that demonstrate her acumen; (2) selectively seek, accept, and retain information that confirms her sagacity; and (3) attempt to convince others that she possesses a brilliant mind.

Two considerations are thought to drive the search for self-verifying feedback (Swann, Stein-Seroussi, & Giesler, 1992). First, we feel more comfortable and secure when we believe that other people see us as we see ourselves. Imagine how unsettling it would be if you suddenly learned you were not the person you thought you were. Seeking self-verifying feedback helps people avoid this anxiety and epistemic confusion. The search for self-verifying feedback is also fueled by more pragmatic, interpersonal concerns. Self-verification theory assumes that our social interactions proceed more smoothly and profitably when other people view us as we view ourselves. This consideration gives people a second reason to selectively seek self-verifying feedback.

An especially controversial aspect of self-verification theory is the predictions it makes when people hold negative views of themselves. The theory asserts that people are just as interested in confirming their negative self-views as they are in corroborating their positive self-views. We will examine the support for this prediction later in this chapter.

SOURCES OF SELF-KNOWLEDGE

Suppose one day you read about a characteristic you have never heard of. How would you go about finding out whether you have this characteristic or not? Generally speaking, you have three sources of information at your disposal: the physical world, the social world, and the inner (psychological) world of thoughts and feelings.

Physical World

Physical reality provides one means by which you can learn about yourself. If you want to know how tall you are, you can measure your height; if you want to know how many pounds you can lift, you can go to a health club and take note of how many pounds you can lift. In these cases, you are using the physical world to gain knowledge of yourself.

Though useful as a source of self-knowledge, the physical world is limited in two important respects. First, many attributes are not anchored in physical reality (Festinger, 1954). Suppose you want to know how *kind* you are. You can't simply get out a yardstick and measure your kindness. The same is true if you want to know how clever or sincere you are. A physical basis for gaining knowledge in these domains (and many others) is lacking.

A second, and related point, is that even when attributes can be assessed with reference to the physical world, the knowledge we gain from the physical world isn't necessarily the knowledge we are after. Knowing your height doesn't really tell you whether or not you are tall. You need to know how tall other people are, and whether you are taller or shorter than they are. The same is true when it comes to knowing how many pounds you can lift. Before you can know whether you're strong or not, you need to know how many pounds other people can lift.

The larger point here is that attributes like tall and strong acquire meaning only with respect to the attributes of others. This is true of many of the ways people think about themselves. Most of our personal identities are couched in comparative terms. When we say we are independent, we are implicitly saying that we think we are more independent than are other people; when we say we are talented, we are implicitly saying that we think we are more talented than are most others.

Social World

The comparative nature of self-views means that people must rely heavily on the social world when seeking to understand who they are and what they are like. Two social processes are particularly important.

Social Comparison

First, as just indicated, people engage in a process of social comparison. They compare their attributes with others and draw inferences about what they are like. Research on social comparison processes was initiated by Leon Festinger (1954). Festinger postulated that people have a drive to know what they are really like, and that often they can satisfy this desire only by comparing themselves with others. To illustrate, suppose you find out that you can run a mile in seven minutes. In order to know whether you're fast or slow, you need to know how long it takes other people to run a mile.

Of course, any conclusions you draw about yourself greatly depend on those with whom you compare yourself. The need for *accurate* self-knowledge was originally thought to guide the social comparison process (Festinger, 1954), and researchers assumed that comparing with others who are similar to us in important ways is most informative. From this perspective, you would best be able to tell how fast you really are by comparing with other people of your sex and age group. To the extent that you run a mile faster than these *similar others,* you would think of yourself as fast. Comparing your time with people of the opposite sex, or with those who are much older or younger than you, is less informative. These people are too different from you in areas relevant to running to serve as suitable targets of comparison.

There is considerable evidence that people do compare themselves with others who are similar to them in important ways (Wood, 1989). But this is not always true (Collins, 1996; Goethals & Darley, 1977; Taylor & Lobel, 1989; Wills, 1981; Wood, 1989). People also compare themselves with those who are slightly better off than they are (a process called *upward comparison*) and with those who are slightly worse off or somehow disadvantaged on the dimension under consideration (a process called *downward comparison*). There is also substantial evidence that the need for accurate self-knowledge is not the only, or even the most important, factor that guides the social comparison process (Helgeson & Mickelson, 1995). Under many circumstances, the need to feel good about ourselves affects the social comparison process (Wood, 1989).

Reflected Appraisals

Another way people gain self-knowledge is by observing how others respond to them. Imagine, for example, that a person tells a joke and perceives that other people are laughing at it. The person might reasonably infer that she is witty. Formally, this process is known as the *reflected appraisal* process.

Charles Horton Cooley, a turn-of-the-century American sociologist, first articulated this perspective in his discussion of the *looking-glass self*. Cooley (1902) was particularly concerned with how people's feelings toward themselves develop. He argued that these feelings are socially determined. We imagine how we are regarded by another person, and this perception determines how we feel about ourselves. The term *looking-glass self* was used to call attention to the fact that other people serve as a mirror; that is, we see ourselves reflected in other people's eyes.

> In a very large and interesting class of cases the social reference takes the form of a somewhat definite imagination of how one's self . . . appears in a particular mind, and the kind of self-feeling one has is determined by the attitude toward this attributed to that other mind. A social self of this sort might be called the reflected or looking-glass self. (Cooley, 1902, pp. 152–153)

Cooley went on to propose a three-step process. First, we imagine how we appear in the eyes of another person; second, we imagine how that person is evaluating us; third, we feel good or bad in accordance with this imagined judgment. Note the phenomenological nature of Cooley's model. It is our imagined judgment, not what the person actually thinks of us, that makes us feel proud or ashamed of ourselves.

> A self-idea of this sort seems to have three principal elements: the imagination of our appearance to the other person; the imagination of his judgment of that appearance; and some sort of self-feeling, such as pride or mortification. The comparison with a looking-glass hardly suggests the second element, the imagined judgment, which is quite essential. The thing that moves us to pride or shame is not the mere mechanical reflection of ourselves, but an imputed sentiment, the imagined effect of this reflection upon another's mind. (Cooley, 1902, p. 153)

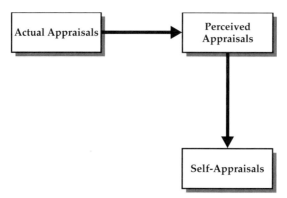

FIGURE 3.1. A schematic representation of the reflected appraisal model. In this model, what other people think of us (actual appraisals) influences our self-appraisals indirectly, via perceived appraisals.

Although Cooley was concerned with how people's feelings toward themselves develop, Kinch (1963) adapted these ideas to explain how people's thoughts about themselves develop. Kinch's model, which is shown in Figure 3.1, also has three components: (1) what other people actually think of us (the actual appraisals of others); (2) our perception of these appraisals (our perceived appraisals); and (3) our own ideas about what we are like (our self-appraisals). The model assumes that actual appraisals determine perceived appraisals, and perceived appraisals, in turn, determine self-appraisals. As an example, the model assumes (1) that another person thinks you are attractive (actual appraisal), (2) that you are aware of this (perceived appraisal), and (3) that, because of this, you think you are attractive. Note again the phenomenological nature of the model. The lack of a direct arrow linking actual appraisals to self-appraisals means that it is our perception of what other people think of us, rather than what they actually think of us, that determines our self-appraisals.

In recent years, a great deal of research has tested the model shown in Figure 3.1 (for reviews, see Felson, 1993; Kenny & DePaulo, 1993). A typical investigation with college students involves a group of friends, roommates, or acquaintances. The students rate themselves and each other on a number of dimensions (e.g., how attractive, intelligent, and sociable do you think person X is?). The students are also asked to predict how they are being rated by others (e.g., how attractive do you think person Y thinks you are?). Finally, the relations among actual appraisals, perceived appraisals, and self-appraisals are examined.

In general, this research has turned up only limited support for the reflected appraisal model. First, contrary to the model, people are not very good at knowing what any particular individual thinks of them. Felson (1993) believes this is because communication barriers and social norms limit the information we receive from others. This is especially true when the feedback would be negative. People rarely give one another negative feedback ("if you don't

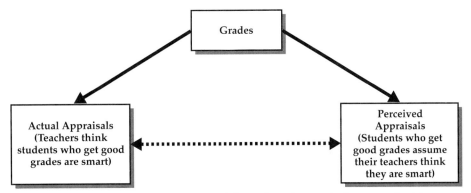

FIGURE 3.2. A schematic representation of the reflected appraisal process. In this example, grades function as a common third variable that leads to an association between actual appraisals and perceived appraisals.

have anything nice to say about someone, don't say anything at all"), so people rarely conclude that other people dislike them or evaluate them negatively.

Despite being largely unaware of how any particular person evaluates them, people are better at knowing what people *in general* think of them. At the same time, the nature of this association may not conform to the one specified in Figure 3.1. The reflected appraisal model assumes that actual appraisals determine perceived appraisals (e.g., other people think you are smart, somehow communicate this information to you, and you correctly perceive that they think you are smart). Although this pattern may occur, the influence of a common third variable could also produce a spurious association between actual appraisals and perceived appraisals (Felson, 1993; Kenny & DePaulo, 1993).

Performance in the classroom provides a suitable example (see Figure 3.2). Some students get better grades in school than do others. Teachers think students who get good grades are smart, and students who get good grades assume their teachers think they are smart. In this case, actual appraisals and perceived appraisals will be correlated, but there is no causal relation between them. They are correlated simply because they are both associated with grades.

A related problem clouds the interpretation of the association between perceived appraisals and self-appraisals. As shown in Figure 3.1, these variables are highly correlated (Felson, 1993; Kenny & DePaulo, 1993; Shrauger & Schoeneman, 1979), but the causal association between them is unclear. The reflected appraisal model assumes that perceived appraisals determine self-appraisals (e.g., if we think other people think we are clever, then we think we are clever), but the reverse causal sequence is also possible (e.g., if we think we are clever, we assume other people think so, too). Although correlational studies do not afford a definitive test of this issue, the tendency to assume that others see us as we see ourselves seems to account for most of the correlation between perceived appraisals and self-appraisals (Felson, 1993).

These findings suggest some important qualifications to the reflected appraisal model. As originally conceived, the model assumed that people see themselves as others see them. Person A forms an opinion about Person B, and Person B pliantly registers this opinion and incorporates it into her self-concept. This sequence may accurately characterize matters in early childhood (parents give their children lots of personal feedback, and children incorporate this feedback into their ideas about themselves), but it appears to be less relevant later in life. This is because people are not as passive as the model assumes; they actively and selectively process information from the social world. Once people's ideas about themselves take shape, these ideas influence the manner in which new information is gathered and interpreted.

Inner (Psychological) World

Three processes of a more personal nature also influence the way people acquire knowledge of themselves.

Introspection

One of these processes, introspection, involves looking inward and directly consulting our attitudes, feelings, and motives. Suppose, for example, I want to know whether I'm a sentimental person. I can look inward and ask myself how I generally feel at weddings, funerals, and other occasions that are relevant to sentimentality. If I feel soft and warm inside on these occasions, I'm apt to conclude that I am a sentimental person.

Introspection would seem to be a very reliable way of knowing what we are like. After all, what better way to know ourselves than to examine our own thoughts and feelings? This perception appears to be widely shared. Andersen and Ross (1984) asked college students whether another person would know them better (1) if they knew their private thoughts and feelings for one day, or (2) if they were able to observe their behavior over a period of several months. By a wide margin, the students believed that other people would know them best if they were privy to their inner world of thoughts and feelings.

Andersen (1984) conducted a follow-up investigation to test this assumption. Andersen had participants describe themselves to people they did not know, emphasizing either their private thoughts and feelings, their behavior, or a mixture of the two. Later, the observers rated the participants on a number of dimensions, and Andersen calculated the correspondence between these ratings and the participants' own self-assessments.

The results from this investigation, which are displayed in Figure 3.3, show that observers produced ratings that most closely matched the participants' own ratings when the participants had described their thoughts and feelings. These findings indicate that your thoughts and feelings provide other people with valuable information about what you are like. By extension, these findings suggest that consulting your own thoughts and feelings can yield meaningful self-knowledge (see also, Hixon & Swann, 1993; Johnson & Boyd, 1995; Millar & Tesser, 1989).

Whether introspection always fosters self-insight is not entirely clear, however. Wilson and his colleagues have argued that thinking too much

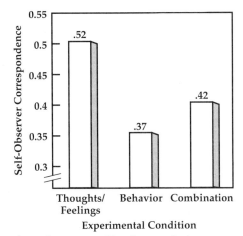

FIGURE 3.3. Correspondence between self-ratings and observer ratings as a function of whether people revealed their thoughts and feelings, their behavior, or a combination. The data show that observers learn more about what a person is like when the person reveals his or her thoughts and feelings.
(Adapted from Andersen, 1984, *Journal of Personality and Social Psychology, 46,* 294–307. Copyright 1984. Adapted by permission of The American Psychological Association.)

about *why* we feel the way we do about some person, object, or issue can confuse us and undermine accurate self-knowledge (for a review, see Wilson & Hodges, 1992). Wilson's research is built on the premise that people do not always know why they feel the way they do (Freud, 1957; Lyons, 1986; Nisbett & Wilson, 1977). Nevertheless, people have little difficulty generating plausible explanations for their feelings. The problem is that these reasons often reflect common cultural assumptions rather than private, accurate self-knowledge. For example, if you were asked why you like your boyfriend or girlfriend, you would probably say it has something to do with the person's personality (e.g., the person's warmth or kindness). In fact, these reasons are imperfectly related to why you feel the way you do. Other reasons, such as the person's physical attractiveness or even the way the person walks, laughs, or gestures, may be equally or more important.

Wilson and his associates have conducted numerous studies demonstrating that problems can arise when people introspect about reasons. In these studies, some participants (those in the introspection condition) are encouraged to carefully consider why they feel the way they do about some person, object, or issue before making a decision. Other participants (those in the control condition) make their decision without being asked to analyze the basis of their feelings. The results show that participants in the introspection condition are less accurate when predicting their future behavior (Wilson & LaFleur, 1995) and are less satisfied with their choices and decisions (Wilson et al., 1993) than are participants in the control condition. On the basis of these and other findings, Wilson concludes that thinking too much about why we feel the way we do can diminish, rather than promote, accurate self-knowledge.

Self-Perception Processes

Wilson's work is based on the assumption that people are not always aware of why they feel the way they do. Bem's (1972) *self-perception* theory makes a similar assumption. Self-perception theory is concerned with how people explain their behavior. The theory argues that people do not always know why they do what they do. When this occurs, they infer the causes of their behavior by analyzing their behavior in the context in which it occurs.

To illustrate, suppose you ask me whether I like country music. To answer this question, I might recall that every time I'm in my car I keep my radio tuned to a country music station. So I answer, "Yes, I like country music." After all, what other reason can there be? No one makes me listen to country music, so the only reasonable explanation for why I listen to it all the time is that I like it.

Note that an outside observer would have reached a similar conclusion. If you knew I always listened to country music, you would also infer that I like country music. This equivalence is a hallmark of Bem's theory. The theory assumes that people often gain self-knowledge simply by observing their own behavior, and drawing logical conclusions about why they behaved as they did.

> Individuals come to "know" their own attitudes, emotions, and other internal states partially by inferring them from observations of their own overt behavior and/or the circumstances in which this behavior occurs. Thus, to the extent that internal cues are weak, ambiguous, or uninterpretable, the individual is functionally in the same position as an outside observer, an observer who must necessarily rely upon those same external cues to infer the individual's inner states. (Bem, 1972, p. 2)

Self-perception theory has been applied to a wide range of phenomena. Under certain conditions, people have been shown to infer their attitudes (Olson & Hafer, 1990), emotions (Laird, 1974; Schachter & Singer, 1962), and motives (Lepper, Greene, & Nisbett, 1973) in the manner specified by the theory. Some of the most intriguing demonstrations of the theory come from research on emotion. In one study (Laird, 1974), participants were induced to smile or frown while reading a series of cartoons to themselves. Those who read the cartoons while smiling thought the cartoons were funnier and liked them more than did those who read the cartoons while frowning. According to self-perception theory, the participants thought, "Well, I'm smiling a lot. I guess I think these cartoons are really amusing" (but see also, Strack, Martin, & Stepper, 1988 for a different interpretation).

Self-perception processes are akin to introspection, but there is an important difference. With introspection, we directly examine our attitudes, feelings, and motives; with self-perception, we indirectly infer our attitudes, feelings, and motives by analyzing our behavior. Another way of saying this is that only introspection involves directly consulting our internal states; the self-perception process is an indirect one that does not require direct access to our internal states.

Causal Attributions

The explanations people give for their actions are the key elements in self-perception theory. Formally, these explanations are known as causal attributions. Causal attributions are answers to *why* questions (Weiner, 1985). Imagine that we see a person staggering as he walks across the street. We ask, "Why?" Is it because the person is injured, mentally unstable, physically challenged, drunk, or high on drugs? The explanation we settle on is a causal attribution; we attribute the person's behavior to a cause. People also make attributions for their own behavior. In our previous example, I decided that the reason I always listen to country music is that I like it. This is a causal attribution.

The attributions people make for events in their lives constitute an important source of self-knowledge. This is especially true when people make attributions for positive and negative events. Imagine, for example, that you take a math course and fail all of the tests. You might decide it's because you're not good at math. In this case, the attribution you made for your poor test performance led you to conclude that you have low ability in this area. If you had decided that you failed the exams for some other reason (e.g., you didn't study hard enough; you studied the wrong material; or the tests were unfair) you would not have concluded that your ability was low.

Finally, people can gain self-knowledge by making attributions for *other* people's behavior. Imagine, for example, that I ask several people to play bridge with me and they all say "no." If I decide the reason they won't play with me is because I'm not a good bridge player, the attribution I have made for other people's behavior has influenced what I think about myself.

Section Summary

In this section we have discussed a number of ways people learn about themselves. They can (1) consult the physical world; (2) compare themselves with others (social comparison); (3) incorporate the opinions of others toward them (reflected appraisals); (4) look inward (introspection); and (5) examine their behavior in the context in which it occurs and draw an appropriate inference (self-perception and attributions).

Not all of these sources of information are relevant for every attribute, but most are. Consider, for example, how these processes could lead a person to think of herself as shy and introverted. To begin, she might examine how she behaves at parties. If she's always standing off to the side, apart from others, she might come to regard herself as introverted through a self-perception process. She could also engage in introspection and examine her feelings in social situations. If she feels anxious and uncomfortable in the company of others, she might conclude that she is shy. People may also have told her she was shy. If she accurately perceived what they were saying, and she incorporated this information into her self-concept, she could come to believe that she was shy through the reflected appraisal process. Finally, she could also compare her level of social activity with others and conclude that she is less socially inclined than most other people. From that information, she might also infer that she is introverted.

WHAT DO PEOPLE THINK OF THEMSELVES?

Having identified the motives that guide the search for self-knowledge and examined various sources of information that people consult to learn what they are like, it is time to look more closely at what people think of themselves. To begin, let's note that so far we have characterized the manner in which people acquire knowledge of themselves as a fairly logical and rational process. We think we are smart *if* we can solve difficult problems, *if* we outperform our peers in school, *if* other people think we are smart, and so forth. In short, we think we are smart *if* we *are* smart. This characterization implies that there should be a strong correspondence between what people think they are like and what they are really like.

Positivity Bias

This is not really the case, however. When it comes to their ideas about their socially valued qualities and abilities (e.g., their kindness, attractiveness, and intelligence), many (if not most) people do not have entirely accurate views of themselves. They regard themselves as better than they really are.

The data shown in Table 3.1 provide initial support for this assertion. The data come from a group of undergraduates attending the University of Washington. As part of a class project, I asked these students to indicate how well a number of attributes described them, most other people, and most University of Washington students (1 – not at all; 5 – very much). Several things about the data are of interest. First, note the extent to which these students regard themselves in very positive terms. They rated themselves above the scale midpoint of 3 on all of the positively valued attributes, and far below the scale midpoint of 3 on all of the negatively valued attributes. This tendency shows that people generally think of themselves in very positive terms. They think of themselves as very loyal, sincere, kind, and intelligent, and not at all as inconsiderate, phony, insensitive, and unintelligent.

The second thing to notice is that this positivity bias is less apparent when the students rate "most other people." In fact, ratings of "most other people" hover around the scale midpoint. Consequently, the students regard themselves in more positive and far less negative terms than they regard most other people. This bias is apparent for every single attribute, and it is particularly strong for attributes that refer to important interpersonal qualities (e.g., kindness, loyalty, sincerity).[1] Moreover, the bias is quite general and is not due to extreme ratings from only a few students. Collapsed across the various attributes, 89 percent of the students rated themselves more positively than they

---

[1]This finding has an important implication. Colvin and Block (1994) have argued that it is entirely appropriate for college students to believe they are better than others on dimensions that are relevant to college admission (e.g., intelligence). Although this may be true, the data shown in Table 3.1 indicate that the tendency for these students to see themselves as "better than others" is actually strongest for attributes that bear no relevance whatsoever to college attendance (e.g., loyalty, sincerity, kindness).

TABLE 3.1. Evaluations of Self and Others

	Target		
Attribute	Self	Others	UW
Positive Attributes			
Loyal	4.25$_a$	2.59$_b$	2.74$_b$
Sincere	4.03$_a$	2.63$_b$	2.74$_b$
Kind	3.99$_a$	2.90$_b$	2.86$_b$
Intelligent	3.85$_a$	2.90$_b$	3.74$_a$
Athletic	3.22$_a$	2.61$_b$	3.29$_a$
Well-liked	3.58$_a$	3.03$_b$	3.23$_c$
Talented	3.46$_a$	3.08$_b$	3.60$_a$
Attractive	3.26$_a$	2.91$_b$	3.20$_a$
$M =$	3.71$_a$	2.83$_b$	3.18$_c$
Negative Attributes			
Inconsiderate	1.43$_a$	3.02$_b$	2.70$_c$
Phony	1.44$_a$	2.91$_b$	2.97$_b$
Insensitive	1.46$_a$	2.91$_b$	2.53$_c$
Unintelligent	1.25$_a$	2.30$_b$	1.70$_c$
Dumb	1.10$_a$	2.11$_b$	1.48$_c$
Unattractive	1.64$_a$	2.43$_b$	2.10$_c$
Unwise	1.52$_a$	2.42$_b$	2.00$_c$
Unpopular	1.82$_a$	2.31$_b$	2.09$_c$
$M =$	1.46$_a$	2.55$_b$	2.20$_c$

Note: Values could range from 1 (not at all) to 5 (very much). Others = Most other people; UW = most University of Washington students. Within each row, means with different subscripts differ at $p < .05$ or less.

rated most other people, and 92 percent of the students rated themselves less negatively than they rated most other people. In short, there is a widespread tendency for these students to regard themselves in more favorable terms than they regard most other people.

Table 3.1 shows one other effect of interest. The tendency to see oneself as "better than others" is reduced when the students' self-ratings are compared with their ratings of most University of Washington students. But it is not completely eliminated. It is still very apparent for the socially valued interpersonal qualities (e.g., loyal, sincere, kind). There is also a corresponding tendency for the students to appraise their fellow University of Washington students in very positive terms. In almost all cases, students regard their fellow students in more positive and less negative terms than they regard most other people. This tendency, which was discussed in Chapter 2, is known as ingroup favoritism (Tajfel & Turner, 1986). The term refers to the fact that people not only regard themselves in more favorable terms than they regard most other people, they also regard their family, friends, and fellow group members as better than others (Brown, 1986).

The tendency to regard oneself as somehow better than others is pervasive. People think they are more fair than others (Messick, Bloom, Boldizar, & Samuelson, 1985), possess richer and more adaptive personalities than others (Sande, Goethals, & Radloff, 1988), drive better than others (Svenson, 1981), and have more satisfying interpersonal relationships than others (Buunk & van der Eijnden, 1997; Van Lange & Rusbult, 1995). One of the most dramatic illustrations of this tendency was provided in a 1976 College Board survey, in which nearly 1 million high school students were asked to compare themselves with their peers (cited in Dunning, Meyerowitz, & Holzberg, 1989). Seventy percent of the students rated themselves above the median in leadership ability, 60 percent rated themselves above the median in athletic ability, and 85 percent rated themselves above the median in their ability to get along well with others. Of these, 25 percent placed themselves in the top 1 percent!

It would be one thing if these tendencies were simply due to the excesses of youth, but similar results are found with adults. In one survey, 90 percent of business managers rated their performance as superior to other managers, and 86 percent rated themselves as more ethical than their peers (cited in Myers, 1993). Another study found that 94 percent of college professors believe they do above average work (Cross, 1977). Finally, people facing threats to their health (e.g., cancer patients, people with HIV) show the same self-aggrandizing bias when evaluating themselves relative to other patients with their disease (Buunk, Collins, Taylor, VanYperen, & Dakof, 1990; Helgeson & Taylor, 1993; Taylor, Kemeny, Reed, & Aspinwall, 1991).

To summarize, there is extensive evidence that most people regard themselves in highly favorable terms (Alicke, 1985; Brown, 1986, 1991; Brown & Dutton, 1995a; Greenwald, 1980; Taylor & Brown, 1988, 1994). They believe they have many fine qualities and few negative qualities. This is particularly true when we compare people's self-evaluations with their evaluations of most other people. The majority of individuals regard themselves (and members of their extended self) in far more desirable terms than they regard people in general.

Assessing the Accuracy of People's Self-Views

Because most people can't be *better* than most people, the data shown in Table 3.1 speak to the accuracy of people's self-views. They suggest that people's views of themselves are not only highly positive, they are also inaccurate. But caution is indicated when drawing this conclusion. It is possible (though not likely) that this is an exceptional sample. These students could, in fact, be exceedingly loyal, sincere, and kind (though none too modest!). It is not likely, but it is possible. Determining whether people's ideas about themselves are accurate requires a firmer standard against which these ideas can be measured.

Finding these standards is not as straightforward as it may seem. Multiple constructions of reality are the rule, not the exception (Watzlawick, 1976). Two people can be looking at the same stimulus and legitimately disagree about what they are seeing. This is especially true when it comes to social perception

(Funder, 1987; Kenny, 1991; Kruglanski, 1989; Swann, 1984). Suppose Mary thinks Larry is friendly and warm, but Carrie thinks Larry is cold and detached. Both may be right: Larry may be amicable with Mary but aloof with Carrie. Problems like these only get worse when we try to assess the validity of people's thoughts about themselves (Robins & John, 1997). If Barry thinks he has a wonderful sense of humor, who's to say he's wrong? If he laughs at all of his jokes, to him, he has a good sense of humor.

Despite these difficulties, attempts have been made to assess the accuracy of people's self-views. The following research areas speak to this issue.

Correspondence between Self-Views and Objective Criteria

The most obvious (and decisive) way to determine whether people's views of themselves are accurate is to compare these views with some objective criterion. Unfortunately, this is rarely done, in part because physical reality is lacking for most attributes.

One (albeit imperfect) exception is people's perceptions of their intelligence. Considering the importance of intelligence in our culture and the fact that people routinely receive feedback on their intellectual abilities throughout schooling, we might expect that people are quite accurate with respect to where they fall on this dimension. This is not the case. People's self-appraisals of their intelligence and their scores on standardized IQ tests hover around .3 (Borkenau & Liebler, 1993; Hansford & Hattie, 1982). Importantly, these values are not just found with college students. They are also found with community samples, ruling out the possibility that the modest correlations are due to an attenuated range of intelligence scores.

Intelligence is a broad construct with many components, and this generality may make it difficult to judge. People's ideas about themselves may be more accurate when a narrower, more specific domain is considered. There is some reason to believe this is so. Students' self-appraisals of ability in school ("How good a student are you?") are substantially correlated with their actual classroom performance (Cauce, 1987; Faunce, 1984; Felson, 1984). This is especially true when we look at the association between self-ratings of ability and performance in particular subject areas. For example, students' judgments of how good they are in math are highly correlated with their classroom performance in this area (Marsh, 1993a). This suggests that people's ideas about themselves in very specific domains may be rather accurate.

Unfortunately, the use of correlations to assess the accuracy of people's self-views limits the informational value of these findings. To illustrate the problems involved, consider the information presented in Table 3.2. In these hypothetical examples, we have asked three students to estimate their class rank. The data show that one of the students is in the 25th percentile, one is in the 50th percentile, and one is in the 75th percentile.

In both examples, the correlation between actual class rank and self-reported class rank is 1.0. But only Example 1 shows strong evidence of accuracy. In Example 2, all three students vastly overestimate their class rank. This illustration shows why correlation coefficients are largely uninformative as to

TABLE 3.2. Two Hypothetical Examples Showing the Relation between Actual Class Rank and Self-Reported Class Rank

Example 1		Example 2	
Actual Class Rank	Self-Reported Class Rank	Actual Class Rank	Self-Reported Class Rank
25	25	25	93
50	50	50	96
75	75	75	99
Correlation $r = 1.0$		$r = 1.0$	

Note: In both examples, the correlation between actual class rank and self-reported class rank is 1.0. However, only Example 1 provides evidence of accuracy. In Example 2, all three students substantially overestimated their class standing.

whether people truly know what they are really like. They can tell us whether people are *relatively* accurate, but they cannot tell us whether people are accurate in any absolute sense. Although this issue was raised some time ago (Cronbach, 1955), and more appropriate methods for analyzing data like these are available (Gonzales & Griffin, 1995), researchers have generally ignored the importance of this issue when assessing the accuracy of people's self-views (for an exception, see Sheppard, 1993).

Correspondence between Self-Views and the Judgments of Others

In contrast to the paucity of research relating self-assessments to objective criteria, many studies have related people's self-appraisals to the judgments of others. Although self–other agreement does not constitute accuracy (i.e., reliability is not validity), some attributes, such as attractiveness and popularity, are socially defined. In such cases, the judgments of others provide an appropriate standard for gauging the accuracy of people's self-views.

Consider first, people's perceptions of their attractiveness. In a meta analysis involving over 5,000 participants, Feingold (1992) reported that the correlation between people's perceptions of their own attractiveness and how attractive they are regarded by others was .24. It is important to note that this rather modest value does not arise because observers disagree on who is attractive and who is not. In fact, just the opposite is true: Inter-rater agreement in these studies is generally high, typically exceeding .60. Thus, people are in strong agreement about the attractiveness of others, but these consensual judgments do not coincide with people's perceptions of their own attractiveness.

Felson (1981) found a similar pattern in an examination of college football players' estimates of their ability. In this investigation, each player rated his athletic ability, and these ratings were compared to the ratings made by the players' coaches. There was substantial agreement between coaches about the players' abilities ($r = .65$), but little agreement between the players' assessments and the coaches' assessments ($r = .16$).

An investigation using popularity as a criterion produced similar results. Bohrnstedt and Felson (1983) had 415 children in grades 6 through 8 indicate how well liked they were by the boys or girls in their class. These judgments were then compared with how popular the students actually were. Averaging across the two sexes, Bohrnstedt and Felson found a .32 correlation between children's beliefs about how popular they were in class and their actual classroom popularity. These values provide additional evidence that people's self-perceptions are not strongly tied to the perceptions of others (Malloy, Yarlas, Montvilo, & Sugarman, 1996).

The situation is somewhat different when we examine the correspondence between people's perceptions of their *personality traits* and the way they are perceived by others. Research in this area has found substantial self–other agreement for traits that are unambiguous (Hayes & Dunning, 1997) or clearly manifested in behavior (Funder & Dobroth, 1987). For example, people who are very talkative, outgoing, and sociable tend to think of themselves as being extroverted, and they are judged by others to be extroverted. This leads to a substantial correlation between self-ratings and the ratings of others. Conscientiousness shows a similar effect. People who are meticulous in their appearance and fastidious in their bearing recognize that they are conscientious and are rated that way by others. These effects are so robust that they are found with only minimal acquaintanceship: After knowing someone for only a few minutes, our impressions of the person along these attributes correlate highly with what the person thinks he or she is like (Albright, Kenny, & Malloy, 1988; Borkenau & Liebler, 1992; Watson, 1989).

Of course, this last finding does not mean that strangers know you as well as your good friends or family. Funder and Colvin (1988) found consistent evidence that the personality judgments of friends correlated more highly with people's self-assessments than did the judgments of strangers. Husbands and wives also show substantial agreement regarding one another's personality traits (Costa & McCrae, 1988; McCrae, 1982). These effects appear to be particularly large for attributes that are *hidden from view* (i.e., attributes that do not have clear behavioral referents). For example, although strangers are able to judge your sociability, only your family and friends can gauge how intellectually curious you are (Paulhus & Bruce, 1992; Paunonen, 1989).

A final variable that influences the strength of self–other agreement is the desirability of the trait. The more desirable the trait, the less correspondence there is between people's self-ratings and the way they are rated by others (John & Robins, 1993; Park & Judd, 1989). One interpretation of this finding is that people's ideas about themselves in nonevaluative domains are largely accurate, but their thoughts about themselves in highly evaluative domains are not.

To summarize, people's ratings of their personality traits often are correlated (sometimes substantially) with the judgments of others (Funder, 1987, 1995). This correspondence may indicate that people know what they are really like. At the same time, agreement does not constitute accuracy. My wife and I may agree that I am creative, but this concordance doesn't make it so (Costa & McCrae, 1988; McCrae, 1982). Furthermore, as noted earlier, correlations do not provide an unambiguous estimate of accuracy. Finally, it's also important to bear in mind that the agreement that exists is limited to evaluatively neutral traits. People's judgments of themselves in evaluative domains do not correspond highly with the judgments of others.

Correspondence between Self-Views and Behavior

Another domain relevant to the accuracy issue is the agreement between people's ideas about themselves and their actual behavior. For example, does a person who says he is kind act compassionately? Does a person who says she is generous behave charitably? Several research areas address issues of this nature.

First, there is a vast literature that has looked at the correspondence between personality and behavior. Personality is often measured with self-report, so much of this research is relevant to whether people's views of themselves accurately predict their behavior. This research has found only limited evidence that they do. To illustrate, those who describe themselves as "extremely honest" are only slightly less likely to refrain from cheating when given the opportunity to do so than are those who claim simply to be "rather honest" (Mischel, 1968). In a similar vein, people's attitudes (as expressed by self-report) do not always predict their overt behavior. For example, people who describe themselves as "environmentally conscious" do not always act in an environmentally responsible manner (Wicker, 1969).

Finally, people overestimate their ability to predict their own behavior. A study by Vallone, Griffin, Lin, and Ross (1990) examined this issue (see also, Osberg & Shrauger, 1986). At the beginning of an academic term, university students indicated the likelihood that they would engage in a variety of behaviors in the coming weeks (e.g., declare a major, vote in an upcoming election). They then indicated how certain or confident they were in their judgments. Despite the obvious difficulties involved in predicting one's future behavior, the students were very confident in their prognostications. This confidence turned out to be unfounded. Less than two-thirds of the students' behavioral predictions came true, a value well under the degree of certainty they had expressed. One interpretation of these findings is that people mistakenly believe that their self-knowledge is accurate enough to allow them to unerringly predict their own behavior.

Prediction errors are especially likely for positively valued outcomes. For example, most students predict their grades in class will be better than they actually are (Robins & John, 1997). People also overestimate the likelihood that they will engage in socially desirable behaviors. To illustrate, Sherman (1980, Experiment 3) asked college students whether they would spend three hours collecting for the American Cancer Society if they were ever asked to do so. Nearly half of the students (47.8 percent) said they would. Yet when they were contacted later and asked to donate three hours of their time, less than one-third (31.1 percent) of the students actually agreed to do so. Along with other research (Greenwald, Carnot, Beach, & Young, 1987), these findings support the claim that people exaggerate the degree to which they will behave in socially desirable ways.

Section Summary

In summary, people's ideas about themselves in evaluative domains are rarely a faithful representation of what they are really like. Most people regard themselves (and those who are part of their extended selves) in more positive terms than they regard people in general. Insofar as it is logically impossible for most people to be *better* than most people, these tendencies suggest that people's views of themselves are not entirely accurate.

Also consistent with this conclusion is the modest agreement that exists between people's self-views and their standing in domains that are objectively defined (e.g., intelligence) and in domains that are consensually determined (e.g., attractiveness, popularity). Additionally, although people's judgments of their personality traits are related to the judgments of others, this agreement occurs largely in nonevaluative domains. Finally, people are not very good at predicting how they will behave in particular situations. Considering all of the evidence, it seems fair to conclude that people's beliefs about themselves in socially valued domains are overly positive.

In a moment, we will examine factors that contribute to this state of affairs. Before we do, several points should be kept in mind. First, we have only used self-reports to examine how people think of themselves. A number of factors may taint these reports, including a desire to present oneself to others in a positive manner and a tendency to defensively distort what one truly thinks of oneself. We will consider these issues in Chapters 7 and 10.

Another important factor to keep in mind is that the research we've reviewed comes from Western cultures. As we have noted, these countries are very competitive and individualistic, and these factors may lead people to try and distinguish themselves from others by exaggerating their virtues. Although research on this point is in its infancy, overly positive self-views seem to be less apparent among people from Eastern cultures (Heine & Lehman, 1995; but see also, Falbo, Poston, Triscari, & Zhang, 1997; Kurman & Sriram, 1995).

It is also worth mentioning again that the present discussion is limited to people's beliefs about their socially valued abilities and psychological qualities. People show greater accuracy when it comes to qualities that are less evaluative (e.g., their tidiness; their punctuality). Moreover, the degree of bias is not excessive. People are not completely unaware of what they are like. A student who gets very poor grades is unlikely to think of herself as being the smartest person in class; a person who has no friends is unlikely to think he's the most popular child in school. Instead, people's views of themselves in evaluative domains tend, on average, to be just slightly more positive than can be justified.

Finally, not everyone is self-enhancing (John & Robins, 1994). Some people's self-views are more modest, and some people are even self-deprecating. Sometimes these differences are associated with greater accuracy; sometimes they are linked to inaccuracy. We will discuss these differences in Chapters 8, 9, and 10. At that time we will also consider whether these biases are beneficial or detrimental to psychological and physical well-being.

HOW DO PEOPLE MAINTAIN POSITIVE SELF-VIEWS?

At this point, let's consider how people are able to maintain positive beliefs about themselves. How, for example, are the majority of people able to sustain a belief that they are kinder, more loyal, and more sincere than their peers? Several processes conspire to sustain these beliefs.

Perhaps the most important one is that most personality attributes are inherently ambiguous. Consider, for example, what it means to be *honest.* Does it mean you never fudge on your income taxes? Regularly tell your friends what you think of their new clothes and hair styles? Always correct a waiter when he forgets to charge you for some item? All of these examples, and more, are indicative of honesty, but none is necessary or defining. This opens the door for individuals to define honesty in ways that cast them in a favorable light.

Dunning and his associates have provided considerable evidence that people do define traits in self-serving ways (for a review, see Dunning, 1993). For example, Dunning, Perie, and Story (1991) had participants rate themselves on two sets of attributes relevant to leadership. One set of attributes emphasized task-oriented qualities (e.g., ambitious, independent, and competitive); the other set emphasized interpersonal skills (e.g., friendly, agreeable, pleasant). Later, participants were asked what qualities are important to leadership. The results showed that participants who believed they possessed many task-oriented qualities also believed that successful leaders were ambitious, independent, and competitive. In contrast, participants who thought they possessed well-developed interpersonal skills believed that successful leaders were friendly, agreeable, and pleasant. In short, participants defined leadership in ways that matched how they thought of themselves (see also Kunda & Sanitioso, 1989). In follow-up research, Dunning, Leuenberger, and Sherman (1995) found that self-serving trait definitions are especially apparent after people receive negative feedback about themselves, suggesting that the tendency is motivated by a desire to enhance feelings of self-worth.

The tendency to define traits in self-serving ways is most evident for attributes that cannot easily be verified. An investigation by Felson (1981) documents this point. As discussed earlier, Felson had college football players rate themselves on a number of attributes relevant to performance in football; the players' coaches also evaluated the players along these dimensions. Some of the abilities (e.g., speed, size) were considered relatively unambiguous and verifiable, insofar as clear standards exist for assessing one's standing on these attributes (speed can be measured, for instance). The remaining abilities (e.g., mental toughness, football sense) were deemed to be more ambiguous and subjective, insofar as one's standing on these measures cannot easily be determined. The prediction was that the players' estimates would be more likely to exceed the coaches' on the ambiguous attributes than on the unambiguous attributes. This prediction was confirmed, suggesting that people's most aggrandizing self-assessments occur for attributes that are more subjective in nature (see also Dunning et al., 1989).

The indeterminate nature of most attributes is one factor that allows individuals to maintain highly positive views of themselves. But it is not the only factor. Other processes are also relevant. We can begin to appreciate these factors by reconsidering the sources of self-knowledge we discussed earlier. These were (1) direct self-assessment with the physical world, (2) social comparison, (3) reflected appraisals, (4) introspection, (5) self-perception, and (6) attribution processes. All of these processes involve a good deal of inference and selectivity. We *decide* when to assess ourselves against physical criteria; we *choose* targets of social comparison; we *interpret* how others feel about us; we *label* our emotions; we *infer* our dispositions. Very little (if any) of the information we receive about ourselves reaches us without first being filtered somehow.

Generally speaking, these filters reflect two of the motivations we discussed earlier. The self-enhancement motive (i.e., the desire to feel good about ourselves) leads people to process information in ways that allows them to believe they have many favorable characteristics. The self-consistency motive (i.e., the desire to preserve our self-views) leads people to process information in ways that ensure that their present self-views endure. In the following section, we'll see how these filters affect the way people gather and process information about themselves.

Behavioral Factors That Promote Positive Self-Views

Selective Exposure to Favorable Feedback

One way people could develop and maintain positive self-views is by only seeking favorable information about themselves. Completely insulating oneself from negative feedback is doomed to be maladaptive, however. Individuals who remain completely oblivious to their lack of ability in some domain would be condemned to experience repeated failure in that aspect of life. A more modest, but adaptive, strategy would involve approaching positive self-relevant information more vigorously than negative self-relevant information. In this manner, the preponderance of the feedback one received would be positive, but negative feedback, though not actively sought, would still be encountered from time to time.

Evidence supporting such a biased pattern of information-seeking behavior has been reported. In one study (Brown, 1990), participants were first led to believe that they had high ability or low ability at an intellectual task. Later, they were given the opportunity to learn more about their ability. Those in the high-ability condition expressed a good deal of interest in learning more about themselves, whereas those in the low-ability condition were more ambivalent. This pattern, which was especially pronounced when participants sought information under private (rather than public) conditions, suggests that people enthusiastically seek feedback about their abilities when they expect it to be positive but not when they expect it to be negative (see also, Sachs, 1982; Sedikides, 1993).

This tendency is not restricted to achievement-related situations. Several investigations have documented that positive information about one's health is preferentially sought and accepted (e.g., Croyle, Sun, & Louie, 1993; Ditto & Lopez, 1992; Quattrone & Tversky, 1984). In keeping with this evidence, many people at risk for HIV and other serious medical conditions (e.g., Huntington's disease) choose not to learn whether they have the condition, despite the availability of diagnostic tests (Bloch, Fahy, Fox, & Hayden, 1989; Myers, Orr, Locker, & Jackson, 1993).

Self-Handicapping

Occasionally, individuals will even work to obscure the informational value of negative feedback (Berglas & Jones, 1978; Darley & Goethals, 1980; Jones & Berglas, 1978; Snyder & Wicklund, 1981). Berglas and Jones (1978) coined the term self-handicapping strategies to refer to situations in which people erect barriers to their own success. A student who doesn't study for an exam or an athlete who doesn't practice before an important competition is exhibiting self-handicapping behavior. These behaviors make success less likely, but they allow individuals to dismiss failure as nondiagnostic and uninformative of their underlying abilities.

Self-handicapping also occurs in interpersonal settings. When I was in high school, my friends and I used to wait until the last minute to ask a girl for a date. In part, this was because we were scared to make the phone call! But it also gave us a good excuse if the girl said no. Instead of attributing her refusal to anything about *us*, we consoled ourselves by saying that we had just asked too late.

Berglas and Jones (1978) tested the conditions that promote self-handicapping behavior. They first led some male participants to believe that they were likely to succeed on an upcoming test; other participants were led to believe that future success was unlikely. All of the participants were then told that the second part of the experiment involved testing the effects of two new drugs on test performance. One of the drugs purportedly facilitated test performance; the other supposedly impaired test performance. The participants were then given a choice as to which drug they wished to ingest. Participants who doubted their ability to succeed preferred the performance-inhibiting drug, even though the drug made success even less likely.

Findings like these make an important point about psychological life. Often, what's important to people is not simply whether they succeed or fail, it's whether these outcomes reveal something positive or negative about the self. With self-handicapping, people actively risk failure because doing so ensures that failure does not implicate valued aspects of the self (e.g., low ability). In this manner, people are able to cling to an image of competency even if they fail.

Task Choice in Achievement Settings

To this point we have seen that people avidly seek positive feedback but indifferently approach or actively avoid negative feedback. One research program, Trope's (1986) research on task choice in achievement settings, seems inconsistent with this tendency. In these studies, participants are first told that they are about to take a test of an intellectual ability. They are then offered a choice between various kinds of tests. Some of the tests are allegedly very good at identifying whether or not a person has the ability; others are allegedly not very good at identifying whether or not a person has the ability. In several investigations (e.g., Strube, Lott, Le-Xuan-Hy, Oxenberg, & Deichmann, 1986; Trope, 1975, 1979), participants have been shown to prefer tests that promise to provide them with information about their ability. Moreover, this is true even if the test is good at disclosing whether a person has low ability.

These findings have led some theorists to conclude that people characteristically strive to learn the truth about themselves (Strube et al., 1986; Trope, 1986). There is a problem with this conclusion, however. The vast majority of participants in these studies believe they have high ability and expect to succeed at the task. Consequently, the interest they show in learning more about themselves may represent a desire to confirm an image of competency and gain additional favorable information about themselves, rather than any genuine interest in learning the truth about themselves. Only if people seek feedback without regard for whether they will learn something good or bad about themselves can they truly be said to be seeking accurate feedback. These conditions have generally not been met in the studies of task choice in achievement settings (for an elaboration of these views, see Brown, 1990; Brown & Dutton, 1995a).

Further Evidence of Strategic Information-Seeking Behavior

Two additional points about selective exposure to positive feedback are worth making. First, avoidance of negative feedback is not always obvious or deliberate (Greenwald, 1988). Often, people believe they possess some ability or talent, but they are not sure. They can evade finding out whether the ability is truly present or not by avoiding situations that call for its display (Shrauger, 1982). Suppose, for instance, that in the privacy of his mind (or shower) an individual believes his singing voice is second only to Sinatra's. By judiciously avoiding situations that call for public singing, he will never have to put this belief to a test. As a result, he will forever be free to cling to the belief that he is a spellbinding vocalist.

Second, people do seek diagnostic feedback on attributes that are modifiable (Brown, 1990; Dunning, 1995). Many professors, for example, ask their colleagues to comment on their manuscripts. To some extent, this practice stems from an expectation that the remarks they receive will be favorable (few professors send their papers to their enemies and critics), but it also reflects a genuine desire to improve the quality of one's work. But seeking feedback about the *products* of one's ability is not the same as seeking feedback about one's underlying ability. One's work is subject to modification and improvement; one's abilities are relatively fixed. Consequently, although they may ask for feedback on what they have written, few professors ask their colleagues to let them know whether they think they truly possess the intellectual ability to make a contribution to the field, whether they have any innate ability as a writer, and so forth.

Social Factors That Promote Positive Self-Views

Numerous social factors enable individuals to maintain positive views of themselves. At an early age, most (though not all) children receive a great deal of praise from their parents. They are fussed over, complimented, and adored. Social feedback continues to be positive as children age. Teachers are encouraged to find each child's "gift" and to let children know that they are valued and respected. Social norms also actively discourage peers from giving one another negative feedback. With the exception of anonymous journal reviews, we rarely hear what our peers really think of us, especially when this feedback is negative (Blumberg, 1972; Felson, 1993; Tesser & Rosen, 1975).

Selective Interaction

Selective affiliation also allows people to maintain positive self-views. The vast majority of people choose to associate with others who like them, not with those who dislike them. Think about your friends for a moment. Don't you think they have many positive qualities? Chances are, they think the same way about you (otherwise they wouldn't be your friends)! Choosing to interact with people who like and admire us ensures that most of the interpersonal feedback we receive is positive. To the extent that we incorporate this feedback into our self-views (as the reflected appraisal model maintains), this means we end up thinking positively about ourselves.

Biased Social Comparison

People also use social comparison processes to develop and maintain positive views of themselves. One way they do this is by strategically choosing targets of comparison. If I compare my athletic ability with most Nobel laureates, I'm apt to conclude that I am pretty athletic. If I compare my intellectual ability with most professional athletes, I'm likely to conclude that I am pretty smart. Had I reversed the targets of these comparisons, I would undoubtedly have come to some very different conclusions about myself!

Comparing ourselves with others who are worse off on a relevant dimension is known as downward social comparison (Wills, 1981). Wheeler and Miyake (1992) found that this type of social comparison activity is quite common. They asked University of Rochester students to keep track of how often they compared themselves with another person over a 10-day period. The students also indicated whether the person they compared with was better than they were on the relevant dimension (my roommate is more popular than I am), the same as them (my roommate and I both get good grades), or worse than them (my roommate is more phony and superficial than I am). Downward comparisons were most frequent and made people feel better about themselves (see also, Aspinwall & Taylor, 1993; Gibbons & Gerrard, 1991).

When there's nobody around to feel better than, people sometimes invent *worse-off others*. For example, a student may simply assume that other students are having great difficulty with their homework. Tendencies like these increase when people feel threatened in some manner, either because they have just failed at some important activity (Brown & Gallagher, 1992; Crocker, Thompson, McGraw, & Ingerman, 1987) or because they are facing a threat to their health (e.g., Affleck & Tennen, 1991; Taylor & Lobel, 1989). An investigation by Wood, Taylor, and Lichtman (1985) documents these effects. In a sample of breast cancer patients, these investigators found that the vast majority of women consoled themselves by comparing themselves with women who were worse off than they were. In essence, the women said "Yes things are bad, but they could be worse. I'm a lot better off than are other women who have cancer." Often, these *worse-off* others were manufactured; they represented a composite or fictional portrait of someone who was suffering more and coping less well with the trauma. Inventing a worse-off other allowed these women to feel good about themselves in comparison.

Downward comparison is not the only form of social comparison. People also compare themselves with others who are similar to them in important ways, and even with people who are better off than they are. The effects of upward comparison have received a lot of attention in recent years. Initially, researchers assumed that upward comparison had only negative effects. After all, when you compare yourself with someone who is better than you, you look worse by comparison (Brickman & Bulman, 1977). Although this sometimes occurs, it is not always the case. Upward comparisons can also make people feel better about themselves, either because they serve as a source of inspiration and hope, or because people bask in the reflected glory of another person's positive qualities and achievements (Buunk et al., 1990; Brown, Novick, Lord, & Richards, 1992; Cialdini et al., 1976; Collins, 1996; Brewer & Weber, 1994; Major, Testa, & Bylsma, 1991; Taylor & Lobel, 1989; Wood, 1989). It is for this reason, perhaps, that cancer patients prefer to affiliate with someone who is doing better than they are, rather than with someone who is doing worse (Taylor & Lobel, 1989).

Tesser's Self-Evaluation Maintenance Model

Tesser's (1988, 1991) research examines the conditions under which upward comparison has positive or negative effects. The model is most concerned with situations in which people compare themselves with close friends, family members, and the like. How does it feel, for example, to have a "super smart sister" or a "gorgeous roommate"? Do these positive qualities make your own attributes seem paltry in comparison, or are you able to derive some benefit from the other person's talents and virtues? These are the questions that Tesser's model seeks to answer.

According to Tesser, the personal relevance of the comparison domain is the key variable to consider. In domains of low personal relevance, being outperformed by someone who is close to you has positive psychological effects. For example, if your sister is a concert pianist and you don't care much about music, you can bask in the reflected glory of her accomplishments. In this case, your sister's achievements make you feel good about yourself. The situation is quite different when the domain is something you care a lot about, however. Here, being outperformed by someone close to you has negative consequences. For example, if you and your sister are trying to cultivate active social lives and only your sister is succeeding, you're apt to feel envious, threatened, and diminished by her achievements. In short, upward comparison is assumed to have positive consequences in domains of low personal importance but negative consequences in domains of high personal importance.

Tesser's model is a self-enhancement model. It assumes that people approach situations that make them feel good about themselves and avoid situations that make them feel bad about themselves. Building on these assumptions, the model makes some interesting predictions about friendship patterns. It predicts that people will choose to be friends with those who perform worse than they do in domains of high personal relevance, but better than they do in domains of low personal relevance. For example, a person who cares a lot about his athletic ability and little about his intellectual ability will prefer a friend who is less coordinated but more intelligent than he is. Tesser, Campbell, and Smith (1984) tested and found support for this prediction in a study of school-aged children. Beach and Tesser (1995) have recently applied these ideas to the study of close personal relationships. They believe husbands and wives often arrange matters so that each spouse excels in domains of low importance to the other. This arrangement allows people to have their cake and eat it too: People outperform their mate in areas about which they care deeply, but they bask in the reflected glory of their mate's accomplishments in areas about which they care very little.

Personal Factors That Promote Positive Self-Views

To this point, we have considered behavioral and social factors that allow individuals to acquire and maintain positive self-views. Processes of a more psychological nature are also relevant. These processes center around the unbalanced way people deal with positive and negative self-relevant information (Taylor, 1991). Most people (1) uncritically accept positive self-relevant feedback but carefully scrutinize and refute negative self-relevant feedback (Ditto & Lopez, 1992; Kunda, 1990; Liberman & Chaiken, 1992; Pyszczynski & Greenberg, 1987); (2) show better memory for positive self-relevant information than for negative self-relevant information (Kuiper & Derry, 1982); (3) recall their past in ways that allow them to lay claim to possessing desired attributes (Conway & Ross, 1984; Klein & Kunda, 1993; Sanitioso, Kunda, & Fong, 1990); and (4) introspect about themselves in ways that enable them to confirm the possession of positive traits and disconfirm the possession of negative traits (Sedikides, 1993).

Self-serving attributions are another factor that help people maintain positive self-views. One of the most reliable findings in social psychology over the last 20 years is the pervasive tendency for individuals to make asymmetric attributions for positive and negative outcomes (for reviews, see Greenwald, 1980; Snyder & Higgins, 1988; Taylor & Brown, 1988; Zuckerman, 1979). Positive outcomes are attributed to stable, central aspects of the self (e.g., "I received a high test grade because I am smart"), but negative outcomes are attributed either to external factors (e.g., "I received a low test grade because the test was unclear") or less central aspects of the self (e.g., "I received a low test grade because I studied the wrong material"). By denying that negative outcomes are due to one's enduring character, abilities, or traits, individuals are able to hold on to their self-enhancing beliefs even when confronted with negative feedback.

In an early and influential review of this phenomenon, Miller and Ross (1975) reported that self-serving attributions were more apparent given success than given failure. Subsequent research has failed to support this conclusion. If anything, just the opposite is true (Brown & Rogers, 1991; Campbell & Fairey, 1985; Zuckerman, 1979). Individuals will occasionally concede that they succeeded because of good fortune or an easy test, but they will rarely attribute failure to enduring characteristics of the self.

Part of the confusion may have arisen because researchers were comparing internal attributions (attributions to personal factors) versus external attributions (attributions to factors other than oneself). This distinction ignores a crucial matter. The critical issue is not whether negative outcomes are attributed to *personal* factors, but whether they are attributed to highly valued and stable aspects of oneself. Students, for example, will freely admit that they did poorly on an exam because they didn't try hard or because they studied the wrong material. Indeed, self-handicapping research shows that people sometimes actively create these impediments to success. What students don't do, however, is readily attribute a poor performance to a general lack of intelligence.

This finding bears on another issue. It is widely assumed that people are generally disposed to make dispositional attributions for behavior (Gilbert & Malone, 1995; Ross, 1977). A dispositional attribution is an attribution to a stable, inherent property of a person, such as the person's character, ability, or personality. No such bias exists when people make attributes for their own behavior. Instead, it depends entirely on whether the outcome in question is good or bad. People routinely make dispositional attributions for positive outcomes (e.g., "I got promoted because I am smart, dependable, and energetic"), but they rarely make dispositional attributions for negative outcomes (e.g., "I got fired because I am dumb, undependable, and lazy). Instead, people attribute negative outcomes to external factors (e.g., "The boss doesn't like me") or to less valued aspects of themselves (e.g., "I'm just not suited for this particular line of work").

This tendency also occurs when we make attributions for members of our extended self. Earlier we discussed ingroup favoritism. This term refers, in part, to the fact that people evaluate ingroup members (i.e., people we feel close to or otherwise connected with) in a highly positive manner. Causal

attributions are also affected by ingroup favoritism. We make dispositional attributions for the successes of ingroup members, but we make situational attributions for their failures. This bias does not occur when we make attributions
for the behavior of people with whom we share no association or connection
(Islam & Hewstone, 1993; Pettigrew, 1979; Weber, 1994).

REVISITING THE MOTIVES THAT GUIDE
THE SEARCH FOR SELF-KNOWLEDGE

Having identified a variety of tactics that permit most people to believe they
possess many positive qualities and few negative qualities, let's reconsider
what these tactics tell us about the motives that guide the acquisition of self-
knowledge. According to the self-enhancement model, people want to feel
good about themselves. In Western cultures, this motive leads people to seek
information in such a manner that they are apt to conclude they possess many
positive qualities and few negative qualities. According to the accuracy model,
people want to know what they are really like. This leads them to seek the
truth about themselves, without regard to whether they will gain positive or
negative self-knowledge. Finally, the self-consistency model assumes that people are motivated to preserve and strengthen their present self-views. As represented in Swann's (1990, 1996) self-verification theory, self-consistency
needs lead people to seek and embrace information that is consistent with
how they think of themselves, and to avoid and reject information that is inconsistent with how they think of themselves.

What can we conclude about the strength of these motives on the basis of
our review? The fact that most people have overly positive self-views that do
not correspond closely with objective reality or the judgments of others poses
problems for the accuracy position. The issue is this: If people actively seek the
truth about themselves, why don't they possess it? Although there is some
reason to believe that people would have difficulty finding the truth even if
they looked for it (Felson, 1993), the bulk of the evidence indicates that most
people don't look all that hard to begin with. When it comes to attributes that
are highly desirable, people seek positive, rather than necessarily accurate,
feedback (Brown, 1990; Brown & Dutton, 1995a; Sedikides, 1993).

Both the self-enhancement model and self-verification theory can explain
these findings. Both models assume that people with positive views of themselves preferentially seek and embrace positive feedback. Because most people
think of themselves in positive terms, both models assume that this biased
pattern characterizes most people.

But what about people with negative self-views? According to the self-
enhancement model, these people also desire positive feedback; according to
the self-verification model, these people desire negative feedback. As counter-
intuitive as this latter position may seem, it is not without apparent support.
Virtually all of the effects discussed earlier are less characteristic of people
with negative self-views than of people with positive self-views (see Swann,

1990, 1996 for reviews). For example, people who believe they have low ability at some task are less apt to attribute failure to external factors than are people who think they are highly able (Swann, Griffin, Predmore, & Gaines, 1987).

Self-verification theory makes its most provocative predictions when applied to the study of interpersonal relationships. The theory asserts that "people want others to validate and confirm their [self-views], even when those [self-views] are negative" (McNulty & Swann, 1984, p. 1013). This means that people who think negatively of themselves prefer to associate with someone who shares this negative perception, rather than with someone who views them more positively (see also, Secord & Backman, 1965).

Swann and his colleagues have tested this hypothesis in two ways. In laboratory studies, participants first learn that another person has evaluated them in either a positive or negative manner. For example, a participant in one of these studies might give a speech and be told that another person observing through a one-way mirror thought the participant was socially poised or socially awkward. Participants then indicate how interested they are in interacting with the (alleged) evaluator. Participants who think of themselves in positive terms (in this case as socially poised) overwhelmingly prefer to interact with the positive evaluator. This is less true for those who think of themselves in negative terms (in this case as socially awkward). These individuals generally show only a reduced preference for the positive evaluator or no preference either way.

Similar findings have been found in naturalistic settings. In a study of college roommates, people with many positive views of themselves wished to remain roommates with another person who evaluated them positively, but this preference was less apparent among people who did not think highly of themselves (Swann, 1990). Married couples seem to be especially interested in receiving congruent (as opposed to merely positive) feedback from their spouses (Swann, De La Ronde, & Hixon, 1994).

In sum, the desire for positive feedback is clearly less apparent among people with negative self-views than among people with positive self-views. This does not mean, however, that people with negative self-views want others to dislike them (Alloy & Lipman, 1992; Hooley & Richters, 1992; Swann, Wenzlaff, Krull, & Pelham, 1992). They desire positive feedback, but only if it is believable (Swann, Pelham, & Krull, 1989).

In consideration of this evidence, Swann and his colleagues (De La Ronde & Swann, 1993; Swann, 1990, 1996) have concluded that people possess two independent motives: a desire for favorable feedback and a desire for self-verifying (congruent) feedback. Normally, people satisfy these dual needs by seeking favorable feedback for their positive self-views (Swann et al., 1989). For example, a person who thinks she is smart but uncoordinated ordinarily seeks confirmation from others that she is intelligent, but she does not try and convince other people that she is clumsy. However, if circumstances are such that she is forced to confront this issue (e.g., she is asked to pitch for the office softball team), she will take aims to ensure that others see her as she sees herself. Under these circumstances, people prefer authentic negative feedback to inauthentic positive feedback.

CHAPTER SUMMARY

This chapter examined the way people think about themselves in socially valued domains. We began by identifying three broad motivations that guide the search for self-knowledge. These were self-enhancement needs, accuracy needs, and self-consistency needs. Next, we discussed various sources of information that people consult when seeking to learn what they are like. These sources include physical factors, social factors, and psychological factors (such as introspection and self-perception processes).

We then looked at what people think of themselves in highly evaluative domains. Here we saw that most people think of themselves in very positive terms, especially compared to their beliefs about most other people. We also noted that people's self-views are not entirely accurate. In highly evaluative domains, people's self-views are only moderately correlated with what they are really like.

Finally, we examined various mechanisms that enable people to maintain their positive self-views. Some of these mechanisms ensure that individuals receive predominantly positive feedback in their lives; others are designed to minimize the degree to which negative feedback implicates central aspects of the self. We concluded by considering the relevance of these findings to understanding the motivations that drive the search for self-knowledge. The desire to feel good about ourselves seems to be the major motivational factor to consider.

- People actively acquire knowledge of themselves throughout their lives. The search for self-knowledge is shaped by three broad concerns: self-enhancement needs (a desire to feel good about ourselves and to avoid feeling bad about ourselves); accuracy needs (the need to know what we are really like); and consistency needs (a desire to keep our self-views consistent and to protect them against change).
- People consult various sources of self-knowledge when seeking to learn what they are like. They (1) consult the physical world; (2) compare themselves with others (social comparison); (3) incorporate the opinions of others toward them (reflected appraisals); (4) look inward (introspection); and (5) examine their behavior in the context in which it occurs and draw an appropriate inference (self-perception and attributions).
- Most people regard themselves (and those who are part of their extended selves) in highly positive terms. They believe they have many positive qualities and few negative qualities. This bias is especially apparent when we compare the way people evaluate themselves with the way they evaluate most other people. Many (if not most) people believe they are *better* than are most other people.
- Research assessing the accuracy of people's self-views has turned up mixed evidence that people know what they are really like. People's self-views in nonevaluative domains (e.g., "How punctual and conscientious are you?") are fairly accurate, but their self-views in highly evaluative domains (e.g., "How intelligent and attractive are you?") are not. People are also overly confident about their ability to predict their future behavior, particularly behaviors that are socially desirable or positive. Taken together, these findings suggest that people's ideas about themselves in evaluative domains are rarely a faithful representation of what they are really like.
- Various mechanisms help people maintain their positive self-views. Most people eagerly seek self-relevant feedback when they think it will be positive, but they reluctantly seek self-relevant feedback when they think it will be negative. Under some circumstances, people actively obscure the informational value of negative

feedback by erecting barriers to their own success. People also selectively affiliate with those who like them, and compare themselves with others in ways that are designed to promote and maintain positive self-views. Finally, the attributions people make for positive and negative outcomes further serve to bolster their positive self-views.

- Not everyone holds positive views of themselves, and not everyone seeks positive self-relevant feedback. Under some circumstances, people with negative self-views seek negative information about themselves. This is most apt to occur in interpersonal settings, when people fear they won't be able to live up to other people's positive perceptions of them.

For Further Reading

DUNNING, D. (1993). Words to live by: The self and definitions of social concepts and categories. In J. Suls (Ed.), *Psychological perspectives on the self* (Vol. 4, pp. 99–126). Hillsdale, NJ: Lawrence Erlbaum Associates.

FELSON, R. B. (1993). The (somewhat) social self: How others affect self-appraisals. In J. Suls (Ed.), *Psychological perspectives on the self* (Vol. 4, pp. 1–27). Hillsdale, NJ: Lawrence Erlbaum Associates.

KENNY, D. A., & DEPAULO, B. M. (1993). Do people know how others view them? An empirical and theoretical account. *Psychological Bulletin, 114,* 145–161.

Self-Development

It is almost certain that people everywhere have a concept of self. The way they think about themselves differs, of course, but for several thousand of years at least, people have been aware of their own continued existence and have thought about what they are like (Jaynes, 1976). Understanding how these ideas develop and change with age is the focus of Chapter 4.

The chapter begins by covering three theories of self-development. The first of these theories is sociological in nature; the second is cognitive in nature; and the third emphasizes interpersonal and emotional processes. In combination, these perspectives help us understand the development of the self.

The next section of this chapter examines the origins of self-awareness in humans and animals. For centuries, self-awareness was thought to be a uniquely human capacity. Recent research has challenged this assumption, providing suggestive evidence that other species besides humans possess self-awareness. There is also evidence that self-awareness emerges in humans at a very young age and may even be present at birth.

The final section of this chapter examines developmental shifts in self-understanding. Although the greatest developments in the self occur during our early years, people's thoughts about themselves change throughout life. Changes that occur during adolescence are particularly noteworthy, and we will cover this period of life in some detail.

One more word before we begin. For the most part, this chapter will focus on how people's *thoughts* about themselves develop and change. A thorough discussion of the origins and development of *self-esteem* (an examination of how people's *feelings* toward themselves develop and change) will be delayed until Chapter 8.

THEORIES OF SELF-DEVELOPMENT

Mead's Symbolic Interactionism Theory

The first theory we will consider was offered by the American sociologist, George Herbert Mead. Actually, we have already encountered some of Mead's ideas when we considered Cooley's (1902) notion of the looking-glass self (see Chapter 3). Cooley argued that people's feelings toward themselves develop through a perspective-taking process: We imagine how we are regarded by other people, and we feel good or bad in accordance with that imagined judgment.

Mead greatly extended these ideas.[1] Whereas Cooley had linked perspective taking to the development of self-related *feelings,* Mead believed that perspective taking comprised the very genesis of the self. The basis for these ideas resides in a theory known as symbolic interactionism (for reviews of this theory, see Hewitt, 1997; Meltzer, Petras, & Reynolds, 1975; Stryker & Statham, 1985). Symbolic interactionism is concerned with understanding the socialization process. How is culture acquired and perpetuated? How do people come to adopt the values, standards, and norms of the society into which they are born? In short, how are individuals transformed from asocial creatures at birth into socialized beings?

Perspective Taking, Socialization, and the Emergence of Self

Mead (1934) believed that the emergence of self provides the key to understanding this metamorphosis. Mead argued that individuals become socialized when they adopt the perspective of others and imagine how they appear from other people's point of view. For Mead, this perspective-taking ability is synonymous with the acquisition of self.

To illustrate, imagine a very young child is scribbling on the walls with a crayon. Because the child is not yet able to ask, "I wonder what mom and dad would think of my behavior?" the child is not acting with reference to self and is not acting in a socialized manner. As the child matures, this ability to adopt the perspective of others toward the self develops ("I bet mom and dad wouldn't be happy with what I'm doing to the walls"). According to Mead, this capacity to imagine how we appear in the eyes of others heralds the emergence of self. When we are further able to modify our behavior to conform to the perceived wishes of others, we are socialized beings.

Symbolic Communication and the Development of Self

Mead also speculated about how this perspective-taking ability develops. "How can an individual get outside himself," he asked, ". . . in such a way as to become an object to himself" (1934, p. 138). Mead believed that interpersonal communication, particularly the use of symbolic communication in the form of language, was the key to understanding this "essential problem of selfhood."

Mead based his analysis on Darwin's theory of the evolution of emotional expressions. In his book *Expression of the Emotions in Man and Animals,* Darwin (1872) asserted that certain emotional states are associated with specific bodily and facial expressions. For example, anger is associated with a baring of the

[1]Cooley and Mead were colleagues at the University of Chicago and developed their theories at approximately the same time. However, Mead did not publish his ideas during his lifetime; his work was published posthumously by his students, assembled from their lecture notes. For this reason, Mead's work carries a later publication date than does Cooley's, even though the two worked concurrently.

teeth. Darwin believed that these facial expressions reveal something about the inner state of the animal. They serve as a sign of what the animal is feeling and indicate what the animal is likely to do. In this sense, these gestures (as Mead called them) constitute a form of communication; they let other animals know what is about to occur.

Communication in lower animals is largely instinctive. An angry wolf doesn't ask itself, "How can I let this other wolf know I'm angry?" It instinctively bares its teeth and communicates the internal state. Humans also communicate through instinctive facial expressions (Ekman, 1993), but these displays represent only a small portion of human communication. People also communicate symbolically, using *significant* gestures. (In this context, the word *significant* means "having the qualities of a sign.") In order to do so, Mead argued, we must adopt the perspective of the other person toward ourselves and imagine how our gestures will be regarded by that person. For Mead, this perspective-taking ability is synonymous with the acquisition of self.

To illustrate, imagine that I want you to know that you are welcome in my home. How can I communicate this information to you? According to Mead, I need to put myself in your shoes and ask myself, "What behavior or gesture on my part would let you know that you are welcome here?" After engaging in this process, I might conclude that opening up my arms in the form of a hug would do the trick. This gesture would signify (have the qualities of a sign) that you are welcome. In this fashion, the need to adopt the perspective of others in order to communicate with symbols creates the self in Mead's theory.

Social Interaction and the Development of Self

It is important to note the strong emphasis Mead gives to social interaction in his analysis of the development of self. In the absence of social interaction, symbolic communication would be unnecessary and the self would not develop through the perspective-taking process Mead describes. For Mead, then, social interaction is essential to the emergence of self.

Once the self has developed, however, it continues to exist even when others are not around. This is the case because people can mentally represent others and imagine how their behavior would appear in another person's eyes. Most people, for example, do not steal items from a store even when no one is around to watch them. One explanation is that they mentally represent how others would react to their behavior if they were present, and behave accordingly. In more general terms, we can say that once people acquire a self and are socialized, they internalize the anticipated reactions of others and continue to act in a socialized manner even when they are alone. But they would not develop this capacity, Mead argued, if they were not raised in social surroundings.

> The self, as that which can be an object to itself, is essentially a social structure, and it arises in social experience. After a self has arisen, it in a certain sense provides for itself its social experiences and we can conceive of an absolutely solitary self. *But it is impossible to conceive of a self arising outside of social experience.* When it has arisen, we can think of a person in solitary confinement for the rest of his life, but who still has himself as a companion, and is

able to think and to converse with himself as he had communicated with others. (Mead, 1934, p. 140, emphasis added)

This doesn't mean that people are always acting in a self-conscious and socialized fashion. Sometimes people act without reference to self, without looking back on themselves from the (imagined) perspective of others. If, for example, we are walking along, mindlessly humming a tune, we are not, in Mead's scheme, acting with reference to self. Only when something happens that causes us to become the object of our own attention (e.g., someone calls our name) are we swept out of our unsocialized reverie back into the self-conscious state that is socialized behavior.

The Generalized Other

To this point, we have been concerned with the individual's ability to adopt the perspective of another person toward the self. When this capacity emerges, the self develops. Ultimately, Mead argued, socialization requires more than the ability to adopt the perspective of a *particular* other toward the self; to be truly socialized, people must come to adopt the perspective of society at large. We must view ourselves through the eyes of an abstract, generalized other that represents the broader society and culture into which we are born.

Mead believed the foundation for this ability could be found in the type of games children play. Initially, young children play in an asocial manner. Their play is entirely autonomous and does not involve others. In time, children play with particular others. Sometimes these are imaginary playmates who take turns "speaking to one another." Mead believed this form of play was very important for the development of self, as it requires adopting the perspective of a particular other and seeing yourself from the other person's point of view. Role-playing is also characteristic of children at this stage. For example, a child may play "firefighter" and mimic the behaviors and language of a firefighter. This also involves the ability to adopt the perspective of a particular other and lays the groundwork for the development of self.

The game stage is the next stage in Mead's analysis. In the game stage, there are multiple others and the individual must simultaneously be aware of many people's perspectives. Mead used the game of baseball to illustrate this stage.

> The child who plays in a game must be ready to take the attitude of everyone else involved in that game. . . . If he gets in a [baseball game] he must have the responses of each position involved in his own position. He must know what everyone else is going to do in order to carry out his own play. He has to take all of these roles. They do not all have to be present in consciousness at the same time, but at some moments he has to have three or four individuals present in his own attitude, such as the one who is going to throw the ball, the one who is going to catch it, and so on. . . . In the game, then, there is a set of responses of such others so organized that the attitude of one calls out the appropriate attitudes of the others. (Mead, 1934, p. 151)

The key difference, then, between play and the game is that in the former the child adopts only the attitudes of one other person, but in the latter the child adopts the attitudes of many other people.

Ultimately, the ability to adopt multiple perspectives toward the self pre-pares the individual to adopt the perspective of an abstract, generalized other that represents the society at large. When this occurs, the self is said to be fully developed and socialization is complete.

> If the given human individual is to develop a self in the fullest sense, it is not sufficient for him merely to take the attitudes of other human individuals to-ward himself. . . ; he must also . . . take the attitude of the generalized other toward himself. Only insofar as he takes the attitudes of the organized social attitudes of the given social group or community to which he belongs, does he develop a complete self. (paraphrased from Mead, 1934, pp. 155–156)
>
> [Thus] there are two general stages in the full development of the self. At the first of these stages, the individual's self is constituted simply by an organi-zation of the particular attitudes of other individuals toward himself. . . . But at the second stage in the full development of the individual's self, that self is constituted not only by an organization of these particular individual attitudes, but also by an organization of the social attitudes of the generalized other. . . . So the self reaches its full development by organizing these individual attitudes of others into the organized social or group attitudes. (Mead, 1934, p. 158)

Cognitions, Not Emotions, as Central to the Self

Another important aspect of Mead's theory is its emphasis on cognitive rather than affective processes. In Chapter 3 we noted that Cooley emphasized the development of self-feelings. In fact, feelings were paramount throughout his analysis. "There can be no test of the self," Cooley wrote, "except the way we feel" (1902, p. 172). This emphasis on emotion also characterized William James's (1890) treatment of self (see Chapter 2).

Mead offered a very different view of the self. For Mead, cognition, not emotion, is the central element of self.

> Emphasis should be laid on the central position of thinking when considering the nature of the self. Self-consciousness, rather than affective experience . . . , provides the core and primary structure of the self, which is thus essen-tially a cognitive rather than an emotional phenomenon. . . . Cooley and James, it is true, endeavor to find the basis of the self in . . . affective experi-ences, i.e., in experiences involving "self-feeling"; but the theory that the na-ture of the self is to be found in such experiences does not account for the ori-gin of the self. . . . The individual need not take the attitudes of others toward himself in these experiences. The essence of the self . . . is cognitive. . . . (Mead, 1934, p. 173)

Piaget's Model of Cognitive Development

With its emphasis on perspective-taking ability and the acquisition of lan-guage, Mead's model assumes that self-development requires a good deal of cognitive sophistication. Cognitive abilities are also the focus of Piaget's (1952) theory of child development. Although his theory is a general theory of cogni-tive development and is not explicitly concerned with self-development, re-searchers have applied many of Piaget's insights to the study of the self.

As is widely known, Piaget developed his theory by observing the way his own children attempted to solve various problems. On the basis of these observations, Piaget concluded that human cognitive development proceeds through a series of stages. Each stage is characterized by qualitatively distinct ways of understanding the world. This understanding changes very little within each stage, but it changes abruptly across stages. Transitions from one stage to another are brought about by cognitive and physical maturation.

Sensory-Motor Stage

The first stage in Piaget's theory is the sensory-motor phase (first 15 months).[2] This stage is characterized by extreme egocentrism, in that children's knowledge is centered on their own thoughts and feelings. This stage could also be called the prerepresentational stage, as children at this stage have yet to fully develop representational thought. Representational thought involves the ability to mentally represent people, places, and events. With this ability, one can consider events not currently taking place and think about people and objects not presently in sight.

The lack of representational thought at this stage is inferred from tests of object permanence. If we show a very young infant an object and then cover or otherwise hide the object, the infant shows no sign of knowing that the object continues to exist even when it is hidden from view ("out of sight, out of mind"). This capacity emerges by the end of the sensory-motor phase. At this point, children will search for the hidden object, suggesting that they know the object continues to exist even when it cannot be seen.

Preoperational Stage

The second stage in Piaget's scheme is the preoperational stage (15 months to 6 years). Although children at this age remain embedded in their own point of view, they begin to develop the ability to think abstractly (i.e., they are able to use symbols to represent things). This capacity greatly facilitates the acquisition of language.

The ability to think abstractly is also reflected in the emergence of imaginary play. Recall that Mead believed that imaginary play was central to the development of self and progressed through a series of stages. Research using Piaget's model largely supports Mead's conjecture (Bretherton, 1984; McCune Nicolich, 1981). At first, imaginary play involves only self-directed actions (e.g., the child pretends to feed herself). This is consistent with the egocentrism that characterizes this stage of life. Later, between 15 and 21 months of age, children begin to include others in their imaginary play. For example, a child may pretend to "feed her kitty-cat." Between 19 and 24 months, turn taking in imaginary play emerges. Here, the child combines action sequences and

[2]Although researchers generally accept that children pass through the stages Piaget described, there is disagreement about just when these stages occur. In general, it seems that Piaget was conservative in his estimates, and that many of the cognitive changes he described occur earlier (in some cases much earlier) than he believed (Mandler, 1990; Meltzoff, 1990). Because these issues are not yet resolved, the time frames I present should be regarded as approximate, not definitive.

switches between one role and another. Pretend play continues to become increasingly more elaborate until about 6 years of age, when it starts to abate.

Concrete Operational Stage

The third stage in Piaget's model is the concrete operational stage (6 years to 11 years). Thinking during this stage becomes increasingly logical with respect to time, space, and number. It is at this stage when (most) children stop believing in Santa Claus and the Tooth Fairy, simply because it isn't *possible* for one person (or fairy) to visit everyone in a single evening! Children at this stage also understand that sequences can be reversed, and they use this knowledge to demonstrate conservation (i.e., they understand that the amount of water in a tall, thin glass may be equal to the amount of water in a short, wide glass).

Formal Operations Stage

The final stage in Piaget's model is the formal operations stage (11 years and up). One of the hallmarks of this stage is the ability to think about hypothetical events and situations. For example, when attempting to solve a problem, young adolescents at this stage are able to ask, "What would happen if I did *X*?" Individuals at this stage are also able to effectively use inductive and deductive reasoning. These cognitive advances help free people from their egocentric point of view, as individuals are now capable of imagining that others might have a perspective on matters that is different than their own.

Erikson's Model of Psychosocial Development

Psychoanalytic models offer a third approach to understanding the development of the self. While recognizing the importance of social interaction and cognitive development, these models emphasize affective factors as well, presenting a more dynamically charged account of self-development.

There are a number of such theories (see, for example, Mahler, Pine, & Bergman, 1975), but the most influential theory for the study of the self is Erikson's (1963) model of psychosocial development. Along with Freud, Erikson assumed that particular needs arise at particular stages of life. If these needs are met, development proceeds to the next stage; if these needs are not met, development stagnates or regresses. For Freud, these needs were somatic in nature (e.g., anal gratification; oral gratification). In his award-winning book *Childhood and Society*, Erikson (1963) modified Freud's ideas to include eight needs of a more psychological nature. Each of these needs has particular relevance to how people think and feel about themselves.

Table 4.1 shows that the first issue an infant faces is the capacity to trust others, particularly the mother. Trust is established when the infant receives warm, consistent care; mistrust develops when care is inadequate or unpredictable. These initial feelings of trust or wariness set the stage for subsequent interpersonal relationships. Individuals who do not develop trust at this stage may have difficulty getting close to people throughout life.

TABLE 4.1. Erik Erikson's Eight-Stage Model of Psychosocial Development

Stage of Life	Psychosocial Conflict	Characterization
First year	Trust vs. Mistrust	Trust develops when infants receive warm, consistent care; inadequate or unpredictable care instills mistrust.
1–3 years	Autonomy vs. Shame and Doubt	Feelings of autonomy develop when children are encouraged to explore themselves and their environment. Feelings of shame and doubt arise when children's natural inclination to explore is thwarted.
3–5 years	Initiative vs. Guilt	Initiative is fostered when children are given the freedom to try (and fail) at various activities. Parents instill guilt by ridiculing their children or by being overly critical of them.
6–12 years	Industry vs. Inferiority	Children learn a sense of industry when they are praised for producing socially valued goods or for performing socially valued services. Feelings of inferiority result if these efforts are regarded as inadequate or inferior.
Adolescence	Identity vs. Role Confusion	The need to answer the question, "Who am I?" is the critical issue people face at this stage of life. Those who forge a dependable and integrated identity are said to be identity achieved; those who fail to establish a consistent and unified identity suffer from role confusion.
Early adulthood	Intimacy vs. Isolation	Erikson regards the need to establish a committed and intimate interpersonal relationship to be the critical issue people face at this stage of life. Failure to do so leads to feelings of loneliness and isolation.
Middle adulthood	Generativity vs. Stagnation	Generativity involves the belief that one is a productive member of society, contributing in a meaningful way and helping to build future generations. This can be accomplished through work, volunteer efforts, or child rearing. The alternative is stagnation, which is characterized by an excessive concern with one's own welfare or a belief that life is meaningless.
Late adulthood	Integrity vs. Despair	Integrity is achieved when one is able to look back on one's life with acceptance and satisfaction. The belief that things have gone as they should allows people to face death with dignity. If regret dominates, people feel despair.

Issues of independence and mastery assume importance during the second stage of life. Feelings of autonomy develop when children are given the freedom to explore themselves and their environment. Feelings of shame and doubt arise when children's natural inclination to explore is thwarted or subverted.

During the third stage of life, children strive to actively manipulate (rather than simply explore) the environment. Feelings of initiative arise when children are allowed to create, construct, and modify their world (e.g., to build things; to draw or paint). Feelings of guilt arise if parents ridicule or are overly critical of their child's efforts to modify the environment.

The fourth stage of life coincides with the beginning of formal education. Erikson characterizes this stage in terms of a conflict between feelings of industry and inferiority. The term industry refers to the child's ability to master socially appropriate tools and skills. It is an apprenticeship period, during which the child learns to assume adult responsibilities. Those who do so successfully, Erikson argued, acquire a sense of industry; they learn to "win recognition by producing things" (1963, p. 259). Those who do not, develop feelings of inferiority.

The next stage of life is adolescence. According to Erikson, the adolescent faces an *identity crisis* as he or she confronts the need to answer the question, "Who am I?" Adolescents who forge a dependable and integrated identity are said to be identity achieved; those who fail to establish a consistent and unified identity suffer from role confusion.

Erikson regards the need to establish an intimate interpersonal relationship to be the central issue people face during early adulthood. At this stage of life, many (though not all) individuals enter into a committed and lasting relationship. Failure to do so leads to feelings of loneliness and isolation.

In middle adulthood, the paramount issue is the perception that one is a productive member of society, contributing in a meaningful way and helping to build future generations. This can be accomplished through work, volunteer efforts, or child rearing. The alternative is stagnation, which is characterized by an excessive concern with one's own welfare or a belief that one's life is essentially meaningless.

The final issue individuals face in late adulthood is labeled "integrity versus despair." Integrity is achieved when one is able to look back on one's life with acceptance and satisfaction. It is the belief that one's life is something that "had to be and that, by necessity, permitted of no substitution" (Erikson, 1963, p. 268). This belief allows a person to face death with dignity. If regret dominates, the person feels despair and is afraid of dying.

To summarize, Erikson proposed an eight-stage model of psychological development. At each stage, individuals confront an important self-relevant issue. The model is not perfect. It is culturally bound and rigid with respect to the sequence of stages it describes (e.g., many people now marry later in life than they used to and, therefore, may encounter issues of generativity before confronting issues of intimacy). These limitations should not blind us to the importance of Erikson's work, however. Erikson acknowledged that the conflicts he describes can resurface throughout life and may never be entirely resolved. In this sense, it's best to think of these conflicts as general issues people face in their lives, rather than as a fixed sequence that everyone experiences in the same order.

THE COURSE OF SELF-DEVELOPMENT

Having outlined three theoretical models, we are ready to look at how researchers have used these ideas to understand the emergence and development of the self. Our discussion will be organized around four questions: (1) Is self-recognition a uniquely human capacity? (2) At what age does self-recognition emerge in humans? (3) Are the origins of self-awareness present at birth? and (4) How do people's ideas about themselves change during childhood?

The first three questions concern the genesis and development of the *I*; the fourth question concerns the developmental course of the *ME*. Accordingly, let's begin by reviewing the distinction we've made between these two aspects of self. The *I* refers to our sense that we are a distinct and unified entity, continuous over time and capable of willful action. The *ME* refers to our more specific ideas about what we are like. These ideas include beliefs about our physical appearance; social roles and relationships; and likes, values, and personality characteristics.

The development of the *I* precedes the development of the *ME*. Before we can know what we are like, we first need to know that we exist. To illustrate, imagine that someone has suddenly become aware of their own existence. If at this very moment we were to ask the person, "What are you like?" they would say "I don't yet know what I am like; I have only at this very instant become aware that I am." This is what we mean when we say that the development of the *I* precedes the development of the *ME*.

Visual Self-Recognition in Nonhumans

The first issue we will consider is the question of whether humans alone are capable of taking themselves as the object of their own attention. Mead believed that they were. In fact, Mead believed that this uniquely human capacity was the most important difference between humans and other animals.

> Man's behavior is such in his social group that he is able to become an object to himself, a fact which constitutes him a more advanced product of evolutionary development than are the lower animals. Fundamentally, it is this social fact—and not his alleged possession of a soul or mind with which he, as an individual, has been mysteriously and supernaturally endowed, and with which the lower animals have not been endowed—that differentiates him from them. (Mead, 1934, p. 137)

Mirror Recognition in Chimpanzees

In an ingenious series of experiments, Gallup (1977) tested whether animals other than humans are able to take themselves as an object of their own attention.

Gallup's experiments used a mirror-recognition task, in which an animal's ability to recognize itself in a mirror was assessed. Gallup reasoned that mirror recognition implies the existence of a rudimentary self-concept, as it requires knowing that you and the image in the mirror are one and the same.

In an initial investigation, Gallup exposed chimpanzees to a full-length mirror and unobtrusively recorded their behavior over a 10-day period. At first, Gallup notes, the animal responds to the mirror image as if it were another chimpanzee. Gradually, this behavior is replaced by activities of a distinctively self-directed nature. For example, while looking into the mirror, the animal begins to groom parts of the body that cannot be seen directly and pick material out of its teeth. Gallup argued that this switch in behavior meant that the chimpanzees had come to recognize that the *animal* in the mirror was their own reflection.

Follow-up research provided even stronger support for this assertion. In a subsequent study, Gallup (1977) anesthetized each chimpanzee and, while they were unconscious, painted the uppermost portion of their eyebrow with a tasteless, odorless, red dye. The dye was applied so that it was visible to the chimpanzees only when they viewed themselves in a mirror. Upon awakening, the animals were again exposed to their mirror image, and the number of behaviors they directed to the spot where the dye had been applied was recorded. In comparison with their earlier behavior, Gallup found that the chimpanzees were over 25 times more likely to touch the spot where the dye had been applied when they saw their reflection in the mirror. Moreover, this increased activity did not occur among a control group of chimpanzees who were not given prior exposure to their mirror image. These findings imply that the experimental group had earlier learned to recognize themselves in a mirror and were aware that the red-stained image in the mirror was indeed themselves.

A number of investigations have now replicated Gallup's (1977) basic results and have also tested whether other animals show signs of self-recognition (e.g., Meddin, 1979; Povinelli, Rulf, Landau, & Bierschwale, 1993). This research suggests that only two species besides humans (chimpanzees and orangutans) are capable of recognizing themselves in a mirror. For reasons not yet known, gorillas, despite being highly similar to humans, do not pass the mirror-recognition test.

The Social Bases of Self-Recognition

If we concede that self-recognition implies a concept of self (see Heyes, 1994, for a discussion of this issue), Gallup's findings challenge Mead's assertion that self-awareness is a uniquely human capacity. But what of Mead's more specific claim that self-awareness arises only in the context of social interaction? Must one have the opportunity to view oneself from the perspective of another before one can develop a concept of self?

Gallup (1977) conducted additional research to test this idea. He repeated his earlier experiments using chimpanzees who had been reared in isolation, without ever having seen another chimpanzee. If, as Mead claimed, social interaction is necessary to the development of self, chimpanzees who have never had the opportunity to view themselves through the "eyes of others" should fail to recognize themselves in the mirror. This is precisely what occurred. The chimpanzees reared in isolation showed no indication of knowing that they were the object in the mirror. Only after three months of social interaction did they begin to show signs of self-recognition. Although alternative explanations for these results can be generated (e.g., being reared in isolation may have created a general cognitive deficit), the data are in accordance with Mead's claim that the opportunity to adopt the perspective of others is critical to the development of self.

Visual Self-Recognition in Infants

A modified version of the facial mark test (sans anesthesia!) has been used to assess self-recognition in infants. Lewis and Brooks-Gunn (1979) conducted some of the most comprehensive research in this area. These researchers began by noting that mirror images contain two sources of self-relevant information: contingency cues (when "I" move, the person in the mirror also moves) and featural cues (the person in the mirror looks like "me"). To see which of these sources of information is critical to self-recognition, Lewis and Brooks-Gunn added other recognition tasks. These included (1) still photographs (which provide only featural cues); (2) simultaneous video displays (which provide both featural and contingency cues as an infant sees herself on a TV screen while she moves); and (3) delayed video displays (which provide featural cues and delayed contingency cues).

The participants in Lewis and Brooks-Gunn's research were 9- to 36-month-old infants, and self-recognition was assessed in multiple ways, including (1) self-directed behavior (touching a mark on one's nose while looking in the mirror); (2) verbal pronouncements (referring to oneself with a proper noun or a personal pronoun); and (3) self-conscious emotions (responding with embarrassment when viewing oneself but not when viewing others).

Using these various methods, Lewis and Brooks-Gunn found evidence for the following pattern of development. From 9 to 12 months of age, there is evidence of visual self-recognition with contingent stimuli. Most infants show signs of recognizing themselves when seeing themselves in a mirror or when viewing a simultaneous videotape display. They smile, attend to themselves intently, and touch their bodies. At this point, however, there is only limited and variable recognition of self with the noncontingent stimuli (i.e., the photographs and the delayed videotapes). These findings suggest that contingency is necessary for self-recognition at this stage of life.

At 15 to 18 months of age, most infants pass the facial mark test. When presented with their mirror image, they respond by pointing to the appropriate spot on their face where the rouge has been applied. Many 15- to 18-month-old infants are also able to distinguish themselves from others in photographs and to point to themselves in pictures. These findings suggest that contingency cues are no longer needed for self-recognition at this age.

These abilities continue to develop between 18 and 21 months of age. By this time, nearly all normally developed children are able to recognize themselves with contingent stimuli, and over three-fourths show evidence of self-recognition with noncontingent stimuli. Two-thirds of infants at this age also begin using personal pronouns when viewing photographs of themselves. By 21 months of age, self-recognition is well established.

Self-Awareness in the First Weeks of Life

Lewis and Brooks-Gunn's (1979) research suggests that visual self-recognition is apparent at nine months of age. Other researchers (e.g., Butterworth, 1992; Meltzoff, 1990; Neisser, 1988) have examined whether even younger infants possess self-awareness. These investigators do not rely on the visual recognition tests used by Lewis and Brooks-Gunn. They note that visual recognition demands a relatively advanced form of self-awareness; in order to recognize oneself in a mirror, one needs to have both self-awareness and an understanding of how mirrors work. For this reason, other measures are needed to determine whether self-awareness is present earlier in development.

Butterworth (1992) provided a review of this research. He began by distinguishing three aspects of self-awareness: (1) self–nonself differentiation (the ability to distinguish oneself from others and from the external world); (2) a sense of volition (comprehending that we can control some events but not others); and (3) perceived continuity of self over time (understanding that we have a stable existence). These aspects correspond to the three functions of the *I* we described in Chapter 1, and they accord with our definition of the *I* as "our awareness that we are a distinct and unified entity, continuous over time and capable of willful action."

Butterworth (1992) believes that infants come into the world with the *capacity* to make these discriminations. Among the findings he cites to buttress his claim are the following:

1. Newborns can visually orient themselves and maintain body postures in a changing environment, suggesting that self–world (self–environment) differentiation is present at birth.
2. Newborns cry harder to the sound of another infant's cry but not to the sound of their own cry, suggesting that self–other differentiation is present at birth.
3. Newborns rapidly learn to control the movements of objects and show delight when doing so, suggesting an early awareness that they can produce desired outcomes.
4. In newborns, the mouth anticipates the arrival of the hand, suggesting the presence of an innate body schema.

Imitation in Early Infancy

Research on imitation provides further support for the claim that self-awareness is present early in infancy. Imitation has long been thought to be integral to self-development. Cooley and Mead emphasized processes akin to imitation when they claimed that the self develops by taking the perspective of others: We put ourselves in other people's shoes and adopt their attitudes toward us. The role of imitation in self-development was made even more explicit by an earlier theorist, James Mark Baldwin, who wrote:

> My sense of myself grows by imitation of you, and my sense of yourself grows in terms of my sense of myself. Both [self] and [other] are thus essentially social; each is . . . an imitative creation. (Baldwin, 1897, p. 7)

Meltzoff and Moore (1977) studied facial imitation in infants who were 12 to 21 days old. An infant and an adult were brought together, and the adult made various faces (e.g., stuck his tongue out, pursed his lips together) while the infant watched. The infant's facial behavior was then recorded, and observers unaware of the adult's facial expression coded the infant's expression. There was clear evidence that infants imitated the faces they saw. A follow-up study (Meltzoff & Moore, 1993) found that imitation of this sort can be documented in 2- to 3-day-old infants!

Meltzoff and Moore (1994) discussed two explanations for these findings. One possibility is that the adult's facial expression *automatically* triggers a matching facial expression in the infant. This account is similar to a "reflex-arc" model, because it does not assume that any higher-order processes, including ones involving self-awareness, are implicated in imitative behavior. A second possibility is that newborns possess a rudimentary body schema that allows them to *deliberately* mimic the expressions they see. According to this account, infants see the adult's expression and are able to translate what they have seen into an expression of their own.

Research on these competing explanations is just beginning (Meltzoff & Moore, 1994), but the initial evidence provides support for the notion that facial imitation is deliberate rather than reflexive. On the basis of these and other findings, Meltzoff believes that the seeds of self-awareness are part of the infant's normal biological endowment:

> The young infant possesses an embryonic "body scheme" . . . [Although] this body scheme develops [with age], some body-scheme kernel is present as a "psychological primitive" right from the earliest phases of infancy. This nascent notion of self is a foundation from which self development proceeds, not an endpoint that is reached after months or years of interaction with the social environment. (Meltzoff, 1990, p. 160)

Summary

It is important to underscore just what is and is not being claimed here. Butterworth and Meltzoff acknowledge that each of the effects we have discussed is subject to alternative explanations, and that none is sufficient to establish self-awareness in the neonate. Moreover, these theorists do not dispute the fact that self-awareness develops with age. Rather, they claim that the *basis* for self-awareness is present at birth. Infants possess an innate *capacity* to distinguish self from "not self," to recognize their ability to produce desired outcomes, and to coordinate their movements via an inchoate body schema. These findings suggest that newborns enter the world with a rudimentary sense of self that sets the stage for subsequent development. Social interaction and language may (as Mead claimed) be necessary for the complete development of the self, but they may not be necessary for its birth.

The Developmental Course of the ME

To this point we have been concerned with the development of the *I*, with the infant's awareness that it is a distinct and continuous entity. We have yet to consider the development of the *ME*. A focus on the *ME* would lead us to ask: How do people's thoughts *about themselves* change with age? For example, do 6-year-olds think of themselves differently than do 16-year-olds? Research in this area (for reviews, see Damon & Hart, 1988; Harter, 1983; Lewis & Brooks-Gunn, 1979) suggests the following developmental trends.

Early Childhood (Ages 2–6)

Gender and age appear to be the first characteristics applied to the self. By age two, most children correctly identify themselves as a boy or a girl, although they may not be fully aware that gender is constant until several years later (Harter, 1983). At this age, children also tend to describe themselves in terms of concrete, observable characteristics (e.g., I have brown hair; I have an older brother) and typical behaviors and activities (e.g., I play games; I like soccer). In short, young children tend to think of themselves in terms of their observable, verifiable characteristics.

Middle Childhood (Ages 7–11)

Several changes in self-descriptions occur during middle childhood. First, self-descriptions become more general. For example, instead of thinking of themselves in terms of specific activities (I like soccer; I like skating), children start applying broader labels to themselves (I like sports). Children at this age also begin defining themselves (and others) in psychological terms that emphasize perceived traits. Many of these qualities refer to important social characteristics (e.g., nice, likable, or friendly).

Cognitive maturity accounts for many of these changes. Middle childhood encompasses the concrete operational phase in Piaget's model. During this stage, children acquire the ability to think logically and to organize their thinking through the use of inductive reasoning. These abilities enable them to construct a more general view of themselves than was possible during early childhood.

Children at this age also acquire the capacity to take the perspective of others (in the manner specified by Mead) and to see themselves from another person's point of view. Social comparison processes also become more influential at this stage of life. Children compare themselves with others and draw inferences about themselves on the basis of what these comparisons show ("Jimmy has more trouble solving problems than I do, so I must be smart"). Before the age of six, social comparison is not thought to strongly influence the way children evaluate themselves (Ruble, 1983).

TABLE 4.2. Developmental Changes in Self-Descriptions

Stage of Development	Dominant Self-Descriptions	Examples	Parallels to James's Empirical Self
Early childhood (approximate ages: 2–6)	Observable, verifiable characteristics Specific interests and activities	I am a girl. I have brown hair. I have a younger brother. I like playing soccer.	Material self
Middle childhood (approximate ages: 7–11)	General interests Use of social comparison Interpersonal qualities	I like sports. I'm smarter than Meredith. I am nice.	Social self
Adolescence (approximate ages: 12–18)	Hidden, abstract "psychological" qualities	I am moody. I am self-conscious.	Spiritual self

Adolescence (Ages 12–18)

Adolescence brings another shift in self-understanding. Adolescents define themselves in abstract qualities that emphasize their perceived inner emotions and psychological characteristics. For example, an adolescent might be inclined to say he is moody or insecure. These assessments reflect a more sophisticated, analytical approach to self-definition, one that emphasizes private qualities not necessarily known to others.

Table 4.2 summarizes these developmental trends in self-description. The table also shows the parallels between these stages and the three components of the empirical self discussed by William James (1890) (see Chapter 2). In early childhood, children emphasize the material self (physical attributes, possessions); in middle childhood, children focus on the social self (they use social comparison information and emphasize their interpersonal qualities); in adolescence, the focus is on the spiritual self (one's perceived inner psychological qualities).

SELF-DEVELOPMENT ACROSS THE LIFE SPAN

Self-development is most rapid during infancy and early childhood, but people's ideas about themselves change (at least somewhat) throughout their lives. In the final section of this chapter, we will broaden our scope and look more closely at self-development across the life span.

The Developmental Course of Self-Evaluation

We will begin by considering age-related changes in the way people *evaluate* themselves. In Chapter 3 we noted that most people evaluate themselves in very favorable terms. Several investigators have examined whether this "positivity bias" is equally apparent at all stages of life.

An investigation by Ruble, Eisenberg, and Higgins (1994) sheds light on this issue. These investigators tested children at three age levels: 5–6, 7–8, and 9–10. Approximately half of the children succeeded or failed at an experimental task; the other half observed another child (of the same age and sex) succeed or fail at the task. The children then rated their own (or the other child's) ability.

At all three age levels, the children rated their own ability more favorably than they rated the other child's ability. Moreover, this tendency was especially pronounced given failure, leading Ruble and her colleagues to conclude that children's highly positive self-evaluations are driven by a desire to maximize feelings of self-worth.

Ruble et al. also found that self-evaluations were most favorable among the youngest children (5–6-year-olds) and least favorable among the oldest children (9–10-year-olds). This is a common pattern. Figure 4.1, which is based on the results of a number of studies (for reviews, see Demo, 1992; Eccles, Wigfield, Harold, & Blumenfeld, 1993; Marsh, 1989; Stipek, 1984), presents a schematic representation of findings in this area. The figure shows that young children (3–8-year-olds) evaluate themselves in very positive terms. Sometime around age 9 or 10, these evaluations become less positive. They are still favorable in an absolute sense (and compared to children's evaluations of others), but they are not as favorable as they were a few years ago. This downward trend continues into early adolescence, as children make the transition from elementary school to junior high (or middle school), but begins to reverse itself around age 15. From that point on, self-evaluations become increasingly positive until they level off in early adulthood.

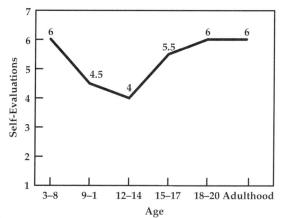

FIGURE 4.1. Schematic representation of the relation between self-evaluations and age. For this example, self-evaluations range from 1 to 7, with 7 being the most favorable. The data show that self-evaluations are very positive in childhood, become less positive during early adolescence, and rebound in late adolescence and early adulthood.

Adolescence

The fact that self-evaluations become more negative at the start of adolescence is consistent with the notion that adolescence is a difficult stage of life. These difficulties are thought to arise from the many changes adolescence brings. These include physical changes (brought about by the onset of puberty), cognitive changes (brought about by the emergence of formal operational thinking), and social changes (brought about by shifting societal expectations and changing friendship patterns).

The Adolescent Identity Crisis

Erik Erikson (1963, 1968) introduced the term "identity crisis" to describe the manner in which these changes can affect the way adolescents think and feel about themselves. He noted that many of the changes that accompany adolescence are abrupt and discontinuous, rather than smooth and gradual. This disjunction can create confusion and instability in the self-concept. Adolescents can become "unsure of who they are." To resolve this crisis, adolescents must find a way to establish continuity between their prepubertal self and the way they look, think, and feel about themselves now. They must also integrate the various ideas they have about themselves (including those involving new social roles and obligations) into a unified self-concept. In other words, as they first did in infancy, adolescents must fashion a stable and integrated self-view.

> The young person, in order to experience wholeness, must feel a progressive continuity between that which he has come to be during the long years of childhood and that which he promises to become in the anticipated future; between that which he conceives himself to be and that which he perceives others to see in him and to expect of him. (Erikson, 1968, p. 87) The sense of [identity], then, is the accrued confidence that the inner sameness and continuity prepared in the past are matched by the sameness and continuity of [the present]. (Erikson, 1963, p. 261)

Erikson believed that these issues are resolved when adolescents make commitments in three broad areas: (1) occupation (i.e., choose a profession); (2) ideology (i.e., establish a religious preference, political affiliation, and general world view); and (3) sexual orientation (i.e., define their sexual orientation and adopt age-appropriate sex-role behavior).

Historically, these commitments were not difficult to make (Baumeister & Tice, 1986). Before the industrial revolution, adolescents worked on the family farm or served an apprenticeship that prepared them to assume the family business. They also tended to adopt their parents' religious and political beliefs, and very often allowed their parents to determine whom and when they married. This is much less true today. At least in contemporary Western societies, adolescents are free to choose their occupation, ideology, and marriage partners. This freedom has obvious advantages, but it is not without costs. Today, adolescents must decide who they are and what they will be, leading to the type of identity crisis Erikson depicted (Baumeister & Tice, 1986).

TABLE 4.3. Four Levels of Identity Commitment in College Students

Identity Level	Description
Identity achieved	Individual has resolved an identity crisis by making identity commitments
Moratorium	Individual is currently in the midst of an identity crisis and is actively working toward resolution
Identity diffused	Individual is mired in an identity crisis and is not making progress toward resolution
Foreclosure	Individual has made identity commitments in the absence of an identity crisis

Source: Adapted from Marcia, 1966, *Journal of Personality and Social Psychology, 5,* 551–558. Copyright 1966. Adapted by permission of The American Pyschological Association.

Having the freedom (and responsibility) to forge an identity suggests that adolescents will differ with respect to how far along they are in making their identity commitments. Marcia (1966) considered this issue and distinguished four levels of identity commitment in college students. As shown in Table 4.3, individuals who have successfully weathered an identity crisis and have made the occupational, ideological, and sexual commitments Erikson described are said to be in the *identity achieved* stage. In effect, these individuals have "found themselves" after a period of searching. Those who are actively working toward resolving their crisis but have yet to do so successfully are said to be in the *moratorium* stage. Individuals who are mired in an identity crisis and are not making any discernible progress toward resolving it are said to be in the *identity diffused* stage. Finally, individuals who have made commitments in the absence of any crisis are said to be in the *foreclosure* stage. Typically, these individuals have accepted the commitments of their parents without attempting to define these commitments for themselves. As one might expect, there is a developmental shift across the college years, with identity achievers being more common among college seniors than among college freshmen (Waterman, 1982).

Self-Awareness in Adolescence

In addition to being a time of identity confusion, adolescence is also a time of increased self-consciousness. This heightened self-awareness takes two forms. The first is a private preoccupation with oneself, epitomized by the soul-searching Erikson emphasized. The second is an excessive (some would say obsessive) concern with how one appears to others. Adolescents are renown for believing that others are scrutinizing them, talking about them, and evaluating them (Elkind, 1967). These feelings appear to be particularly acute during early adolescence (Rosenberg, 1979) and decline as adolescents begin to make their identity commitments (Adams, Abraham, & Markstrom, 1987; Ryan & Kuczkowski, 1994).

Sex Differences in Self-Evaluation during Adolescence

Another issue that has received attention is whether there are sex differences in the way adolescents think and feel about themselves. One widely cited study by Simmons and her associates found a sharp decline in the self-esteem of white females entering junior high school (Simmons, Blyth, Van Cleave, & Bush, 1979). Subsequent research has failed to replicate this finding (see, for example, Hirsch & Rapkin, 1987). Thus, although there is a general decline in self-related feelings at the start of adolescence (see Figure 4.1), this decline does *not* vary as a function of sex (or race).

There are, however, sex differences when it comes to the way adolescents evaluate their specific qualities (Marsh, 1989). For some attributes (e.g., perceived ability in math), boys evaluate themselves more positively than do girls; for other attributes (e.g., perceived verbal ability), girls evaluate themselves more positively than do boys. These differences generally follow cultural stereotypes and may be specific to Western societies.

Pubertal development also differentially affects the way boys and girls evaluate themselves. Among boys, early pubertal development is associated with a more positive view of one's body; among girls, early development is associated with a more negative view of one's body (for a review, see Buchanan, Eccles, & Becker, 1992). Again, these differences may well be specific to particular cultures, rather than universal.

Is Adolescence Invariably Stressful?

Adolescence is clearly a psychologically rich period of life. The dramatic physical, cognitive, and social changes that occur can have many negative consequences, as evidenced by the disproportionately high rates of unwanted teenage pregnancy, alcohol and drug abuse, accidents related to high-risk behavior, and suicide rates (Quadrel, Fischhoff, & Davis, 1993). Unfortunately, these problems seem only to be increasing as we enter the twenty-first century (Garland & Zigler, 1993).

But is adolescence invariably stressful? The answer appears to be "no." Although many adolescents confront the sorts of issues Erikson and others have spoken of, and may experience temporary *disturbances* in the self-concept, these changes are rarely extreme or long-lasting. Moreover, many positive changes occur during adolescence as well, including strong ties to peer groups and a new sense of freedom and control. For these reasons, the majority of adolescents do not experience the kind of anguish and turmoil that the term "identity crisis" implies.

The majority of adolescents of both genders successfully negotiate this developmental period without any major psychological or emotional disorder, develop a positive sense of personal identity, and manage to forge adaptive peer relationships at the same time they maintain close relationships with their families. (Petersen et al., 1993)

Self-Conceptions in Adulthood

And the years are rolling by me, they are rocking evenly,
I am older than I once was, and younger than I'll be, that's not unusual.
No it isn't strange, after changes upon changes we are more or less the same.
After changes we are more or less the same.

—P. SIMON, "The Boxer"

Although relatively serene in comparison to the many changes that characterize adolescence, adulthood is also marked by a number of important transitions. People get married, begin careers, have children, relocate to new cities, and so forth. Despite these many changes, the adult personality is remarkably stable (McCrae & Costa, 1994). Whether we look at mean levels (are the elderly more conscientious than the middle-aged?), or the rank-ordering of individuals (do people who score high on conscientious in middle age score high on conscientious later in life?), the story is the same: Personality changes little after the age of 30. This stability also characterizes people's ideas about themselves. Self-ratings obtained in early adulthood are highly similar to self-ratings obtained many years later (Mortimer, Finch, & Kumka, 1982). Identities are added and lost, of course, but our ideas about ourselves remain consistent.

Several theorists (e.g., Cohler, 1982; Filipp & Klauer, 1986; Gergen & Gergen, 1983) believe this stability arises from a constructive process in which individuals create stability by generating a coherent narrative of their life's story. This approach emphasizes that individuals are not passive witnesses to their life; they are active historians. They interpret their past in ways that allow them to maintain a strong sense of continuity (McAdams, 1996). Viewing experiences in this manner allows people to perceive the continuity that James (1890) noted was so critical to the preservation of identity.

These interpretive processes extend into late adulthood. Although advancing age often brings many changes, including impairment in visual, auditory, and motor functioning, there is little consistent evidence that people's views of themselves change appreciably in their later years (Brandtstädter & Greve, 1994). Nor does research support the claim that elderly people are lonely, depressed, and filled with despair. Absent any serious health problems, people's feelings toward themselves and the perceived quality of their lives do not decline with age. Again, this is because people do not passively register the circumstances of their lives, they actively transform them. Among other things, they adjust their goals and adopt different targets for purposes of social comparison. Age also brings positive changes as well (Carstensen & Freund, 1994; Cross & Markus, 1991). As was true with adolescence, then, most people are not filled with angst at this stage of life.

> The processes of aging involve a multitude of changes and discontinuities that challenge the person's construction of self. . . . It seems plausible to assume, as many researchers in the field of adult development and aging have done, that such experiences should translate into problems of self-esteem, reduced well-being, and in increased vulnerability to depression. Despite their seeming theoretical consistency, these assumptions have received little empirical

support. On the contrary, the picture that begins to emerge from recent research gives testimony to a remarkable stability, resilience, and resourcefulness of the aging self. (Brandstädter & Greve, 1994, p. 71)

CHAPTER SUMMARY

In this chapter we have charted the developmental course of the self. We began by considering three theories that have guided research in this area. These were (1) Mead's (1934) theory of symbolic interactionism; (2) Piaget's (1952) theory of cognitive development; and (3) Erikson's (1963) eight-stage theory of psychosocial development.

We then examined the origins of self-awareness. Using self-recognition as an index of self-awareness, research has found (1) that self-awareness is not uniquely human, and (2) that self-awareness in humans emerges during the first year of life. Research using other means of assessing self-awareness (e.g., imitation) suggests that even newborns may possess a rudimentary self-schema.

Next, we discussed how people's thoughts about themselves change as they age. Self-descriptions show a shift toward increasing generality. Young children describe themselves in very concrete terms; during middle childhood, children's self-descriptions become more socially oriented; and adolescents focus more on their inner (psychological) qualities.

Finally, we examined self-development across the life span. We noted that the tendency for people to evaluate themselves in very positive terms declines a bit during early adolescence but then rebounds during early adulthood. We also noted that although adolescence is a time of great change in the self, most individuals weather these changes with a strong sense of identity. The same principle applies to the aging process. Most individuals retain a positive self-view as they age.

- Mead presented a theory of the self that tied its development to social interaction. Individuals enter the world as unsocialized beings, but they come to adopt the standards and norms of the culture into which they are born. They do so, Mead argued, by developing self—by acquiring the capacity to look back on themselves through the eyes of others. Two activities—the need to communicate with symbols, and play—facilitate the development of this perspective-taking ability. At first, these activities lead individuals to adopt the perspective of *particular* others toward the self; later, individuals come to adopt the perspective of an abstract, generalized other. When this perspective-taking sequence is completed, the self is said to be fully developed and the individual is said to be fully socialized.
- Piaget's model of development assumes that individuals progress through a series of cognitive stages. Each stage is characterized by qualitatively different modes of thinking. The stages move toward increasing sophistication in the use of abstract reasoning, perspective-taking capacity, and problem-solving ability. These stages affect self-understanding, as people's ideas about themselves grow increasingly complex as they age.
- Erikson outlined an eight-stage model of psychological development. Each stage is characterized by a particular psychological need or conflict that centers around a self-relevant issue. Failure to resolve these conflicts leads to later psychological difficulties.
- Research using a mirror-recognition task has found that two species besides humans (chimpanzees and orangutans) are capable of recognizing themselves in a

mirror. Chimpanzees raised in social isolation fail to show mirror recognition, supporting Mead's claim that self-development requires social interaction.

- Self-recognition in infants begins with the ability to recognize oneself through contingent movement (as indexed by a mirror-recognition task). This ability is apparent around nine months of age. At around 15 months of age, infants are able to recognize themselves with noncontingent stimuli (e.g., a photograph) and pass the facial mark test. By 21 months of age, most infants are further able to identify themselves using personal pronouns.

- Self-awareness in humans may be present at birth. Infants appear to possess an innate *capacity* to distinguish self from "not self," to recognize their ability to produce desired outcomes, and to coordinate their own movements (suggesting the existence of a primitive body schema). These findings are consistent with the claim that newborns enter the world with a rudimentary sense of self that sets the stage for later development.

- People's thoughts about themselves follow a developmental sequence of increasing generality and abstraction. Young children focus on specific concrete, observable aspects of themselves, such as their physical characteristics and typical activities. As they age, children increasingly couch their self-descriptions in terms of more general traits and qualities that subsume these more specific attributes. They also begin to define themselves in social terms. Self-descriptions become increasingly more general and abstract during adolescence, with an emphasis on hidden, psychological characteristics (e.g., feelings, motives) rather than observable, physical ones.

- Self-evaluations also show a developmental pattern. Young children evaluate themselves very positively. This positivity declines a bit during early adolescence, as children make the transition from elementary school to middle school. Positive self-evaluations return as adolescents enter high school, and they remain generally positive throughout adulthood.

- Adolescence is a critical time in self-development. Erik Erikson coined the term "identity crisis" to describe the process many adolescents go through in their attempt to (re)define themselves. Not all adolescents suffer difficulties during this stage of life, however, and most weather the storms of adolescence unscathed.

- People's ideas about themselves remain rather stable during adulthood. New identities are added as people's lives change, but people actively interpret these experiences in ways that allow them to maintain a sense of continuity.

For Further Reading

DAMON, W., & HART, D. (1988). *Self-understanding in childhood and adolescence.* New York: Cambridge University Press.

HARTER, S. (1983). Developmental perspectives on the self-system. In M. Hetherington (Ed.), *Handbook of child psychology: Social and personality development* (Vol. 4, pp. 275–385). New York: Wiley.

LEWIS, M., & BROOKS-GUNN, J. (1979). *Social cognition and the acquisition of self.* New York: Plenum Press.

CHAPTER 5

The Self from
a Cognitive Perspective

The 1960s were a time of great change in American culture. They were also a time of change in American psychology. Behaviorism, which had dominated the field for nearly 50 years, was giving way to a new movement known as the cognitive revolution. Although the two movements share some core assumptions, they differ in a fundamental respect. Behaviorism pays scant attention to internal, mental processes, whereas the cognitive approach treats mental processes as the key object of study.

Much of cognitive psychology is concerned with the way people process information. This concern includes a consideration of (1) attentional processes (what we notice), (2) interpretation (how we interpret and explain what we notice), and (3) memory (what we remember). For many years, psychologists characterized these operations as *data-driven* or *bottom-up* processes, because it was assumed that people passively register stimuli in the external world. What we see, hear, and understand, depends entirely on what is "out there."

A different view of information processing emerged in the late 1950s. Building on Gestalt principles of perception, Bruner (1957) argued that information processing is not solely a data-driven process; it is also a *theory-driven, top-down* process. People do not simply register stimuli in the external world. Instead, they actively construct the world they experience, and this constructive process depends on prior knowledge and expectations about what the world is like.

Let's look at an example (adapted from Anderson, 1983). Consider the statement "The robber ran from the bank." Even though the word "bank" could refer to either a monetary institution or a river's edge, you probably assumed that the word referred to a monetary institution. That's because you expect to find a robber running from a monetary institution, rather than a river's edge. Now consider the statement "The otter ran from the bank." Now you are more likely to think of a river's edge, because that's where you expect to find otters running. The point here is that the way we interpret the sentence depends on prior knowledge. This is what we mean when we say that perception and information processing are theory-driven (top-down) processes.

Seymour Epstein was one of the first psychologists to fully appreciate the implications of this perspective for the study of the self. In an influential paper, Epstein (1973) argued that people's ideas about themselves are one form of knowledge that guides the way they process information. In pursuing this theme, Epstein likened self-knowledge to a theory (see also, Kelly, 1963; Sarbin, 1952). Much as a scientist's theories organize and give meaning to a body of data, so, too, do people's ideas about themselves organize and give meaning to their experiences.

> I submit that the self-concept is a self-theory. It is a theory that the individual has unwittingly constructed about himself as an experiencing, functioning individual. . . . Like most theories, the self-theory is a conceptual tool for accomplishing a purpose. [One of these purposes] is to organize the data of experience in a manner that can be coped with effectively. (Epstein, 1973, p. 407)

Along with other papers by Markus (1977), and Rogers, Kuiper, and Kirker (1977), Epstein's information-processing approach led to an important change in the way researchers approached the study of self. Instead of looking only at why people think of themselves as they do, researchers began exploring how people's thoughts about themselves influence their interpretation of events and experiences. This shift represents the most significant development in self-psychology over the last 30 years (Markus & Wurf, 1987). Particularly within the fields of personality and social psychology, researchers now generously apply the theory and methods of cognitive psychology to the study of self-relevant processes.

The purpose of this chapter is to familiarize you with this research approach. The first issue we will consider is the cognitive representation of self-knowledge. People have many ideas about themselves, but these ideas do not exist in a haphazard fashion. They are linked to one another in an organized configuration. The first section of this chapter will examine this organizational structure.

Next we will consider the manner in which self-knowledge is activated. At any moment, only some of our self-knowledge is active and guiding our behavior. What determines this activation? What factors bring one or another self-view into awareness? These are the issues we will explore in the second section of this chapter.

The third issue we will consider is the way self-relevant information is processed. Only a portion of the information we attend to everyday implicates the self, yet this information is somehow *special.* For example, it is easily noticed and well remembered. In the third part of this chapter, we will consider why this is so and examine how motivational forces and cognitive processes combine to influence the processing of personal information.

THE REPRESENTATION OF SELF-KNOWLEDGE

Cognitive psychologists assume our knowledge of the world is organized into cognitive structures. Although there is disagreement about the precise form these structures take, one possibility is that knowledge is organized in a hierarchical fashion. A general concept sits at the top of the hierarchy, and more specific knowledge occupies a subordinate status.

The top half of Figure 5.1 presents a greatly simplified example of this type of model for the general concept of "animal." Various kinds of animals are associated with this general heading (e.g., birds, fish, and mammals). Examples of each type of animal reside at a subordinate level, and linked to each of these specific animals are characteristic behaviors and attributes.

People's ideas about themselves may be represented in a similar manner (Kihlstrom & Cantor, 1984). The bottom half of Figure 5.1 shows such a model (again, very simplified). At the top of the hierarchy is the self. Underlying this concept are three more specific headings: physical attributes, self-esteem, and social identities. Under each of the social identities are various characteristics and traits.

Although not all psychologists endorse the particular model shown in Figure 5.1, most agree that people's ideas about themselves form a complex and highly organized knowledge structure, and that this structure becomes increasingly differentiated with age as people acquire additional knowledge of themselves. There is also agreement on the general implications of the model

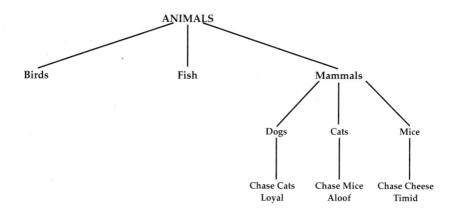

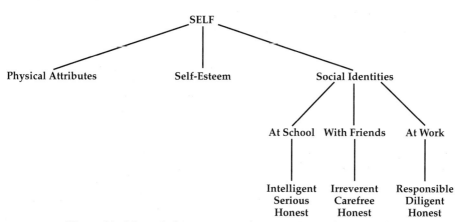

FIGURE 5.1. Hierarchical knowledge structures for animals and for oneself.

(Greenwald & Pratkanis, 1984; Linville & Carlston, 1994; Markus & Wurf, 1984). For example, note the contextual basis of self-knowledge. How we think of ourselves depends on the social context (James, 1890; Rosenberg & Gara, 1985). A person might think of himself as intelligent at school, irreverent when he's with his friends, and responsible when he's at work. Another thing to notice is that people have knowledge of themselves that is somewhat contradictory. For example, we might think of ourselves as serious at school, carefree with our friends, and diligent when we are working. Finally, people have views of themselves that are common to more than one role, relationship, or situation. "Honest" is such a trait in the example shown in Figure 5.1.

Self-Complexity

A number of important issues flow from this structural model. First, we can ask "How full is the self-concept?" Does a person think of herself in many different ways or in only a few ways? Linville (1985, 1987) coined the term "self-complexity" to refer to such differences. People who think of themselves in many different ways are high in self-complexity; those who think of themselves in relatively few ways are low in self-complexity.

Linville uses a card-sorting task to measure self-complexity. People are given a number of index cards, each containing a trait term or characteristic (e.g., lazy, outgoing, rebellious). They are then asked to group the cards into piles that describe themselves in various settings or relationships. The more groups the person forms, and the less overlap there is among groups, the higher the person's self-complexity score.

Table 5.1 depicts individual differences in self-complexity. The person in the top half of the table is high in self-complexity. This person thinks of himself in many different ways, and there is little overlap among the various identities the person has described. The person in the bottom half of the table is low in self-complexity. This person thinks of himself in only a few ways, and there is a good deal of overlap among the groups.

Linville (1985, 1987) argued that differences in self-complexity affect people's responses to positive and negative events. The less complex the person's self-representation, the more extreme the person's response to positive and negative events. As an example, suppose you are a single-minded lawyer. Your entire life revolves around your law practice. If you win a case, you will feel ecstatic, but if you lose a case, you may feel devastated. According to Linville, this is because you do not have other identities to fall back on. Now consider the situation if you think of yourself in many ways (e.g., as a hardworking lawyer, but also as an understanding friend, a loving spouse, a caring parent, and so on). Under these circumstances, losing a case may not be so devastating, because you have many other identities to help cushion the blow (see also Dixon & Baumeister, 1991; Niedenthal, Setterlund, & Wherry, 1992; Steele, 1988; Thoits, 1983).

Although multiple identities may generally be healthy, there is a point at which highly complex self-concepts may get us into trouble. The problem, as

TABLE 5.1. Examples of Self-Concepts That are High in Self-Complexity and Low in Self-Complexity

High Self-Complexity

With Men	With Friends	With Family	At School	Alone	At Parties
outgoing	humorous	emotional	quiet	individualistic	humorous
playful	relaxed	playful	studious	reflective	playful
reflective	assertive	reflective	organized	industrious	outgoing
mature	outgoing	mature	mature	quiet	sophisticated
emotional	mature	assertive	reserved		affectionate
assertive	emotional	humorous	industrious		competitive
competitive	reflective	outgoing	individualistic		imaginative
relaxed	soft-hearted	individualistic			impulsive
humorous	not studious	unconventional			mature
affectionate	affectionate				
soft-hearted	individualistic				
individualistic					
sophisticated					

Low Self-Complexity

At School	With Friends	Alone
relaxed	playful	playful
reserved	relaxed	relaxed
organized	assertive	imaginative
energetic	individualistic	impulsive
secure		energetic

Adapted from Linville, 1987, *Journal of Personality and Social Psychology*, 52, 663–676. Copyright 1987. Adapted by permission of The American Psychological Association.

William James noted over a century ago, is that we cannot be all the things we would like to be.

> I am often confronted by the necessity of standing by one of my empirical selves and relinquishing the rest. Not that I would not, if I could, be both handsome and fat and well-dressed, and a great athlete, and make a million a year, be a wit, a *bon-vivant*, and a lady-killer, as well as a philosopher, a phil-anthropist, statesman, warrior and African explorer, as well as a "tone-poet" and saint. But the thing is simply impossible. The millionaire's work would run counter to the saint's; the *bon-vivant* and the philanthropist would trip each other up; the philosopher and the lady-killer could not well keep house in the same tenement of clay. (James, 1890, pp. 309–310)

The point here is that each additional identity can be a burden as well as a blessing. Ultimately, it depends on whether these identities fit well with each other. We hear often in modern society about role conflict. Women, for exam-ple, are expected to be wage earners, wives, mothers, educators, athletes, chauffeurs, doctors, and more. These multiple social identities may create con-flict. Women may also experience friction among their various personal identi-ties. After the birth of a child, they may experience a conflict between a desire to be nurturing and caring versus a desire to be tough and competitive. Whether more is better, then, is likely to depend on whether the fit among the various identities is good. Otherwise, too many identities can create as many problems as too few identities.

A study by Donahue, Robins, Roberts, and John (1993) illustrates this point. These investigators had college students describe themselves in each of five social roles (e.g., "How responsible are you as a student, friend, romantic partner, son/daughter, and worker?"). Donahue et al. then calculated an index of self-concept differentiation to capture the extent to which students described themselves differently in each role. High self-concept differentiation was associated with depression, neuroticism, and low self-esteem. These find-ings pose an interesting challenge to Linville's (1985, 1987) research on self-complexity, suggesting that multiple identities are beneficial *only* if they are well integrated with one another (see also, Woolfolk, Novalany, Gara, Allen, & Polino, 1995).

Self-Concept Certainty and Importance

The certainty of people's self-knowledge is another facet of the self-concept. We hold some views of ourselves with great certainty. We are absolutely sure we are outgoing, and positive we are not mechanically inclined. Other views of ourselves are ill defined and subject to equivocation. We're not sure if we're intuitive or not. This issue is important because self-views that are held with great certainty are less likely to change than are self-views about which we are uncertain (Pelham, 1991; Swann & Ely, 1984). There is also evidence that the more certain people are of their self-views, the better they feel about them-selves (Baumgardner, 1990; Campbell, 1990).

In addition to considering the certainty of people's self-views, we can also consider their importance. Some of our self-views are particularly central and self-defining; others are peripheral or unimportant. In general, the importance of an identity varies as a function of goal relevance. Identities of high personal importance tend to be ones that are instrumental to our goals and ambitions; identities of low personal importance tend to be unrelated to our goals and ambitions (Pelham, 1991). To illustrate, a professional athlete might primarily think of herself in terms of her athleticism and competitive drive, but an artist might think of herself chiefly in terms of her spontaneity and creativity.

People also vary in the importance they attach to their various *social* identities (McCall & Simmons, 1978; Stryker, 1980). One person might think of himself principally in terms of his work; another might think of himself primarily in terms of his family. These differences influence people's emotional lives. People show stronger emotional reactions to outcomes that touch important identities than to outcomes that implicate unimportant identities (Brunstein, 1993; James, 1890; Lavallee & Campbell, 1995; Pelham, 1991).

Differences like these highlight a more general point about the nature of self-knowledge. It is not simply *what* people think about themselves that is important; it is also the meaning people give to each identity element (Pelham, 1991; Rosenberg, 1979). It is conceivable, though highly unlikely, that the self-concepts of two individuals could be comprised of exactly the same identities. But their self-concepts would still be different if the two people varied in how certain they were of these identities or in how important these identities were to them.

An appropriate analogy here would be the relation between the notes of a song and the song's melody. If we rearrange the notes of a melody, we have a very different tune—even though the notes themselves remained unchanged. This idea can be derived from Gestalt principles of perception, which hold that "the whole is greater than the sum of the parts." As applied to the self-concept, this principle tells us that in order to understand a person's self-concept, we need to know more than what the individual thinks of when she thinks of herself. We also need to know how these conceptions are related and arranged, and what meaning they hold for the individual.

Self-Schemas

Markus (1977) believes that self-views that are important and are held with great certainty function as *self-schemas*.[1] Schemas are hypothetical knowledge structures that guide the processing of information. People have schemas about many different things, including other people, social groups, social

[1]The term *self-schema* has been the source of controversy and confusion. Some (e.g., Burke, Kraut, & Dworkin, 1984) have questioned whether the term is needed at all; others (e.g., Rogers, Kuiper, & Kirker, 1977) have used the term to refer to the entire self-concept, rather than to specific self-conceptions of high personal importance. Without taking a position on this debate, I will use the term in the manner specified by Markus (1977): Self-schemas will be used to refer to those attributes that people regard as particularly self-defining and of which they are highly certain.

events, and objects (Fiske & Taylor, 1991). These schemas influence what information we notice, how we interpret and explain the information we take in, and what we remember.

Self-schemas have similar effects. In an initial demonstration, Markus (1977) first identified people who are *schematic* with respect to their perceived independence. These people think of themselves as very independent or very dependent, and they regard this characteristic as very important. Other people were identified as being *aschematic* with respect to this dimension. Aschematic people don't think of themselves as very independent or as very dependent, and they don't regard this trait as important.

In the second part of the experiment, the participants were shown a list of words that related to independence, and they were asked to indicate whether the word described them or not (e.g., How assertive are you? How conforming are you?). Schematic participants made these judgments faster than did aschematic participants, indicating that being schematic influences the ease with which people process information for that characteristic (see also, Bargh, 1982). Additional findings showed that, in comparison with aschematics, schematic participants remembered more examples from their life when they had acted in an independent or dependent manner, and made more confident predictions regarding their future behavior in this realm.

Self-schemas also influence the way we process social information. People who are schematic for a trait readily accept information that confirms their self-view but actively refute or reject information that runs counter to how they think of themselves (Markus, 1977; Swann 1990). If, for example, you are certain that you are very graceful, you will quickly accept feedback that suggests you are agile but you will carefully scrutinize or dismiss feedback that suggests you are ungainly.

Our perceptions of other people are also affected by self-schemas (Fong & Markus, 1982; Markus & Smith, 1981). For example, people who are schematic with respect to their own weight are quick to notice other people's weight and to categorize other people along this dimension (i.e., they classify other people as fat or thin). This tendency reflects a more general inclination to use the self as a reference point when judging others. The more important an attribute is to the way we think about ourselves, the more inclined we are to use that attribute when perceiving other people (Dunning & Hayes, 1996; Lewicki, 1983, 1984; Prentice, 1990; Shrauger & Patterson, 1976).

Finally, self-schemas influence behavior. People who are schematic in a given domain act more consistently than do those who are aschematic (Bem & Allen, 1974; Markus, 1983). For example, compared to people who are aschematic for independence, people who are schematic for independence are more apt to act in an independent manner across various situations. This may be true even though both aschematics and schematics regard themselves as independent. The key difference is that people who are schematic for this trait are highly certain of their independence and regard the trait as particularly self-defining. These features account for the greater behavioral consistency schematic individuals display.

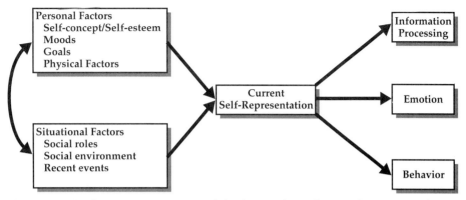

FIGURE 5.2. A schematic presentation of the factors that influence the way people currently think about themselves, and the influence these thoughts have on other aspects of psychological life.

THE ACTIVATION OF SELF-KNOWLEDGE

Individuals think of themselves in many ways, but only some of these ideas are active at any one time. A person who thinks of himself as idealistic and sentimental at one moment may think of himself as diffident and indecisive at another point in time. In this section, we will consider factors that activate one or another of our various self-conceptions.

The model shown in Figure 5.2 will guide our discussion. In the middle of the model is a box labeled "Current Self-Representation." We will use this term to refer to the way people are thinking of themselves at a given moment. Other theorists have referred to these momentary representations of self as "the phenomenal self" (Jones & Gerard, 1967), "the spontaneous self-concept" (McGuire & McGuire, 1981, 1988), "self-identifications" (Schlenker & Weigold, 1989), or aspects of the "working self-concept" (Markus & Kunda, 1986).

Figure 5.2 shows that personal and situational factors influence a person's current self-representation, and that these self-representations influence information processing, emotion, and behavior. The curved line connecting the two antecedent variables (i.e., Personal Factors and Situational Factors) indicates that these variables are interrelated. In the present context, this means that personal variables interact with situational factors to influence current self-representations.

Personal Factors That Influence the Activation of Self-Knowledge

Self-Concept/Self-Esteem

The most important factor affecting self-representations is the way people usually think of themselves. To illustrate, all else being equal, a person who usually thinks of herself as intelligent is more likely to be thinking of herself that way than is a person who does not usually think of herself as intelligent. This is especially true for attributes that are important and self-defining. These self-schemas, as we have called them, tend to be chronically accessible (Markus & Kunda, 1986; see also Higgins & King, 1981).

Self-esteem also affects the way people think about themselves. At any given moment, high self-esteem people are more apt to be thinking of themselves in positive terms than are low self-esteem people (Brown & Mankowski, 1993).

Mood States

Mood states also influence the accessibility of positive and negative self-views. All of us have things we like about ourselves and things we don't like about ourselves. When we are happy, we tend to think about our positive qualities and attributes; when we are sad, our negative qualities and attributes become more accessible (Brown & Taylor, 1986; Sedikides, 1995; Teasdale & Fogarty, 1979; Teasdale, Taylor, & Fogarty, 1980).

The link between mood states and self-views is particularly strong for low self-esteem people. Brown and Mankowski (1993) had students record their moods and complete a self-evaluation questionnaire (e.g., "How intelligent are you?" "How attractive are you?") on a daily basis over an eight-week period. Overall, the sadder people were, the more negatively they evaluated themselves. This was especially true for low self-esteem people, indicating that mood states are especially apt to influence the way low self-esteem people think of themselves (see also, Smith & Petty, 1995).

Goals

People can deliberately activate self-views. Very often, we survey a situation, figure out who we want to be or what role we want to play, and then activate an appropriate image of ourselves (Schlenker & Weigold, 1988; Snyder, 1979). For example, when interviewing for an important job, people try and project an image of themselves as industrious, competent, and responsible. Actively recruiting these self-images is one factor that helps people project these qualities (Feltz & Landers, 1983).

A desire to feel good about ourselves is another goal that influences the activation of self-views. A study by Kunda and Sanitioso (1989) illustrates this point. Kunda and Sanitioso had participants read a story about another student who was either doing well in school or was doing poorly in school. The participants were further told that the student was either very extraverted or very introverted. Later, participants rated their own levels of extraversion and introversion.

Kunda and Sanitioso (1989) assume that people want to believe they possess qualities associated with success, not qualities associated with failure. Accordingly, they predicted that their participants would want to think of themselves as extraverted when extraversion was linked to academic success, but introverted when introversion was linked to academic success. This is just what occurred. The participants described themselves as relatively outgoing and congenial when they believed extraversion predicted success, but they described themselves as relatively shy and reserved when they believed introversion predicted success. Follow-up research (Sanitioso, Kunda, & Fong, 1990) revealed that this occurred because participants selectively searched their memories for times they had acted in either an extraverted or introverted fashion. Along with other findings (e.g., Gump & Kulik, 1995; Kunda, 1990), these data show that a desire to feel good about ourselves influences the particular self-views we activate at any given time.

Physical Factors

Physical factors also affect the way people think about themselves. Research on the neurological basis of depression, for example, finds that particular chemical imbalances in the brain can trigger positive and negative thoughts about oneself. Other physical factors, such as hunger, lack of sleep, and hormonal changes, also alter the way people think about themselves.

Drugs can have a similar effect. Lithium, Prozac, and other medications alter the way people think about themselves (Kramer, 1993). Some of the effect is mediated through mood (the medication alters mood, and mood influences self-evaluations), but some of the effect is direct (self-evaluations are directly responsive to alterations in brain chemistry).

Situational Factors That Influence the Activation of Self-Knowledge

Personal factors are not the only things that influence the way people think about themselves. Situational factors also play an important role. Many of these factors derive from the nature of the social environment.

Social Roles

How we think about ourselves depends largely on the social role we are presently playing (Roberts & Donahue, 1994). For example, I am more apt to think of myself as a professor when I am teaching than when I am coaching my son's baseball team. Social roles also influence our personal identities. You are probably more apt to think of yourself as studious when you are studying in the library than when you are out on a date. The larger point here, which we noted in Chapter 2, is that "who we are" depends on where we are and with whom we are in contact.

Social Context and Self-Descriptions

If you've ever attended a meeting where everyone but you was dressed up, you were probably keenly aware of how you differed from the others. McGuire and McGuire (1981, 1988) have argued that situations like these influence the way people think about themselves, such that people tend to think of themselves in ways that distinguish them from their social surroundings (see also, Nelson & Miller, 1995).

McGuire and McGuire (1981, 1988) have tested their ideas using an open-ended questionnaire. Participants are asked to describe themselves in any terms they choose, and the descriptions they give are then coded along a number of dimensions. Finally, the researchers examine the distinctiveness of each description in the context of the person's social environment.

The results have shown clear support for the McGuires' *distinctiveness postulate*. In one study of school-age children, 27 percent of very tall or very short children spontaneously mentioned their height, but only 17 percent of children of average height did so. Similar results were found for weight, hair color, and birthplace. The more distinctive the attribute, the more likely children were to use it to describe themselves.

Distinctiveness also influences the salience of *group* identities. Self-categorization theory (Turner, Hogg, Oakes, Reicher, & Wetherell, 1987) proposes that whether people are thinking of themselves in terms of their various social groups (e.g., as an American, Protestant, or teamster) or in terms of their various personal identities (e.g., as ambitious, dependable, or outgoing) depends, in part, on the social context. In general, group identities are more salient in intergroup contexts. An American, for example, is more likely to think of himself as an American when he is in Paris, France, than when he is in Paris, Texas. This is because his nationality is distinctive when he is in a foreign land.

Group size is another factor that affects the salience of group identities. Almost by definition, minority groups tend to be statistically distinctive (in part, this is what it means to be a minority). Because of this distinctiveness, group identity should be more salient among minority group members than among majority group members. To illustrate, consider the salience of a person's racial identity. In America, there are far fewer people of Asian descent than of European descent. All else being equal, then, racial identity should be more prominently represented in the self-concept of Asian Americans than in the self-concept of European Americans. This prediction is another application of the McGuires' distinctiveness postulate.

The salience of group identities may further depend on group status (Tajfel & Turner, 1986). Simon and Hamilton (1994) had participants indicate how much they liked a series of paintings. Participants in the majority group condition were told that their preferences were shared by many other students, whereas participants in the minority group condition were led to believe that very few students shared their preferences. Independent of this manipulation, half of the participants were led to believe that their group was of high status and half were led to believe that their group was of low status. Finally, participants indicated how similar they thought they were to the average group member.

The results of this investigation are shown in Figure 5.3. The data show that group size (majority versus minority) and group status (high or low) interacted to affect the salience of social identities. Minority group members rated themselves as more like a typical group member only if the minority group was also of high status. When the group's status was low, minority group members distanced themselves from their group by denying that they were like a typical group member (for related findings, see Brewer, Manzi, & Shaw, 1993; Jackson, Sullivan, Harnish, & Hodge, 1996; Simon, Pantaleo, & Mummendey, 1995).

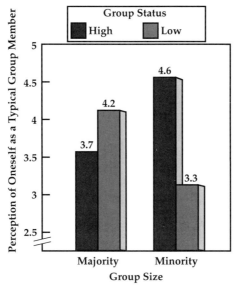

FIGURE 5.3. Self-descriptions as a function of group size and group status. The data show that minority group members think of themselves as highly typical of their group *only* when their group is also of high status.
(Adapted from Simon & Hamilton, 1994, *Journal of Personality and Social Psychology, 66,* 699–711. Copyright 1994. Adapted by permission of The American Pyschological Association.)

Social Context and Self-Evaluation

So far we've been discussing how the social context affects the salience of various identities. The social environment also influences the way people *evaluate* themselves. Most research shows evidence for a contrast effect. For example, we tend to regard ourselves as more attractive when we are in the company of unattractive people than when we are among people who are very attractive. In a similar vein, we are more apt to think of ourselves as sophisticated and knowledgeable when discussing world affairs with the ill-informed than when we are conversing with the politically astute. These effects occur as a result of social comparison processes (see Chapter 3). We use those in the immediate social environment as a target of comparison, and contrast our characteristics against theirs.

An investigation by Morse and Gergen (1970) first documented these tendencies. These investigators led participants to believe they were interviewing for a position as a research assistant. Participants were asked to wait for the alleged interview in the company of another applicant—a confederate. In one condition, the confederate was impeccably well mannered and professional in all respects; in the other condition, the confederate was disheveled and slovenly. Participants waiting with the highly desirable confederate later reported feeling worse about themselves than did participants waiting with the undesirable confederate.

Contrast effects of this sort can have important real-world consequences (Pettigrew, 1967; Stouffer et al., 1949). Davis (1966) examined how students' perceptions of their academic abilities are related to the ability level of their classmates. He found evidence for a contrast effect: With actual ability level held constant, students attending high-achieving schools evaluated their ability less favorably than did students attending low-achieving schools (see also, Bachman & O'Malley, 1986; Marsh & Parker, 1984). This finding does not mean that students attending high-achieving schools think they are less intelligent than do students attending low-achieving schools; it means that, at every ability level, a given student is less likely to think she is smart when attending a school with highly able classmates than when attending a school with less able classmates. In less formal terms, it appears that when it comes to how people evaluate themselves, it pays to be a big fish in a little pond!

Not all research shows evidence of a contrast effect in self-evaluations, however. Under some circumstances, people show an assimilation effect; that is, they evaluate themselves more positively when they are in the company of others who are exemplary on some dimension. Psychological closeness is one factor that determines when contrast and assimilation effects occur (Brewer & Weber, 1994; Brown, Novick, Lord, & Richards, 1992; Pelham & Wachsmuth, 1995). Contrast effects occur when people feel psychologically disconnected from their social surroundings, but assimilation effects occur when people feel psychologically connected to their social surroundings.

Brown et al. (1992) tested these ideas under the guise of a study on the impression formation process. During the first part of the experiment, female participants were shown a photograph of another woman. For some of the participants, the woman in the photograph was highly attractive; for other participants, the woman in the photograph was relatively unattractive. To establish psychological closeness, some of the participants were led to believe that they and the woman in the photograph were born on the same day; other participants (those in a control condition) were not given this information.

Brown et al. (1992) reasoned that the shared birthday manipulation would lead participants to feel psychologically connected to the woman in the photograph (Cialdini & De Nicholas, 1989; Finch & Cialdini, 1989), and that these feelings of relatedness would lead participants to assimilate to the woman's attractiveness. The data shown in Figure 5.4 are in accord with these predictions. The usual contrast effect was found in the control condition: Participants viewing the attractive photograph rated themselves as less attractive than did participants viewing the unattractive photograph. Just the opposite occurred, however, in the shared-birthday condition. Here, participants rated themselves as more attractive when viewing the attractive photograph than when viewing the unattractive photograph.

The data shown in Figure 5.4 indicate that people assimilate to the characteristics of others when they feel psychologically close to them. Brewer and Weber (1994) reported additional evidence for this effect in the context

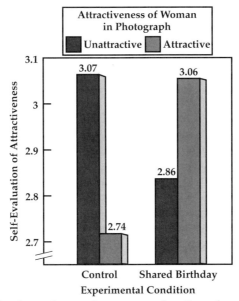

FIGURE 5.4. Self-evaluations of attractiveness as a function of psychological closeness and the attractiveness of others. The data show a contrast effect in the control condition but an assimilation effect in the shared-birthday condition.
(Adapted from Brown, Novick, Lord, & Richards, 1992, *Journal of Personality and Social Psychology, 60*, 717–727. Copyright 1992. Adapted by permission of The American Psychological Association.)

of research on group processes. They found that people show assimilation effects when a relevant group identity is salient but show contrast effects when personal identities are salient (see also, McFarland & Buehler, 1995). To illustrate, imagine you are a member of some group and that your group identity is currently prominent. When one of your fellow group members does something exemplary, you will share in the person's achievements. This is an assimilation effect; you feel joined to the person by virtue of your shared group identity, and you bask in the reflected glory of the person's success. Now imagine that your group identity is not salient, and you are focusing on ways in which you and the other person are different. In this case, the other person's accomplishments tend to diminish your own achievements.

Significant Others and Self-Evaluations

Comparing ourselves with others is not the only way social factors can affect the self-concept. Imagining how we appear to others also influences the way we think about ourselves. Consider, for example, a teenager who dresses in the latest fashion. If he focuses on what his friends are thinking of him, he probably feels "cool." If he focuses on what his parents are thinking of him, he might feel "foolish."

Baldwin and his colleagues (Baldwin, 1994; Baldwin, Carrell, & Lopez, 1990) have demonstrated these effects experimentally. In one investigation (Baldwin et al., 1990), graduate students in psychology were asked to evaluate their research ideas after viewing (at levels below conscious awareness) the disapproving face of their advisor or the approving face of a fellow student. Those exposed to the disapproving face subsequently evaluated their work more negatively than did those exposed to the approving face. Subsequent work replicated and extended these findings (Baldwin, 1994), providing additional evidence that variations in the salience of an "internal audience" can influence the way people evaluate themselves.

It is especially noteworthy that the participants in Baldwin's research were not consciously aware that they had viewed an approving or disapproving face, even though seeing these faces affected the way participants thought about themselves. This suggests that even incidental stimuli (stimuli to which we are not deliberately paying attention) can activate particular self-views (Bargh, 1982; Higgins, 1987; Strauman & Higgins, 1987). You might, for example, catch a glimpse of someone who reminds you of your father. Without even realizing it, you might start seeing yourself through his eyes and begin thinking of yourself from his point of view (for related research, see Andersen & Baum, 1994).

Recent Events

Recent events can also cue particular views of the self. A person who falls while running may momentarily regard himself as clumsy. In a similar vein, failing an exam can cue thoughts of personal inadequacy. This might occur as a direct result of failure, or via mood: Failure creates a bad mood; bad moods cue negative thoughts about the self. This point recognizes the link that exists between personal and situational factors (which is represented by the curved arrow in Figure 5.2).

The manner in which recent events affect self-representations often depends on personality variables. To illustrate, my students and I have examined how self-esteem (a personality variable) interacts with success and failure (a recent event) to influence the way people think about themselves. We have found that failure is especially apt to lead low self-esteem people to think of themselves in negative terms (Brown & Dutton, 1995b; Brown & Smart, 1991).

High self-esteem people do not show this effect. In fact, sometimes they do just the opposite. Under some conditions, high self-esteem people evaluate themselves a bit more positively after failure, particularly on attributes that are unrelated to their intellectual ability. For example, after failing an intellectual test, high self-esteem people rate themselves as extremely socially skilled and kind (Baumeister, 1982; Brown & Smart, 1991). This suggests that high self-esteem people actively recruit positive images of themselves in an attempt to offset the negative implications of failure (Greenberg & Pyszczynski, 1985; Steele, 1988). We will have more to say about this type of compensatory self-enhancement effect in Chapter 8.

Finally, people's memory for prior events influences the way they think about themselves (Kunda, 1990; Salancik & Conway, 1975). Fazio, Effrein, and Falender (1981) asked participants a series of questions relating to either extraversion or introversion. By manipulating the content of these questions, half of the participants were led to focus on times they had acted in an extraverted manner, and half of the participants were led to focus on times they had acted in an introverted manner. Later, participants who had been asked questions that focused on extraverted behavior rated themselves as more sociable than did participants who had been asked questions that focused on introverted behavior.

The experiment did not stop there, however. After rating their sociability, participants were told to wait in another room while the experimenter got the next part of the experiment ready. Another person was sitting in the room, but the rest of the chairs were stacked up against the wall. The critical dependent variable was a measure of how close participants would put their chair to the person sitting in the room. The prediction was that participants who had just been coaxed into thinking of themselves as extraverted would sit closer to the other participant than would participants who were thinking of themselves as introverted. This prediction was confirmed.

The study by Fazio et al. (1981) thus makes two important points. It demonstrates (1) that selective memory for prior events can temporarily activate self-representations, and (2) that, once activated, these representations guide our behavior.

Stability versus Malleability in the Self-Concept

The findings we have been discussing show that people's ideas about themselves are subject to change. Indeed, some of the research we have reviewed makes it seem as if these views can be modified with apparent ease. Are people's ideas about themselves really this pliant and ephemeral, so easily altered by shifting circumstances, or are people's ideas about themselves firmer and more resistant to change?

Although some theorists have argued that there is no core, stable set of beliefs when it comes to the self (e.g., Gergen, 1982), most of the evidence suggests otherwise. For one thing, as was noted in Chapter 4, people's views of themselves are highly stable after the age of 30 (McCrae & Costa, 1994; Mortimer, Finch, & Kumka, 1982). It is also the case that therapists struggle for years to change the self-views of their clients, often with only limited success. Why, then, does it seem as if researchers have been able to so readily alter people's beliefs about themselves in experimental settings?

The first thing to note is that there is a difference between self-concept *activation* and self-concept *change*. Some of the research we've reviewed is concerned with factors that influence which one of a person's many self-views will be active at a given time. The evidence here is clear and straightforward: Numerous factors (e.g., the social context) influence the salience or accessibility of our various self-views.

The second issue under discussion—self-concept *change*—is more controversial. Here the question is whether people's ideas about themselves can be easily modified. Can people who generally think of themselves as attractive easily be made to think of themselves as homely? Several things should be kept in mind when considering this question.

First, the changes we have documented are often not large in any absolute sense. People who typically regard themselves as reticent and shy do not suddenly report being gregarious and outgoing. Rather, people's self-ratings merely shift a bit toward one or the other self-view depending on the factors we have discussed.

Another thing to consider is that in most of the investigations we have reviewed, the participants were college students. There is good reason to believe that people's ideas about themselves have yet to crystallize at this stage of life (Sears, 1986). This fact undoubtedly contributes to the ease with which self-conceptions can be modified. In a related vein, participants may not have been highly certain of the self-conceptions being altered. Kunda, Fong, Sanitioso, and Reber (1993) found that leading questions of the type Fazio et al. (1981) used did not alter the self-views of people who were highly certain of their extraversion or introversion (see also, Swann & Ely, 1984).

Finally, the experimental sessions extract people from their normal social environments (Swann, 1984). In the real world, people typically choose their targets of social comparison and decide who to take as an object of their reflected appraisals. These choices give people much greater freedom in determining the outcome of these processes. People also structure their social environments in predictable ways. For example, they choose to enter social environments, and these choices are often influenced by what people think about themselves (Niedenthal, Cantor, & Kihlstrom, 1985; Snyder, 1979). A person who thinks she is competitive, for example, chooses to engage in competitive activities. These situations, in turn, activate competitive views of the self. People also enlist the aid of others to help them maintain their self-views (Swann, 1990; Swann & Hill, 1982). These aspects of social life contribute to the stability of people's self-conceptions.

What, then, can we conclude from the research we reviewed earlier? The most reasonable conclusion is that although people's ideas about themselves *can* be changed, they typically do not. Constructive processes and the way people structure their life promotes stability in the real world. Indeed, the very processes that experimenters have exploited to demonstrate change generally ensure that people's beliefs about themselves do not dramatically shift from one moment to the next.

PROCESSING SELF-RELEVANT INFORMATION

Many people have had the following experience: You're talking to someone at a party, when you hear your name mentioned from across a crowded room. This familiar experience, known as the "cocktail-party effect," shows that peoplc are highly attuned to self-relevant information. They are especially apt to notice such information and to process it efficiently and deeply. In this section, we will discuss research that has examined how people process self-relevant information.

Memory for Self-Relevant Material

> The phenomenon of Self and that of Memory are merely two sides of the same fact. We may, as psychologists, set out from either of them, and refer the other to it. (James Mill, 1829)

Self and memory are closely related. In Chapter 2, we noted that Locke and Hume argued that memory provides the very foundation for our sense of personal identity. James (1890) agreed, adding that our identity depends on our ability to remember what it feels like to be *us*. These assumptions are supported by clinical evidence indicating that memory loss and identity disturbances often go hand in hand (Jacoby & Witherspoon, 1982).

Further evidence for a link between self and memory comes from research on the relative memorability of personal versus impersonal material. This research confirms what school teachers have long known: Memory is facilitated when people forge a connection between the material they are attempting to learn and their own experiences. In one early investigation, Bartlett (1932, cited in Keenan & Baillet, 1980) found that people were better able to remember a face or a detail in a story when it reminded them of themselves. Research has also shown that self-*generated* material is very well remembered. In group settings, people show better memory for their own actions than for the actions of others (Ross & Sicoly, 1979), and better memory for statements they have uttered than for statements other people have voiced (see Greenwald, 1981, for a review).

The Self-Reference Effect

One of the most productive attempts to study memory for self-relevant information was launched by Rogers, Kuiper, and Kirker (1977). These researchers used a depth-of-processing task (Craik & Tulving, 1975), in which participants were asked to answer one of four questions about a series of target words. Some of the words were judged for their self-relevance (e.g., Does *honest* describe you?), some of the words were judged according to their semantic properties (e.g., Does *kind* mean the same as nice?), some of the words were judged according to their phonemic features (e.g., Does *shy* rhyme with sky?), and some of the words were judged according to their structural properties (e.g., Is the word *rude* printed in lowercase letters?). After making these judgments, participants were unexpectedly asked to recall as many of the target words as they could remember.

Figure 5.5 shows that words referenced to the self produced the highest rates of recall, indicating that people's ideas about themselves serve as a powerful memory aid. Numerous investigations have subsequently replicated this "self-reference effect" (for reviews, see Greenwald & Banaji, 1989; Klein & Kihlstrom, 1986).

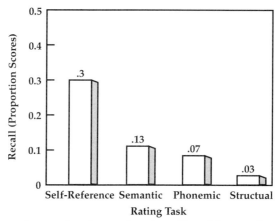

FIGURE 5.5. Memory for words referenced to the self, and for words rated according to their semantic, phonemic, or structural properties. The data show that self-referent words were more memorable than were words rated according to their nonself-relevant properties.
(Adapted from Rogers, Kuiper, & Kirker, 1977, *Journal of Personality and Social Psychology, 35,* 677–688. Copyright 1977. Adapted by permission of The American Psychological Association.)

To explain their findings, Rogers, Kuiper, and Kirker (1977) proposed that self-knowledge forms a unique cognitive structure with special properties (e.g., high degree of differentiation and elaboration). Follow-up research tested the assertion that self-knowledge was somehow special and unique in its memorability. Some investigators examined whether material that referred to other people produced similarly high rates of recall. In general, the more familiar the other person, the less advantage self-reference yields (Bower & Gilligan, 1979; Keenan & Baillet, 1980). For example, deciding whether a word describes "your best friend" produces rates of recall comparable to those produced by the self-reference task, but deciding whether a word describes "Walter Cronkite" does not. Other research examined whether the memorial advantage of material referenced to the self occurred only for evaluative words, such as the trait adjectives Rogers et al. (1977) had used. Keenan and Baillet (1980) found that the self-reference effect was greatly diminished when nonevaluative nouns (e.g., Do you have legs?) were used instead of adjectives. These and other limits to the self-reference effect have led researchers to conclude that self-knowledge does *not* represent a unique cognitive structure. Rather, material referenced to oneself is well recalled simply because it is highly organized and well elaborated (Greenwald & Banaji, 1989; Klein & Kihlstrom, 1986; Klein & Loftus, 1988; Lord, 1980; Symons & Johnson, 1997).

The Accuracy of Personal Memory

Although personal material is generally well recalled, this is not always the case. Consider people's memory for what they used to be like. Suppose someone tells you that he used to be more liberal, unconventional, and promiscuous. Should you naturally assume his recollections are valid? Research by Ross (1989) suggests that you might want to accept such proclamations cautiously.

Ross's (1989) research builds on evidence that memory is a schema-driven, (re)constructive process. What we remember about an event depends not only on the experience itself but also on the conditions prevailing at the time of recall. Implicit theories or subtle biases in the way we search for memories can alter what we remember (Loftus, 1980). As George Orwell observed in a rather different context, "[he] who controls the present, controls the past" (Orwell, 1949, p. 32).

Applying Orwell's insight, Ross (1989) suggests that when people are asked to recall their prior standing on a personal attribute, they begin by reviewing their present standing on the attribute. They then ask themselves whether there is any reason to believe they have changed. Typically, these reasons center around culturally shared theories. Some of these theories emphasize stability (e.g., "You can't teach an old dog new tricks"); some point toward change (e.g., "You're never too old to learn"). Whether people believe they have changed or not depends, in large part, on which theory is invoked.

Conway and Ross (1984) used these ideas to understand people's evaluation of self-improvement programs (e.g., weight-loss programs; memory-improvement programs). People often believe that these programs produce dramatic changes, even though the evidence indicates that the changes that occur are only modest at best (Pratkanis, Eskenazi, & Greenwald, 1994). One possible explanation for this gap between perception and reality is that people *misremember* what they used to be like. They recall being worse off than they actually were, with the result that they now seem better by comparison.

To test this hypothesis, Conway and Ross (1984) conducted a study-skills course for college students. At an initial meeting, students expressing an interest in the course evaluated their current study skills. The students were then randomly assigned to one of two groups: Students in the experimental group completed a three-week study-skills course; students in the control condition did not. After three weeks both groups of students (1) evaluated their current study skills, (2) recalled how they had initially evaluated their skills, and (3) gave the researchers permission to track their grades over the rest of the academic term.

The results showed students attending the program believed that their study skills had improved, even though their grades were actually no better than the grades of students assigned to the waiting list. To see whether this perceived improvement depended on revising the past, the researchers looked at students' memory for how they had earlier evaluated their study skills. Students attending the program recalled their original evaluations as being worse than they had actually been. By misremembering their past, the students were able to believe they had improved even when they had not (see also, Klein & Kunda, 1993).

Coping with Inconsistent Personal Information

Conway and Ross (1984) interpreted their findings in cognitive terms. They argued that participants misremembered their past because they relied on a theory that emphasized behavioral change rather than on one that emphasized behavioral stability. Motivational explanations for this effect are also possible.

Cognitive Dissonance Theory and Effort Justification

In Chapter 3 we discussed cognitive dissonance theory. As formulated by Aronson (1968, 1992), the theory asserts that people experience an aversive state of discomfort (termed cognitive dissonance) when they say or do things that are inconsistent with how they think about themselves. To reduce this discomfort, people rationalize, justify, or otherwise attempt to excuse their actions.

Let's look at how dissonance theory would explain the effects Conway and Ross (1984) reported. Participants had just spent time in a study-improvement course. Most people do not like to think they engage in activities of this sort without getting something in return; it doesn't feel good to think we wasted our time and effort (Aronson & Mills, 1959; Axsom, 1989; Axsom & Cooper, 1985). To avoid this psychological discomfort, people convince themselves that they have benefited from the program by exaggerating how badly off they were before enrolling in the program. Notice how this explanation has a more motivational flavor than the one Conway and Ross favored. Conway and Ross assume that people just *happen* to believe they have improved because of the particular theory that guided their memory search. The dissonance explanation says that people purposefully arrange their perceptions in order to feel good about the effort they have invested in the program.

Cognitive Dissonance Theory and Attitude Change

Dissonance theory has also been applied to situations in which people say or do things that are inconsistent with their attitudes. To illustrate, suppose you believe that it's important to recycle soda pop cans. Now suppose, for whatever reason, that you repeatedly find yourself throwing soda pop cans in the trash. This act should create cognitive dissonance: presumably, doing something that runs counter to your beliefs violates your perception of yourself as a decent, trustworthy person. One way to reduce dissonance is to change your attitude. In this case, you could decide that recycling is not all that important after all. Now you are no longer acting in a hypocritical fashion, because your behavior matches your attitude.

Dozens of studies have been conducted to test the predictions dissonance theory makes in situations of the sort just described (for a review, see Aronson, 1992). In general, the research shows that people change their attitudes to match their behavior (1) if they perceive that their behavior was freely chosen, and (2) if they perceive that their behavior has negative consequences, either for themselves or for other people (Cooper & Fazio, 1984).

Self-Affirmation Theory

Steele's (1988) self-affirmation theory is also concerned with how people handle inconsistencies between their behavior and their self-image. The theory assumes (1) that people strive to think of themselves in positive terms (e.g., as competent and decent), and (2) that people experience discomfort whenever they do something that violates these self-ideals.

So far, the theory has much in common with Aronson's (1969, 1992) version of dissonance theory. The two theories differ, however, when it comes to the predictions they make for how people can reduce discomfort. Dissonance theory maintains that people must resolve the specific inconsistency that is causing dissonance in order to make themselves feel better; self-affirmation theory maintains that in order to reduce discomfort, all people must do is reestablish a global sense of adequacy or decency.

To illustrate these different perspectives, let's return to our example regarding recycling. Dissonance theory assumes that in order to reduce dissonance, you must change your attitude toward recycling. That is, you must come to believe that recycling is not always a good idea. Self-affirmation theory makes a different prediction. Self-affirmation theory assumes that all you have to do to reduce dissonance is to remind yourself that you are a good person. For example, you could remind yourself that you are a caring friend, an outstanding student, an accomplished pianist, or a creative poet. Although none of these perceptions alters the fact that you are doing something that goes against your beliefs, they do imply that you are not really a bad person after all.

Steele and Lui (1983) conducted three experiments to test self-affirmation theory against dissonance theory. The participants in this experiment were induced to write an essay advocating tuition hikes at their university. (All participants had earlier indicated that they were opposed to tuition hikes.) After writing their essays, participants in a self-affirmation condition were given an opportunity to affirm important self-relevant values and identities; other participants (those in the control condition) were given no such opportunity. Later, all participants indicated their support for tuition hikes. The participants who were in the control condition subsequently changed their attitudes to match their behavior, but participants in the self-affirmation condition did not. Along with related findings (Steele, 1988), these findings suggest that people can tolerate inconsistency if they are given the opportunity to reestablish a positive self-image.

Motivated Information Processing

Dissonance theory and self-affirmation theory assume that needs and motives influence the processing of personal information. This idea has its roots in Freud's psychoanalytic theory.

> For psychoanalysis, it is axiomatic that cognition is largely if not entirely in the service of affective and motivational processes, and that needs, wishes, and conflicts are involved in categorizing and selecting information to be consciously perceived and processed. (Westen, 1990, p. 43)

Although this idea has been around for a long time, attempts to specify *how* motives and needs influence the processing of personal information have been lacking (for an exception, see Erdelyi, 1974). One possibility is that motives exert their effect by guiding the manner in which people generate and test hypotheses about why events have occurred (Kunda, 1990; Pyszczynski & Greenberg, 1987).

Self-Serving Causal Attributions

To illustrate this approach, let's consider the manner in which people make attributions for success and failure. As noted in Chapter 3, people generally (though not always) accept greater responsibility for positive outcomes than for negative outcomes. They attribute positive outcomes to stable, central aspects of the self (e.g., "I won the tennis match because I'm the better player"), but they attribute negative outcomes either to external factors (e.g., "I lost the match because the sun was in my eyes") or less central aspects of the self (e.g., "I lost the match because I had an off day").

According to the motivational model, a need to enhance feelings of self-worth underlies this attributional pattern. People accept greater credit for success than for failure *because* it makes them feel better about themselves to do so (Bowerman, 1978; Heider, 1958; Zuckerman, 1979). In support of this claim, self-serving attributions (1) increase as the importance of the outcome increases (Miller, 1976); (2) are affected by physiological arousal (Brown & Rogers, 1991; Gollwitzer, Earle, & Stephan, 1982; Stephan & Gollwitzer, 1981); (3) are observed in private as well as in public situations (Greenberg, Pyszczynski, & Solomon, 1982); and occur even when (4) strong constraints to be honest are present (Reiss, Rosenfeld, Melburg, & Tedeschi, 1981) and (5) the person's pattern of performance logically dictates otherwise (Stevens & Jones, 1976). Although it is possible to generate alternative explanations for these findings (Dawes, 1976; Miller & Ross, 1975; Nisbett & Ross, 1981; Ross, 1977a, 1977b; Tetlock & Levi, 1982), most researchers accept that motivational processes strongly influence the attributions people make for success and failure (e.g., Fiske & Taylor, 1991; Kunda, 1990; Pyszczynski & Greenberg, 1987).

This does not mean, however, that people simply settle on a cause that "feels good" when making causal attributions. Most people like to think of themselves as being rational, thoughtful, and usually quite logical. To completely disregard all rules of logic when making causal judgments would threaten this image. Moreover, explanations for events that are wholly without logical underpinnings would be easily discredited and vulnerable to disconfirmation. For these reasons, then, it is unlikely that self-enhancing attributions are reached in a careless, thoughtless fashion.

Instead, self-serving attributions are apt to be generated by a process that, at least to the attributor, seems logical (Anderson & Slusher, 1986; Kruglanski, 1990; Kunda, 1990; Pyszczynski and Greenberg, 1987). Pyszczynski and Greenberg (1987) have attempted to specify how this process proceeds. Their model begins by assuming that after an event occurs, a plausible causal hypothesis is generated. Inference rules needed for testing the hypothesis are then settled on. Subsequently, data relevant to testing the hypothesis are gathered, and the validity of the data are evaluated. Finally, the data are weighted and integrated and a final causal judgment is reached.

TABLE 5.2. Steps Leading to a Self-Serving Attribution for a Poor Test Performance

Step	Example
Generate a self-serving causal hypothesis	The test questions were unclear.
Devise inference rules for testing the hypothesis	Find out if anyone else thought the questions were unclear.
Gather data relevant to the hypothesis	Ask only people who did poorly on the exam what they thought of the questions.
Evaluate the validity of the data	Accept as valid the perceptions of people who thought the questions were unclear, and dismiss as invalid the perceptions of anyone who thought the test questions were clear.
Integrate the data to form a final attribution	Weigh the data and decide that the test questions lacked clarity.

Table 5.2 shows how this process can lead to a self-serving attribution. In this example, a student has done poorly on an important exam. Initially, the student may generate a self-serving causal hypothesis (Kunda, 1987). She may decide that the poor performance was probably due to ambiguous test questions rather than to her own lack of ability. At this point, she might settle on an inference rule that is especially congenial to her self-serving hypothesis. Perhaps she concludes that in order to properly test her hypothesis, she need only determine whether any one of her fellow students also found the questions to be lacking in clarity. When gathering data relevant to testing this proposition, she might then be prone to sample from the population in such a way that her hypothesis is apt to be supported. For example, she might query only students who did at least as poorly, if not worse, on the exam as she did (Pyszczynski, Greenberg, & LaPrelle, 1985). If these students also found the test questions to be vague and equivocal, her hypothesis would seemingly have received support. In the event that any evidence inconsistent with the hypothesis is encountered, it can be dismissed as invalid or, at the very least, less relevant. For instance, if another student who did poorly didn't find the questions confusing, the attributor may dismiss that student's perceptions as atypical and aberrant (e.g., "He's so out of it, he probably didn't even read the questions!"). By adhering to such a strategy, the student is able to cling to the belief that her conclusion regarding the causal role of the ambiguous test questions is fully justified on the basis of the available evidence.

Self-Serving Evaluation of Information

Other researchers have extended these ideas to explain similar self-serving biases (for a review, see Kunda, 1990). For example, people tend to view positive self-relevant information as more credible than negative self-relevant information. Ditto and Lopez (1992) suggested that this occurs because people uncritically accept positive feedback at face value but carefully scrutinize and thoughtfully consider alternative explanations for negative feedback.

To test their ideas, Ditto and Lopez (1992) told participants they were testing for the presence of a medical condition that makes people susceptible to pancreatic disorders. (In fact, the condition was fictitious.) Participants were further told that they would test themselves for the presence of the disorder, using a self-administered saliva test in which a strip of test paper, dabbed with each participant's own saliva, was dipped into a solution. Ditto and Lopez found that participants who were led to believe that they possessed the deficiency (1) took longer to decide that their test results were complete; (2) were more likely to repeat the test; and (3) rated the test as less accurate than did participants given a favorable test result (see also, Croyle, Sun, & Louie, 1993; Kunda, 1987; Liberman & Chaiken, 1992). These findings show how seemingly logical processes can be used to justify self-serving conclusions. (They also explain the common observation that few people seek out a second opinion when the diagnosis is good!)

CHAPTER SUMMARY

In this chapter we examined cognitive approaches to the study of self. We began by discussing how self-knowledge is represented in memory. We noted that people's ideas about themselves are not arranged in a haphazard fashion but are linked in an organized structure. We then discussed several aspects of the self-concept, including self-complexity and self-schemas.

The next issue we considered was self-concept activation. Although people think of themselves in many ways, only a subset of this knowledge is active at any time. Numerous factors affect the activation of self-knowledge, including personal factors and various social factors.

We ended the chapter by considering the manner in which personal information is processed. We saw that people show superior memory for personal information, and that the processing of personal information is often biased in a self-serving fashion. These biases are produced by motivational and cognitive processes.

- Cognitive psychologists believe that information processing depends on prior knowledge and expectancies. People's ideas about themselves are one type of knowledge that influences how information is processed.
- Self-knowledge is organized in memory, perhaps conforming to a hierarchical structure. For some people, this structure is complex and well integrated. For others, this structure is simple and highly differentiated.
- Self-conceptions that are important and held with great certainty function as *self-schemas*. Self-schemas influence a variety of psychological processes, including what we attend to, what we remember, how we perceive and judge other people, and how we behave.
- Only a subset of our self-knowledge is active at any given time. This activation depends on personal factors (including our moods and goals) and situational factors (including recent events and the composition of the social environment).

- People tend to think of themselves in ways that distinguish them from their social surroundings. In general, the more distinctive an attribute is, the more likely it is to be represented in the person's self-concept.
- Contrast effects in self-evaluation are common. People evaluate themselves more negatively when they are surrounded by other people who are somehow "better off" than they are. This does not always occur, however. Assimilation effects occur when people feel psychologically close to other people.
- Although people's ideas about themselves change as a function of the situations they are in, these shifts are typically only moderate and short lived. People's ideas about themselves also show a good deal of stability across both situations and time.
- Personal (or self-relevant) information is generally remembered better than *impersonal* material. This occurs because personal information is well elaborated in memory, not because self-knowledge forms a unique cognitive structure.
- Personal information is often biased in a self-serving manner. Motivational and cognitive processes combine to produce these biases. People use information-processing strategies to justify and support their self-enhancing beliefs. These strategies involve biases in memory, and the generation and evaluation of self-serving causal theories.

For Further Reading

GREENWALD, A. G., & PRATKANIS, A. R. (1984). The self. In R. S. Wyer & T. K. Srull (Eds.), *Handbook of social cognition* (Vol. 3, pp. 3–26). Hillsdale, NJ: Lawrence Erlbaum Associates.

LINVILLE, P. W., & CARLSTON, D. (1994). Social cognition of the self. In P. G. Devine, D. L. Hamilton, & T. M. Ostrom (Eds.), *Social cognition: Its impact on social psychology* (pp. 143–193). New York: Academic Press.

MARKUS, H., & WURF, E. (1987). The dynamic self-concept: A social psychological perspective. *Annual Review of Psychology, 38,* 299–337.

CHAPTER 6

Self-Regulation of Behavior

Chances are you know people who work really hard at what they do. They always try their best and rarely give up. When the going gets tough, these people get going. You probably also know people who aren't like that at all. They're content to settle for "second best" or are easily frustrated when encountering difficulties.

In this chapter we will apply principles from the field of motivation to examine differences of this sort. Motivational psychologists are concerned with why people (and animals) behave as they do. Why do people choose to do one activity and not another? Why does one person persist in the face of difficulties, while another person withdraws and quits? These are the sorts of questions motivational psychologists pose.

We will begin by outlining a general model of motivated behavior. This model (referred to as a model of self-regulation) assumes that behavior is goal directed or purposive. This means that people select a goal from among various alternatives and then set about trying to reach their goal. Clearly, not all behavior is of this type. Often, people act out of habit, reflex, or impulse. This type of nonpurposive behavior is not covered in the analysis that follows.

Next, we will focus on how self-relevant processes affect goal-directed behavior. Numerous factors influence what people choose to do in life and whether or not they meet their goals. In the second section of this chapter, we will see that people's thoughts and feelings about themselves are among the most important of these factors.

The third section of this chapter will focus on behavior in achievement situations. Here we will examine how self-relevant thoughts and feelings influence persistence and performance in classroom settings.

Finally, we will consider situations in which people fail to effectively regulate their actions. Our concern here will be with understanding how people's self-relevant thoughts and feelings can contribute to negative behaviors, such as alcoholism, aggression, and suicide.

A GENERAL MODEL OF SELF-REGULATION

Three Component Processes

Self-regulation models are concerned with what individuals choose to do and how they go about trying to accomplish their goals. In more formal terms, we can distinguish three components of the self-regulation process: (1) goal selection, (2) preparation for action, and (3) a cybernetic cycle of behavior (made up of several component processes) (Markus & Wurf, 1987).

Goal Selection

The first stage in the self-regulation process is the goal-selection stage. Before they can effectively regulate their behavior, people must select a goal; they must decide what they intend to do.

Many motivational theorists assume that goals arise in the context of an *expectancy-value* framework (Atkinson, 1964; Rotter, 1954). Expectancy-value models assume that people select goals according to their expectancy of reaching the goal, in conjunction with the positive value they place on attaining the goal and the negative value they place on not attaining the goal. The idea here is really quite simple. If, for example, we want to predict whether a person will adopt getting a Ph.D. in psychology as a goal, we would want to know how likely the person thought it was that she would successfully complete the Ph.D. requirements and the value she places on receiving versus not receiving a Ph.D.

In an expectancy-value model, these factors are assumed to combine in a multiplicative fashion. This means that we multiply (rather than add) the two factors together to determine the strength of an individual's motivation to engage in some behavior. This assumption has an interesting and important consequence. It means that if either value is set at zero, the goal will not be adopted. If a person sees no possibility that she can successfully complete a Ph.D. program (i.e., if expectancy = 0), she will not apply to graduate school, no matter how much she might value getting a degree. Conversely, if she places absolutely no value on getting the degree (i.e., if value = 0), she will not apply to graduate school no matter how probable she thinks success would be.

Goals can be conceived at different levels of abstraction (Powers, 1973; Vallacher & Wegner, 1987). Some of these interpretations are specific and concrete; others are broad and abstract. For example, reading this passage may be relevant to several of your goals, such as "learning the material," "doing well on a test," or "preparing for graduate school." Generally speaking, goals conceived in broad terms assume greater value than do goals conceived in specific terms (Vallacher & Wegner, 1987).

At the most general level, people's goals center around who they want to be or what they want to become. For example, a person might be striving to "be independent" or even to "be a good person." Self-relevant goals like these have been studied by numerous researchers (e.g., Emmons, 1986; Klinger, 1977; Little, 1981; Zirkel & Cantor, 1990) and are often the most highly valued goals in life.

Preparation for Action

Having adopted a goal, people prepare to attain it. This is the second stage in the self-regulation process. Here, people gather information, construct scenarios regarding possible outcomes, and engage in behavioral practice (rehearsal). In short, they design and prepare to implement a plan to achieve their goal. Of course, not all behavior fits this model. As noted earlier, sometimes people act impulsively without a good deal of forethought. Impulsive behavior of this type is not considered in this framework.

Cybernetic Cycle of Behavior

The third stage in the self-regulation process has been conceptualized as a cybernetic cycle of action. Cybernetics is the study of how entities use information to regulate their actions (Wiener, 1948). It is also called control theory, as it emphasizes negative feedback control as the means by which machines (e.g., thermostats, guided missiles, cruise control settings in automobiles) as well as animals adjust their behavior to match some standard. In this context, negative feedback doesn't mean bad or unfavorable; it means discrepancy reducing.

A prototypic example from the field of engineering would be a thermostat and furnace. A thermostat is equipped to sense the temperature in a room. The room temperature is then compared against a desired value. If the present temperature in the room is below the desired value, the thermostat ignites the furnace, the heat comes on, and the discrepancy is reduced. When the standard is met, the furnace turns off.

Formally, this process is known by the acronym *TOTE*, as it involves four stages: (1) a *test* phase, in which a present value is compared against some relevant standard (the current temperature in the room is compared with the desired temperature); (2) an *operate* stage, in which an action is undertaken to bring the present value in line with the standard (the heat comes on if the room temperature is below the standard); (3) another *test* phase, in which the new value is compared with the standard (the new room temperature is compared with the desired temperature); and (4) an *exit*, or quit, stage, which occurs when the desired goal is reached (the furnace shuts off when the room reaches the selected temperature).

Table 6.1 describes this process, extending it to better capture the complexities of human behavior. The sequence begins after a person has selected a goal and has prepared to attain it. For purposes of illustration, imagine that someone has adopted the goal of running a mile in a specified time. After spending some time training (preparing), the person heads for the track. There, the person (1) runs a mile, (2) observes his behavior (times himself), and (3) compares his time against the adopted goal.

Thus far, the sequence is no different than what was described with the thermostat. The complexities of human behavior enter into the analysis in the next two steps, labeled expectancy and emotional reaction in Table 6.1. As-

TABLE 6.1. The Processes That Make Up the Cybernetic Cycle of Behavior

1. Initial behavior (Run a mile)
2. Observe behavior (Time oneself)
3. Compare against some standard (Compare time against goal)
4. Expectancy (Form an expectancy that future behavior will reduce the discrepancy between present behavior and the standard)
5. Emotional reaction (React emotionally to discrepancy between performance and goal)
6. Behavioral adjustment (Continue striving toward goal or quit)

Note: In this example, a person has set a goal of running a mile in a specified time. The table describes the various stages that occur once the person has prepared to reach the goal.

sume that the person has fallen short of his goal (i.e., his time was slower than his specified goal). The person then forms an expectancy about the likelihood that the discrepancy can be reduced. We will treat this expectancy as a binary, either-or decision; that is, the person has either a favorable or unfavorable expectation of being able to close the gap (Carver & Scheier, 1981).

At the same time the person is forming a cognitive expectancy, he will experience an emotional reaction to his performance. These emotional reactions can take many forms, ranging from positive emotions of pride and self-satisfaction to negative emotions of disappointment and despair. Finally, based on the expectancies he has formed and the emotion he is experiencing, the person will readjust his behavior. If his expectancies of success are high and his emotional reaction is positive, he will probably continue working toward his goal, perhaps fine-tuning his training regimen. If his expectancies of success are low and his emotional reaction is largely negative, he may give up the goal altogether (and take up painting!).

Three Self-Relevant Phenomena

To this point we have looked only at a generic model of the self-regulation process, without considering where and how self-relevant processes come into play. We will explore this issue by first discussing three self-relevant processes that influence people's efforts to regulate their behavior. After describing these processes, we will examine their effect on motivated behavior.

Self-Efficacy Beliefs

People's beliefs about their ability to succeed exert a strong influence on the self-regulation process. Bandura (1986, 1989) refers to such beliefs as self-efficacy beliefs. People with high self-efficacy beliefs think they have the ability to succeed at a task, to overcome obstacles, and to reach their goals. People with low self-efficacy beliefs doubt their ability to succeed and do not believe they have what it takes to reach their goals. Importantly, these beliefs are only partly based on people's actual abilities. In any given domain, people with high self-efficacy beliefs are not necessarily more able than are those with low self-efficacy beliefs.

The classic tale of *The Little Engine That Could* illustrates these differences. The little blue engine that ultimately carried the toys over the mountain to the waiting children had high self-efficacy beliefs ("I think I can; I think I can"). Many of the other trains doubted their ability to make the trek over the mountain; they would be classified as having low self-efficacy beliefs. As we shall see momentarily, people's beliefs about their capabilities exert an important influence at virtually all stages of the self-regulation process.

Possible Selves

People's ideas about what they may be like in the future also influence motivated behavior. Markus and her colleagues (Markus & Nurius, 1986; Markus & Ruvolo, 1989) coined the term *possible selves* to refer to these beliefs. To illustrate, an aspiring gymnast might have a clearly articulated "Me winning an Olympic gold medal" possible self. This person is able to vividly imagine herself on the victory stand with the national anthem playing in the background and the crowd cheering while she receives her medal.[1]

Most of our possible selves are positive (Markus & Nurius, 1986), but people have negative possible selves as well. Typically, these negative possible selves involve fears of what we may become if we fail to take some course of action. A recovering alcoholic, for example, may have a clear image of what he will be like if he returns to drinking. These negative possible selves can also serve a motivational function, to the extent that people are motivated to avoid them (Oyserman & Markus, 1990).

Self-Awareness

A third variable of interest to a motivational analysis of behavior is self-awareness. As discussed throughout this text, the self has a reflexive quality: People are capable of taking themselves as the object of their own attention. But our attention is not always focused inward. Much of the time (perhaps most of the time) our attention is focused outward on the environment. This means that attentional focus is variable and that self-awareness is a transient state. Sometimes we are aware of ourselves; other times we are not.

Duval and Wicklund (1972) were among the first theorists to propose that differences in attentional focus have important motivational consequences. They argued that when people focus their attention inward (i.e., when they become self-aware), they tend to compare their present state with a relevant standard. Positive emotion arises when people believe they are meeting or exceeding a relevant standard; negative emotion arises when people believe they are falling short of a relevant standard. Duval and Wicklund further proposed that the negative emotion that arises from a perceived discrepancy is experienced as an aversive state of discomfort that people are motivated to reduce in

---

[1]America's newest figure skating champion, Tara Lipinski, exemplifies this phenomenon. When she was six years old, Lipinski watched the 1988 Olympics on television. Mesmerized by the winning gold medalists, she had her father construct a cardboard podium so that she could stand on a pretend victory stand when the athletes received their medals. Eight years later, at age 14, Lipinski won the World's Figure Skating Championship, becoming the youngest person in history to achieve that goal.

one of two ways: (1) People can try and reduce the discrepancy by working to bring their behavior in line with the standard, or (2) they can attempt to avoid thinking about the discrepancy by shifting their attention away from themselves and onto the environment.

Let's look at an example. Imagine you are passing by a department store window when you see your reflection in the glass. As you gaze at yourself, you notice that your hair is not as neat as you would like it to be. You then run your fingers through your hair in an attempt to fix it. In the language of the theory, seeing your reflection in the window shifted your attention away from the environment and onto yourself. This attentional shift led you to notice a discrepancy between your present state and some relevant standard. The noticed discrepancy then engendered negative emotion, which you were motivated to reduce by fixing your hair. If, for some reason, you could not fix your hair, the theory would predict that you would try and reduce discomfort by shifting your attention away from your own reflection.

Carver and Scheier (1981) offered an elaboration and modification of these ideas. In agreement with Duval and Wicklund (1972), Carver and Scheier believe that self-awareness leads people to compare their present state with a relevant standard. Carver and Scheier do not, however, believe that the presence of a discrepancy inevitably produces discomfort in people. Instead, they contend that negative feelings arise only if the person believes the discrepancy cannot be reduced. In their model, then, it is *not* the presence of a discrepancy that determines the person's emotional reaction; rather, it is the person's expectancy about whether or not the discrepancy can be reduced.

Carver and Scheier (1981) also took issue with Duval and Wicklund's claim that behavioral regulation is driven by a desire to reduce an aversive state of discomfort. Applying the principles of control theory, they argued that information processes, not emotional ones, guide the behavioral regulation process. For these theorists, "information regarding the outcome of one's action and the subsequent guidance it provides are [the basic elements of] self-regulation" (Carver & Scheier, 1982a, p. 124). We will examine the importance of these claims in the sections that follow.

PUTTING THE SELF INTO SELF-REGULATION

Having defined three aspects of the self-regulation process (goal selection, preparation for action, and the cybernetic cycle of behavior) and discussed three self-relevant processes (self-efficacy beliefs, possible selves, and self-awareness), we are ready now to put these pieces together and look at how people's thoughts and feelings about themselves influence motivated behavior.

The Self and Goal Selection

We will begin by looking at what determines the goals people adopt in life. Earlier we noted that goals are adopted according to an expectancy-value framework. When making a choice among various courses of action, people take into account the likelihood that they will reach some goal and the positive value they place on doing so (relative to the negative value they place on failing to reach their goal).

Self-efficacy beliefs are directly relevant to the expectancy component in this model. All else being equal, people select goals they believe they can achieve. Because people with high self-efficacy beliefs assume that they have high ability, they adopt more challenging goals than do people with low self-efficacy beliefs. And because adopting more difficult goals is linked with superior performance (Locke & Latham, 1990), people with high self-efficacy beliefs tend to perform better on tasks than do those who doubt their ability to succeed.

People's ideas about themselves also influence goal selection through the value component in an expectancy-value model. What people value in life is tied to how they think about themselves. The person who thinks of herself as an intellectual values intellectual pursuits; the person who regards herself as an athlete values athletic pursuits. In more general terms, we can say that people value activities that match or reaffirm what they think they are like (Swann, 1990).

Possible selves also influence goal selection. People not only value activities that allow them to reaffirm who they think they are now, they also value activities that allow them to lay claim to possessing future identities. The youngster who clearly imagines himself pitching in the World Series one day values activities related to baseball. When choosing how to spend a Saturday afternoon, it is a pretty good bet this youngster will opt to play ball. This process is a bit different than the one just discussed, because here it is a *future* identity that the person is wishing to establish, not a present identity he is wishing to affirm.

There is another way in which possible selves influence motivation. This occurs when people tie goal attainment to the establishment of a desired identity. To illustrate, suppose I decide my house needs painting and I connect this goal to a future conception of "Me as handyman." I then set about the task of painting my house. The connection I have forged between the goal and how I think about myself means that having a freshly painted house is no longer my only goal. Painting the house is also important for what it says about me as a person; completing the goal allows me to lay claim to the desired identity of "handyman." At an even broader level, it might even signify that "I am a competent and responsible person who can accomplish what I set out to do." In this manner, goal attainment implicates how I think and feel *about myself.* These connections add to the value of the goal, thereby increasing my motivation to succeed.

One way to think about these processes is in terms of the hierarchy of goals we discussed earlier. Painting my house can be conceptualized at many different levels of abstraction. At one level, I could be said to simply be painting the house. At an even lower level, I could be said to be dipping my brush in paint; or lower still, to be tensing my muscles. At higher levels, I could be said to be demonstrating my ability as a handyman, an artisan, or even a competent, worthwhile person. Ordinarily, then, the more general and abstract our conception of an activity becomes, the more relevant self-processes become (Vallacher & Wegner, 1987). By construing goals at very broad levels and tying them to how we think (or wish to think) about ourselves, we increase the value of goal attainment.

The Self and Preparation for Action

Self-relevant phenomena also influence behavior during the preparation for action state. Recall that during this stage, people gather information, plan and rehearse various courses of action, and engage in behavioral practice. Self-efficacy beliefs have been linked to these processes. People with high self-efficacy beliefs seek more information and spend more time practicing than do those who doubt their ability to succeed (Bandura, 1986, 1989).

At first, these effects may seem paradoxical: Why should those who are highly confident of success spend more time in preparation than those who doubt their ability to succeed? The difficulty and familiarity of the task is relevant to this apparent contradiction. For tasks that are easy, familiar, or well learned, high self-efficacy beliefs do not necessarily lead to greater preparation. But when a task is difficult or is being approached for the first time, people who believe they have what it takes to succeed spend more time and energy preparing to attain their goals than do those who are beset by doubt.

Self-efficacy beliefs and possible selves also influence the mental scenarios people construct prior to engaging in some activity. Often people anticipate what is likely to happen before undertaking a task. For example, athletes are encouraged to develop a clear mental picture of themselves succeeding before participating in an important competition. Self-efficacy beliefs influence these mental pictures. People with high self-efficacy beliefs are more apt to imagine themselves succeeding than are those who doubt their ability to succeed. The same is true for those who have clearly articulated positive possible selves.

Visual images of this sort can influence performance. In general, people who are able to clearly visualize themselves attaining a goal are more likely to reach it than are people who have difficulty forming such a mental image (Feltz & Landers, 1983; Markus, Cross, & Wurf, 1990). A study by Sherman, Skov, Hervitz, and Stock (1981) illustrates this effect. In this study, participants were told that they were about to take an anagram test. Prior to taking the test, one-third of the participants were asked to spend a few minutes imagining they had already taken the test and had done very well. Another one-third of the participants were asked to spend a few minutes imagining they had already taken the test and had done very poorly. A third group of participants were in a control condition and were given no imagination instructions. Finally, participants rated their performance expectancies and took the anagram test.[2]

Figure 6.1 presents the results from the anagram task. The figure shows that participants who were asked to imagine themselves succeeding at the task

[2]This is only a partial description of the study by Sherman et al. (1981). Additional experimental conditions were included but are not discussed here.

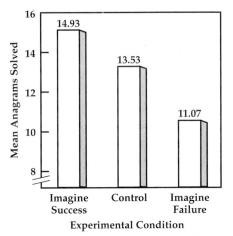

FIGURE 6.1. Mean number of anagrams solved among participants who had been asked to imagine they had succeeded or failed (or were given no instructions). The data show that participants who imagined themselves succeeding solved more problems than did control participants, and that control participants solved more problems than did participants who imagined themselves failing. These findings support the claim that mental images of success or failure influence task performance.
(Adapted from Sherman, Skov, Hervitz, & Stock, 1981, *Journal of Experimental Social Psychology, 17,* 142–158. Copyright 1981. Reprinted by permission of Academic Press, Inc.)

solved more problems than did participants in the control condition, and that participants in the control condition solved more problems than did participants who were asked to imagine themselves failing at the task. These findings support the claim that the mental scenarios people construct prior to undertaking a task can influence their level of performance (Campbell & Fairey, 1985).

The Self and the Cybernetic Cycle of Behavior

The next stage in the self-regulation process is the cybernetic cycle. Having adopted a goal and formulated a plan of action, individuals set out to achieve it. Generally speaking, success at any activity depends on four factors: ability, effort, strategy, and luck (Heider, 1958). Whether I win my next tennis match, for example, depends on (1) how skillful I am relative to how skillful my opponent is; (2) how hard I try; (3) the strategies—both cognitive and behavioral—I use during the match; and (4) luck.

For purposes of our discussion, we will regard ability as a fixed quality—akin to aptitude. As we use the term, then, ability refers to actual underlying capacity. In this sense, it is more a property of personality than of the self. Luck resides outside of the person's influence, so it, too, is not a property of the self. But the other two factors that influence goal attainment, effort and strategy, are strongly influenced by self-relevant thoughts and feelings.

Self and Effort

As concerns effort expenditure, self-efficacy judgments influence how hard and long people will work at attaining a goal. All else being equal, people work harder and persist longer when they believe they have the wherewithal to succeed than when they have doubts about their abilities (Bandura, 1986). This is particularly true when obstacles to success are encountered, which is the case with almost all important goals in life.

The important role these beliefs play in performance was documented by John White (1982) in his book *Rejection*. White notes that a common characteristic of many eminent scientists, artists, and writers is an unshakable belief in their abilities. These beliefs allowed them to weather rejection and overcome disappointment. Gertrude Stein, for example, submitted poems to editors for over 20 years before finally having one accepted. Similarly, over 20 publishers rejected James Joyce's book *Dubliners*. A resolute belief in their ability allowed these writers to continue trying, ultimately leading them to succeed.

Possible selves have also been linked to this stage of the motivation process. People who can vividly imagine themselves reaching some goal work harder than do those who lack this capability. This may be particularly true when the positive possible self is accompanied by a negative possible self (Oyserman & Markus, 1990). Imagine, for example, a person who enters medical school with both a clearly articulated positive possible self (myself winning the Nobel prize in medicine) and a clearly articulated negative possible self (myself flunking out and ending up on the streets). The positive self-image provides a powerful incentive to succeed (a carrot) and the negative self-image provides a powerful reason not to fail (a stick). As long as the positive image is more powerful than the negative, the two images working in concert can boost motivation more than either one alone.

Self and Strategy

Self-processes also influence the strategies people adopt in their pursuit of goals. People who believe they have the ability to succeed adopt more efficient and sophisticated problem-solving strategies than do those who doubt their ability to succeed (Bandura & Wood, 1989). Being high in self-efficacy also reduces anxiety and keeps one's attention focused on the task. This is particularly true when initial difficulties are encountered. Because anxiety itself can be debilitating and impair performance, the link between self-efficacy and anxiety reduction provides another means by which self-efficacy beliefs promote success.

The ability to stay focused on the task at hand is related to another important factor that affects whether or not people achieve their goals. This factor is the ability to suppress the attractiveness of competing activities. For example, in order to finish writing this chapter, I need to put thoughts of alternative activities out of my mind. Kuhl (1985) refers to this process as the shielding of an intention. Bandura's (1986) research suggests that people who are confident of their abilities to succeed are better able to shield their intentions than are those who are plagued by doubt. They are less apt to become distracted or enticed by competing activities. This, then, constitutes another avenue through which self-efficacy beliefs affect performance.

Self and the Comparison Process

After working on some activity, people monitor their behavior and compare their performance against some reference value or standard. This comparison process is an important part of the self-regulation process. It tells us whether or not we are making progress toward our goal and what, if any, kinds of adjustments need to be made.

Earlier we noted that self-awareness is an important element of this process. People are more apt to compare their current behavior with a relevant standard when their attention is focused on themselves than when their attention is focused on the environment (Carver & Scheier 1981; Duval & Wicklund, 1972).

A study by Scheier and Carver (1983) tested the hypothesis that self-awareness increases the likelihood that people will compare their present behavior against a relevant standard. The subjects in this study were asked to reproduce a series of geometric shapes from memory. To help them with the task, they were allowed to momentarily view the geometric shape as many times as they wished. The number of times subjects asked to view the shape was used as an index of the degree to which they were comparing their present behavior (i.e., their drawing) against a standard.

To determine whether self-awareness affects this comparison process, Scheier and Carver (1983) experimentally manipulated the extent to which the participants' attention was focused on themselves. Half of the participants performed the task in front of a mirror, in which their own reflection was visually salient. The remaining participants did not perform the task in front of a mirror. On the assumption that seeing oneself in a mirror focuses one's attention on oneself, and that self-awareness leads people to compare their present behavior against a relevant standard, Scheier and Carver predicted that participants situated in front of the mirror would examine the geometric shapes more frequently than would participants who were not situated in front of the mirror. This proved to be the case. Although there are alternative explanations for this finding, the data are consistent with the claim that self-awareness leads people to compare their present situation with a relevant standard.

Self, Expectancies, and Behavioral Adjustment

After comparing their performance with a relevant standard, people form an expectancy regarding the likelihood that future efforts will meet with success. They then adjust their behavior. Broadly speaking, this adjustment involves persistence (continued striving toward the goal, perhaps with a different strategy) or disengagement (quitting or otherwise psychologically withdrawing from the task) (Carver & Scheier, 1981).

Self-relevant phenomena influence which route people take. As noted earlier, people who have high self-efficacy beliefs persist longer and work harder at attaining their goals than do those with low self-efficacy beliefs (Bandura, 1986). In a similar vein, people who have favorable possible selves persist longer than do people who have failed to forge a connection between themselves and their goals (Markus & Nurius, 1986).

Attentional processes also enter into the relation between expectancies and behavioral adjustment (Carver & Scheier, 1981). When expectancies are favorable, self-awareness promotes high effort and high persistence; when expectancies are unfavorable, self-awareness leads to low effort and low persistence. Formally, we say the two variables (expectancies and self-awareness) interact. The effect of one variable depends on the other variable. Whether self-awareness leads to more or less effort depends on whether expectancies are favorable or unfavorable.

An investigation by Carver, Blaney, and Scheier (1979) demonstrates these effects. All of the participants in this experiment first performed poorly on a set of difficult anagram problems. This was done to ensure that a discrepancy between current behavior and some standard (a desire to do well) was present. The participants were then told that they would be taking a second test. Half of the participants were led to believe that they were likely to do very well on the second test (high expectancy condition) and half were led to believe that they were likely to do very poorly on the second test (low expectancy condition). After receiving this information, the second test was administered. Half of the participants took the test while seated in front of a large mirror (the high self-awareness condition); the remaining participants took the test under controlled conditions, with no mirror present (the low self-awareness condition). These manipulations enabled the investigators to experimentally vary participants' expectancies of success at the second task and their level of self-awareness.

The results of this study are shown in Figure 6.2. The figure shows that participants with high expectancies of success were *more* persistent when seated in front of a mirror, but that participants with low expectancies of success were *less* persistent when seated in front of a mirror. These findings support the contention that self-awareness promotes persistence when expectancies are high but leads to withdrawal when expectancies are low.

Scheier and Carver (1982a) extended these findings in a subsequent investigation. They began by noting that people vary with regard to how much they generally think about themselves. Some people are very aware of themselves and spend a lot of time examining their thoughts and feelings. These individuals are said to be high in *private self-consciousness.* Other people are not very attentive to themselves and are less introspective. These individuals are said to be low in private self-consciousness. Table 6.2 presents the scale Scheier and Carver used to measure these differences.

Scheier and Carver (1982a) wanted to see whether individual differences in private self-consciousness produce effects comparable to those found with situationally induced variations in self-awareness. Toward this end, they adapted the procedures of the Carver et al. (1979) study, using scores on the private self-consciousness scale in place of the experimental manipulation of

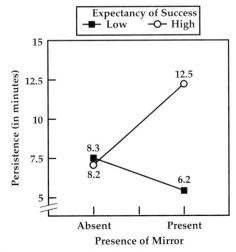

FIGURE 6.2. Task persistence as a function of performance expectancy and self-awareness. The data show that participants with high expectancies of success persisted longer at the task when self-awareness was high than when it was low, but participants with low expectancies of success did just the opposite. These findings support the claim that self-awareness has positive effects when expectancies are favorable, but negative effects when expectancies are unfavorable.
(Adapted from Carver, Blaney, & Scheier, 1979, *Journal of Personality and Social Psychology, 37,* 1859–1870. Copyright 1979. Adapted by permission of The American Psychological Association.)

self-awareness. The findings paralleled the data displayed in Figure 6.2: High scores on the private self-consciousness scale were associated with high persistence when expectancies were favorable, but low persistence when expectancies were unfavorable.

Self-awareness and expectancies not only influence task persistence, they also interact to affect *task performance.* Self-awareness leads to superior performance among people with high expectancies of success, but it leads to inferior performance among people with low expectancies of success (Brockner, 1979; Carver & Scheier, 1982b). These findings provide further evidence that self-focused attention can have beneficial effects when expectancies are favorable, but detrimental effects when expectancies are unfavorable.

Self, Emotion, and Behavioral Adjustment

Earlier we noted that in addition to forming expectancies of success, people also react emotionally to their task performances. They feel happy and proud or unhappy and dejected. The source of these feelings and the role they play in guiding behavior is the subject of some debate. One possibility is that the perceived *distance* from a goal is the critical determinant of emotion. Positive emotion arises when goals are judged to be within reach; negative emotion arises when goals are judged to be out of reach.

TABLE 6.2. The Private Self-Consciousness Scale

Please indicate the extent to which each of the following items describes you by choosing one number on the rating scale next to each item.

	0	1	2	3	4
	Extremely Uncharacteristic			Extremely Characteristic	
1. I'm always trying to figure myself out.	0	1	2	3	4
2. Generally, I'm not very aware of myself.	0	1	2	3	4
3. I reflect about myself a lot.	0	1	2	3	4
4. I'm often the subject of my own fantasies.	0	1	2	3	4
5. I never scrutinize myself.	0	1	2	3	4
6. I'm generally attentive to my inner feelings.	0	1	2	3	4
7. I'm constantly examining my motives.	0	1	2	3	4
8. I sometimes have the feeling that I'm off somewhere watching myself.	0	1	2	3	4
9. I'm alert to changes in my mood.	0	1	2	3	4
10. I'm aware of the way my mind works when I work through a problem.	0	1	2	3	4

Note: To determine your score, reverse the scoring for items 2 and 5 (0 = 4, 1 = 3, 2 = 2, 3 = 1, 4 = 0), and then add up your score to all 10 items. The higher the score, the higher your level of private self-consciousness.
Source: Adapted from Fenigstein, Scheier, & Buss, 1975, *Journal of Consulting and Clinical Psychology,* 43, 522–528. Copyright 1975. Adapted by permission of The American Psychological Association.

Carver and Scheier (1990) have offered an intriguing modification of this position. They have argued that the perceived rate of progress toward a goal is a more important determinant of emotion than is the absolute distance from a goal. Positive emotion arises when people believe they are making adequate progress toward their goals; negative emotion arises when people believe they are not making adequate progress toward their goals. This means that people can still feel good when they are far from their goals, as long as they perceive that they are making progress. For example, an aspiring pianist who has "playing Carnegie Hall" as her goal may feel elated after her first piano recital because it signifies that she is on her way. Research testing these ideas has just begun, but the evidence suggests that both factors (i.e., distance from the goal and progress toward it) influence emotion (Hsee & Abelson, 1991; Hsee, Salovey, & Abelson, 1994).

Another unresolved issue is the extent to which the emotional reaction (whether it be determined by distance from the goal or rate of progress) guides behavioral adjustment. As noted earlier, Duval and Wicklund (1972) proposed (1) that negative emotion arises whenever people become aware of a discrepancy between their current state and a relevant standard and (2) that this negative emotion is the main force that drives further attempts at discrepancy reduction. A similar position has been espoused by Pyszczynski and Greenberg (1987b).

Bandura (1986) has also argued that emotions play a critical role in the behavioral regulation process. In addition to discussing the role of negative emotions, he emphasizes that positive emotions, such as pride and self-satisfaction, motivate behavior by virtue of their capacity to function as positive reinforcers. The idea is that people are motivated to experience these positive emotions and that they regulate their behavior in an attempt to maximize these feelings of self-worth. For Bandura, these feelings, not information, govern people's behavior.

Carver and Scheier (1981) have disagreed with these positions. They maintain that informational factors, not emotional ones, guide the self-regulation process. If people believe that further efforts at discrepancy reduction will be successful, they persevere; if people do not believe that further efforts at discrepancy reduction will be successful, they withdraw and quit. People may also experience various emotions when making these decisions, but the emotions themselves play no role in guiding behavior. The only important factor to consider, according to Carver and Scheier, is the expectancy of success.

Summary

To summarize, the self is implicated in virtually all aspects of the self-regulation process. Table 6.3 documents this involvement. Self-relevant phenomena influence (1) goal selection, via their effect on people's values and expectancies; (2) preparation for action, via their effect on information seeking, practice, and mental rehearsal; and (3) goal attainment, via their effect on various aspects of the cybernetic cycle of behavior.

TABLE 6.3. Summary of the Role Self-Relevant Phenomena Play in the Self-Regulation Process

I. GOAL SELECTION (within an expectancy-value framework)
  A. Self and Expectancies
    1. Self-efficacy beliefs: People undertake activities they believe they can successfully complete and avoid activities they think they cannot successfully complete.
    2. Possible selves: People who can vividly imagine themselves succeeding hold higher expectancies of success than do those who lack such an image.
  B. Self and Values
    1. Current self-conceptions imply values (e.g., a person who thinks of herself as an artist values artistic pursuits).
    2. Possible selves (future self-conceptions) influence values. People want to think of themselves a certain way. Anything that promotes these possible selves assumes value. For example, attending medical school assumes value for a person who wishes to think of himself as a physician.
    3. Goals construed at broad, abstract levels almost always implicate the self. For example, a person may be striving to "be independent" or to "be a good person."

II. PREPARATION FOR ACTION
  A. Gather Information
    People with high self-efficacy beliefs engage in greater information-seeking than do those who doubt their ability to succeed.

TABLE 6.3. Summary of the Role Self-Relevant Phenomena Play in the Self-Regulation Process—*Concluded*

    B. **Mental Rehearsal**

       People with high self-efficacy beliefs and people with clearly articulated possible selves are able to imagine themselves succeeding. These images, in turn, generally make success more likely.

    C. **Practice**

       People with high self-efficacy beliefs spend more time in preparation than do those with low self-efficacy beliefs.

III. **CYBERNETIC CYCLE OF BEHAVIOR**

    A. **Initial Behavior**

       1. Ability—a component of personality, not self-relevant.

       2. Effort—self-efficacy beliefs influence how long and how hard people try.

       3. Strategy—self-efficacy beliefs and possible selves influence strategies, particularly the ability to tune out distracting thoughts and suppress competing activities.

       4. Luck—not influenced by self.

    B. **Observe Behavior**

       Not directly related to self-relevant processes.

    C. **Compare Against Some Standard**

       Self-focused attention: People are more apt to compare their current behavior with a relevant standard when self-awareness is high.

    D. **Expectancy**

       Self-efficacy beliefs: People who believe they have the ability to succeed are more optimistic that they can overcome obstacles to goal attainment than are those who doubt their ability to succeed.

       Self-awareness: Self-awareness and expectancies interact to influence whether a person persists or withdraws. When expectancies are favorable, self-awareness leads to persistence; when expectancies are low, self-awareness leads to withdrawal.

    E. **Emotional Reaction**

       Duval and Wicklund (1972) believe that emotion is a critical component of the self-regulation process. Becoming aware of a discrepancy produces negative emotion which people are motivated to reduce.

       Bandura (1986) also believes that emotion is critical to the self-regulation process. He has emphasized that self-relevant emotions (e.g., feelings of pride for finishing a job) serve as powerful incentives and reinforcers.

       Carver and Scheier (1981) believe that emotion is not a critical component of the self-regulation process.

    F. **Behavioral Adjustment**

APPLICATIONS TO THE ACHIEVEMENT DOMAIN

The theoretical ideas we have been discussing in this chapter have been applied to a wide range of human behaviors. One of the most commonly studied areas is performance in achievement-related situations. In this section, we will consider three ways in which people's thoughts and feelings toward themselves influence their performance at achievement tasks.

Defensive Pessimism

I had a friend in college who used to exasperate me. Before every test, she would tell me how nervous she was and how bad she was going to do. Invariably, she would then proceed to set the curve for the test by getting the highest score. The first few times this happened, I figured my friend was just trying to save face in case she did poorly on the test. But as I got to know her better, I realized this strategy of expecting the worst was an important element in her success.

Norem and Cantor (1986; Cantor & Norem, 1989) coined the term *defensive pessimism* to describe my friend's behavior. Despite having a history of success in achievement situations, defensive pessimists doubt their ability to succeed in the future. Instead of imagining themselves doing well, they exaggerate their odds of failing and dwell on all the ways things could go wrong.

This does not mean that defensive pessimists adopt a passive, "what's the use" attitude. In fact, just the opposite is true. Focusing on potential problems prods defensive pessimists to make sure these calamities don't occur. This is the key component to making defensive pessimism work. Defensive pessimists feel anxious and out of control when they approach a performance situation. To quell their anxiety, they painstakingly work through all the ways things could go wrong, and then "cover their bases" by taking active steps to avoid these pitfalls. In this manner, imagining the worse motivates the defensive pessimist to work harder and perform better.

An investigation by Spencer and Norem (1996) showed how important these strategies are to a defensive pessimist. Spencer and Norem had participants perform a test of manual dexterity (a dart-throwing task). Before the performance, participants were randomly assigned to one of three mental rehearsal conditions. Participants in a mastery-imagery condition were asked to imagine themselves turning in a stellar performance, entirely free of mistakes. Participants in the coping-imagery condition were asked to imagine they had made some mistakes during the performance, and then to think about how they would recover from those mistakes and make necessary corrections. Another third of the participants (i.e., those in a relaxation-imagery condition) were instructed to relax prior to the performance.

Spencer and Norem (1996) reasoned that although most people perform best when they imagine themselves succeeding, defensive pessimists perform best when they are given the opportunity to plan for how things could go wrong. This proved to be the case. Defensive pessimists performed better in the coping-imagery condition than in either of the other two conditions. These results show that high expectations of success do not always improve performance. For some people, imagining worst-case scenarios can be beneficial, as long as this pessimism is accompanied by active attempts to find solutions.

Goal Orientations in Achievement Settings

Expectancies of success are not the only factor that influences performance in achievement settings. The goals individuals pursue also affect performance. Research by Carol Dweck and her colleagues is particularly relevant to some of the ideas we have been discussing in this chapter (for reviews, see Dweck, 1991; Dweck & Leggett, 1988).

Dweck's early work was conducted with young children. At the beginning of an experimental session, the children were given several problems to solve. All of these problems were of easy or moderate difficulty, and the children were able to solve most of them. Later, the children were given a very difficult problem to solve. Dweck noted strong differences in how the children responded to this challenge. Some of the children exhibited signs of helplessness. These helpless-oriented children (as Dweck refers to them) became frustrated and angry, and they indicated that they did not want to continue working on the task. Other children were more mastery oriented. They became interested and engaged in the activity, and they expressed a strong desire to keep working on the task, often increasing their efforts to solve the problem. Interestingly, these differences did not depend on ability level. On average, the helpless-oriented children did not have lower ability (as measured by performance on the set of initial problems) than did the mastery-oriented children.

The key question to Dweck and her colleagues was "why?" Why do some children respond to obstacles with frustration and withdrawal, while others respond to obstacles with excitement and engagement? Dweck hypothesized that the goals individuals adopt when entering an achievement situation guide the way they respond to performance feedback (see also, Ames & Ames, 1984; Nicholls, 1984). According to Dweck, helpless-oriented children adopt *performance* goals in achievement settings. Their goal is to demonstrate competence—to prove to themselves and others that they are intelligent and capable. In contrast, mastery-oriented children adopt *learning* goals in achievement settings. Their goal is to cultivate competence—to acquire knowledge, attain skills, and grow and develop as an individual.

Dweck's research has shown how these different goal orientations shape people's reactions to achievement setbacks (Dweck & Leggett, 1988). People with performance goals generally respond poorly to obstacles and setbacks. They view poor performance as an indication that they lack ability, and they disengage from the task and quit. People with learning goals show a different reaction. Instead of attributing failure to a lack of ability, they attribute it to insufficient effort or an ineffective strategy; and instead of viewing setbacks as threats to be endured, they view them as challenges to be mastered.

In her more recent work, Dweck has considered how these different goal orientations develop. She believes that the goals are a product of the theories people hold about the nature of intelligence. People with performance goals hold an *entity* theory of intelligence. They view intelligence as a fixed, immutable quality. Intelligence is something you either have or don't have (like blue eyes), and your goal in an achievement setting is to demonstrate that you have it. People with learning goals adopt an *incremental* theory of intelligence. They view intelligence as a fluid, malleable quality that can be developed and cultivated. This perspective leads them to enter achievement situations with the goal of increasing their ability level, of becoming more proficient and skillful.

Table 6.4 summarizes the two different orientations and shows how different theories about the nature of intelligence influence people's performances in achievement settings. One thing is missing from Table 6.4, however.

TABLE 6.4. Summary of Helpless- and Mastery-Oriented Achievement Orientations

Achievement Orientation	Theory of Intelligence	Dominant Goal	Attributions	Task Preference	Persistence and Performance
Helpless	Entity (intelligence is fixed)	Performance (goal is to demonstrate competence to self and others)	Ability	Avoid challenging tasks that threaten to reveal low ability	Quit easily in the face of difficulty; show performance decrements when confronting obstacles and setbacks
Mastery	Incremental (intelligence is malleable)	Learning (goal is to cultivate competence and increase ability)	Strategy or effort	Seek challenging tasks that foster learning and skill acquisition	Remain focused on task in the face of difficulty; maintain a high level of performance when confronting obstacles and setbacks

Source: Adapted from Dweck & Leggett, 1988, *Psychological Review, 95,* 256–273. Copyright 1988. Adapted by permission of The American Psychological Association.

Performance goals aren't always maladaptive. Elliott and Dweck (1988) found that people who hold performance goals *and* believe their ability is high actively seek opportunities to demonstrate this competence and do not shy away from challenging tasks. This suggests that performance goals are detrimental only when they are accompanied by low perceptions of competence (see also Harackiewicz & Elliot, 1988).

Intrinsic versus Extrinsic Motivation

The goal orientations Dweck describes are closely related to another issue of importance in achievement settings. This is the issue of whether behavior is motivated from within (i.e., intrinsically motivated) or driven by a desire to gain external rewards (i.e., extrinsically motivated). People who are intrinsically motivated strive to do well in achievement situations for personal reasons. They take pleasure in learning and find the educational process to be inherently interesting and enjoyable. People who are extrinsically motivated

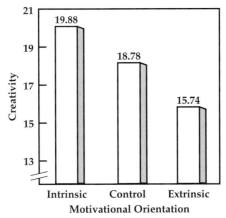

FIGURE 6.3. Judged creativity of a poem as a function of motivational orientation. The data show that participants who were led to focus on extrinsic reasons for creative writing wrote less-creative poems than did control participants or participants who were led to focus on intrinsic reasons for writing.
(Adapted from Amabile, 1985, *Journal of Personality and Social Psychology, 48,* 393–399. Copyright 1985. Adapted by permission of The American Psychological Association.)

strive to do well in achievement situations in order to gain external rewards. These rewards can include positive attention from teachers, parents, or peers, or material rewards, such as money or related privileges (e.g., you can use my car if you maintain a 3.0 average).

Extrinsic Motivation Impairs Task Performance

Although the differences are not always large, students who are extrinsically motivated tend to perform worse in school than students who are intrinsically motivated (Deci, Vallerand, Pelletier, & Ryan, 1991). An extrinsic orientation can also dampen creativity. In one experiment, Amabile (1985) randomly assigned some students in a creative-writing class to focus on extrinsic reasons for writing (e.g., the market for freelance writers is expanding; you enjoy public recognition of your work). Another group was led to focus on the intrinsic rewards associated with writing (e.g., I write because I like to express myself; I feel relaxed when I write). A third group was given no instructions. Later, all three groups of students wrote a poem, and the poems were rated for creative expression by an independent set of judges.

Figure 6.3 shows that students who were in the extrinsic motivation condition wrote poems that were less creative than those written by students in the other two conditions. Along with the results from other investigations (e.g., Amabile, 1983; Amabile, Hill, Hennessey, & Tighe, 1994), these findings reveal that extrinsic motivation can stifle creativity.

Extrinsic Motivation Undermines Intrinsic Interest

Thinking too much about external rewards can have other negative consequences. For example, Lepper, Greene, and Nisbett (1973) found that students

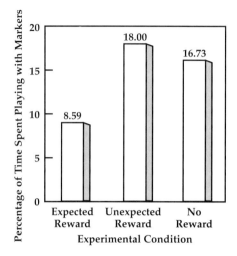

FIGURE 6.4. Time spent playing with markers as a function of reward condition. The data show that children who earlier had received an expected reward for playing with felt-tip markers subsequently showed less interest in the markers than did children who received either an unexpected reward or no reward at all. These findings document that expected rewards can sometimes undermine intrinsic motivation.
(Adapted from Lepper, Greene, & Nisbett, 1973, *Journal of Personality and Social Psychology, 28,* 129–137. Copyright 1973. Adapted by permission of The American Psychological Association.)

who perform an activity with the expectation of receiving an award subsequently show less interest in the activity than students who perform the activity without the promise of an external reward. In this study, nursery school children were encouraged to draw with some felt-tip markers. One-third of the children were in the *expected-reward* condition. These children were told they would receive a reward (in the form of a special certificate) if they drew with the markers. Another one-third of the children were in the *unexpected-reward* condition. They also received a reward for playing with the markers, but they didn't know they were going to get it when they chose to play with the markers. Finally, children in a control condition neither expected nor received an award for playing with the markers.

Several days later, the children were brought back into the laboratory and were given the opportunity to play with a number of attractive toys, including the felt-tip markers. No rewards were mentioned or administered during this phase of the experiment. The results from this study, which are shown in Figure 6.4, revealed that the children in the expected-reward condition spent less time playing with the markers during the second stage of the experiment than did children in the other two conditions (for related research, see Boggiano & Main, 1986; Higgins, Lee, Kwon, & Trope, 1995).

Although the data shown in Figure 6.4 indicate that expected external rewards can undermine intrinsic motivation, this is not always the case. Deci

(1975) noted that external rewards contain two aspects. On the one hand, they tend to reduce choice and constrain behavioral freedom by coercing or seducing people to behave in ways they normally would not. A bribe aptly illustrates this controlling function of rewards. But external rewards can also provide important information about the quality of one's efforts and performance (as when a person receives a sticker for trying hard or for turning in an exemplary performance). Rewards appear to undermine intrinsic interest *only* when the controlling aspect of the reward is more prominent than its informational value (Ryan, Mims, & Koestner, 1983). This means that rewarding someone for a job well done does not necessarily dampen the person's enthusiasm for performing the task.

SELF-REGULATION FAILURE

To this point, we have focused on how self-relevant processes promote successful self-regulation. People are not always successful in their efforts to regulate their own behavior, however. Indeed, many of the problems that currently plague American society—alcoholism, domestic violence, drug use, drunk-driving, excessive gambling, smoking, and unsafe sexual practices—reflect, to some extent, people's inability to control themselves. Even our national debt represents an inability to control our collective spending.

Using principles discussed in this chapter, Baumeister, Heatherton, and Tice (1994; see also Baumeister & Heatherton, 1996) have developed a theoretical model of self-regulation failure. The model begins by assuming that people must often choose between conflicting goals. A person wants to save for the future *and* buy a new CD player; a person wants to act responsibly *and* gratify sexual desires. Successful self-regulation occurs when higher-order goals and desires (the desire to save money and act responsibly) override or supersede lower-order impulses and desires (the desire to own a new stereo or satisfy sexual urges).

As noted earlier, higher-order goals are ones that involve self-images (Vallacher & Wegner, 1987). They represent the way people wish to think of themselves; the kind of person they want to be. Successful self-regulation requires activating these superordinate, higher-order goals and making sure they are sufficiently strong to guide behavior.

Baumeister et al. (1994) refer to this process as one of *transcendence*. Transcendence occurs when individuals are able to see beyond the present situation (which may offer immediate gratification) and focus upon more distant goals involving desired self-images. A person who focuses on how smoking will kill him in the long run is engaging in transcendence. He is focusing on distant concerns and ignoring the immediate gratification a cigarette would bring.

Finally, Baumeister et al. (1994) assume that a person's ability to transcend the present situation and override impulses and urges varies as a function of situational factors. These factors include fatigue, stress, and distraction. This approach does not deny that some individuals generally are more proficient at self-control than others (Mischel, Shoda, & Peake, 1988); it simply underscores that several factors can impede everyone's ability to regulate their own behavior.

Negative Effects of Too Little Self-Awareness

One of these factors is a lack of self-awareness. As noted throughout this chapter, successful self-regulation demands that people compare their behavior against a relevant standard, and this comparison process is more apt to occur when people are aware of themselves. Anything that diminishes self-awareness, then, can hinder self-regulatory efforts.

Deindividuation and Moral Behavior

Deindividuation illustrates this effect. Deindividuation occurs when people lose their sense of individuality. Deindividuation tends to occur in group situations, and it is often accompanied by a loosening of moral behavior. For example, deindividuation has been shown to increase aggression (Mullen, 1986). The kind of rioting that can characterize a mob provides a suitable example. Being anonymous (or deindividuated) by virtue of their immersion in a group, normally law-abiding citizens can run amok and cause considerable financial and physical damage. The riots that sometimes occur following soccer games in Europe provide a fitting example of this phenomenon.

Deindividuation can also give rise to other forms of antisocial behavior. In one study, Diener and Wallbom (1976) gave college students an alleged intelligence test. The students were told they had only 5 minutes to work on the test, but that the experimenter would not be back for 10 minutes. This gave the students an opportunity to cheat on the test by working past the allotted time. Half of the students were seated in front of a large mirror while they worked on the test (and thus were in a state of heightened self-awareness); the remaining students (those in the low self-awareness condition) did not sit in front of a mirror. In accordance with the claim that diminished self-awareness undermines moral behavior, 71 percent of the students who took the test in the low self-awareness condition cheated on the test by working past the allotted time, but only 7 percent of the students who took the test in the high self-awareness condition did so. These and similar findings (e.g., Beaman, Klentz, Diener, & Svanum, 1979) suggest that people are less likely to act on higher-order moral principles when self-awareness is low.

Alcohol Consumption and Self-Regulatory Failure

Alcohol is implicated in many instances of self-regulatory failure. Domestic violence, aggression, unsafe sexual practices, and many other troublesome behaviors are more likely to occur when people have been drinking. There are many explanations for this effect, but one is that alcohol reduces self-awareness (Hull, 1981). When intoxicated, individuals become less aware of themselves, and they fail to compare their present behavior with appropriate, higher-order standards. Consequently, they do things they would ordinarily not do.

Hull, Levenson, Young, and Sher (1983) conducted a study to see whether alcohol reduces self-awareness. The participants in this study were asked to give a short speech, and the researchers took note of how often participants referred to themselves during the speech. Half of the participants consumed alcohol before giving the speech; the rest of the participants consumed tonic water. Consistent with the notion that alcohol reduces self-awareness, participants who drank alcohol referred to themselves less often during their speeches than did participants who drank tonic water. Because self-awareness is an essential component of successful self-regulation, alcohol's ability to diminish self-awareness can explain why it is often associated with self-regulation failure.

There is another, related, way in which alcohol can lead to self-regulatory failure. Steele and Josephs (1990) have argued that alcohol restricts people's attention to immediate cues and reduces their ability to think abstractly. This tendency (which Steele and Josephs refer to as *alcohol myopia*) may explain why people fail to consider the broader implications of their actions when intoxicated. Instead of focusing on the general implications of their behavior (e.g., on what kind of person they want to be), they focus on the immediate pleasures of the action they are contemplating. In more formal terms, we can say that alcohol interferes with the transcendence process identified by Baumeister et al. (1994). This interference may explain why alcohol is implicated in so many instances of self-regulatory failure, including date rape and unsafe sexual practices (MacDonald, Zanna, & Fong, 1996).

Unfortunately, the positive effects of alcohol are also alluring. Alcohol not only makes people feel better physically (e.g., it relaxes them), it also makes people feel better about themselves. Banaji and Steele (1989) found that many people evaluate themselves more positively after they have ingested moderate amounts of alcohol. People also tend to drink after they have suffered a threat to their self-image, and doing so helps them feel better about themselves (Steele, Southwick, & Critchlow, 1981). These effects provide powerful psychological reasons for drinking alcohol.

Negative Effects of Too Much Self-Awareness

In the preceding section we discussed situations in which a lack of self-awareness can impair self-regulation. Somewhat paradoxically, too much self-awareness can also be harmful.

Choking

Choking provides one instance of this effect. Choking occurs when individuals fail to perform at optimal levels under conditions in which optimal performance is desired. Athletic competitions provide the prototypic example. The annals of sports lore abound with fabled stories of teams or individuals who have been in a winning position only to lose because of a series of flagrant errors. For example, the Australian golfer, Greg Norman, led by six strokes going into the final round of the 1996 Masters Golf Tournament. Despite having this commanding lead, Norman ended up losing by five strokes, largely due to a spate of errors he committed.

Baumeister (1984; Baumeister, Hamilton, & Tice, 1985) linked choking to heightened self-awareness. Baumeister argued that choking occurs when situational pressures (such as those induced by competition or the presence of an audience) heighten self-awareness. This increased attention to oneself leads people to compare their present behavior with a relevant standard and to think too much about what they're doing. This, in turn, interferes with the execution of well-learned, highly demanding skills. Interestingly, both anticipation of success (Baumeister & Steinhilber, 1984) and fear of failure (Schlenker, Phillips, Boniecki, & Schlenker, 1995) can increase self-awareness and produce choking.

Steele and Aronson (1995) have used these ideas to explain racial differences in academic performance. There is considerable evidence that many Black Americans fail to perform up to their intellectual potential in achievement situations (Steele, 1992). Steele and Aronson suggested that heightened self-awareness may account for this effect. They argued that Black Americans feel intense pressure to perform well at achievement tasks in an attempt to disconfirm cultural stereotypes of intellectual inferiority. This pressure, which Steele and Aronson refer to as *stereotype threat,* increases self-awareness and ultimately undermines performance (i.e., causes choking).

To test their ideas, Steele and Aronson administered an intellectual test to Black and White college students. Before taking the test, half of the students were instructed to indicate their race on a pretest questionnaire; the other half of the students were not asked to indicate their race. Steele and Aronson assumed that asking students to indicate their race would make race salient and that, for Black students, racial salience would lead to heightened self-awareness and poor task performance.

Figure 6.5 presents the results for the task performance measure. In accordance with predictions, the figure shows that Black students performed worse than White students only in the racial-prime condition. When race was not made salient, Black students actually performed a bit better on the test than did White students. Additional data suggested that this effect was due to heightened self-awareness on the part of Blacks in the racial-prime conditions (for related research, see, Schneider, Major, Luhtanen, & Crocker, 1996).

Self-Destructive Behavior As Escape from Self-Awareness

Excessive self-awareness has also been implicated in acts of self-destruction (Baumeister & Scher, 1988). Substance abuse provides the best example. Earlier we noted that alcohol reduces self-awareness (Hull, 1981) and that drinking alcohol can make people feel better about themselves (Banaji & Steele, 1989). Many people who drink to excess do so for these reasons. They turn to alcohol as a means of reducing self-awareness, particularly when things are going poorly in life (Hull & Young, 1983). Nearly 1,000 years ago, the Persian poet Omar Khayyam described the experience in this way:

> I drink not from mere joy in wine nor to scoff at faith—no, only to forget myself for a moment, that only do I want of intoxication, that alone.

Baumeister and Scher (1988) have argued that a desire to reduce self-awareness plays a role in many other acts of self-destruction (e.g., smoking,

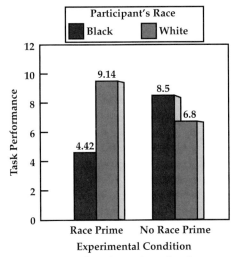

FIGURE 6.5. Task performance as a function of student's race and whether race was primed or not primed. The data show that Black students performed significantly worse than did White students when race was primed, but not when race was not primed. Other findings suggested that this occurred because Black students became highly aware of themselves in the race-primed condition.
(Adapted from Steele & Aronson, 1995, *Journal of Personality and Social Psychology, 69*, 797–811. Copyright 1995. Adapted by permission of The American Psychological Association.)

thrill seeking, and masochism). When self-awareness becomes too intense and aversive, people turn to these activities in an attempt to escape from themselves.

A desire to escape self-awareness may even underlie suicide. According to Baumeister (1990), suicide can arise when negative experiences, such as a business failure or the break-up of an important interpersonal relationship, lead to an intense state of heightened self-awareness. When other efforts to eliminate this aversive state fail to bring relief, people begin to contemplate suicide. For these people, suicide represents a last-ditch attempt to escape an acute state of self-awareness.

CHAPTER SUMMARY

In this chapter we explored how self-relevant processes influence motivated behavior. We began by outlining a general model of self-regulation. This model is concerned with the goals people adopt and the manner in which people go about trying to attain their goals. We then identified three self-relevant processes that influence self-regulation. These are (1) self-efficacy beliefs (the extent to which people believe they have the ability to reach their goals); (2) possible selves (people's ideas about what they will be like in the future); and (3) self-awareness (the extent to which people's attention is focused on themselves or is focused on the environment). Finally, we reviewed research showing that these phenomena affect virtually every aspect of the self-regulation process.

Next, we discussed task performance in achievement situations. Most people function best when they imagine themselves succeeding and have high expectancies of success. But some people (called defensive pessimists) function best when they are allowed to think about all the ways things could go wrong. Task performance is also influenced by the goals people adopt in achievement settings. Some people strive to demonstrate to themselves and others that they are competent; other people strive to cultivate competence and to improve themselves. These different goal orientations influence people's responses to setbacks and obstacles. In a similar vein, some people are motivated by intrinsic (or personal) concerns when they enter an achievement situation, whereas others are driven to gain external rewards or attention from others. Under some circumstances, an extrinsic orientation can stifle creativity and reduce task enjoyment.

Finally, we looked at situations in which self-relevant processes can interfere with self-regulatory efforts. Here we saw that both a lack of self-awareness and an excess of self-awareness can lead to self-regulatory failure.

- Self-regulation models of motivated behavior are concerned with what individuals choose to do and how they go about trying to accomplish their goals. There are three aspects of the model: (1) goal selection (which can be understood in terms of an expectancy-value model); (2) preparation for action; and (3) a cybernetic cycle of behavior.
- Cybernetic models of behavior assume that people use information to regulate their behavior. After adopting a goal or standard, people periodically monitor their behavior and compare it against some standard. This comparison process yields (1) an expectancy that future efforts will be worthwhile, and (2) an emotional reaction. These factors, in turn, determine whether people continue to pursue their goals or abandon them.
- Self-efficacy beliefs refer to people's ideas about their ability to bring about desired outcomes. People with high self-efficacy beliefs are confident they have what it takes to succeed; people with low self-efficacy beliefs doubt their ability to succeed. These beliefs play an important role in the behavioral regulation process, influencing (1) the goals people adopt; (2) how thoroughly people prepare to attain their goals; and (3) how long, hard, and effectively people work at achieving their goals.
- Possible selves refers to people's ideas about what they will be like in the future. Some of these possible selves are positive; others are negative. Vivid and clearly defined possible selves affect goal selection by influencing what people value in life. Possible selves also help people to remain focused on their goals by suppressing the attractiveness of competing activities.
- Attentional focus varies from a state of heightened self-awareness to a relative lack of self-awareness. People whose attention is focused on themselves are more apt to compare their current state with a relevant standard than are people who are less aware of themselves. When expectancies are favorable, self-focused attention leads to high effort, continued persistence, and superior task performance; when expectancies are unfavorable, self-focused attention leads to low effort, a lack of persistence, and poor task performance.
- Defensive pessimists perform best in achievement settings when they are allowed to focus on all the ways things might go wrong. This occurs because planning for the worst reduces anxiety.
- Some people enter achievement situations with the goal of demonstrating to themselves and to others that they possess high ability. These individuals tend to be-

lieve that intelligence is a fixed quality that you either have or do not have. Other people enter achievement settings with the goal of cultivating competence. These individuals tend to believe that intelligence is a malleable quality that you can acquire and develop.

- External rewards can reduce creativity and undermine intrinsic interest in an activity. This occurs when the controlling aspect of the reward (I'll pay you if you do your homework) is more salient than the reward's informational value (here's a reward for doing such a good job on your homework).

- Self-awareness can interfere with effective self-regulation. When self-awareness is too low, people fail to compare their current behavior with appropriate higher-order standards. This can lead to aggression and irresponsible behavior (such as unsafe sexual practices). Excessive self-awareness can also be harmful. People who become too aware of themselves sometimes turn to self-destructive behaviors (such as drinking or thrill seeking) in an attempt to reduce self-awareness. In extreme cases, suicide can result when efforts to escape self-awareness fail.

For Further Reading

BANDURA, A. (1986). *Social foundations of thought and action.* Englewood Cliffs, NJ: Prentice Hall.

BAUMEISTER, R. F., HEATHERTON, T. F., & TICE, D. M. (1994). *Losing control: How and why people fail at self-regulation.* San Diego: Academic Press.

CARVER, C. S., & SCHEIER, M. F. (1981). *Attention and self-regulation: A control-theory approach to human behavior.* New York: Springer-Verlag.

DECI, E. L. (1975). *Intrinsic motivation.* New York: Plenum Press.

CHAPTER 7

Self-Presentation

There will be time, there will be time, to prepare a face to meet the faces that you meet.

—T. S. Eliot, *The Lovesong of J. Alfred Prufrock*

The self-concept seems like a very private phenomenon. After all, people's thoughts about themselves are hidden and are often highly personal. Yet the self-concept is also very much a social phenomenon. It has social roots (e.g., reflected appraisals, social comparison), it includes social identities and roles, and it guides our perception of others and our behavior in social settings.

In this chapter we will explore the social side of the self in the context of self-presentational behavior. Self-presentational behavior is any behavior intended to create, modify, or maintain an impression of ourselves in the minds of others.[1] According to this definition, whenever we are attempting to lead people to think of us in a particular way, we are engaging in self-presentation.

Because much of our time is spent in the company of other people, self-presentation is a pervasive feature of social life. We even engage in self-presentation when we are alone; for example, we rehearse what we are going to say or do in public, molding our behavior to an imaginary or anticipated audience. Sometimes this rehearsal is deliberate and noticeable (as when we prepare for a job interview or a public speaking engagement); other times it is automatic and almost imperceptible (as when we mindlessly check our hair in the mirror before stepping out the front door).

Self-presentation is not only a prevalent aspect of our lives, it is also a very important one. Our success at leading others to believe we possess various characteristics has a profound influence on our outcomes in life (Hogan & Briggs, 1986). Who we marry, who our friends are, whether we get ahead at work, and many other outcomes depend, to a great extent, on our ability to convince people that we are worthy of their love, their friendship, their trust, and their respect. Undoubtedly, this need to create a positive impression is one reason that people spend billions of dollars a year on cosmetics and other

---

[1]The term *impression management* has also been used to describe people's efforts to manage the impressions others form of them. Although the two terms (self-presentation and impression management) differ in certain respects (see Schlenker, 1980), I use them interchangeably throughout this chapter.

personal-appearance products. Self-presentational concerns also lead people to engage in behaviors that enhance their appearance to others but simultaneously jeopardize their own physical well-being (e.g., overexposure to the sun; excessive dieting) (Leary, Tchividijian, & Kraxberger, 1994). Self-presentational concerns can even underlie self-destructive behaviors, such as cigarette smoking and substance abuse (Sharp & Getz, 1996).

The chapter begins by considering the nature of self-presentational behavior. Why do people engage in self-presentation, and when and how do they go about creating impressions of themselves in the minds of other people? In the second section of the chapter, we will look at the kinds of images people create and the obstacles they face when trying to create these images. Here, we will also examine some of the things people do when they fail to make a desired impression. The third part of the chapter explores the close connection between public behavior and private self-conceptions. We will see that people are very often audiences for their own behavior, and in the course of trying to convince others that they possess particular qualities, they end up convincing themselves. Finally, we will consider the extent to which public behavior is a faithful reflection of what people really think about themselves.

THE NATURE OF SELF-PRESENTATION

Why Do People Engage in Self-Presentation?

We begin our discussion by considering why people engage in self-presentation. Why do we bother to lead people to see us in one way or another?

Facilitate Social Interaction

The most basic function of self-presentation is to define the nature of a social situation (Goffman, 1959). Most social interactions are very role governed. Each person has a role to play, and the interaction proceeds smoothly when these roles are enacted effectively. For example, airline pilots are expected to be poised and dignified. As long as they convince their passengers that they possess these qualities, their passengers remain calm and behave in an orderly fashion. (Imagine, for example, how unsettling it would be if your airline pilot acted like the character "Kramer" on the television show Seinfeld!)

This function of self-presentation was first highlighted by Erving Goffman (1959). Goffman noted that social life is highly structured. In some cases, this structure is formalized (e.g., state dinners at the White House are characterized by strict rules of protocol), but most often it is informal and tacitly understood (e.g., norms of politeness and etiquette guide our social interactions). Among these norms is one that mandates that people support, rather than undermine, one another's public identities. Goffman refers to these efforts as *face work*. Each participant in an interaction is obliged to honor and uphold the other person's public persona. Toward this end, people may misrepresent themselves or otherwise refrain from saying what they really think or feel. For example, people publicly claim to like the presents they receive, find another person's new clothes or hairstyle attractive, or make excuses for why they cannot get together for some social encounter. This kind of self-presentational behavior seems to be primarily driven by a desire to avoid social conflict and reduce tension (DePaulo, Kashy, Kirkendol, Wyer, & Epstein, 1996).

Gain Material and Social Rewards

People also strive to create impressions of themselves in the minds of others in order to gain material and social rewards (or avoid material and social punishments). As discussed earlier, it is usually in our best interests to have others view us in a particular way. Employees generally have a material interest in being perceived as bright, committed, and promising. To the extent that they are successful in inducing these impressions in the minds of their employers, they are apt to be promoted and given raises. Social rewards also depend on our ability to convince others that we possess particular qualities. Being liked entails convincing others that we are likable; being a leader involves convincing others that we are capable of leading.

Jones (1990; see also, Tedeschi & Norman, 1985) notes that this type of *strategic self-presentation* represents a form of social influence in which one person (the self-presenter) attempts to gain power over another (the audience). This approach assumes that we are in a better position to influence the nature of social interaction in a manner that suits our purposes if we are able to control how others see us. This emphasis is apparent in many popular books, which carry titles like *How to Win Friends and Influence People* (Carnegie, 1936) and *Winning through Intimidation* (Ringer, 1973).

To some, the idea that people actively strive to manipulate how they are viewed by others conjures up images of duplicity and Machiavellianism. This need not be the case, however. Strategic self-presentation does not necessarily mean that we are trying to deceive others (though sometimes we are). It can also involve genuine attempts to bring our (self-perceived) positive qualities to the attention of others. In fact, for reasons to be discussed later, misrepresentation and lying tend to be the exception rather than the rule. Most of the time, strategic self-presentation involves "selective disclosures and omissions, or matters of emphasis and timing, rather than blatant deceit or dissimulation" (Jones, 1990, p. 175).

Self-Construction

Another reason we try and create impressions of ourselves in the minds of others is to construct a particular identity for ourselves (Baumeister, 1982b; Rosenberg, 1979; Schlenker, 1980). This type of self-presentational behavior serves a more private, personal function. Convincing others that we possess some quality or attribute is a means of convincing ourselves.

Sometimes, self-construction is initiated in order to create an identity. Rosenberg (1979) notes that this is particularly prevalent during adolescence. Adolescents routinely try out different identities. They adopt the dress and mannerisms of various social types (e.g., the sophisticate; the rebel), and studiously note people's reactions to these displays in an attempt to fashion an identity that fits. Other times, self-construction is undertaken to confirm an already established self-view. The successful Wall Street banker may wear suspenders, carry a beeper, and drive a Lexus to signal to others that he is indeed a man of "wealth and taste." Swann (1990) calls this form of self-construction "self-verification," and Wicklund and Gollwitzer (1982) refer to such behavior as "self-symbolizing."

Self-enhancement needs also underlie self-construction. Most people like to think of themselves as being competent, likable, talented, and so forth. By convincing others that they possess these positive attributes, people are better able to convince themselves. This, in turn, makes people feel better about themselves. In this sense, we can say that people seek to create impressions in the minds of others because it makes them feel good about themselves to do so.

Finally, self-construction can serve a motivational function. People are expected to be who they claim to be (Goffman, 1959; Schlenker, 1980). When they publicly announce an intention or otherwise stake a claim to an identity, people experience additional pressures to make *good* on their claims. The reformed alcoholic who proclaims his sobriety is utilizing this function. By publicly renouncing the use of alcohol, he increases his commitment to stay sober. We also see this in the world of sports. Before the 1968 Super Bowl, Joe Namath boldly predicted that his New York Jets would beat the Baltimore Colts (which they did). The great boxer, Muhammad Ali, also routinely predicted the outcomes of his fights. Under some circumstances, this kind of public boasting can serve to make the idea a reality.

Summary

In this section, we distinguished three functions of self-presentation. Although conceptually distinct, the three functions often operate simultaneously in the real world. For example, airline pilots project an air of dignity because doing so (1) makes the plane ride go smoother; (2) helps them retain their jobs; and (3) leads them to think of themselves as dignified people, which in turn makes them feel good about themselves.

When and How Do People Manage Impressions?

People form impressions of us whenever we are in public, but we are not always actively monitoring or regulating those impressions. In many situations, our self-presentations are automatic or habitual, and we are devoting little conscious attention to how we are being perceived by others. In other situations, we become acutely aware of the impressions we are creating, and we actively strive to take control of these impressions (Leary, 1993; Schlenker & Weigold, 1992). In this section, we will discuss factors that influence when we are most likely to actively engage in self-presentation and what it takes to successfully present ourselves to others.

Situational Variables That Influence Impression Motivation

The first component of self-presentation is a motivational one. Before we can create a desired impression, we have to be motivated to do so. Several factors can arouse this motive. One of the most important occurs when desired external rewards depend on the judgments of others (Buss & Briggs, 1984; Leary & Kowalski, 1990; Schlenker, 1980). Job interviews and first dates are two prototypic examples. In these situations, we are highly concerned with making a positive impression and we try to "put our best foot forward."

The motivation to engage in self-presentation also tends to increase when we are the focus of other people's attention. For some people, speaking in front of a group or audience is an aversive experience, in part because it causes them to become highly aware of their public identities. Certain stimuli, such as cameras and tape recorders, can also make us aware of our public appearance, as they remind us of how we are seen by others (Carver & Scheier, 1985; Scheier & Carver, 1982b).

Paradoxically, perhaps, being ignored or shunned by others can also increase self-presentational concerns (Buss, 1980). Think of how you would feel if you were being ignored by others at a party. Chances are this would make you feel acutely aware of yourself and motivate you to make a positive impression. This occurs, in large part, because being alone at a party is not a desired identity. In more general terms, we can say that a motive to actively engage in self-presentation increases whenever we encounter obstacles to creating a desired impression (Schlenker, 1985, 1986).

Familiarity with an audience is another factor that influences the nature of self-presentational behavior (Leary, Nezlek, Downs, Radford-Davenport, Martin, & McMullen, 1994; Tice, Butler, Muraven, & Stillwell, 1995). Although there are exceptions, people are generally more attentive to the impressions they are creating when they are interacting with casual acquaintances and business associates than when they are interacting with close friends, family members, and loved ones. Many people, for example, walk around the house with their hair uncombed, but they wouldn't go out to a business meeting that way. People also tend to be more modest and authentic when interacting with those they feel close to (particularly those of the same sex) than when interacting with people they don't know well. In the vernacular of the 1960s, people are more apt to "let their hair down and be themselves" when they are in the company of people they feel comfortable with and know well.

Social Acuity

Once we are motivated to create a particular impression, we need to possess an awareness of how that impression can best be created. This cognitive ability is called social acuity (Hogan & Briggs, 1986). Social acuity refers to our ability to know what we would need to do in order to successfully create a desired impression. Usually this involves adopting the perspective of other people and inferring what particular behaviors will give rise to a particular impression in their minds. Imagine, for example, that I want to convince you that I am witty. In order to do so, I must figure out what is required. I need to know what behaviors I must execute in order to create the desired impression. This perspective-taking ability is what we mean by social acuity.

Mead's influence is apparent here. As discussed in Chapter 4, Mead (1934) argued that in order to communicate effectively, people must be able to anticipate how their own symbolic gestures will be interpreted by others. The same is true for successful self-presentation. To create a desired impression, we must put ourselves in other people's shoes and discern what behaviors would produce a given impression. If we are inept at adopting the other person's perspective, we are unlikely to create the impressions we desire.

Behavioral Skills

Behavioral skills are the third component of successful self-presentation. People need to be capable of performing the behaviors they believe will create a desired impression. To return to an earlier example, I may be motivated to create the impression that I have the wit of Noel Coward, and I may recognize that in order to create this impression I need to toss out one *bon mot* after another. But wanting to create a particular impression and knowing what it would take do not guarantee that I can pull it off. I also need to be able to enact the desired behavior.

Numerous tactics are used to create a desired impression. Verbal claims are perhaps the most common strategy. People selectively disclose, *accidentally* mention, or overtly boast as a means of creating a particular impression. Like actors, we also use props to establish our characters. Our hair, physique, figure, and clothing all serve to create particular impressions of us in the minds of others. Although we may deny that self-presentation is the most important consideration that guides our decisions in such matters, few people claim that such decisions are made without any regard for the social consequences. Those that do make such claims are typically trying to create an impression of nonconformity or independence (Schlenker & Weigold, 1990)!

Even our movements signal to others what we are like. People draw inferences about what we are like from observing our mannerisms and gestures and the way we stand and walk (McArthur & Baron, 1983). Aware of this, people actively regulate their movements to control the impressions others form of them. For example, *unattached* people at a party or bar typically carry themselves differently than do those who are accompanied by someone. Their behavior signals to others that they are *available.*

Summary

To summarize, successful self-presentation involves a mix of motivation and ability. People can be motivated to make a particular impression, but they may fail to do so because they are unaware of what behaviors are needed or because they aren't able to perform the appropriate behaviors. Viewed in this way, it can be seen that successful self-presentation is a complicated affair. It requires a good deal of skill and sophistication. Recognizing this complexity, Schlenker and Leary (1982a) theorized that social anxiety arises when individuals are motivated to make a positive impression but they see little likelihood that they will do so. In extreme cases, these doubts can be paralyzing and lead to social phobias.

Individual Differences in Self-Presentation

Although everyone engages in self-presentation, people vary with respect to how concerned they are with their public image and with the kinds of impressions they try to convey. Before reading further about these differences, complete the scale shown in Table 7.1. When you are through, return to the text and learn more about this issue.

Self-Monitoring

Mark Snyder (1974) developed the scale shown in Table 7.1 to measure the degree to which people monitor and control their behavior in public situations. High self-monitors regard themselves as highly pragmatic and flexible people who strive to be the *right* person for every occasion. When entering a social situation, they try to discern what the model or prototypic person would do in that situation. They then use this knowledge to guide their own behavior. Low self-monitors adopt a different orientation. They regard themselves as highly principled people who value consistency between who they are and what they do. When entering a social situation, they look inward and use their attitudes, beliefs, and feelings to guide their behavior. Instead of striving to be the *right person* for the situation, they strive to *be themselves* in social settings.

Individual differences in self-monitoring influence a wide range of social behaviors (see Snyder, 1979, 1987, for reviews). In comparison with low self-monitors, high self-monitors (1) pay more attention to the behavior of others in social situations; (2) prefer to enter situations that provide clear guidelines for behavior; and (3) are more attracted to careers that emphasize the importance of public behavior, such as acting, sales, and public relations. High self-monitors also (4) are more adept at reading other people's facial expressions, and (5) are better at communicating a wider variety of emotions than are low self-monitors.

High self-monitors also exhibit less congruence between their underlying attitudes and their public behavior. They might, for example, say or do things they don't believe in if doing so seems like the appropriate thing to do. This is less true for low self-monitors. These individuals value congruence between their attitudes and their behavior. What they say and do is more often a faithful reflection of what they truly believe. To illustrate these differences, imagine that you and another person are discussing recent movies, and that the person tells you she liked a particular movie that you did not like. What will you do? Basically, you have three choices. You can (1) say you also liked the movie, even though you didn't; (2) voice your true opinion and admit that you didn't like the movie; or (3) avoid taking a stand, perhaps by changing the subject. All else being equal, high self-monitors are more apt to choose the first option than are low self-monitors.

Friendship patterns are also influenced by differences in self-monitoring. High self-monitors tend to have many different friends, each suitable for a different activity. For example, they play sports with one friend, go to the theater with another, and talk politics with yet another. This pattern allows them to

TABLE 7.1. The Self-Monitoring Scale

Please answer each of the following items True or False by circling T or F.

T F 1. I find it hard to imitate the behavior of other people.
T F 2. My behavior is usually an expression of my true inner feelings, attitudes, and beliefs.
T F 3. At parties and social gatherings, I do not attempt to do or say things that others will like.
T F 4. I can only argue for ideas which I already believe.
T F 5. I can make impromptu speeches even on topics about which I have almost no information.
T F 6. I guess I put on a show to impress or entertain people.
T F 7. When I am uncertain how to act in a social situation, I look to the behavior of others for cues.
T F 8. I would probably make a good actor.
T F 9. I rarely seek advice of my friends to choose movies, books, or music.
T F 10. I sometimes appear to others to be experiencing deeper emotions than I actually am.
T F 11. I laugh more when I watch a comedy with others than when alone.
T F 12. In a group of people I am rarely the center of attention.
T F 13. In different situations and with different people, I often act like very different persons.
T F 14. I am not particularly good at making other people like me.
T F 15. Even if I am not enjoying myself, I often pretend to be having a good time.
T F 16. I'm not always the person I appear to be.
T F 17. I would not change my opinions (or the way I do things) in order to please someone else or win their favor.
T F 18. I have considered being an entertainer.
T F 19. In order to get along and be liked, I tend to be what people expect me to be rather than anything else.
T F 20. I have never been good at games like charades or improvisational acting.
T F 21. I have trouble changing my behavior to suit different people and different situations.
T F 22. At a party I let others keep the jokes and stories going.
T F 23. I feel a bit awkward in company and do not show up quite so well as I should.
T F 24. I can look anyone in the eye and tell a lie with a straight face (if for a right end).
T F 25. I may deceive people by being friendly when I really dislike them.

Note: To determine your score, give yourself 1 point if you answered true to items 5, 6, 7, 8, 10, 11, 13, 15, 16, 18, 19, 24, and 25, and 1 point if you answered false to items 1, 2, 3, 4, 9, 12, 14, 17, 20, 21, 22, and 23. Add up your total score. Scores of 12 or less are characteristic of a low self-monitor; scores of 13 or more are characteristic of a high self-monitor.
Source: Snyder, 1974, *Journal of Personality and Social Psychology, 30,* 526–537. Copyright 1974. Adapted by permission of The American Psychological Association.

꘏꘏꘏꘏꘏

TABLE 7.2. A Comparison of High Self-Monitors and Low Self-Monitors

Component Processes	High Self-Monitors	Low Self-Monitors
Goals	Be the *right person* for the situation.	Be *me* in this situation.
Social Acuity	Highly adept at reading the character of the situation and the behavior of others, and able and willing to use this knowledge to construct a prototype of the model person for the situation.	Less adept at reading the character of the situation and the behavior of others. They base their behavior on inner attitudes, values, and dispositions.
Acting Ability	Superior acting ability allows them to modify their behavior to match the requirements of the situation.	Limited acting skills lead them to play similar roles in various situations.

express their characteristic orientation to be a different person in different situations. In contrast, low self-monitors have relatively few friends, and they engage in multiple activities with each one. They are more inclined to play sports, go to the theater, and talk politics with the same friend. This pattern is conducive to being the *same person* in all situations.

Table 7.2 summarizes the different orientations of high self-monitors and low self-monitors with reference to the three components of self-presentation we discussed earlier. High self-monitors are social chameleons. They enjoy being different people in different situations, and they possess the cognitive and behavioral skills needed to play many roles. In contrast, low self-monitors think of themselves as highly principled individuals who cherish being "true to themselves" in various situations. They are also somewhat less adept at reading the character of the social situation and their acting skills are not as well developed.[2]

Public Self-Consciousness

Related to differences in self-monitoring are differences in *public* self-consciousness. In Chapter 6, we noted that people differ in the degree to which they focus on their private, internal states. Fenigstein, Scheier, and Buss (1975) used the term *private* self-consciousness to refer to these differences, and they developed a scale to measure them. Fenigstein et al. also developed a scale to assess the degree to which people focus on the public, observable aspects of

---

[2]Important questions have been raised about the self-monitoring construct and the scale Snyder (1974) developed to measure self-monitoring. A thorough discussion of these issues can be found in Briggs, Cheek, and Buss (1980) and Gangestad and Snyder (1985).

TABLE 7.3. The Public Self-Consciousness Scale

Please indicate the extent to which each of the following items describes you by choosing one number on the rating scale next to each item.

	0 1	2	3 4
	Extremely Uncharacteristic		Extremely Characteristic
1. I'm concerned about my style of doing things.	0 1	2	3 4
2. I'm concerned about the way I present myself.	0 1	2	3 4
3. I'm self-conscious about the way I look.	0 1	2	3 4
4. I usually worry about making a good impression.	0 1	2	3 4
5. One of the last things I do before I leave my house is look in the mirror.	0 1	2	3 4
6. I'm concerned about what other people think of me.	0 1	2	3 4
7. I'm usually aware of my appearance.	0 1	2	3 4

Note: To determine your score, add up your scores for all seven items. Higher scores mean higher public self-consciousness.
Source: Adapted from Fenigstein, Scheier, & Buss, 1975, *Journal of Consulting and Clinical Psychology, 43,* 522–528. Copyright 1975. Adapted by permission of The American Psychological Association.

themselves (see Table 7.3). People who score high in public self-consciousness are very aware of themselves as a social object and think a lot about their public appearance. Those who score low in public self-consciousness are less aware of themselves as a social object and do not think as much about their public appearance (Buss, 1980; Carver & Scheier, 1985; Scheier & Carver, 1982b).

Public self-consciousness and self-monitoring share some similarities, and people who score high in self-monitoring tend to also score high in public self-consciousness (Tomarelli & Shaffer, 1985). The two constructs are not identical, however. Self-monitoring is a motivational orientation. High self-monitors strive to be the right person for the situation. Public self-consciousness is not a motivational orientation. People who score high in public self-consciousness don't necessarily try to be the right person for the situation; they simply are highly aware of themselves in social situations. Another key difference is that high self-monitors enjoy opportunities for social interactions that allow them to display their (self-perceived) acting skills, but people who are high in public self-consciousness do not necessarily seek out opportunities to "put on a show."

CREATING DESIRED IMPRESSIONS

What Impressions Do People Try to Create?

The number of impressions people try and create of themselves in the minds of others is almost limitless. At the same time, these impressions tend to fall

TABLE 7.4. Five Common Self-Presentational Strategies

Self-Presentational Strategy	Impression Sought	Prototypical Behaviors	Self-Presentational Risks
Ingratiation	Likable	Compliments, favors	Insincere, deceitful
Self-Promotion	Competent	Boasting, showing off	Conceited, fraudulent
Intimidation	Powerful, ruthless	Threats	Reviled, ineffectual
Exemplification	Virtuous, moral	Self-denial, martyrdom	Hypocritical, sanctimonious
Supplication	Helpless	Self-deprecation	Manipulative, demanding

into a smaller number of classes. Jones (1990; Jones & Pittman, 1982) distinguished five common self-presentational strategies (see Table 7.4).

Ingratiation

Ingratiation is probably the most familiar impression management strategy. The goal of ingratiation is to get the other person to like you. Since we tend to like people who agree with us, say nice things about us, do favors for us, and possess positive interpersonal qualities (e.g., warmth and kindness), it should come as no surprise that ingratiation can be accomplished through imitation, flattery, doing favors for someone, and displaying positive personal characteristics (Jones, 1990).

Ingratiation may backfire if it is too blatant. If your audience knows you are trying to manipulate them, they may come to distrust or dislike you. This problem is rarely acute. People want to believe they are likable and are liked by others. Consequently, they are disinclined to believe that a show of admiration or affection from another person is inauthentic or derives from an ulterior motive, even when such a motive is obvious to an impartial observer (Jones & Wortman, 1973). For this reason, ingratiation (if it is at least somewhat subtle) is often a highly successful self-presentational ploy.

Self-Promotion

Self-promotion is another common self-presentational strategy. Here we seek to convince people of our competence. This is not the same as ingratiation. With ingratiation, we are trying to get people to like us. With self-promotion, we are trying to get people to think we are capable, intelligent, or talented.

In many situations, it is beneficial to be seen as both likable and competent. In academia, for example, job offers are extended to applicants who are perceived as highly competent and pleasant to be around. Unfortunately, it is not always easy to simultaneously display both of these qualities. For example, modesty can be an effective form of ingratiation, but it rarely instills a perception of competence. Conversely, blowing one's own horn may convince people that you are competent, but it rarely leads to strong feelings of liking. For this reason, people are often forced to blend or balance these two self-presentational strategies. Many braggarts do not seem to understand this point, or else they are willing to sacrifice being liked for being considered competent.

Intimidation

Ingratiation and self-promotion are the most common self-presentational strategies. But there are others. Sometimes people want to be feared. This is intimidation. An employer, for example, might want to be viewed as tough, powerful, or ruthless. These views might serve to increase her workers' productivity and soften their demands for salary increases and other benefits. Former White House aide John Sununu once remarked that he didn't care if he was disliked as long as he was respected and feared.

Exemplification

Another form of self-presentation is exemplification. With exemplification, people attempt to create the impression that they are morally superior, virtuous, or righteous. Exemplification is often portrayed by exaggerating the degree to which one has suffered poor treatment at the hands of others or has endured excessive hardships.

Supplication

A final form of self-presentation is supplication. Supplication occurs when people publicly exaggerate their weaknesses and deficiencies. For example, in earlier times, women were expected to play helpless (rather than appear competent) in order to attract a mate. Men do this as well, of course, as when a husband claims to not know how to use the dishwasher or washing machine. The more general point is that people will sometimes exaggerate their incompetence and frailties if doing so gets them what they want. In extreme cases, these tendencies may underlie depression and other psychological difficulties (Gove, Hughes, & Geerken, 1980; Leary & Miller, 1986).

What Constitutes a Desirable Impression?

No matter which impressions people try to convey, these impressions will be effective only if they are accepted by others. Schlenker (1980, 1985; Schlenker & Weigold, 1989) has proposed that successful self-presentation always involves a trade-off between two considerations: (1) *beneficiality* (presenting the most advantageous image possible) and (2) *believability* (making sure the image you present is believable). To return to an earlier example, job candidates strive to be seen as competent and diligent. But if they go overboard and describe themselves in almost superhuman terms, they risk arousing suspicion and inadvertently creating a bad impression.

The Role of Accountability

Several factors influence the believability of a self-presentational claim (Schlenker, 1980, 1985; Schlenker & Weigold, 1989). These factors include the acting ability of the self-presenter (highly skilled actors can make more self-aggrandizing claims) and the ambiguity of the performance domain (the more ambiguous the domain, the more self-aggrandizing a person can be). Accountability is another important factor. People are accountable when their claims can be checked against relevant facts. It is one thing to boast that you are an expert at chess if no one is around to challenge you to a game; it's quite another if there is a chess board handy and another person waiting to test your claims. The broader point is that people's self-presentational claims should be more truthful when audiences are able to assess the veracity of these proclamations.

Schlenker (1975) tested this hypothesis. In this study, participants were led to believe that they would do very well or very poorly on an upcoming test. They were then given the chance to present themselves to other people who either would or would not learn how they did on the upcoming test.

Figure 7.1 displays some of the findings from this investigation. The figure shows that the only condition in which participants did *not* present themselves in highly positive terms (e.g., as having high ability at the task) was when they expected to do poorly *and* believed the audience would learn how they did. When participants believed the audience would *not* know how they performed, they publicly claimed high ability even though they privately doubted that their ability was high.

Audience Reactions to Self-Presentational Claims

Presumably, the participants in Schlenker's (1975) study modified their claims in the public performance condition because they feared being evaluated negatively if their positive claims were shown to be nothing more than hollow boasts. Schlenker and Leary (1982b) conducted a follow-up investigation to see whether such a pattern does, in fact, evoke condemnation. Using a simulational methodology, they had participants evaluate students whose claims about a test varied in their positivity. In some conditions, the participants were told whether these claims were consistent with the student's actual performance (e.g., the student said he had done well and participants knew he had or hadn't); in other conditions, the participants were given no information about how the student had actually performed (e.g., the student said he had done well and participants didn't know whether he had done well or not).

The upper portion of Figure 7.2 shows participants' evaluations (judgment of liking) for the student under the various conditions. It can be seen that participants generally admired congruence between public claims and performance. Students whose performance claims matched their performance were evaluated more positively than were students whose performance claims did not match their performance. Participants particularly disliked students who falsely claimed to have high ability.

The situation is different when it comes to competence ratings (see the bottom portion of Figure 7.2). Performance claims had little effect here. In-

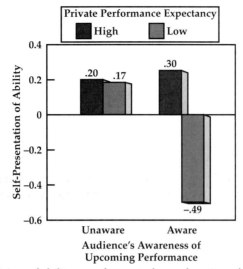

FIGURE 7.1. Public claims of ability on a future task as a function of private performance expectancy and public accountability. The data show that the only condition in which participants did not present themselves as highly competent was when they expected to do poorly *and* believed the audience would learn how they did.
(Adapted from Schlenker, 1975, *Journal of Personality and Social Psychology, 32,* 1030–1037. Copyright 1975. Adapted by permission of The American Psychological Association.)

stead, students who did well were judged to be more competent than students who did poorly, and it really didn't make much difference whether the students claimed that their ability was high or low.

There is one interesting qualification to this conclusion, however. Notice that in the unknown performance condition, students who claimed to have high ability were considered more competent than students who claimed to have medium or low ability. Apparently, in the absence of any contradictory information, people take a person's self-presentational claims at face value: If you say you have high ability, people assume you do have high ability. From a purely self-presentational point of view, then, the data suggest that it will often be to your advantage to present yourself as reasonably competent and able. Unless the audience knows you are deliberately misrepresenting yourself, they will give you the benefit of the doubt and believe your claims.

Self-Promotion versus Self-Protection

The preceding analysis assumes that the benefits of making a positive impression outweigh the costs of making a negative impression. This is not always the case, however. In politics, for example, the candidate who wins an election is often the one with the lowest negative rating rather than the one with the highest positive rating. This is why politicians often equivocate or refrain from taking stands; it is often more important to avoid alienating a block of voters than it is to favorably impress one.

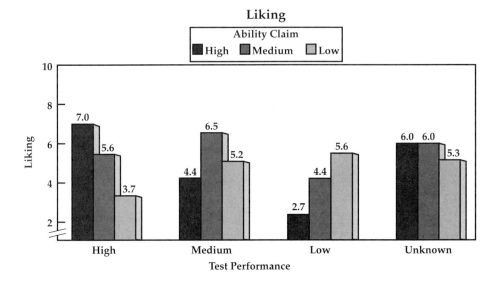

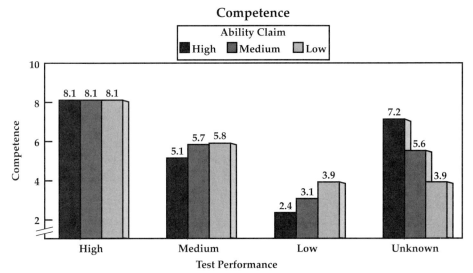

FIGURE 7.2. Audience evaluations of a person who claimed to have high, medium, or low ability. The top half of the figure shows that audiences generally admire congruence between claims and performance. The bottom half of the figure shows that audiences base their judgments of competence on test performance information if it is available, but on self-presentational claims of ability if test performance data are not available.

(Adapted from Schlenker & Leary, 1982, *Journal of Experimental Social Psychology, 18,* 89–104. Copyright 1982. Adapted by permission of Academic Press, Inc.)

Arkin (1981) has noted that individuals also differ in this regard. Some individuals are especially motivated to avoid making a negative public impression. Such individuals tend to "play it safe" in social situations, presenting themselves in relatively neutral, modest, or noncommittal terms. This protective self-presentational style rarely leads to highly favorable interpersonal reactions, but it also rarely leads to highly negative ones.

Several personality variables are thought to incorporate a heightened concern for public self-protection. These personality variables include shyness (Arkin, 1987), low self-esteem (Baumeister, Tice, & Hutton, 1989; Schlenker, Weigold, & Hallam, 1990), depression (Hill, Weary, & Williams, 1986), and social anxiety (Baumgardner & Brownlee, 1987). In rare cases, fear of negative public evaluations can lead to social isolation (e.g., agoraphobia) or excessively self-defeating behavior patterns (Baumeister & Scher, 1988; Schlenker, Weigold, & Doherty, 1991).

Identity Predicaments

Try as they might to avoid them, most people confront situations in which their public identity is threatened. Some of these situations are relatively minor—what the French call a contretemps: We slurp our soup, get caught singing aloud in the car, or otherwise embarrass ourselves by making a gaffe or faux pas. (Judging from how many terms they have, it seems that this happens a lot in France!) Ordinarily, people extricate themselves from such situations with only minimal effort.

Other identity predicaments are more consequential. One such situation occurs when people are seen as responsible for bringing about a negative event or outcome (Schlenker, 1982; Snyder, 1985; Weiner, Amirkhan, Folkes, & Verette, 1987). You might, for example, keep people waiting by coming late to an important meeting; forget your spouse's birthday; or get caught in a "white lie" regarding your absence from a social engagement.

Account Giving

People call upon a number of ingenious artifices to mitigate the negative implications of these identity predicaments (Schlenker, 1980, 1982; Scott & Lyman, 1960). Table 7.5 shows five such strategies in the context of an all-too-common situation that arises in my house—the case where one brother accuses the other of hitting him.

The first line of defense people use when confronting a threat to their identity is often a claim of innocence. Here, people completely deny responsibility for a negative outcome by asserting that they played no role in producing the event. If that doesn't work, they might attempt to reinterpret the event in positive terms. This is a common ploy among politicians, who habitually try and put a positive spin on a seemingly negative outcome. ("Yes, we came in third, but that's a victory for us. We were vastly outspent and had hoped only to finish fifth. So actually, we won.")

TABLE 7.5. Five Types of Account Giving

In this example, one brother has accused another of hitting him, and the parent is trying to find out what happened.

Actor's Account	Underlying Aim	Example
Claim of innocence	Deny responsibility	I didn't hit him. He fell on his face reaching for the remote control.
Reinterpretation	Alter the meaning of the event	I didn't *hit* him. I was patting him on the face for being such a good brother.
Justification	Legitimize behavior	Yes, I hit him, but he hit me first.
Excuse	Excuse behavior by reducing intentionality	Yes, I hit him, but it was an accident. I was trying to swat a fly when his face got in the way.
Apology	Accept responsibility and seek forgiveness	Yes, I hit him. I'm sorry. I won't do it again.

In the next two accounts (justification and excuse), people admit responsibility for a negative event, but they attempt to escape punishment by altering the audience's perception of the circumstances that surrounded the event. With justification, the person attempts to legitimize the negative behavior by making it seem warranted; with excuses, the person attempts to rationalize the behavior by making it seem accidental or inadvertent. Finally, when all else fails, one can admit full responsibility, apologize, and throw oneself on the mercy of the court.

The saga of former Senator Bob Packwood provides a current, real-world example of these strategies. Numerous women accused the senator of making unwanted sexual advances over a period of many years. Initially, Packwood denied the events took place (or at least remembering that they ever took place). He then attempted to reinterpret the events. "These were not lascivious sexual advances," he argued, "but friendly kisses, no different than when two men shake hands with one another." After it became evident that these kisses were *not* platonic in nature, Packwood attempted to justify his behavior. "I come from a different generation," he said, "one in which men were expected to be macho and force themselves on women." When this account failed to appease the nation, Packwood tried to excuse his behavior, claiming he was an alcoholic and wasn't responsible for his actions. Finally, in a last ditch attempt to salvage his career, Packwood accepted responsibility and apologized to any of the women he "may have offended." Alas, even this (belated) apology failed to mollify his critics, and Packwood was forced to resign from the U.S. Senate in disgrace. (But don't feel too sorry for him. He's now a well-paid lobbyist, peddling influence in the very Senate corridors he once walked.)

Preemptive Excuse Making

In the examples just discussed, account giving occurred after the behavior in question had taken place. People also engage in preemptive excuse making. ("I should probably warn you, I'm not very good at this sort of thing."). Sometimes this excuse making involves pointing out to others that we possess a characteristic that negatively affects performance. Consider, for example, a study by Baumgardner, Lake, and Arkin (1985). The participants in this study were led to believe that they would do poorly on an upcoming memory test. Half of the participants (those in the experimental condition) were further told that a bad mood could negatively affect their performance; other participants (those in the control condition) were given no information about whether mood affected performance. All participants then rated their moods before taking the test. The results showed that participants in the experimental group reported being in a worse mood than did control participants. Presumably, publicly claiming a bad mood allowed them to preemptively excuse their expected poor performance on the upcoming task.

Snyder and Smith (1982) have suggested that many clinically relevant conditions, such as depression, substance abuse, and anxiety, serve a similar function (see also, Hill, Weary, & Williams, 1986). An investigation by Smith, Snyder, and Perkins (1983) illustrates this effect. These investigators hypothesized that hypochondriacs use self-reports of physical illness and symptoms as a preemptive excuse-making strategy. To test this hypothesis, they led participants to believe that poor health either could or could not negatively affect one's performance on a test. All participants then filled out a questionnaire that assessed their health. Hypochondriacal participants complained more than nonhypochondriacal participants *only* when they believed that poor health could explain a poor performance. These and similar findings (e.g., Smith, Snyder, & Handelsman, 1982; Snyder, Smith, Augelli, & Ingram, 1985) suggest that some people use chronic symptoms to escape responsibility for an anticipated negative performance or outcome.

Self-Handicapping Behavior

In some situations, people may even go so far as to actively create an excuse for failure. This is self-handicapping behavior (Berglas & Jones, 1978; Jones & Berglas, 1978). As discussed in Chapter 3, self-handicapping behavior occurs when people create obstacles to their own success. Consider, for example, an athlete who fails to prepare properly for an upcoming competition. Lack of preparation makes success less likely, but it also gives the person a ready-made excuse for failure.

Self-handicapping was originally thought to be a private phenomenon that occurred independent of the social context (Berglas & Jones, 1978; Jones & Berglas, 1978). More recent research suggests, however, that self-handicapping is most apt to occur under public performance conditions (Arkin & Baumgardner, 1985). For example, Kolditz and Arkin (1982) found that only participants who believed their performance would be known to others actively handicapped themselves on an upcoming task.

As a self-presentational tactic, self-handicapping is a double-edged sword. On the one hand, creating an impediment to success makes it less likely that people will assume you have low ability if your performance is poor. At the same time, people disapprove of those who fail to maximize their potential by creating obstacles to their own success (Luginbuhl & Palmer, 1991; Rhodewalt, Sanbonmatsu, Tschanz, Feick, & Waller, 1995; Weiner, 1993). For these reasons, public self-handicapping would seem to be a last-ditch impression-management tactic, useful only when success is highly unlikely and being disliked is less aversive than being seen as incompetent.

Identity-Repair Tactics

Active attempts to repair a tarnished public identity are a final way of dealing with an identity predicament. An investigation by Baumeister and Jones (1978) illustrates this effect. The participants in this study were told that another person had negative information about some of their personality characteristics (e.g., the other person had learned the participant was somewhat insensitive or immature on the basis of some personality scales the participant had completed earlier). The participants were then given the opportunity to describe themselves on a questionnaire that was to be shown to the other person. Some of the items on the questionnaire were relevant to information the other person allegedly had; other items were new ones. Baumeister and Jones found that participants tried to compensate for an initially bad impression by elevating their ratings on the unrelated items. For example, if the other person thought the participant was insensitive, the participant described herself as very mature; conversely, if the other person thought the participant was immature, the participant described herself as very sensitive. In this manner, participants attempted to rebuild a favorable public image without contradicting the information the other person had about them (see also, Baumeister, 1982a).

An additional way to restore a negative public image is to point out a connection you share with another person who is somehow special or exemplary. For example, I might tell you I once had dinner with Bob Dylan's mother (now, aren't you impressed?!). Cialdini and his colleagues (Cialdini & De Nicholas, 1989; Cialdini & Richardson, 1980; Cialdini et al., 1976) call this strategy *basking in reflected glory*. In an early demonstration of this tendency, Cialdini et al. (1976) found that students were more likely to use the pronoun *we* when discussing a football game their university team had won ("We won!") than when talking about a game their team had lost ("They lost"). Moreover, this tendency was most apparent after students had first experienced a public failure, suggesting that it represented an attempt to restore a positive social identity.

SELF-PRESENTATIONS AND PRIVATE SELF-CONCEPTIONS

To this point we have focused exclusively on the *public* side of self-presentational behavior. But self-presentational behavior also has a very private side. Most obviously, how people think about themselves influences how they present themselves to others. For example, the person who thinks he is a connoisseur of fine wines is the one who is most apt to try and impress his friends with his knowledge of a fine Bordeaux. Although theorists disagree about just how strong this relation is, none deny that people's ideas about themselves are one factor that determines the public impressions they try and create.

More interesting, perhaps, is the manner in which public behavior influences private self-conceptions. People are audiences for their own behavior. Just as our behavior might convince others that we possess a given quality or attribute, so, too, might we convince ourselves. Research from a variety of different quarters supports this claim.

Role Internalization

> Everyone is always and everywhere, more or less consciously, playing a role. . . . It is in these roles that we know each other; it is in these roles that we know ourselves. (Park, 1926, p. 137)

We all play many roles in social life. We are children, siblings, and parents; students, friends, and employees; and so on. These roles figure prominently in the way people think about themselves. When asked to describe themselves, people often respond with reference to the social roles they play (e.g., I am a professor, a father, a husband).

This tendency to define ourselves in terms of our social roles is not the only link between social roles and self-conceptions, however. Each role we play carries with it a set of behavioral expectations (e.g., judges are expected to uphold the law) and assumptions about personal characteristics (firefighters are expected to be brave). These personal characteristics are of concern here. In the course of playing social roles, people often come to internalize role-relevant personal characteristics. They come to see themselves as possessing the qualities suggested by the roles they play (McCall & Simmons, 1966; Sarbin & Allen, 1968; Stryker & Statham, 1985).

Role internalization occurs for many reasons. According to the reflected appraisal process (see Chapter 3), social interaction is essential to the development of self-conceptions. People form views of themselves based on the (perceived) reactions of others. Before too long, the police officer who sees fear in the eyes of those she arrests comes to regard herself as strong and powerful. Self-perception processes (Bem, 1972) also operate here. People are often passive observers of their own behavior. A teacher who helps struggling students with their homework might reasonably infer that he is a caring, helpful person.

Of course, people gravitate toward roles that allow them to express their self-perceived qualities, so the road between self-conceptions and roles goes in both directions. But sometimes people's self-views are initially at odds with the roles they adopt. Imagine an employee who regards herself as a shy and deferent person. What becomes of such self-views when she is promoted to a managerial position? Very often, she comes to adopt the attitudes and beliefs that accompany her new title. She comes to think of herself as tough and demanding—because this is how she thinks others perceive her (reflected appraisals), because this is how she is behaving (self-perception), or because to do otherwise would create psychological inconsistency (or cognitive dissonance) between her actions and self-relevant beliefs.

In summary, people thrust into new social roles often come to view themselves as having the very qualities that the role demands. In effect, by playing the *role,* they become the *part.* This does not mean, however, that individuals passively adopt the labels implied by their social roles. Although the expectations of some roles are rigid and unyielding, most are pliant and allow room for interpretation. This allows people to bring their own distinctive stamp to the roles they play. The same is true in the theater. All actors who play Hamlet are obliged to recite his famous "To be or not to be" soliloquy, but each actor is allowed to emphasize different facets of the character. In more general terms, we can say that people both create and are created by the social roles they play (Backman & Secord, 1968; Stryker & Statham, 1985). This is why expectations for social roles can change over time. With every new role occupant, the role is reinvented (although the core expectations tend to remain relatively constant).

Carry-Over Effects in Self-Presentation

Further evidence that public behavior alters private self-conceptions comes from experimental research on carry-over effects in self-presentation. In these studies, participants are asked to present themselves in specified ways to an audience. For example, some participants might be asked to convince an interviewer that they are extraverted and sociable; other participants are asked to convince an interviewer that they are introverted and reserved. Later, as part of an ostensibly unrelated investigation, participants are asked to evaluate themselves along this dimension. The typical finding is that self-presentational behavior carries over to affect private self-conceptions. People who present themselves to others as outgoing and gregarious subsequently regard themselves as more sociable than do those who present themselves to others as shy and retiring (Fazio, Effrein, & Falender, 1981; Jones, Rhodewalt, Berglas, & Skelton, 1981; Rhodewalt & Agustsdottir, 1986; Schlenker, Dlugolecki, & Doherty, 1994; Tice, 1992).

Theoretical Explanations

At least two explanations for this carry-over effect can be distinguished. One possibility, which we'll call the *cognitive accessibility* model, traces the effect to a private, intrapsychic process. According to this account, presenting oneself to others in a certain manner (e.g., as sociable) activates or makes accessible certain behaviors and beliefs consistent with that presentation (e.g., times we have behaved sociably). When people are later asked whether they possess these qualities, the greater accessibility of these recently enacted behaviors leads them to believe that they do. Note how this explanation views public behavior as largely incidental to the carry-over effect. The effect reflects greater cognitive accessibility, which is a private, intrapersonal process, not a public, interpersonal one. Presumably, privately reviewing our past behaviors would produce a comparable effect.

Another explanation, which we'll call the *reflected appraisal* model, views public behavior as essential to the carry-over effect. This account builds on the notion that people's ideas about themselves are forged in the crucible of social life; that is, we come to know ourselves by imagining how we appear in the eyes of others. According to this view, public behavior is more consequential than private behavior. Publicly presenting ourselves to another and seeing ourselves through that person's eyes has a greater impact on the way we see ourselves than does private behavior.

Empirical Findings

In a test of these competing explanations, Tice (1992, Study 2) had participants portray themselves as either extraverted or introverted. Half of the participants did this publicly, in the context of a one-on-one interview; the other half did this privately, by anonymously completing a questionnaire while seated alone in a room. The accessibility model predicts carry-over effects in both conditions, whereas the reflected appraisal model predicts that carry-over effects will be especially strong in the public condition.

Figure 7.3 presents the results of this investigation. In support of the reflected appraisal model, it can be seen that carry-over effects were much stronger among participants who presented themselves to another person

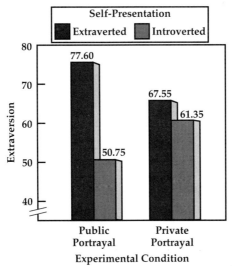

FIGURE 7.3. Self-ratings of extraversion after presenting oneself as extraverted or introverted under public or private conditions. The data show that carry-over effects were stronger when self-presentations were made in public than when they were made in private.
(Adapted from Tice, 1992, *Journal of Personality and Social Psychology, 63,* 435–451. Copyright 1992. Adapted by permission of The American Psychological Association.)

than among participants who merely completed a questionnaire under private and anonymous conditions (see also Schlenker, Dlugolecki, & Doherty, 1994). These results suggest that public behavior is uniquely potent when it comes to producing self-concept change. Perhaps this is why many self-help therapies (such as Alcoholic Anonymous) operate in a group setting, where people are asked to stand and publicly commit themselves to a course of action.

This does not mean, however, that public behavior drastically changes the way people think about themselves. Those who regard themselves as outgoing do not suddenly claim to be wallflowers after presenting themselves as socially awkward. Instead, the person's self-view simply shifts a bit in the direction implied by the behavior. Moreover, to be effective, the self-presentational behavior must be at least somewhat consistent with how the person already thinks of herself. Finally, the more certain you are of where you stand on a given trait, the less likely it is that public behavior will alter your self-view (Rhodewalt & Agustsdottir, 1986; Schlenker & Trudeau, 1990).

Symbolic Self-Completion Theory

The link between public behavior and private self-conceptions is also the focus of Wicklund and Gollwitzer's (1982) symbolic self-completion theory. Before turning to the specifics of this theory, let's review a point we made earlier in this chapter. When discussing the various functions of self-presentational behavior, we noted that people sometimes engage in self-presentational behavior in order to privately establish an identity for themselves (Schlenker, 1980). We called such behavior a form of self-construction (Baumeister, 1982b). With self-construction, people use audiences as a means to an end. They seek to convince others that they possess particular qualities because doing so helps them convince themselves.

Social Validation of Identities

Symbolic self-completion theory builds on this function of self-presentational behavior. The theory assumes that most important identities require social validation. Before individuals can fully lay claim to possessing an identity (and experience a sense of self-completion in the words of the theory), other people must recognize and acknowledge their right to claim the identity. As an example, consider what it means to be a physician. To be a physician in the truest sense of the word, other people need to acknowledge your expertise and consult you in matters of personal health. Otherwise, you are a physician in name only. This type of social validation is most obviously needed for the various social roles we play, but it is also true for many personal identities. It is difficult for a person to think he is popular if no one ever seeks his company.

Because most identities require social validation, people actively try and convince others that they are entitled to claim the identity. According to symbolic self-completion theory, one way they do this is by displaying socially defined, identity-relevant symbols (hence the name, *symbolic* self-completion). In the case of a physician, this might entail wearing a white lab coat, draping a stethoscope around one's neck, and learning to write a prescription in an unintelligible scrawl! When recognized by others, these identity-relevant symbols give people a sense of self-completion; they give people the sense that they truly possess an identity or characteristic.

Gollwitzer (1986) tested the hypothesis that symbolic activities are more effective in furnishing people with a sense of self-completion when these symbols are noticed and recognized by others. Medical students were given a number of problems frequently confronted by physicians and were asked to suggest some possible solutions (e.g., How would you deal with a diabetic patient who refuses to follow the diet you prescribe?). There were 45 such problems, and the students were told they could work on as many or as few as they wanted. Shortly after the students had begun working on the problems, a confederate appeared. In the social recognition condition, the confederate read through the problems the student had completed and then addressed the student as a physician. In the control condition, the confederate did not take notice of the completed problems and did not address the student as a physician. The results revealed that students in the social recognition condition chose to work on fewer problems than did those in the control condition. Presumably, this occurred because being addressed as a physician by another person provided these medical students with a sense of self-completion.

Seeking Symbolic Self-Completion

Symbolic self-completion theory makes another interesting prediction. Because self-completion is most apt to occur when self-symbolizing efforts are recognized by others, people committed to attaining an identity should be especially interested in finding an audience for their symbolic activities. This should occur, according to the theory, even though doing so might not be an effective self-presentational strategy at the time. Perhaps you have encountered such a situation when chatting with another person at a party. The person seems bent on convincing you that he possesses a certain characteristic (e.g., he is rich, scholarly, dashing, or athletic), even though doing so is making a bad impression. According to symbolic self-completion theory, this occurs because being liked is not the person's goal. Instead, the person is seeking social validation for a desired identity and is using the audience in a self-centered fashion to achieve this goal, without regard for what the social costs might be.

> Self-symbolizing individuals are not at all selective with respect to the people they address. Nor are they interested in engaging in meaningful interactions with the audience at their disposal. Rather, [they] appear to see in audiences nothing more than passive witnesses of identity-related goal striving. (Gollwitzer, 1986, p. 149)
>
> [They] focus only on demonstrating to others that they are in possession of an intended identity, irrespective of others' wishes, needs, or potential responses. (Gollwitzer, 1986, p. 154)

Gollwitzer (1986) reports a study relevant to this issue. The participants were students committed to various academic identities (e.g., mathematician, biologist). During the first part of the experiment, some of the students were led to focus on experiences that suggested they were not well suited for these professions; other students were led to focus on experiences that suggested they were well suited for these professions. These manipulations were intended to arouse different needs for self-completion in the two groups, with those in the negative feedback condition being more in need of self-completion than those in the positive feedback condition.

In the second part of the experiment, the students were told they would engage in a get-acquainted conversation with another student in which they would discuss various topics. Allegedly, the other student had already indicated a preference for certain topics by completing a questionnaire. These preferences revealed a strong *disinterest* in talking about topics related to the participants' interests (e.g., if the participant was a biology major, the other student indicated that he or she was not interested in discussing biology). Finally, the participants indicated which topics they wished to discuss. The results showed that participants whose needs for self-completion had been raised by the negative feedback were more eager to discuss topics related to their major, even though doing so risked making a bad impression with the other person. One explanation for this finding is that needs for self-completion were more powerful in this situation than were needs for social approval.[3]

SELF-PRESENTATION AND SOCIAL BEHAVIOR

The central theme of this chapter—that people actively monitor and regulate their public identities—is relevant to understanding a good deal of social behavior. It also has broad implications for psychological research. Most psychological research occurs in a social context. Experimenters and other participants are often present in the situation, and participants are almost always aware that their responses will be known to others. The public nature of the experimental setting raises the possibility that participants' behavior is driven by a deliberate (or unconscious) desire to manage a particular social identity, rather than by more spontaneous or private psychological processes.

Although this possibility has been known for some time (see, for example, Crowne & Marlowe, 1964; Edwards, 1957; Erdelyi, 1974), interest in this topic blossomed in the 1970s. At that time, many social psychological phenomena that had previously been understood in terms of intrapsychic processes were reinterpreted in terms of self-presentational behavior (Alexander & Knight, 1971). A paper by Tedeschi, Schlenker, and Bonoma (1971) illustrates this perspective.

---

[3]Symbolic self-completion theory shares some similarities with Swann's (1990) self-verification theory. As discussed earlier (e.g., Chapter 3), self-verification theory assumes that people seek social validation for their self-conceptions and strive to get others to see them as they see themselves. The key difference between Swann's approach and symbolic self-completion theory centers around whether the identity in question is desired from the person's point of view. Swann argues that people seek to verify desired and undesired identities, whereas symbolic self-completion theory maintains that people seek social validation only for desired identities.

These theorists were interested in the nature of cognitive dissonance effects (see Chapter 5). Numerous studies had shown that participants change their attitudes when they behave in ways that contradict their values or beliefs. According to cognitive dissonance theory, this occurs because people find inconsistency between beliefs and behavior to be aversive (Festinger, 1957). As a result, they change their attitudes in order to reduce this internal state of distress.

Tedeschi et al. (1971) offered a different explanation (see also, Schlenker, 1982). Instead of tracing attitude change to internal inconsistency, these theorists suggested that people publicly change their attitudes in order to avoid looking like a hypocrite to others. This perspective shifts the emphasis away from the mind's inability to tolerate psychological inconsistency toward a concern with maintaining a positive social identity. Baumeister (1982b) subsequently applied a similar analysis to a wide range of social behavior, including conformity, helping, aggression, and social facilitation effects. In each case, concerns with creating, maintaining, or restoring a positive public identity were invoked to explain effects previously attributed to more private, internal processes.

Self-Presentation and Self-Enhancement

Self-enhancement biases were another topic reinterpreted in self-presentational terms (Tetlock & Manstead, 1985). As noted throughout this book (see especially Chapter 3), people evaluate themselves in very positive terms (Taylor & Brown, 1988). If, for example, you ask people "How kind, thoughtful, intelligent, and attractive are you?" the majority will tell you that they are kinder, more thoughtful, more intelligent, and more attractive than most other people. People also accept greater responsibility for their successes than for their failures, a phenomenon known as the self-serving bias in causal attribution.

Originally, these biases were thought to stem from a motivated desire to feel good about oneself (a desire we have called the self-enhancement motive). In the mid-1970s, alternative explanations emphasizing cognitive processes were developed (see Chapter 5). Toward the end of the 1970s, self-presentational explanations were developed to explain these effects.

Weary Bradley (1978) was one of the first psychologists to articulate this point of view. Weary Bradley noted that in most investigations in which participants accepted greater responsibility for success than for failure, their performance and attributions were known to others. This raised the possibility that participants were *merely* claiming greater responsibility for success than for failure in a self-presentational attempt to convince the experimenter of their competence.

Despite its plausibility, research testing this claim has generally not found that attributions are more self-serving in public than in private. In fact, just the opposite is true: Self-serving attributions are generally stronger in private than in public (Greenberg, Pyszczynski, & Solomon, 1982; Smith & Whitehead, 1988; Weary, Harvey, Schweiger, Olson, Perloff, & Pritchard, 1982). This also occurs for other self-serving biases, such as the tendency to view oneself in more positive terms than one views most other people (Brown & Gallagher, 1992) and the tendency to preferentially seek positive self-relevant information (Brown, 1990).

Along with related work (Riess, Rosenfeld, Melburg, & Tedeschi, 1981; Greenwald & Breckler, 1985), these findings are inconsistent with the claim that self-serving biases reflect nothing more than public posturing. People genuinely believe their self-serving claims. At the same time, people are not oblivious to the impressions they are creating. They modify their public claims, but this modification is generally in the direction of greater public modesty, not greater self-aggrandizement.

An investigation by Frey (1978) reveals the nature of these effects. The participants in this study experienced either success or failure on an alleged intelligence test. Half the participants believed the experimenter was aware of how they had performed (public performance condition); the other half believed the experimenter was unaware of how they had performed (private performance condition). Participants then rated the test's validity under public conditions (they thought the experimenter would see their responses) or under private conditions (they thought the experimenter would not see their responses). In this fashion, Frey independently varied (1) whether the participants' performance was public or private, and (2) whether the participant's assessment of the test's validity was public or private.

The results of this investigation are shown in Figure 7.4. The right-hand side of panel 1 reveals that the self-serving tendency to disparage the validity of the test after failure was strongest when performances were public and evaluations were made in private. This corresponds to the situation in which others know how you have performed on a test and you privately explain

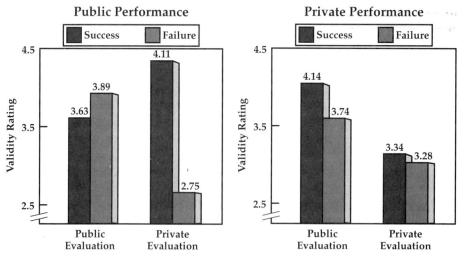

FIGURE 7.4. Evaluation of a test's validity under public performance conditions (panel 1) and private performance conditions (panel 2). The data show that the self-serving tendency to belittle the validity of a test after failure is most apparent when the performance is public and the evaluation is private (see right-hand side of panel 1).

(Adapted from Frey, 1978, *Journal of Experimental Social Psychology, 14,* 172–179. Copyright 1978. Adapted by permission of The American Psychological Association.)

your performance to yourself. Under such circumstances, people's judgments are most self-serving (see also, Greenberg & Pyszczynski, 1985).

The pattern displayed in Figure 7.4 is quite consistent with other evidence we have reviewed in this chapter. It shows again that public behavior is more compelling than is private behavior. In the privacy of their own homes or minds, people are free to try out different behaviors, opinions, and beliefs with little regard for the consequences. This is much less true in public. When we publicly state an opinion or behave in a given fashion, we are expected to be the person we claim to be (Goffman, 1959); and when we display our qualities to others or others are aware of our performance in some domain, we see ourselves reflected in their eyes and these qualities and outcomes assume greater psychological reality. For these reasons, social consensus and public validation bind and strengthen our self-views (Gollwitzer, 1986; Hardin & Higgins, 1996; Schlenker, 1986; Swann, 1990).

Sincerity and Authenticity versus Pretense and Deceit

The final topic we will consider in this chapter is the extent to which people's self-presentations faithfully reflect how they think about themselves. It is obvious that people sometimes misrepresent themselves (and some people do this more than others). But how prevalent is this dissimulation? Do the faces people wear in public generally mask how they privately see themselves, or is pretense and deceit the exception rather than the rule?

Trilling (1971, cited in Baumeister, 1986) notes that interest in this issue was particularly acute during the sixteenth century. At that time, Europeans became virtually obsessed with the disparity between public behavior and private beliefs. This is the era of Machiavelli and of Shakespeare, when the theater abounded with characters whose evil intentions were known to the audience but not to the other actors.

The notion that people cannot be trusted to be who they claim to be persists today. Avon ladies flatter, used car salesmen wheedle, and con men and bunco artists cheat and swindle by hiding their true intentions behind a facade of civility and sincerity. Clearly, people are not always what they seem to be.

But whether most people typically present a false front to others is questionable. After carefully considering this issue, several theorists (e.g., Buss & Briggs, 1984; Leary, 1993; Schlenker, 1986; Tesser & Moore, 1986) have concluded that, in their day-to-day lives, most people present a public identity that corresponds with how they privately view themselves. There are at least two reasons that this is so.

The Risks of Presenting a False Impression

Accountability is one relevant factor. Individuals who present an insincere or inauthentic impression to others run the risk of being exposed as a fake or liar if their attempts to create a false impression are discovered. Being regarded as a fake is not a valued identity. Consequently, this concern keeps people's self-presentations in line with their private self-views.

This concern is particularly acute when future interaction is anticipated or when audiences have knowledge of our past (Schlenker, 1980). These conditions generally exist with people with whom we spend most of our time—our friends, colleagues, and loved ones. It therefore follows that most of our self-presentations are genuine and authentic.

A Desire for Social Validation

The need for social validation is another factor that yields convergence between public behavior and private beliefs. People generally believe positive things about themselves (e.g., that they are intelligent, kind, and generous), and they want others to think they possess these qualities as well. Often, their public behavior is in service of this goal. They actively strive to bring their (self-perceived) positive qualities to the attention of others. For both of these reasons, then, it may generally be the case that "appearances made in the world are not veils but guides to the authentic self of the wearer" (Sennett, 1978, p. 153; cited in Tedeschi, 1986, p. 6).

CHAPTER SUMMARY

"All the world's a stage," Shakespeare tells us, "and all the men and women merely players. They have their exits and their entrances, and one man in his time plays many parts" (*As You Like It,* act II, scene VII). And so it is. Much of our time is spent in the company of others, and much of this time we are playing a role.

In this chapter we explored the connection between these public displays and private self-conceptions. We began by considering the nature of self-presentation—the functions it serves and the manner in which people go about trying to create an impression of themselves in the minds of other people. We also noted that people differ in regard to how actively they monitor and regulate their public behavior.

We then looked more closely at the kinds of impressions people typically try to convey. Here we noted that, in order to be successful, self-presentations must be believed. We then discussed various tactics individuals use when their self-presentational attempts go awry.

In the third part of the chapter, we examined the association between public behavior and the way people privately think about themselves. For a variety of reasons, people often come to view themselves in ways that are consistent with the persona they publicly display.

Finally, we explored the extent to which behavior in social situations can be accounted for in self-presentational terms, paying particular attention to self-enhancement biases and the extent to which people are genuine or insincere in their public behavior. We noted that people's positive self-presentations are generally believed, and that outright dissimulation and deceit are the exceptions rather than the rule in people's day-to-day lives.

- Self-presentation is any behavior that is intended to create, modify, or maintain an impression of ourselves in the minds of other people.
- Self-presentation serves three important functions: (1) it helps facilitate social interaction; (2) it enables individuals to attain material and social rewards; and (3) it helps people privately construct desired identities.

- There are three components of successful self-presentation. First, individuals must be motivated to create a particular impression in the minds of other people. Second, they must possess the cognitive ability to know what particular behaviors will give rise to that impression. Finally, they must be able (and willing) to enact the desired behaviors.
- People differ in their self-presentational styles. High self-monitors enjoy being different people in different situations, and they possess the cognitive and behavioral skills needed to adapt their behavior to match the requirements of the situation. In contrast, low self-monitors value congruence between their actions and their underlying attitudes and are less apt to tailor their behavior to match the requirements of the situation.
- Five common self-presentational strategies were identified: (1) *ingratiation* (we strive to get other people to like us); (2) *self-promotion* (we attempt to convince other people of our competence); (3) *intimidation* (we try to lead others to believe we are tough and ruthless); (4) *exemplification* (we aim to create the impression that we are morally virtuous and righteous); and (5) *supplication* (we seek to convince others that we are weak and helpless).
- Successful self-presentation involves a balance between beneficiality (presenting the most beneficial image for the situation) and believability (making sure the image is believed by others). Aware of these factors, individuals generally modify their behavior to match an audience's knowledge and expectations.
- Accountability is one factor that strongly influences believability. The more accountable people are for their actions, the more likely they are to present themselves in ways that match relevant facts.
- People call upon a variety of strategies when they fail to make a desired impression. These include accounts (people attempt to reinterpret, excuse, or justify their actions) and image repair tactics, such as compensating for a bad impression in one area by inflating the positivity of alternative qualities.
- People are often audiences for their own behavior. In seeking to convince others that they possess particular qualities, they often wind up convincing themselves. Sometimes this process is a rather passive one (as when the roles we play filter down to affect the way we see ourselves), and sometimes it is a very active one (as when we purposefully set out to create a private identity by publicly behaving in a particular fashion).
- People often seek to convince others that they possess positive qualities. For the most part, these attempts genuinely reflect the way people privately think about themselves, rather than representing insincere attempts to deceive or mislead.

For Further Reading

BAUMEISTER, R. F. (1986). (Ed.). *Public self and private life*. New York: Springer-Verlag.

GOFFMAN, E. (1959). *The presentation of self in everyday life*. New York: Anchor Books.

SCHLENKER, B. R. (1980). *Impression management: The self-concept, social identity, and interpersonal relationships*. Monterey, CA: Brooks/Cole.

SCHLENKER, B. R. (1985). (Ed.). *The self and social life*. New York: McGraw-Hill.

SNYDER, M. (1987). *Public appearances/private realities: The psychology of self-monitoring*. New York: W. H. Freeman and Co.

CHAPTER 8

Self-Esteem

Self-esteem is the panacea of modern life. It is seen as the key to financial success, health, and personal fulfillment, and it is regarded as the antidote to un-
derachievement, crime, and drug abuse (Branden, 1994; Mecca, Smelser, &
Vasconcellos, 1989). Self-esteem is also popular in academic circles. In the
fields of personality and social psychology, it has been implicated in models of
conformity (Brockner, 1984), attraction (Hatfield, 1965), persuasion (Rhodes &
Wood, 1992), cognitive dissonance (Steele, Spencer, & Lynch, 1993), subjective
well-being (Diener & Diener, 1995), and social comparison processes (Aspinwall & Taylor, 1993; Gibbons & Gerrard, 1991; Wood, Giordano-Beech, Taylor,
Michela, & Gaus, 1994), just to name a few.

The widespread appeal of self-esteem attests to its importance, but this
popularity has had an undesirable consequence. Self-esteem is currently
spread so thin that it is difficult to know just what it is. It is used as a predictor
variable (some researchers study whether high self-esteem people think, feel,
and behave differently than low self-esteem people), an outcome variable
(some researchers study how various experiences affect the way people feel
about themselves), and a mediating variable (the need for high self-esteem is
presumed to motivate a wide variety of psychological processes). In short,
self-esteem has become a protean concept—so capable of changing form that
its value is in risk of being undermined.

In this chapter we will critically review the nature, origins, and functions
of self-esteem. The chapter begins by considering the nature of self-esteem.
Here we ask: What do we mean by the term "self-esteem," and what characteristics are associated with high self-esteem and with low self-esteem? Next
we examine the genesis of self-esteem. Our concern here will be with understanding what experiences give rise to high self-esteem and to low self-esteem.
We will then consider when self-esteem is important. Here we will ask: What
difference does it make whether a person has high self-esteem or low self-
esteem? Finally, we will consider some unresolved controversies in the field.

A central issue guiding our discussion will involve the nature of self-
esteem itself. Some psychologists (myself included) adopt an affective approach to understanding the nature of self-esteem. This approach asserts that

self-esteem is a *feeling* of affection for oneself that develops largely through visceral or irrational processes (irrational in this case means "not based in logic"). Other psychologists take a more cognitive view. They believe that self-esteem is a judgment people make about themselves. This judgment is largely based on an assessment of one's various abilities and attributes. Whereas the former approach likens self-esteem to feelings of love (which typically are not rational or logical), the latter likens self-esteem to a decision people make about their worth and value as a person. Although not all theories fall neatly into one camp or the other, keeping this affect–cognition distinction in mind will help you organize the material that follows.

One more word before we begin. Self-esteem has been implicated in many psychological phenomena of a clinical nature (e.g., anxiety, depression, eating disorders, and substance abuse) (for a review, see Robson, 1988). Issues of this nature will be discussed in Chapter 9. The current chapter will focus on self-esteem within *normal* (i.e., nonclinical) populations.

WHAT IS SELF-ESTEEM?

Self-esteem is part of everyday language, and at an intuitive level, everyone seems to know what self-esteem "is." It may surprise you then to know that there is less than perfect agreement within the psychological literature. Part of the problem is that the term is used in three different ways.

Three Meanings of Self-Esteem

Global Self-Esteem

Most often, the term "self-esteem" is used to refer to a personality variable that captures the way people generally feel about themselves. Researchers call this form of self-esteem *global* self-esteem or *trait* self-esteem, as it is relatively enduring, both across time and situations. In this book, I have used the term *self-esteem* (without any qualifiers) when referring to this variable.

Attempts to define self-esteem have ranged from an emphasis on primitive libidinal impulses (Kernberg, 1975), to the perception that one is a valuable member of a meaningful universe (Solomon, Greenberg, & Pyszczynski, 1991). I take a decidedly less exotic approach and define self-esteem in terms of feelings of affection for oneself (Brown, 1993; Brown & Dutton, 1995b). Within normal populations, high self-esteem is characterized by a general fondness or love for oneself; low self-esteem is characterized by mildly positive or ambivalent feelings toward oneself. In extreme cases, low self-esteem people hate themselves, but this kind of self-loathing occurs in clinical populations, not in normal populations (Baumeister, Tice, & Hutton, 1989).

Self-Evaluations

The term self-esteem is also used to refer to the way people evaluate their various abilities and attributes. For example, a person who doubts his ability in school is sometimes said to have low academic self-esteem, and a person who thinks she is popular and well liked is said to have high social self-esteem. In a similar vein, people speak of having high self-esteem at work or low self-esteem in sports. The terms self-confidence and self-efficacy have also been used to refer to these beliefs, and many people equate self-confidence with self-esteem. I prefer to call these beliefs *self-evaluations* or *self-appraisals*, as they refer to the way people evaluate or appraise their abilities and personality characteristics.

Self-esteem and self-evaluations are related—people with high self-esteem think they have many more positive qualities than do people with low self-esteem—but they are not the same thing. A person who lacks confidence in school might still like himself a lot. Conversely, a person who thinks she is attractive and popular might not feel good about herself at all. Unfortunately, psychologists don't always make this distinction, often using the terms self-esteem and self-evaluations interchangeably.

The causal association between self-esteem and self-evaluations is also unclear. Cognitive models of self-esteem assume a *bottom-up* process (e.g., Harter, 1986; Marsh, 1990; Pelham & Swann, 1989). They assume that positive evaluations of self in particular domains give rise to high self-esteem. I call this a bottom-up process because it assumes that global self-esteem is built up from these more specific evaluations. Affective models of self-esteem assume a *top-down* process (Brown, 1993; Brown, Dutton, & Cook, 1997). These models assume that the causal arrow goes from global self-esteem to specific self-evaluations: Liking oneself in a general way leads people to believe they have many positive qualities. Later in this chapter we will examine support for these claims.

Feelings of Self-Worth

Finally, the term self-esteem is used to refer to rather momentary emotional states, particularly those that arise from a positive or negative outcome. This is what people mean when they speak of experiences that bolster their self-esteem or threaten their self-esteem. For example, a person might say her self-esteem was sky-high after getting a big promotion, or a person might say his self-esteem was really low after a divorce. Following William James (1890), we will refer to these emotions as *self-feelings* or as *feelings of self-worth*. Feeling proud or pleased with ourselves (on the positive side), or humiliated and ashamed of ourselves (on the negative side) are examples of what we mean by feelings of self-worth.

Because they involve feelings toward oneself, some researchers (e.g., Butler, Hokanson, & Flynn, 1994; Leary, Tambor, Terdal, & Downs, 1995) use the term *state* self-esteem to refer to the emotions we are calling feelings of self-worth, and *trait* self-esteem to refer to the way people generally feel about themselves. These terms connote an equivalency between the two phenomena, implying that the essential difference is simply that global self-esteem is persistent, while feelings of self-worth are temporary.

The trait–state assumption has important consequences. First, it suggests that feeling proud of oneself is akin to having high self-esteem and that feeling ashamed of oneself is akin to having low self-esteem. This, in turn, leads investigators to assume that an analogue of high self-esteem or low self-esteem can be created by temporarily leading people to feel good or bad about themselves (e.g., Greenberg et al., 1992; Heatherton & Polivy, 1991; Leary et al., 1995). This is typically accomplished by giving people positive or negative self-relevant feedback (e.g., telling people they are high or low in some ability). Other researchers disagree with this approach, arguing that these manipulations do not provide a suitable analogue of high self-esteem or low self-esteem (Brown & Dutton, 1995b; Wells & Marwell, 1976).

One more point about feelings of self-worth. Several times in this book we have spoken of a basic human need to feel good about ourselves. Within psychology, this is called the self-enhancement motive. This term refers to the fact that people are motivated to have high feelings of self-worth. People want to feel proud of themselves rather than ashamed of themselves. They strive to maximize and protect their feelings of self-worth. The way people go about trying to meet this need differs across time, cultures, and subcultures, but the need is universal. The conclusion was perhaps best stated by the Pulitzer Prize-winning anthropologist Ernest Becker, who wrote:

> The fundamental datum for our science is a fact that at first seems banal, or irrelevant: it is the fact that—as far as we can tell—*all organisms like to "feel good" about themselves.* . . . Thus in the most brief and direct manner, we have a *law* of human development. . . . (Becker, 1968, p. 328)

Interestingly, there is no consensus on why people are motivated to have positive feelings of self-worth. Some believe these feelings are intrinsically satisfying; as James (1890) put it, "direct and elementary endowments of our nature" (1890, p. 306). Others (Gergen, 1971; Kaplan, 1975) believe that positive feelings of self-worth are preferred simply because they have come to be associated with positive outcomes, such as praise from others or success. Still others believe that feelings of self-worth are desired because they imbue life with meaning and make one's inevitable death more tolerable (Greenberg et al., 1992). Whatever the source of this need may be, a desire to promote, maintain, and protect positive feelings of self-worth has been assumed to motivate a wide range of human behavior. This includes behavior in achievement settings (Covington & Berry, 1976), social settings (Tesser, 1988), and health settings (Ditto & Lopez, 1992).

Measuring Self-Esteem

Now that we have some idea of what we mean by self-esteem, we can look at how it is measured. You probably know someone who you think has low self-esteem. Your intuitions are probably based on what the person says and the things the person does. Psychologists also rely on these cues to measure self-esteem (Demo, 1985).

TABLE 8.1. The Rosenberg (1965) Self-Esteem Scale

Indicate your level of agreement with each of the following statements by circling one number on the rating scale that best describes the way you feel about yourself. Use the following scale as your guide.

	0 Strongly Disagree	1 Disagree	2 Agree	3 Strongly Agree
1. At times I think I am no good at all.	0	1	2	3
2. I take a positive view of myself.	0	1	2	3
3. All in all, I am inclined to feel that I am a failure.	0	1	2	3
4. I wish I could have more respect for myself.	0	1	2	3
5. I certainly feel useless at times.	0	1	2	3
6. I feel that I am a person of worth, at least on an equal plane with others.	0	1	2	3
7. On the whole, I am satisfied with myself.	0	1	2	3
8. I feel I do not have much to be proud of.	0	1	2	3
9. I feel that I have a number of good qualities.	0	1	2	3
10. I am able to do things as well as most other people.	0	1	2	3

Note: To determine your score, first reverse the scoring for the five negatively worded items (1, 3, 4, 5, and 8) as follows: 0 = 3, 1 = 2, 2 = 1, 3 = 0. Then, add up your scores across the 10 items. Your total score should fall between 0 and 30. Higher numbers indicate higher self-esteem.
Source: Rosenberg, 1965, *Society and the Adolescent Self-image.* Princeton, NJ: Princeton University Press. Copyright 1965. Adapted by permission of the Princeton University Press.

Self-Report Measures of Self-Esteem

The Rosenberg (1965) self-esteem scale is one of the most widely used instruments for measuring self-esteem in research settings. This scale, which is shown in Table 8.1, was developed to assess global self-esteem. It focuses on people's general feelings toward themselves, without referring to any specific quality or attribute. Half of the items are worded in a positive direction ("On the whole, I am satisfied with myself"); the other half are worded in a negative direction ("All in all, I am inclined to feel that I am a failure").

Table 8.2 presents another widely used measure of self-esteem, the Texas Social Behavior Inventory (Helmreich & Stapp, 1974). This scale is often used as a measure of global self-esteem, but it actually measures how comfortable and competent a person feels in social situations. Scores on this scale are related to scores on the Rosenberg self-esteem scale ($r = .65$ or so), but the two scales do not measure the same thing. A person can be uncomfortable in social situations and still like himself in general. Alternatively, a person can be relaxed and outgoing with others but not like herself in general. For this reason, the Rosenberg scale is the appropriate one to use for measuring global self-esteem.

TABLE 8.2. The Texas Social Behavior Inventory

Indicate your level of agreement with each of the following statements by circling one number on the rating scale that best describes the way you feel about yourself. Use the following scale as your guide.

1 = not at all characteristic of me
2 = not very characteristic of me
3 = slightly characteristic of me
4 = fairly characteristic of me
5 = very much characteristic of me

1. I am not likely to speak to people until they speak to me.	(1)	2	3	4	5
2. I would describe myself as self-confident.	1	2	3	4	(5)
3. I feel confident of my appearance.	1	2	3	(4)	5
4. I am a good mixer.	1	2	3	(4)	5
5. When in a group of people, I have trouble thinking of the right things to say.	(1)	2	3	4	5
6. When in a group of people, I usually do what the others want rather than make my own suggestions.	(1)	2	3	4	5
7. When I'm in a disagreement with other people, my opinion usually prevails.	1	2	(3)	4	5
8. I would describe myself as one who attempts to master situations.	1	2	3	4	(5)
9. Other people look up to me.	1	2	3	(4)	5
10. I enjoy social gatherings just to be with people.	1	2	3	4	(5)
11. I make a point of looking other people in the eye.	1	2	(3)	4	5
12. I cannot seem to get others to notice me.	1	(2)	3	4	5
13. I would rather not have much responsibility for other people.	1	(2)	3	4	5
14. I feel comfortable being approached by someone in a position of authority over me.	1	2	3	4	(5)
15. I would describe myself as indecisive.	1	2	(3)	4	5
16. I have no doubts about my social competence.	1	2	3	(4)	5

Note: To determine your score, first reverse the scoring for the negatively worded items (numbers 1, 5, 6, 12, 13, and 15) as follows: 1 = 5, 2 = 4, 3= 3, 4 = 2, and 5 = 1). Then, add up your scores for the 16 items. Your total score should fall between 0 and 80. Higher numbers indicate higher self-esteem.
Source: Helmreich & Stapp, 1974, *Bulletin of the Psychonomic Society*, 4, 473–475. Copyright 1974. Adapted by permission of the Psychonomic Society.

Many other self-report instruments are available (Blascovich & Tomaka, 1990). Based on theoretical work by Shavelson, Hubner, and Stanton (1976; see also, Byrne & Shavelson, 1996), Marsh (1990) developed an extensive measure to assess the way people evaluate themselves in various domains of life. Included are items pertaining to one's (perceived) physical abilities, appearance, problem-solving abilities, social skills, peer relationships, opposite-sex relationships, and emotional stability. Harter (1986) has developed a similar scale for children, with subscales assessing (perceived) scholastic competence, athletic competence, social acceptance, physical appearance, and behavioral conduct. Scales of this type focus on the second meaning of self-esteem we discussed earlier: They assume that people have different self-esteem levels for different attributes, situations, and activities. Typically, these scales also include a separate subscale to measure global self-esteem.

Problems with Self-Report Measures

Self-report measures of self-esteem are widely used and possess a high degree of theoretical and predictive validity (Rosenberg, 1979; Wells & Marwell, 1975). But they are not without problems. For example, Baumeister, Tice, and Hutton (1989) have argued that scores on self-report measures of self-esteem are compromised by self-presentational concerns. Rather than rating how they really feel about themselves, people may distort their responses to create a particular impression in the minds of other people. From this perspective, a high self-esteem score represents an assertive, interpersonal style, in which one is willing to present oneself to others in a highly positive manner, and a low self-esteem score reflects a modest interpersonal style, in which one is reluctant to present oneself in a highly positive matter (see also, Arkin, 1981; Hill, Weary, & Williams, 1986). These self-presentational patterns are assumed to be imperfectly correlated with how people privately feel about themselves.

Defensive processes also influence self-report measures of self-esteem (Weinberger, 1990; Westen 1990b). People who score high on self-report measures of self-esteem may be fooling themselves by defensively claiming to feel better about themselves than they really do. On the other hand, some forms of self-deception may actually be healthy and play an integral role in psychological adjustment (Paulhus & Reid, 1991; Sackeim, 1993; Taylor & Brown, 1988, 1994). We will look at this issue more closely in Chapter 10.

Greenwald and Banaji (1995) have suggested adapting methods from cognitive psychology to overcome these potential limitations of self-report measures. These indirect or implicit measures of self-esteem (e.g., response latencies, recognition thresholds) would be less transparent than self-report questionnaires, in that people would be unaware that their self-esteem was being assessed. Although such measures have yet to be developed, it is likely that they will be available in the years to come.

THE NATURE AND ORIGINS OF SELF-ESTEEM

Having defined our terms and discussed ways to measure self-esteem, let's look more closely at the nature of self-esteem. What aspects make up high self-esteem? And where does high self-esteem come from? Several different models have been developed to address these questions.

Affective Models of Self-Esteem

Two Components of Self-Esteem

Affective models of self-esteem assume that self-esteem develops at an early age and is characterized by two types of feelings. One of these feelings (which we will call feelings of *belonging*) is rooted in social experiences; the other (which we will call feelings of *mastery*) is somewhat more personal in nature.

Belonging is the feeling that one is unconditionally loved and valued, not for any particular quality or reason but simply for *who* one is. A sense of belonging gives people a secure base in life. It gives them the feeling that no matter what happens, they are valued and respected. Some years ago, the American psychologist Carl Rogers highlighted this aspect of self-esteem when he discussed people's need for unconditional positive regard (Rogers, 1951; Rogers & Dymond, 1954).

Feelings of belonging are a bit different than reflected appraisals. As discussed in Chapter 3, reflected appraisals represent our conscious perception of how we are viewed by others. If I think other people think I'm funny, then I think I'm witty. Feelings of belonging do not occur at a conscious level. They are more intuitive. Belonging is the *feeling* that we are loved and the security that feeling brings.

The second important aspect of self-esteem is a sense of mastery. Mastery involves the perception that one is having an impact on the world—not necessarily in any large-scale sense, but in one's day-to-day life. Mastery is not the same as perceived competence, although some writers (e.g., Tafarodi & Swann, 1995) use the two terms interchangeably. We needn't think we are an accomplished pianist or an "A" student to develop a sense of mastery. Rather, mastery is the feeling we get when we are immersed in an activity or are striving to overcome some obstacle (e.g., Brissett, 1972; Csikszentmihalyi, 1975; deCharms, 1968; Deci & Ryan, 1995; Erikson, 1963; Franks & Marolla, 1976; Gecas & Schwalbe, 1993; White, 1959).

One way to convey the difference between mastery and perceived competence is to consider a child who is making mud pies. The *squishing,* the feeling of the mud between the child's fingers and the sheer joy that comes from that experience creates feelings of mastery. These feelings promote high self-esteem. But this is not the same as thinking one is a "good mud pie maker." The *squish* is process oriented—it is joy in creating and manipulating; the evaluation is outcome oriented—it is a judgment of whether one is good at something. The affective model maintains that only the former is relevant to the genesis of self-esteem.

The Development of Self-Esteem

Affective models of self-esteem assume that feelings of belonging and mastery normally develop early in life. Erik Erikson's model of psychosocial development (discussed in Chapter 4) provides a useful springboard for considering how these feelings arise. According to Erikson, the first developmental task infants face is establishing feelings of trust with their caregivers. These feelings of trust, which are thought to develop during the first year of life, correspond to the feelings of belonging we have said are integral to a sense of high self-esteem.

The next stage Erikson describes is the "autonomy versus shame and doubt" stage. This stage involves the development of feelings of mastery. Children develop feelings of mastery when they are encouraged to explore, create, and modify their world (e.g., to build things, to draw, or paint); they may fail to develop these feelings when their parents subvert, ridicule, or are overly critical of their efforts (Stipek, Recchia, & McClintic, 1992).

Attachment Bonds and Self-Esteem

The caregiver–child relationship plays a key role in Erikson's theory. This relationship also plays a central role in other theories of self-esteem development (e.g., Baumeister & Leary, 1995; Bowlby, 1969; Epstein, 1980; Sullivan, 1953). Bowlby's (1969) attachment theory is particularly relevant to the present discussion. Bowlby was interested in understanding the basis and functions of attachment bonds. He noted that in humans, as well as in other animals, infants bond with their caregivers (particularly with their mothers). Why? What function do these mother–child bonds serve?

Bowlby surmised that the attachment relationship serves a paradoxical function. By becoming securely attached, the child feels safe enough to leave the mother and explore the environment. In this sense, Bowlby believed that a feeling of belonging (i.e., a secure attachment) facilitates a sense of mastery (willingness to explore the environment).

> When individuals of any age are feeling secure they are likely to explore away from their attachment figure. When alarmed, anxious, tired, or unwell they feel an urge toward proximity. Thus, we see the typical pattern of interaction between child and parent known as exploration from a secure base. Provided the parent is known to be accessible and will be responsive when called upon, a healthy child feels secure enough to explore. (Bowlby, 1979, p. 3)

A series of studies using a procedure known as the *strange situation* (Ainsworth, Blehar, Waters, & Wall, 1978) has documented these effects. In this situation, a young child (typically around 14 months of age) is brought into a psychological laboratory with his or her mother. The room contains a number of interesting toys and objects that most children enjoy looking at and playing with. The extent to which the child initially explores the objects in the room is one variable of interest.

Another variable of interest is how the child reacts to separation from the mother. After being together for a few minutes, the mother unexpectedly leaves the child alone with a stranger. The child's emotional reaction to the mother's departure is noted. Several minutes later, the mother returns and the researcher notes the child's emotional and behavioral reaction to the mother's return. In this manner, the strange situation measures the extent to which a child uses the mother as a secure base from which to explore the environment and as a source of comfort in times of stress.

In studies using this procedure, three different attachment styles have been identified.

1. Approximately 60 percent of American infants are classified as being securely attached. Securely attached infants show a healthy balance between closeness to the mother and independence. During the first phase of the procedure, they readily separate to explore the environment. Although

they may be distressed when their mother leaves, they are eager to see her when she returns and enjoy drawing her into their play and sharing their discoveries with her.

2. Approximately 15 percent of American infants are classified as anxious/ambivalent. These children have difficulty separating during the first phase of the procedure. They are unwilling or afraid to explore the environment. When their mother leaves, they become very distressed and upset. Although they are somewhat comforted when she returns, they cling to her and show other signs of insecure dependence (e.g., they continue whining).

3. Approximately 25 percent of American infants are classified as avoidant children. These children tend to avoid or ignore their mothers altogether. They appear to have little difficulty separating during the first phase of the procedure, and they outwardly exhibit few signs of distress when their mother leaves. Furthermore, they show little interest in her when she returns, preferring instead to play alone rather than to interact with her. Importantly, the indifference these infants display toward their mothers is contradicted by an inner sense of anxiety and distress. Rather than being secure and independent, avoidant children are evading intimacy and closeness with their mothers.

The roots of self-esteem would seem to lie within these different attachment styles. The avoidant infants may develop feelings of mastery (because they willingly explore the environment), but they lack a sense of belonging. They do not exhibit a strong emotional bond to their mother. The anxious/insecure infants may display a sense of belonging, but they are unlikely to develop feelings of mastery. They are easily distressed and are unwilling to meet the world head on. Only the securely attached children exhibit both a strong sense of belonging and a strong sense of mastery. It is these children, then, who are most apt to develop high self-esteem.

Research supports this conjecture. Different attachment styles in infancy predict self-esteem in preschool and kindergarten (Cassidy, 1990; Sroufe, 1983), with securely attached children showing the highest self-esteem. Similar patterns have been found with adolescents and young adults (Bartholomew & Horowitz, 1991; Brennan & Morris, 1997; Collins & Read, 1990; Feeney & Noller, 1990; Griffin & Bartholomew, 1994).

Bowlby (1973) invokes the concept of an "internal working model" to explain why the early attachment relationship has an enduring effect. As children mature, they develop a cognitive representation or working model of the attachment relationship. A child who develops a secure attachment relationship comes to believe she is essentially good and worthy of love; a child who develops an insecure attachment comes to believe she is bad and unworthy of love. These beliefs generalize to other people and situations and form the basis for the development of self-esteem.

> An unwanted child is likely not only to feel unwanted by his parents but to believe that he is essentially unwantable, namely unwanted by anyone.

Conversely, a much-loved child may grow up to be not only confident of his parents' affection but confident that everyone else will find him lovable too. Though logically indefensible, these crude overgeneralizations are nonetheless the rule. Once adapted, moreover, and woven into the fabric of working models, they are apt henceforward never to be seriously questioned. (Bowlby, 1973, pp. 204–205)

Summary

Affective approaches to understanding self-esteem make the following points: (1) unconditional feelings of belonging and a sense of mastery comprise the essence of high self-esteem, and (2) these feelings typically develop early in life, largely as a result of parent–child interactions. This emphasis on early childhood experiences does not mean that self-esteem can never change. It simply means that early experiences lay the foundation for high self-esteem or low self-esteem. Later experiences in life may also affect self-esteem, although none is apt to be as important as the parent–child relationship.

One reason that latter experiences are less consequential is that they are always viewed through the prism or schema that is established earlier. Once high or low self-esteem develops, it guides the way we view ourselves, other people, and the experiences and events we confront. Often, this guiding process occurs at an automatic or preconscious level (Epstein, 1990), making it difficult to detect and even harder to correct. For this reason, self-esteem tends to persist.

Cognitive Models of Self-Esteem

Cognitive models offer a different perspective on the nature and origins of self-esteem. They view self-esteem as a more or less conscious decision people make regarding their worth as a person. If you think you possess many socially desirable qualities, then you will have high self-esteem. In terms of the three meanings of self-esteem we discussed earlier, cognitive models emphasize that how we evaluate ourselves in various domains determines our overall level of self-esteem.

Three Cognitive Models of Self-Esteem Formation

The simplest of these models assumes that self-esteem is the aggregate of the way people evaluate their specific qualities and attributes. The top portion of Table 8.3 illustrates this *add-em-up* approach. Here we have asked two (imaginary) people to indicate how attractive, intelligent, well liked, and athletic they think they are using seven-point scales (e.g., 1 = not at all attractive; 7 = very attractive). Person A thinks he is quite attractive, not terribly intelligent, reasonably well liked, and very athletic; Person B thinks he is not terribly attractive, very intelligent, moderately well liked, and not very athletic.

According to the *add-em-up* approach, we would simply add up these various scores to determine the person's overall level of self-esteem. In this example, we would predict that Person A has higher self-esteem than Person B. This is because Person A evaluates himself more positively than does Person B.

TABLE 8.3. Three Cognitive Models of Self-Esteem Formation

Add-em-up Model

	Attractive	Intelligent	Well Liked	Athletic	Self-Esteem
Person A	5	2	5	7	19
Person B	3	7	4	3	17

The add-em-up model assumes that global self-esteem represents the sum of the way people evaluate their more specific qualities. To test this approach, we would simply add up the four self-evaluation scores to determine each person's self-esteem score. Using this approach, we would predict that Person A has higher self-esteem than Person B.

Weight-em-by-Importance Model

	Attractive	Intelligent	Well Liked	Athletic	Self-Esteem
Person A	5 * (2)	2 * (3)	5 * (4)	7 * (1)	43
Person B	3 * (1)	7 * (4)	4 * (3)	3 * (2)	49

The weight-em-by-importance model assumes that self-esteem depends not only on how you evaluate yourself in specific domains but also on how important you think it is to be good in those domains. To test the model, we have each person rank the four attributes in terms of their personal importance (1 = least important; 4 = most important). We then multiply each self-evaluation score by its corresponding importance rating (in parentheses) and add the products. Using this approach, we would predict that Person B has higher self-esteem than Person A. This is because Person B values what he thinks he is good at more than Person A.

Self-Ideal Model

	Attractive	Intelligent	Well Liked	Athletic	Self-Esteem
Person A	5 – (7)	2 – (6)	5 – (7)	7 – (6)	–7
Person B	3 – (3)	7 – (4)	4 – (7)	3 – (2)	+1

The self-ideal model assumes that self-esteem depends on the difference between who we think we are now and who we would ideally like to be. To test the model, we have each person indicate how attractive, intelligent, well liked, and athletic they would like to be (1 = not at all; 7 = very). We then subtract these ideal self-ratings (in parentheses) from their corresponding self-evaluation score and then sum the differences. Using this approach, we would predict that Person B has higher self-esteem than Person A.

Note: For each example, two (hypothetical) people have indicated how attractive, intelligent, well liked, and athletic they think they are (1 = not at all; 7 = very).

One problem with this method (which you may have already identified) is that it ignores the fact that different things are important to different people. If athletic ability is unimportant to Person A, and intellectual ability is extremely important to Person B, then Person B may feel better about himself than Person A.

The idea that self-esteem depends on what you think about yourself in domains of high personal importance is reminiscent of James's (1890) claim that "self-esteem = success/pretensions." In Chapter 2 we noted that James uses the word *pretensions* in two ways. Sometimes it refers to what we value in life or to what we think is important. Here James is saying that outcomes in domains of high personal importance have a greater effect on self-esteem than do outcomes in domains of low personal importance. James also uses pretensions to refer to a person's level of aspiration. In this case, he is saying that we feel good about ourselves when our outcomes exceed our personal standards and bad about ourselves when our outcomes fall short of our personal standards.

Of the two meanings, most contemporary psychologists have focused on the one that emphasizes the importance of different attributes for self-esteem. Morris Rosenberg stated the case for the "importance of different attributes" as follows:

> Ordinarily, we assume that if someone respects himself in certain particulars, then he respects himself in general. If he thinks he is smart, attractive, likable, moral, interesting, and so on, then he thinks well of himself in general. Yet it should be apparent that . . . a person's global self-esteem is based not solely on an assessment of his constituent qualities but on an assessment of the qualities that *count*. . . . The differential importance of self-concept components is thus critically significant for self-esteem. (Rosenberg, 1979, p. 18)

The middle portion of Table 8.3 illustrates one way to test this *weight-em-by-importance* model. For this example, we have asked the two people to rank the four attributes in terms of their importance (1 = least important; 4 = most important). We have then multiplied their attribute ratings by their importance ratings (in parentheses), and then added up the products to form a weighted self-esteem score. Now we would predict that Person B feels better about himself than does Person A. This is because Person B values what he thinks he is good at more than Person A values what he thinks he is good at (Pelham, 1995; Pelham & Swann, 1989).

Despite its intuitive appeal, research has not found strong support for the *weight-em-by-importance* model (Marsh, 1993b, 1995; Pelham, 1995). Simply adding up the person's self-evaluations and ignoring importance often provides as good an indication (if not better) of the person's level of self-esteem. This may be because people tend to believe all of these attributes are important, so that the importance rating does not add much information. Another possibility is that it is not the individual's own importance rating that is critical, but how important the attribute is to society in general (Hoge & McCarthy, 1984; Marsh, 1993b, 1995). This possibility assumes that individuals are not entirely free to decide what is important and what is not.

A final approach to understanding self-esteem looks at the discrepancy between the way people view their specific qualities and their ideal of who they should be in that domain (Higgins, Klein, & Strauman, 1985; Horney, 1945; Rogers, 1951, 1954). This approach also derives from James's (1890) formula, but here we are treating pretensions as level of aspiration—what kind of person do you want to be, think you should be, or ought to be—rather than as values. The more our current self-image matches these idealized self-images, the higher is our self-esteem.

One way to test this model is to have people indicate how they would like to see themselves in various domains (e.g., "How intelligent would you like to be?"). We then subtract these *ideal self-ratings* from the person's current self-evaluation. The bottom portion of Table 8.3 presents a hypothetical example.

Person A is a perfectionist. He needs to be great at everything. Consequently, although he evaluates himself highly, he falls short of his ideals and we would predict that he has low self-esteem. Person B doesn't evaluate himself as highly, but he doesn't think he has to be "great" at everything either. So, we predict that he has high self-esteem.

Empirical tests of this model have found support for the claim that high self-esteem is associated with small "self–ideal self" discrepancies (Higgins et al., 1985; Ogilvie, 1987; Rogers & Dymond, 1954). Unfortunately methodological problems associated with the use of difference scores cloud the interpretation of these findings (Wylie, 1979).

Self-Esteem and Self-Evaluations

Having examined three models that relate self-esteem to self-evaluations, let's look more closely at the relation between these two variables. Table 8.4 presents data relevant to this issue. The data come from a study I conducted at the University of Washington. In this study, college students evaluated themselves and most other people on a number of abilities and personality attributes. I then examined these ratings as a function of the students' self-esteem level, as measured by the Rosenberg (1965) self-esteem scale.

The table shows a number of interesting effects. The top half of the table shows that self-esteem is strongly related to people's self-evaluations. Using a traditional .05 level of significance, high self-esteem students rated themselves more favorably than did low self-esteem students on 11 of the 14 positively valued traits and on 7 of the 12 negatively valued attributes. This means that self-esteem effects are quite broad. In comparison with low self-esteem people, high self-esteem people think they are *better* at a great many socially valued traits.

The bottom half of Table 8.4 shows that both self-esteem groups describe themselves in more positive (or less negative) terms than they describe most other people, and that this tendency is especially pronounced among high self-esteem students. This finding is of interest because it has been suggested that high self-esteem people show a comparable high regard for others, whereas low self-esteem people derogate others in an attempt to compensate for feelings of inadequacy (e.g., Epstein & Feist, 1988; Fromm, 1963; Rogers, 1951). Although this may occur when people evaluate members of their extended self (e.g., close friends and loved ones), it does not occur when people evaluate "most other people." The tendency to see oneself as "better than average" is far more characteristic of high self-esteem people than of low self-esteem people (Brown, 1986).

A final thing to note is that these low self-esteem students do not really describe themselves in negative terms. Their self-evaluations are less positive than are those of the high self-esteem students, but they are not negative in any absolute sense. In fact, they are quite positive. This is especially true when we compare their self-evaluations with their evaluations of most other people. Low self-esteem students appraised themselves more positively than most other people on 8 of the 14 positive attributes and less negatively than most other people on all 12 of the negative attributes. In many cases, these differences are

TABLE 8.4. Evaluations of Self (top half), and Self and Others (bottom half) as a Function of Self-Esteem

POSITIVE TRAITS			NEGATIVE TRAITS		
	HSE	LSE		HSE	LSE
Athletic	5.56_a	4.81_b	Inadequate	1.36_a	2.17_b
Attractive	5.13_a	4.38_b	Incompetent	1.51_a	2.14_b
Capable	6.15_a	5.62_b	Inconsiderate	1.85_a	2.41_b
Compassionate	5.59	5.21	Insensitive	2.13	2.38
Creative	4.97_a	4.40_b	Insincere	2.05	2.50
Friendly	5.79	5.45	Phony	1.54	1.86
Generous	4.95	4.97	Thoughtless	1.82	2.19
Good Looking	5.21_a	4.33_b	Unattractive	1.67_a	2.60_b
Kind	6.05_a	5.52_b	Uncoordinated	1.56_a	2.21_b
Loyal	6.23_a	5.60_b	Unintelligent	1.41_a	1.95_b
Sexy	4.79_a	3.60_b	Unpopular	1.87_a	2.74_b
Smart	5.67_a	5.05_b	Unwise	1.95	2.33
Talented	5.44_a	4.50_b			
Well Liked	5.74_a	5.02_b			

HIGH SELF-ESTEEM			LOW SELF-ESTEEM		
	Self	Others		Self	Others
Athletic	5.56_a	4.44_b	Athletic	4.81	4.64
Attractive	5.13_a	4.31_b	Attractive	4.38	4.40
Capable	6.15_a	5.26_b	Capable	5.62_a	4.93_b
Compassionate	5.59_a	4.56_b	Compassionate	5.21_a	4.38_b
Creative	4.97_a	4.44_b	Creative	4.40	4.45
Friendly	5.79_a	4.92_b	Friendly	5.45_a	4.69_b
Generous	4.95_a	4.10_b	Generous	4.97_a	4.17_b
Good Looking	5.21_a	4.08_b	Good Looking	4.33	4.17
Kind	6.05_a	4.87_b	Kind	5.52_a	4.76_b
Loyal	6.23_a	4.13_b	Loyal	5.60_a	4.14_b
Sexy	4.79_a	3.64_b	Sexy	3.60	3.67
Smart	5.67_a	4.59_b	Smart	5.05_a	4.62_b
Talented	5.44_a	4.59_b	Talented	4.50	4.52
Well Liked	5.74_a	4.64_b	Well Liked	5.02_a	4.52_b
Inadequate	1.36_a	2.79_b	Inadequate	2.17_a	2.88_b
Incompetent	1.51_a	2.92_b	Incompetent	2.14_a	2.90_b
Inconsiderate	1.85_a	3.41_b	Inconsiderate	2.40_a	3.48_b
Insensitive	2.13_a	3.33_b	Insensitive	2.38_a	3.48_b
Insincere	2.05_a	3.31_b	Insincere	2.50_a	3.52_b
Phony	1.54_a	3.72_b	Phony	1.86_a	3.69_b
Thoughtless	1.82_a	3.26_b	Thoughtless	2.19_a	3.19_b
Unattractive	1.67_a	3.23_b	Unattractive	2.60_a	3.14_b
Uncoordinated	1.56_a	3.00_b	Uncoordinated	2.21_a	3.07_b
Unintelligent	1.41_a	2.79_b	Unintelligent	1.95_a	2.67_b
Unpopular	1.87_a	3.23_b	Unpopular	2.74_a	3.26_b
Unwise	1.95_a	3.21_b	Unwise	2.33_a	2.90

Note: Values could range from 1 (not at all true of me or others) to 7 (very true of me or others). HSE = high self-esteem (top 1/3 of self-esteem distribution); LSE = low self-esteem (bottom 1/3 of self-esteem distribution). Within each pair, means with different subscripts differ at $p < .05$ or less.

substantial. For example, low self-esteem students regarded themselves as much more compassionate, kind, and loyal than are most other people, and as much less inconsiderate, unattractive, and unintelligent.

What we have, then, is a tendency for high self-esteem people to regard themselves as *good* at just about everything and a tendency for low self-esteem people to see themselves in generally, but not excessively, positive terms (Baumeister et al., 1989; Brown, 1986, 1993). Keep these points in mind, as we will come back to them later in this chapter.

Self-Esteem and the Certainty of Self-Knowledge

High self-esteem people not only appraise themselves in more positive terms than do low self-esteem people, they also appear to be more sure of who they are. Campbell and her colleagues (Campbell, 1990; Campbell & Lavallee, 1993) have claimed that high self-esteem people are more apt to possess clearly defined and temporally stable self-views than are low self-esteem people (see also, Baumgardner, 1990; Setterlund & Niedenthal, 1993; Pelham, 1991a). This assertion is based on evidence that low self-esteem people (1) show greater changes in their self-evaluations from one day to the next, (2) take longer to make decisions regarding their attributes, (3) report being less certain of where they stand on various attributes, and (4) display greater inconsistency in their self-evaluations than high self-esteem people. Because people's ideas of themselves are often used as behavioral guides, the self-concept *confusion* low self-esteem people show can have important consequences (Baumgardner, 1990; Campbell, 1990; Setterlund & Niedenthal, 1993). For example, low self-esteem people may be more willing than high self-esteem people to accept self-discrepant feedback.

Sociological Models of Self-Esteem

Sociological models provide another perspective on the nature and origins of self-esteem. Building on Cooley's (1902) model of the "looking-glass self" (discussed in Chapter 3), and Mead's (1934) ideas about perspective taking and the generalized other (discussed in Chapter 4), sociological models assume that self-esteem is influenced by societal factors. If we think we are highly regarded and valued by society at large, then we have high self-esteem. From this perspective, sociological variables, such as occupational prestige, income, education, and social status (e.g., race, religion, and gender) are assumed to affect self-esteem.

In fact, the evidence supporting such associations is weak. The successful, the affluent, the well educated, and the socially privileged do *not* have higher self-esteem than people who are less advantaged in these areas (Crocker & Major, 1989; Wylie, 1979). Indeed, members of stigmatized and minority groups sometimes report higher levels of self-esteem than do those who are more privileged (Rosenberg, 1979).

Group pride may explain why self-esteem is not lower in socially disadvantaged groups. As discussed in Chapter 2, minority groups are currently encouraged to view their minority status as a badge of honor rather than a stigma. This perspective is embodied in the Black pride movement, the Gay pride movement, and other similar social movements.

Group pride, in turn, may affect self-esteem. According to social identity theory (Tajfel & Turner, 1986), self-esteem depends, in part, on our group memberships or social identities. People who evaluate their social groups positively enjoy greater self-esteem than those who evaluate their social groups negatively. Crocker and her colleagues (Crocker, Luhtanen, Blaine, & Broadnax, 1995; Luhtanen & Crocker, 1992) tested these ideas and found that self-esteem (as measured by the Rosenberg scale) is positively correlated with a measure of *collective* self-esteem (the degree to which people evaluate their various social groups in favorable terms). Although this correlation doesn't prove that positive group evaluations promote high self-esteem (it is just as likely that high self-esteem leads people to evaluate their groups positively), it does establish that personal self-esteem and collective self-esteem are related.

Crocker and Major (1989) have offered another explanation for why members of socially disadvantaged groups do not have low self-esteem (see also, Rosenberg, 1979). These theorists have suggested that socially disadvantaged groups protect themselves from prejudice and discrimination (1) by attributing negative feedback to prejudice against their group rather than to themselves; (2) by selectively comparing their own outcomes with other ingroup members rather than with members of the majority group; and (3) by devaluing attributes on which their group is deficient and exaggerating the importance of attributes on which their group excels.

Crocker, Voelkl, Testa, and Major (1991) demonstrated how the first of these processes can insulate socially disadvantaged groups from the negative effects of prejudice and discrimination. In their study, African-American college students completed a questionnaire regarding their attitudes, values, and personal qualities. These students were then told that their responses would be shown to another person (who in all cases was said to be Caucasian), and they would learn whether the other person liked them or not. Finally, students were led to believe that the other person could see them through a one-way mirror (in which case the other person would be aware of their race) or could not see them through a one-way mirror (in which case the other person would be unaware of their race).

In the *unseen* condition, African-American students felt good about themselves when they were told the other person liked them, and they felt bad about themselves when they were told the other person did not like them. These effects did not occur in the *seen* condition, however. Here, the students' feelings toward themselves did not change as a function of the feedback they received. Additional analyses suggested that this occurred because the students attributed the evaluation they received to their race, not to their person-

TABLE 8.5. Sex Differences in Self-Evaluation

Competence	Males	Females	Popularity/ Attractiveness	Males	Females
Capable	5.84	5.88	Attractive	4.81	4.78
Creative	4.73	4.57	Sexy	4.36	4.02
Smart	5.40	5.33	Well liked	5.36	5.42
Talented	5.08	4.72	Unattractive	5.84	6.01
Inadequate	6.14	6.12	Good looking	4.88	4.65
Incompetent	6.23	6.03	Unpopular	5.75	5.57
Unintelligent	6.30	6.40	**Mean**	**5.17**	**5.08**
Unwise	5.81	5.92			
Mean	**5.69**	**5.62**			

Kindness	Males	Females	Athleticism	Males	Females
Compassionate	5.15	5.68	Athletic	5.60	4.43
Friendly	5.59	5.78	Uncoordinated	6.22	5.77
Generous	4.89	5.32	**Mean**	**5.91**	**5.10**
Kind	5.66	6.05			
Loyal	5.77	5.87			
Inconsiderate	5.80	6.20			
Insensitive	5.51	6.10			
Insincere	5.53	6.05			
Phony	6.08	6.45			
Thoughtless	5.88	6.15			
Mean	**5.59**	**5.97**			

Note: Scale values for negative items have been reversed, so that higher numbers equal more favorable self-evaluations.

ality, when they thought the other person had seen them (for related research, see Ruggiero & Taylor, 1997).

Sex Differences in Self-Esteem

Gender is another sociological variable that is thought to influence self-esteem. Here again, however, the effects are weak. Contrary to reports circulating in the popular press, research does *not* show that females have lower global self-esteem than men (Feingold, 1994; Maccoby & Jacklin, 1974; Pliner, Chaiken, & Flett, 1990; Wylie, 1979). Sex differences do emerge, however, with respect to how males and females evaluate certain of their attributes and abilities (Beyer, 1990; Marsh, 1990). For the most part, these differences mirror cultural stereotypes.

The study I conducted with University of Washington undergraduates (described earlier) is relevant to this issue. There were 73 men and 60 women in this sample. The two groups had similar scores on the Rosenberg (1965) self-esteem scale, but they did differ in how they evaluated their various characteristics. Table 8.5 reveals the nature of these effects. The table shows that the 26 items fell into four factors, which I have labeled competence, popularity/ attractiveness, kindness, and athleticism. There were no sex differences for the items that tapped perceived competence and popularity/attractiveness, but women thought they were *kinder* than did men, and men thought they were more *athletic* than did women. Even here, however, the differences were rather small, and both groups evaluated themselves very positively.

The tendency for women to laud their interpersonal qualities fits with evidence that women place particular importance on these attributes. Earlier (in Chapter 2) we noted that women are more apt than men to develop a collectivist or interdependent self-concept, one that emphasizes their connection and relations with others. Men, on the other hand, are more apt to develop an individualistic self-concept, one that emphasizes their achievements and separateness from others (Kashima et al., 1995; Markus & Oyserman, 1989). Josephs, Markus, and Tafarodi (1992) suggested that this tendency may be relevant to understanding sex differences in self-esteem. They hypothesized that men and women base their self-esteem on different attributes: Women base their self-esteem on their interpersonal qualities and men base their self-esteem on their perceived competence and personal achievements. The evidence for this claim is currently mixed (Nolen-Hoeksema & Girgus, 1994), but the notion that self-esteem depends on the way people evaluate themselves in culturally important domains shows how the cognitive and sociological approaches to understanding self-esteem formation can be integrated.

Terror Management Theory

Terror management theory (Solomon et al., 1991) represents another integrated model of self-esteem development. This theory is based on the work of Ernest Becker. Becker (1973) argued (1) that a defining feature of human existence is the capacity to contemplate one's own death, (2) that an awareness of one's own mortality creates anxiety and existential terror, and (3) that cultures function to mollify this terror by prescribing a way of life that is meaningful and valuable and offers some hope for immortality. For example, one culture may emphasize achievement, another charity, and another piety as the appropriate way to live. Extending these ideas, Solomon et al. suggested that high self-esteem develops among people who believe they are upholding the standards and ideals emphasized by their particular culture.

> Self-esteem is made possible by the development of cultural worldviews, which provide a stable and meaningful conception of the universe, social roles with specific prescriptions for behaviors that are deemed valuable, and the promise of safety and immortality to those who satisfy those prescriptions. Self-esteem is therefore a cultural contrivance consisting of two components: a meaningful conception of the universe combined with the perception that one is meeting the standards for value within that culturally contrived reality. (Solomon et al., 1991, pp. 24–25)

Because it emphasizes the cultural bases of self-esteem, terror management theory represents a sociological model of self-esteem formation.

SELF-ESTEEM AND RESPONSES TO EVALUATIVE FEEDBACK

Psychological research has not only looked at the nature and origins of self-esteem, it has also explored the consequences of self-esteem. The questions here are "When does self-esteem matter?" and "What difference does it make whether you have high self-esteem or low self-esteem?"

One area of research that has received a lot of attention is the role self-esteem plays when people confront evaluative feedback. Some research looks at how global self-esteem (a personality variable) influences how people cope with evaluative feedback (e.g., Baumeister & Tice, 1985; Brown, 1993); some research explores how evaluative feedback influences feelings of self-worth (e.g., Leary et al., 1995; MacFarland & Ross, 1982); and other research examines how a presumed need to feel good about ourselves (i.e., a self-enhancement motive) guides the way people deal with evaluative feedback (e.g., Steele, 1988; Tesser, 1988).

Our focus will be on the first of these research areas. We will concentrate on understanding how individual differences in self-esteem influence the way people respond to evaluative feedback. The first thing to note is that self-esteem generally has very little effect on how people deal with positive feedback (Brown & Dutton, 1995b; Campbell, 1990; Zuckerman, 1979). With few exceptions (to be discussed later), everyone likes to *succeed* and feels good when they do.

Where self-esteem matters most is when people confront negative outcomes, such as failure in the achievement domain, interpersonal slights or rejection, and even criticism or disagreement from friends. As a first step toward understanding these effects, consider the following vignettes.

> Your boss asks you to prepare a report offering a recommendation on some project. After giving the project considerable thought, you decide it should be approved. You carefully prepare a report outlining your position and turn it over to your boss. Your boss reads your report and rejects your recommendation.
>
> It is nearing lunch time and you decide to go out and get something to eat. You notice three of your co-workers talking. At 12:00, they leave together to have lunch without inviting you.

How would these experiences affect you? Would they make you feel sad and unhappy? Angry and upset? Would they affect the way you feel about yourself? Your answers may reveal a lot about your level of self-esteem. Experiences like these hurt low self-esteem people a lot; they make them feel humiliated and ashamed of themselves and they lead them to think they are worthless and unloved. This is not true of high self-esteem people. High self-esteem people feel sad and disappointed when they encounter negative feedback, but they do not feel humiliated and ashamed of themselves. They do not take failure as personally as do low self-esteem people.[1]

Emotional Responses to Failure

An investigation by Brown and Dutton (1995b) documents some of these effects. In the first part of this study, we had a large sample of college students complete the Rosenberg (1965) self-esteem scale. Those who scored in the upper third were designated as having high self-esteem, and those who scored in the lower third were designated as having low self-esteem. (We did not test those who fell between these extremes, because it is difficult to tell whether their self-esteem is high or low.) These participants were then given a test that allegedly measured an important intellectual ability. By varying the difficulty of the problems they received, it was possible to lead half of the participants to succeed on the task and to lead the other half to fail.

After learning how they had done, the participants completed an eight-item emotion scale. Four of the items (happy, glad, unhappy, sad) represented very general emotional responses to a positive or negative outcome. The other four items (proud, pleased with myself, ashamed, and humiliated) referred specifically to how people feel about themselves. These latter emotions are examples of what we have called feelings of self-worth.

The left-hand side of Figure 8.1 displays the results for the four general emotions. These data show that participants felt sadder after they had failed than after they had succeeded, and that this was just as true of high self-esteem participants as of low self-esteem participants. The situation is different when we look at how participants felt *about themselves* after learning they had succeeded or failed (see the right side of Figure 8.1). Here we do find an effect of self-esteem. Low self-esteem participants felt good about themselves when they succeeded but they felt bad about themselves when they failed. This was much less true of the high self-esteem participants; how they felt about themselves did not depend so much on whether they had just succeeded or failed.

These data make several points. It's okay to feel unhappy and disappointed when you fail at something. That is an understandable response to failure, and both high self-esteem people and low self-esteem people show it. But only low self-esteem people feel bad about themselves when they fail. They take failure very personally; it humiliates them and makes them feel ashamed of themselves. High self-esteem people do not show this effect; they do not feel bad about themselves when they fail.

There's another way to look at these data. Low self-esteem people's feeling toward themselves are very conditional. If they succeed they feel good

---

[1] I am using the term *failure* here in a generic sense to refer to any situation that involves negative self-relevant feedback. This would include not only achievement-related failure but also defeat in the athletic domain and a wide range of interpersonal outcomes, including rejection, criticism from others, and feeling underappreciated or ignored.

VILLA D'ESTE

Fanlore

67.

0775 7870657

22012 CERNOBBIO - LAGO DI COMO - ITALIA
TEL. 031.348.1 - FAX 031.348.844
Internet site: http://www.villadeste.it - e-mail: info@villadeste.it

A member of
The Leading Hotels of the World®

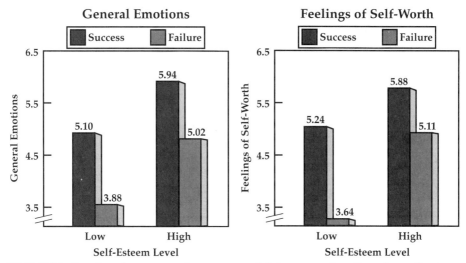

FIGURE 8.1. Emotional responses to success and failure as a function of emotion type and self-esteem. The data show that both self-esteem groups felt sad when they failed (left-hand panel), but only low self-esteem participants felt bad *about themselves* when they failed (right-hand panel).
(Adapted from Brown & Dutton, 1995, *Journal of Personality and Social Psychology, 68*, 712–722. Copyright 1995. Adapted by permission of The American Psychological Association.)

about themselves; if they fail they feel bad about themselves. This is a very precarious approach to emotional life. For low self-esteem people, "you're only as good as your latest outcome." High self-esteem people do not seem to live this way. How they feel about themselves doesn't depend so much on what they have just accomplished (Baldwin & Sinclair, 1996).

Kernis (1993; Kernis, Cornell, Sun, Berry, & Harlow, 1993) has noted that this may not be true of all people who score high on self-esteem scales. By measuring self-esteem on repeated occasions, he has identified people who have unstable high self-esteem; these individuals report having high self-esteem, but their feelings of self-worth fluctuate from day to day.

Unstable high self-esteem represents a kind of pseudo or defensive high self-esteem. Rather than being truly secure in their self-love, people with unstable high self-esteem feel good about themselves only when things are going well. In this sense, unstable high self-esteem appears to be a disguised form of low self-esteem—one in which the person's feelings of self-worth are highly conditional on recent achievements and events. The comedian David Letterman aptly describes the experience:

> Every night you're trying to prove your self-worth. It's like meeting your girlfriend's family for the first time. You want to be the absolute best, wittiest, smartest, most charming, best-smelling version of yourself you can possibly be. That's how I feel every night I go down there to the Ed Sullivan theater. If I can make these 500 people enjoy the experience, and have a higher regard for me

when I'm finished, it makes me feel like an entire person. If I've come short of that, I'm not happy. How things go for me every night is how I feel about myself for the next 24 hours. (David Letterman, *Parade Magazine,* May 26, 1996, p. 6).

Cognitive Responses to Failure

A number of factors could explain why low self-esteem people feel worse about themselves when they fail than do high self-esteem people. One possibility is that the two self-esteem groups evaluate their performances differently. Given comparable levels of performance, low self-esteem people might be more inclined than high self-esteem people to view it as a failure. Another possibility is that low self-esteem people might be more apt to attribute a poor performance to low ability.

These effects do occur (Blaine & Crocker, 1993; Campbell & Fairey, 1985; Jussim, Coleman, & Nassau, 1987; Shrauger, 1972; Zuckerman, 1979), but they do not fully explain why low self-esteem people feel so bad about themselves when they fail (Brown & Dutton, 1995b; Dutton & Brown, 1997). Instead, it seems that failure means something very different to a low self-esteem person than to a high self-esteem person. To a low self-esteem person, failure means you are globally inadequate—really, that you are a bad person. To a high self-esteem person, failure simply means that you didn't do well at some task or that you lack some ability.

An investigation by Dutton (1995) illustrates these effects. After leading participants to succeed or fail on an intellectual task, Dutton had participants evaluate themselves in four different areas: (1) the specific ability measured by the test ("How high/low are you in this ability?"); (2) general intelligence ("How intelligent/unintelligent are you?"); (3) interpersonal qualities ("How kind/phony are you?"); and (4) general perceptions of one's worth as a person ("Overall, how good/bad a person are you?").

Figure 8.2 presents the results of this investigation. The first panel shows that both self-esteem groups thought they were lower in the specific ability when they failed than when they succeeded. This is perfectly reasonable. If you have just done poorly on a test, it is reasonable to assume that you lack ability in this area. Now look at the second panel, which shows participants' perceptions of their general intelligence. Notice the effects of self-esteem here. After failing a test, low self-esteem participants doubt their overall intelligence. They don't simply assume that failure means they lack a specific ability; they assume it means they lack intelligence altogether. High self-esteem participants do not draw this inference. Although they accept that failure means they lack a particular ability, it doesn't lead them to believe they are generally lacking in intelligence.

The results are even more dramatic when we look at how failure influenced participants' perceptions of their interpersonal qualities (e.g., "How kind and warm are you?"). After failing a test of their intellectual ability, low

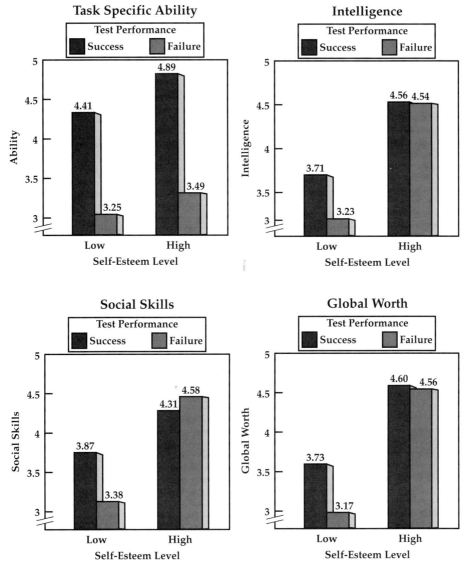

FIGURE 8.2 Self-evaluations as a function of self-esteem, success/failure, and the generality of the evaluation. The data show that low self-esteem people overgeneralize from failure. Failure makes them believe not only that they lack the specific ability measured by the test but also that they are less intelligent, not as socially skilled, and not as good a person. This type of overgeneralization does not occur among high self-esteem people.

(Adapted from Dutton, 1995, unpublished raw data, University of Washington, Seattle.)

self-esteem participants tended to belittle their social qualities. It's as if they were saying, "Not only am I bad at this test and generally unintelligent, but come to think of it, I'm not a very nice person either." High self-esteem participants did not show this tendency. Instead, they tended to compensate for failure by slightly exaggerating their perceived social skills (see also, Baumeister, 1982a; Brown & Dutton, 1995b; Brown & Smart, 1991).

Finally, we can look at how test performance affected participants' perceptions of their general worth as a person (see Panel 4 in Figure 8.2). In comparison with success, failure led low self-esteem participants to disparage their overall worth, not good people, but it did not have this effect on high self-esteem participants (for similar results, see Brown & Dutton, 1995b; Epstein, 1992; Heyman, Dweck, & Cain, 1992; Kernis, Brockner, & Frankel, 1989; Sanbonmatsu, Akimoto, & Moulin, 1994; for related work with depressives, see Beck, 1967; Carver & Ganellen, 1983; Carver, Ganellen, & Behar-Mitrani, 1985; Wenzlaff & Grozier, 1988).

These patterns represent very different responses to failure. Failure hits low-self-esteem people very hard. It makes them feel bad about themselves and it humiliates them. Failure does not have this effect on high self-esteem people. High self-esteem people feel disappointed when they fail, and they may accept that failure means they lack a specific ability. However, they do not treat failure as a global indictment of their character, and they do not feel humiliated and ashamed of themselves.

In my judgment, this is the key difference between having high self-esteem and low self-esteem. The problem with having low self-esteem is that your feelings of self-worth are very conditional. If you succeed, you think you are a good person and feel proud of yourself; but if you fail, you think you are a bad person and feel ashamed of yourself. This is not so for high self-esteem people. They can fail and still feel good about themselves. This capacity to fail without feeling bad about yourself is arguably the chief benefit of having high self-esteem.

Behavioral Responses to Failure

Suppose you were devastated by failure, rejection, disappointment, and the like. How would it affect your behavior? Would you readily seek out opportunities to expose yourself to these negative outcomes, or would you become rather self-protective, choosing to avoid circumstances that put you at risk? Accumulating research shows that low self-esteem people generally adopt the second strategy. They become self-protective, choosing to avoid situations that might lead to negative self-relevant feedback in favor of safe, though often less rewarding outcomes (Baumeister et al., 1989; Tice, 1993).

Risk Taking

Let's look first at the relation between self-esteem and risk-taking behavior. The first thing to note is that people generally prefer a sure gain to a speculative, but potentially more profitable, outcome (i.e., "A bird in the hand is worth two in the bush"). For example, when given a choice between winning $800 or having an 85 percent chance of winning $1,000, people prefer the $800 (despite the fact that the expected utility of the second option is greater) (Tversky & Kahneman, 1981).

Josephs, Larrick, Steele, and Nisbett (1992) showed that low self-esteem people are especially apt to avoid taking risks. These researchers explained their findings in terms of self-protection (see also Larrick, 1993). They noted that pursuing a risky choice of action can not only have negative financial consequences, it can have negative psychological consequences, insofar as a risk that does not pan out casts doubt on one's decision-making ability and judgment. Because low self-esteem people are especially bothered by negative self-relevant feedback, they pursue a psychologically safer (but potentially less rewarding) strategy.

Note, then, that it is not the fear of financial loss that leads low self-esteem people to be more risk averse. Rather, it is the desire to protect themselves from knowing they have made a bad decision. In support of this interpretation, Josephs et al. (1992) found that low self-esteem people were more risk averse than high self-esteem people only when they anticipated learning whether their choices had been good or bad. If there was no chance they would find out they had made a bad decision, they were not more risk averse.

Self-Handicapping

Research on self-handicapping also shows that low self-esteem people are highly concerned with self-protection. As discussed in Chapters 3 and 7, self-handicapping refers to the fact that people sometimes create impediments to their own success if doing so allows them to preserve an image of competency. For example, a student who fails to study for an important exam may be self-handicapping. Self-handicapping simultaneously serves two functions: (1) it offers self-protection from the pain of failure (rather than attributing failure to low ability, the student can blame a lack of preparation), and (2) it offers self-enhancement given success (a student who succeeds without studying can claim to have superior ability).

Building on earlier theoretical work by Arkin (1981), Tice (1991) hypothesized that low self-esteem people are drawn to self-handicapping as a means of self-protection. When they engage in self-handicapping, it is primarily to protect themselves from the pain of failure by avoiding the implication that they have low ability. In contrast, high self-esteem people are drawn to self-handicapping as a means of self-enhancement. When they engage in self-handicapping, it is to augment the perception that they have high ability by succeeding despite a self-imposed impediment.

Tice (1991) tested these ideas in a series of studies. In one investigation, participants were told they were going to take a test that measured an important intellectual ability. In the self-protection condition, participants were told that the test could clearly detect low ability but could not clearly identify high

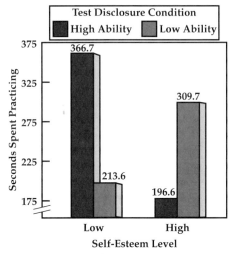

FIGURE 8.3. Seconds spent practicing before taking a test that could either clearly disclose high ability (but not low ability) or clearly disclose low ability (but not high ability). The data show that low self-esteem participants handicapped themselves by not practicing when a poor performance would reveal low ability and that high self-esteem participants handicapped themselves by not practicing when a good performance would reveal high ability. These findings support the claim that low self-esteem people use self-handicapping as a form of self-protection and that high self-esteem people use self-handicapping as a form of self-enhancement.
(Adapted from Tice, 1991, *Journal of Personality and Social Psychology, 60*, 711–725. Copyright 1991. Adapted by permission of The American Psychological Association.)

ability. These instructions were reversed in the self-enhancement condition. Here, participants were told that the test could clearly identify high ability but could not clearly detect low ability.

Tice then gave participants time to practice before taking the test (the assumption being that a lack of practice constitutes a form of self-handicapping). Figure 8.3 presents the results of this investigation. The figure shows that low self-esteem participants handicapped themselves by not practicing when they believed that failure could clearly disclose low ability, whereas high self-esteem participants handicapped themselves by not practicing when they believed that success could clearly reveal high ability. These findings suggest that low self-esteem people use self-handicapping to avoid the perception that they have low ability (i.e., a form of self-protection), and that high self-esteem people use self-handicapping to augment the perception that they have high ability (i.e., a form of self-enhancement). Rhodewalt, Morf, Hazlett, and Fairfield (1991) provided evidence that these self-handicapping strategies do, in fact, cushion the blow of failure among low self-esteem people and increase the glow of success among high self-esteem people.

Task Performance and Task Persistence

Research has also examined how self-esteem affects task performance and task persistence. In the absence of any prior outcome (i.e., under control conditions) or following prior success, self-esteem has virtually no effect on task performance. But after prior failure, low self-esteem people perform worse than high self-esteem people (Brockner, 1979; Brockner et al., 1983; Shrauger & Sorman, 1977; Shrauger & Rosenberg, 1970). Indeed, merely contemplating failure appears to undermine the performance of low self-esteem people (Campbell & Fairey, 1985).

There are at least two reasons why this occurs. First, failure leads low self-esteem people to become preoccupied with themselves. They become self-focused, and this, in turn, impairs their performance because their attention is no longer on the task at hand (Brockner, 1979; Brockner & Guare, 1983; see also, Dweck & Leggett, 1988 for related work). Second, they withdraw effort. Following prior failure, low self-esteem people persist less at a task than do high self-esteem people (McFarlin, 1985; McFarlin, Baumeister, & Blascovich, 1984; Sandelands, Brockner, & Glynn, 1988; Shrauger & Sorman, 1977). Persistence after failure isn't always adaptive, of course (Baumeister & Tice, 1985; McFarlin et al., 1984), but low self-esteem people seem particularly insensitive to the conditions under which it will and will not pay dividends (Janoff-Bulman & Brickman, 1982; McFarlin, 1985; Sandelands et al., 1988).

Social Comparison

Low self-esteem people continue to be self-protective even after they have performed some task or activity. In Chapter 3 we discussed social comparison processes. Comparing ourselves with others can be quite risky when a highly evaluative dimension is involved. When we compare ourselves with someone else, we run the risk of finding out that we are worse off than they are. Because low self-esteem people are highly concerned with self-protection, they ought to be reluctant to take this gamble unless they are quite certain they will learn good things about themselves.

Wood et al. (1994) tested this hypothesis and found considerable support for it. These investigators first gave participants positive or negative feedback on an alleged test of occupational success. All participants were then given the opportunity to engage in social comparison. Low self-esteem participants eagerly sought social comparison when they thought it would be favorable (after receiving positive feedback), but they actively avoided social comparison when they thought it would be unfavorable (after receiving negative feedback). This cautious, "play it safe" strategy provides further evidence that self-protection is a dominant motivational force in the lives of low self-esteem people (for additional research relating self-esteem and social comparison processes, see Aspinwall & Taylor, 1993; Gibbons & Gerrard, 1989, 1991).

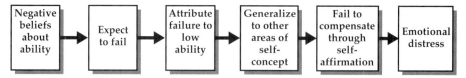

FIGURE 8.4. Schematic model of a cognitive approach to understanding why low self-esteem people suffer greater emotional distress than high self-esteem people when they fail.

Theoretical Explanations

To this point, we have seen that failure humiliates low self-esteem people and leads them to believe that they are globally inadequate. We have also seen that low self-esteem people are especially self-protective and risk averse, even to the point that they may create an impediment to success if doing so means they can avoid confronting the fact that they lack ability. Finally, we have seen that low self-esteem people perform worse and persist less after failure and that they choose to compare themselves with others only when they are reasonably certain that they will learn good things about themselves.

Two broad classes of theories have been developed to explain these findings. One focuses on cognitive factors; the other focuses on affective considerations. We will conclude this section by considering each of these in turn. First, we will look at how these theories explain the fact that low self-esteem people are more adversely affected by failure; then we will consider how they explain the greater risk aversion that low self-esteem people show.

Cognitive Models of Emotional Distress

Figure 8.4 presents a cognitive model of emotional distress. The model begins by assuming that low self-esteem people doubt their ability. This, in turn, leads them to expect to fail and to attribute failure to low ability when they do. Failure then spreads to other areas of the self-concept.

Low self-esteem people then fail to compensate for this overgeneralization. Steele's (1988) self-affirmation theory offers one explanation for why this occurs. As discussed in Chapter 5, self-affirmation theory argues that people can neutralize the effects of failure in one domain by emphasizing their virtues in other, unrelated, domains (see also, Tesser & Cornell, 1991). A student, for example, may offset failure in the classroom by emphasizing her interpersonal virtues. Earlier (see Figure 8.2) we noted that high self-esteem people tend to show this response to failure, but low self-esteem people do not (Baumeister, 1982a; Brown & Dutton, 1995b; Brown & Smart, 1991).

Steele and his colleagues have reasoned that low self-esteem people fail to compensate for failure because they have few positive beliefs about themselves to call upon as resources (Josephs et al., 1992; Spencer, Josephs, & Steele, 1993; Steele et al., 1993). From this perspective, the key difference between high self-esteem people and low self-esteem people lies in how they think about their various abilities and attributes. Low self-esteem people believe they have fewer positive qualities than do high self-esteem people, and this is why they experience greater distress when they fail.[2]

Affective Models of Emotional Distress

In tracing self-esteem differences to the way people think about themselves, cognitive models present a very rational, logical explanation for why low self-esteem people feel worse when they fail than do high self-esteem people. Affective models offer a somewhat different perspective (Brown, 1993; Dutton & Brown, 1997). These models assume that, early in life, low self-esteem people come to feel bad about themselves whenever they make a mistake or otherwise do something wrong. Over time, these feelings come to be evoked whenever failure is encountered. But the feelings are not cognitively mediated; they are largely automatic, visceral, and irrational.

By way of illustration, imagine that a young child spills his milk and, for whatever reason, becomes extremely distraught. The process is not a cognitive one. The child doesn't think "I spilled my milk. This means I lack coordination. Being coordinated is a socially desirable quality. I have few other qualities to offset the impact of this deficiency. Therefore, I'm bad." The reaction is more undifferentiated and automatic than this; the child simply assumes that he is bad when he spills his milk. The affective model argues that low self-esteem people still respond to failure in just this way. Failure automatically makes them feel bad about themselves.

This account draws a parallel between early childhood experiences and later responses to failure. Epstein (1980) also noted these parallels.

> People with high self-esteem, in effect, carry with them a loving parent who is proud of their successes and tolerant of their failures. Such people tend to have an optimistic view about life, and to be able to tolerate external stress without becoming excessively anxious. Although capable of being disappointed and depressed by specific experiences, people with high self-esteem recover quickly, as do children who are secure in their mother's love. In contrast, people with low self-esteem carry within them a disapproving parent who is harshly critical of their failures, and register only short-lived pleasures when they succeed. Such people are apt to be unduly sensitive to failure and to rejection, to have low tolerance for frustration, to take a long time to recover following disappointments, and to have a pessimistic view of life. The picture is not unlike that of children who are insecure in their parent's love. (Epstein, 1980, p. 106)

Theoretical Models of Self-Protection

Cognitive and affective models also offer different explanations for why low self-esteem people are more self-protective and risk averse than are high

---

[2]Steele's (1988) self-affirmation theory is related to Linville's (1975) theory of self-complexity (see Chapter 5). The key difference is that self-affirmation theory maintains that the pain of failure is reduced if the person possesses many other *positive* identities, whereas self-complexity theory claims that the emotional effects of success and failure are less extreme among people who possess many identities, regardless of whether these identities are positive or negative.

self-esteem people. Expectancy-value models of behavior provide a useful framework for understanding these differences. As discussed in Chapter 6, these models assume that freely chosen behavior depends on two factors: a person's expectation that she can achieve some outcome, in conjunction with the value the person places on obtaining versus not obtaining the outcome.

Cognitive theories trace self-esteem differences in behavior to the expectancy component of the expectancy-value model. They assume that low self-esteem people are reluctant to take risks because they have little confidence in their ability to succeed. Affective models emphasize the value component in the expectancy-value model. They assume that the negative incentive value of failure (the pain of failure) is greater for low self-esteem people than for high self-esteem people and that this explains why low self-esteem people are more self-protective.

One way to think about these divergent perspectives is in terms of confidence and consequence. The cognitive model assumes that a lack of confidence guides the behavior of low self-esteem people. Low self-esteem people play it safe because they lack confidence that they will succeed. Presumably, if they thought they were better at things (e.g., thought they had higher ability), they would not be risk averse. The affective model assumes that consequence, not confidence, is the key variable to consider. Low self-esteem people are risk averse not because they don't think they can succeed but because they are afraid to fail. Literally, they are afraid to try.

Brockner (1984) has suggested that the combination of these factors makes low self esteem people especially vulnerable to social influence. Lacking confidence in themselves, and being overly sensitive to rejection and criticism, low self-esteem people conform to the wishes of others. This may explain why low self-esteem is linked to many negative behaviors in adolescence, such as substance abuse and unsafe sexual practices (Hawkins, Catalano, & Miller, 1992). These behaviors often arise as a result of peer pressure, which low self-esteem people may find particularly difficult to withstand.

IMPLICATIONS AND REFLECTIONS

Self-Enhancement and Self-Consistency

The data we have reviewed in this chapter are relevant to two long-standing controversies. The first is known as the "self-enhancement versus self-consistency debate." Self-consistency theories (see Chapter 3) assume that people strive to maintain consistency between their beliefs, attitudes, and behavior, and that inconsistency creates an uncomfortable state of tension that people are driven to reduce. Accordingly, consistency theories predict that people with positive self-views will be less accepting of and more disturbed by negative feedback than will people with negative self-views (because negative feedback is more inconsistent with their positive self-image).

Self-enhancement theories make a different prediction. These theories assume that people strive to feel good about themselves. It is also assumed that this need increases the longer it goes unfulfilled (much as a need for food increases the longer one goes without eating). Accordingly, self-enhancement theories predict that people with negative self-views will be less accepting of and more disturbed by negative feedback than will people with positive self-views.

Shrauger's "Affect–Cognition" Distinction

Shrauger (1975) surveyed the literature and found support for each theory, depending on whether cognitive or emotional reactions to negative feedback were assessed (see also, Swann, Griffin, Predmore, & Gaines, 1987). People's cognitive reactions to negative feedback conform to the self-consistency model: People with negative self-views are more accepting of negative feedback (i.e., they are more inclined to view it as accurate and attribute it to themselves) than are people who have positive self-views. In contrast, people's emotional reactions to negative feedback conform to the self-enhancement model: People with negative self-views are more disturbed by negative feedback than are people with positive self-views.

Although Shrauger's review concerned the effects of task-specific beliefs and expectancies, his analysis also illuminates how global self-esteem affects responses to negative feedback. In accordance with the self-consistency model, low self-esteem people are more inclined to accept negative feedback than are high self-esteem people (Blaine & Crocker, 1993); in accordance with the self-enhancement model, low self-esteem people are more disturbed by negative feedback than are high self-esteem people (Brown & Dutton, 1995b; Dutton & Brown, 1997).

The situation is a bit more complex when we look at responses to positive feedback. Self-consistency theory predicts that low self-esteem people will be uncomfortable with positive feedback because it is inconsistent with how they think and feel about themselves. Although some studies find support for this prediction (e.g., Brown & McGill, 1989; Marecek & Mettee, 1972), most do not. Most studies find that self-esteem has little effect on how people respond to positive feedback (e.g., Brown & Dutton, 1995b; Campbell, 1990; Shrauger & Lund, 1975).

Self-Verification Theory

Swann's (1990, 1996) research on self-verification processes provides an important exception. As discussed in Chapter 3, self-verification theory is concerned with interpersonal behavior. The theory assumes that people "want others to validate and confirm their [self-views], even when those [self-views] are negative" (McNulty & Swann, 1984, p. 1013). This assumption leads

Swann to predict that people with negative self-views will be uneasy receiving positive feedback from others.

Swann and his colleagues (De La Ronde & Swann, 1993; Swann, 1996) have used these ideas to understand the behavior of low self-esteem people. They have argued that low self-esteem people are torn between two competing motives. On the one hand, they want to feel good about themselves, and this leads them to seek and embrace positive feedback from others. On the other hand, they do not want others to think too well of them, because they fear not being able to live up to these expectations. These opposing tendencies place low self-esteem people in a crossfire: They sometimes avoid positive feedback from others (Swann, Pelham, & Krull, 1989) despite evidence that they are especially hurt by interpersonal rejection (Dittes, 1959; Jones, 1973; Smith & Smoll, 1990). In extreme cases, self-verification needs may lead low self-esteem people to seek out or remain in negative interpersonal relationships (Swann, 1996).

Global Self-Esteem and Specific Self-Evaluations

Closely related to the "self-enhancement–self-consistency" debate is the question of whether self-esteem is best treated as a global personality variable or in terms of how people evaluate themselves in specific domains. In keeping with a general movement in the field of personality, many contemporary theorists (e.g., Bandura, 1986; Marsh, 1990; Swann, 1990) have argued that specific self-evaluations are the better predictor of behavior (broadly defined) than is global self-esteem. Some have even gone so far as to claim that global self-esteem is a fiction (Gergen, 1971) or is of limited value:

> [My] research has led me increasingly to the conclusion that general self-concept—no matter how it is inferred—is not a particularly useful construct. General self-concept does not reflect adequately the diversity of specific self-facets. If the role of self-concept [research] is to better understand the complexity of self in different contexts, to predict a wide variety of behaviors, to provide outcome measures for diverse interventions, and to relate self-concept to other constructs, then the specific facets of self-concept are more useful than a global indicator. (Marsh, 1990, p. 100)

The evidence on this point is actually mixed. For example, people's specific beliefs about their academic ability are a better predictor of school performance than is global self-esteem (Marsh, 1990), but global self-esteem is a better predictor of psychological well-being than are domain-specific self-evaluations (Rosenberg, Schooler, Schoenbach, & Rosenberg, 1995). The evidence is also mixed when it comes to understanding people's responses to success and failure. Some investigations have found that specific self-views are better predictors of these reactions than is global self-esteem (e.g., Feather, 1969; Marsh, 1990; Swann et al., 1989); other studies have found the opposite to be true or have reported mixed findings (e.g., Brockner & Hulton; 1978; Dutton & Brown, 1997; Moreland & Sweeney, 1984; Shrauger & Sorman, 1977).

Shrauger's (1975) affect–cognition distinction appears to illuminate this issue as well. Dutton and Brown (1997) found that task-specific self-evaluations (i.e., expectancies of success and beliefs about one's competence) guide people's cognitive reactions to evaluative feedback but that global self-esteem guides people's emotional reactions to evaluative feedback. These findings suggest that both constructs are important and influence different aspects of psychological life.

A Personal Note: Some Thoughts about Feelings

Throughout this chapter, I have contrasted an affective model of self-esteem with one that emphasizes cognitive factors. In doing so, I have tried to describe the main points of each perspective, without commentary or advocacy. In the final section of this chapter, I will depart from this approach and critically examine the two models.

Let me begin by noting that the cognitive view of self-esteem currently dominates contemporary thinking in personality and social psychology. In part, this is because it fits with the more general cognitive zeitgeist. It is also better articulated than the affective model, and it lends itself better to empirical tests and elaborations. These are all highly desirable features of a theory.

Nevertheless, I personally think the theory fails to adequately capture the nature of self-esteem. This is true with respect to the account it offers for the origins of self-esteem and with respect to its explanation for why low self-esteem people feel so bad when they fail. We'll begin by considering the first of these issues.

Self-Esteem Formation

Cognitive models of self-esteem formation adopt an information-integration approach to understanding the origins of self-esteem. They assume that self-esteem develops from a largely rational process. People survey their various characteristics and somehow combine this information into an overall judgment. Stanley Coopersmith (1967), a pioneer in the area of self-esteem research, summarized this approach when he wrote:

> [Self-esteem] is based on a *judgmental* process in which the individual examines his performance, capacities, and attributes according to his personal standards and values, and arrives at a *decision* of his own worthiness. (Coopersmith, 1967, p. 7, emphasis added)

I do not think this is so. In my judgment, people don't examine their various qualities and decide whether or not to like themselves. People's feelings toward themselves are more irrational than this. As the French philosopher Pascal noted, "The heart has its reasons, which reason does not know." Although Pascal was referring to love for others, the same principle applies when we consider how people feel about themselves.

This position was shared by William James. Although his claim that "self-esteem = successes/pretensions" implies that self-esteem is based in cognitive processes, James also believed that self-esteem was not so logical. "There is a certain average tone of self-feeling," James wrote, "which each one of us carries about with him, and which is independent of the objective reasons we may have for satisfaction or discontent" (James, 1890, p. 306). One way to reconcile this apparent contradiction is to assume that James's formula for self-esteem applies to feelings of self-worth (e.g., the pride we feel in a given outcome or achievement) rather than to global self-esteem itself.

Another problem I see with the cognitive approach is that the self-esteem it describes is conditional and fragile. Self-esteem founded on the belief that we possess certain qualities would be unstable (Kernis et al., 1993) and vulnerable to attack. In the event that something happened to undermine our self-evaluations in that domain, our self-esteem would evaporate. If it is to have any value, self-esteem ought to insulate people from just such experiences. High self-esteem people ought to (and do) feel good about themselves even when they find out they are not capable or competent in some domain. This analysis further suggests that high self-esteem is not based on an assessment of one's constituent qualities.

The cognitive model also assumes a high degree of cognitive sophistication. As such, the model predicts that self-esteem doesn't develop until at least middle childhood, when the cognitive abilities necessary to make the various judgments the model describes have developed. Susan Harter, a developmental psychologist, makes this point explicitly, asserting that global self-esteem is "a complex, cognitive construction that does not emerge until approximately the mental age of eight" (Harter, 1986, p. 145). This characterization is at odds with evidence that children show differences reflective of self-esteem at a very young age and that these differences predict self-esteem later in life (Cassidy, 1990; Sroufe, 1983; Sroufe, Carlson, & Shulman, 1993).

Finally, the cognitive model begs the question of what determines self-evaluations in the first place. Consider, for example, people's ideas about how attractive they are. At all ages, and for both sexes, perceived attractiveness is closely related to self-esteem (Harter, 1993; Pliner et al., 1990). People who like the way they look, like themselves (and people who like themselves, like the way they look). The cognitive approach assumes that the causal arrow goes from perceived attractiveness to self-esteem. People somehow come to regard themselves as attractive or unattractive, and this decision affects their level of self-esteem. What this approach leaves unanswered is the question of why some people regard themselves as attractive to begin with.

One possible solution would be to assume that people correctly perceive how attractive they really are. But as we noted in Chapter 3, this is not the case. People's ideas about their attractiveness are not strongly tied to what others think; nor is actual attractiveness related to self-esteem (Feingold, 1992).

The same is true for virtually all highly evaluative attributes. High self-esteem people think they are more competent, intelligent, talented, and well liked than do low self-esteem people, but this is not actually the case. On average, high self-esteem people are no better in these areas than are low self-esteem people, and people who truly possess these qualities do not have higher self-esteem than people who lack them.

What we find, then, is that although self-esteem is strongly related to what people think they are like, it is virtually unrelated to what people are really like. This pattern poses a problem for the cognitive model. The problem is this: If people's ideas about themselves aren't based on what they are really like, where do they come from?

An affective model of self-esteem explains these findings by assuming that self-esteem develops early in life and then functions as a lens through which people view their characteristics and experiences. People who feel good about themselves evaluate themselves positively—they like the way they look, they appreciate their talents, and they believe they are warm, friendly, and liked by others. The relation is a top-down one (from global self-esteem to self-evaluations), rather than a bottom-up one (from self-evaluations to global self-esteem) (Brown, 1993; Brown, Dutton, & Cook, 1997).

Self-Esteem and Failure

Cognitive explanations for why low self-esteem people feel so bad about themselves when they fail may also be incomplete. According to these models, low self-esteem people (1) think they have low ability; (2) expect to fail; (3) are accepting of failure when it occurs; (4) generalize from the failure experience to other areas of the self-concept; and (5) fail to compensate for failure because they don't think they do other things well.

At one time, I was one of the many theorists who endorsed this position (e.g., Brown, Collins, & Schmidt, 1988; Brown & Gallagher, 1992; Brown & Smart, 1991). But now I think it is mistaken. One problem is that the negativity it assumes on the part of low self-esteem people doesn't really exist. Look again at Table 8.4. Notice that low self-esteem people do not describe themselves in negative terms. They don't claim to be unintelligent, incompetent, and homely *losers*. They actually regard themselves quite favorably, believing they are smarter, kinder, and quite a bit better liked than are most other people and that they are certainly every bit as attractive, talented, and sexy. These findings are at odds with a cognitive model that takes as its starting point the idea that low self-esteem people evaluate themselves negatively. It doesn't make sense to claim that low self-esteem people are so adversely affected by failure because they think they can't do anything well and have many negative qualities, when in fact they regard themselves as smarter than most other people and not at all incompetent.

It might be argued that this lack of negativity occurs only among low self-esteem college students. I am not aware of any evidence that college students score higher in self-esteem than do other groups, but true self-deprecation does occur in some populations (e.g., the severely depressed). Nevertheless, the fact remains that self-esteem differences are found with low self-esteem people who do not evaluate themselves in highly negative terms. It must be because these effects are not due to negative thinking per se.

The larger point here is this. Cognitive models assume that the defining feature of low self-esteem is self-criticism. Many low self-esteem people do not fit this pattern. They think they have many fine qualities, yet they feel humiliated and ashamed of themselves when they fail (Bednar, Wells, & Peterson, 1989). The problem is not a lack of positive self-evaluations; rather, it is an almost inexplicable feeling that one is a bad person, a feeling that automatically surfaces whenever failure is encountered. Indeed, one can easily imagine a low self-esteem person who says, "Yes, I know I am smart and attractive and can do many things well, but I just don't *feel good* about myself, especially when I fail or make a mistake."

To summarize, I believe the cognitive model paints too rational a portrait of self-esteem formation and functioning. My claim is not that people's thoughts about themselves are unrelated to how they feel about themselves, it is that self-evaluations aren't the relevant thoughts. The cognitions that underlie self-esteem occur at a preconscious level; they are part of what Epstein (1990) calls the experiential system, rather than the rational system. These automatic thoughts (Bargh & Tota, 1988; Beck, 1967) or irrational beliefs (Ellis, 1962) are undifferentiated and diffuse; they are vague notions about one's general worth as a person (e.g., "I am good versus I am bad"), not ideas about particular competencies and attributes.

Implications for Improving Self-Esteem

The analysis I have offered has implications for the treatment of self-esteem. Many self-esteem improvement programs attempt to instill high self-esteem by encouraging people to focus on their positive qualities (McGuire & McGuire, 1996; Mruk, 1995). This assumes that positive self-evaluations produce high self-esteem. The fact that many low self-esteem people already view themselves positively casts doubt on this assumption.

In a similar vein, attributional retraining programs encourage people to attribute failure to factors other than low ability (Seligman, 1991). The implication is that a perceived lack of ability makes people feel bad about themselves. There is certainly some truth in this. But encouraging people to make such attributions also encourages them to tie their feelings of self-worth to their outcomes and perceived competencies. In the long run, this strategy can be maladaptive. There are many things we can't do well in life, and there is no reason to feel bad about ourselves because of this, *unless* we make our self-esteem dependent on our self-evaluations.

Instead of treating low self-esteem by building people's confidence in themselves ("you can do it"), I believe we should be helping people to understand that "It's OK if you can't do it; it doesn't mean you're a bad person."

Unfortunately, doing so is easier said than done. I am not a clinical psychologist, and my recommendations in this area are little more than intuitions. Still, my intuitions tell me that feelings of belonging and mastery (which I regard as the defining features of high self-esteem) are best created in the context of a secure interpersonal relationship in which a person feels unconditionally loved and accepted.

This position parallels a school of therapy Carl Rogers developed in the 1940s. Rogers (1951) believed that the therapist's role is to accept the client in a nonjudgmental way, to assure the client that he or she is valued as a person. As in the present approach, this strategy assumes that improvements in self-esteem require a focus on global feelings toward oneself rather than cognitively based judgments of one's competencies or qualities. Ultimately, self-esteem is not a decision but a feeling. It is based not on a dispassionate consideration of *what* one is but on feelings of affection for *who* one is.

CHAPTER SUMMARY

In this chapter, we considered the nature, origins, and consequences of self-esteem. We began by noting that the term self-esteem is used in three different ways. Sometimes the term is used to refer to a global personality variable; sometimes the term is used to refer to the way people evaluate their specific abilities and attributes; and sometimes the term is used to refer to particular emotional states.

Next we examined three models of self-esteem development. Affective models assume that self-esteem develops early in life as a function of the parent–child relationship. Cognitive models assume that self-esteem depends on the way people evaluate their various qualities. Sociological models assume that self-esteem depends on how one is regarded by society in general.

We then discussed the role self-esteem plays when people confront negative events, such as failure in the classroom or interpersonal rejection. These types of events lead low self-esteem people (but not high self-esteem people) to believe they are globally inadequate and to feel humiliated and ashamed of themselves. We then saw that low self-esteem people are highly self-protective and risk averse, generally choosing to stay away from situations that expose them to negative feedback. We concluded the chapter by applying these findings to several long-standing controversies and debates regarding the nature and origins of self-esteem.

- The term self-esteem has been used in three ways. Sometimes the term is used to refer to overall feelings of affection for oneself (i.e., global self-esteem); sometimes the term is used to refer to the way people evaluate themselves in specific domains (i.e., domain specific self-esteem); and sometimes the term is used to refer to people's momentary feelings of self-worth (i.e., state self-esteem). In this chapter, we used the term self-esteem only when referring to the way people generally feel about themselves.
- Self-report questionnaires are often used to measure self-esteem. Because such questionnaires explicitly ask people how they feel about themselves, they are subject to self-presentational biases and defensive responding. Indirect measures of self-esteem are being developed to bypass these limitations.

- Affective models of self-esteem development contend that feelings of belonging and a sense of mastery comprise the essence of high self-esteem and that these feelings develop early in life, largely as a result of parent–child interactions. Research on attachment styles supports the notion that the early parent–child interaction is related to the development of self-esteem.
- Cognitive models of self-esteem development assume that self-esteem develops from a rational process. People survey their various qualities and somehow integrate these perceptions into an overall feeling of self-regard. These perceptions may simply be added together or weighted by their importance. Another possibility is that self-esteem depends on whether our current self-image matches our ideal self-image.
- Sociological models maintain that self-esteem depends on how one is regarded by society at large. This position predicts that people who are socially disadvantaged or stigmatized will have lower self-esteem than people who are socially privileged. There is little evidence to support this position, in part because people take great pride in their group membership and in part because people do not passively register and incorporate society's views toward themselves.
- High self-esteem people believe they have many more positive qualities than do low self-esteem people, but even low self-esteem people think of themselves in generally positive terms.
- Self-esteem influences how people cope with negative, self-relevant feedback (such as failure in the classroom or interpersonal rejection). Events of this nature lead low self-esteem people to feel humiliated and ashamed of themselves and to believe that they are globally inadequate. Failure does not have this effect on high self-esteem people. High self-esteem people feel disappointed when they fail, and they may accept that failure means they lack a specific ability; however, they do not treat failure as a global indictment of their character, and failure does not make them feel humiliated and ashamed of themselves.
- Low self-esteem people adopt a self-protective orientation. In a variety of situations, they refrain from taking risks and pursue safe, but often less rewarding, options. High self-esteem people are oriented toward self-enhancement. They are willing to take risks, a factor that often leads to more positive outcomes.
- In attempting to explain the risk aversion low self-esteem people show, cognitive models of self-esteem emphasize the role of negative self-relevant beliefs on the part of low self-esteem people (i.e., a lack of confidence). Affective models emphasize that low self-esteem people are risk averse because they deal poorly with failure (i.e., an emphasis on consequence).
- People's cognitive reactions to evaluative feedback conform to a self-consistency model (people are more apt to accept feedback that matches the way they think about themselves than feedback that doesn't match the way they think about themselves). People's emotional reactions to evaluative feedback conform to a self-enhancement model (low self-esteem people suffer more emotional distress when they fail than do high self-esteem people).
- Global self-esteem and domain-specific self-evaluations are both important psychological constructs, but they should not be used interchangeably. Depending on the situation, they may have independent, additive, or interactive effects on behavior.
- Cognitive models of self-esteem currently dominate social psychological thinking, but the notion that people's feelings toward themselves depend on how they evaluate their various qualities has not been established. Moreover, most low self-esteem people believe they have many positive qualities, suggesting that self-criticism, low confidence, and negative self-evaluations are not the defining feature of low self-esteem.

For Further Reading

BAUMEISTER, R. F. (1993). (Ed.). *Self-esteem: The puzzle of low self-regard*. New York: Plenum Press.

BEDNAR, R. L., WELLS, M. G., & PETERSON, S. R. (1989). *Self-esteem: Paradoxes and innovations in clinical theory and practice*. Washington: American Psychological Association.

KERNIS, M. H. (1995). (Ed.). *Efficacy, agency, and self-esteem*. New York: Plenum Press.

ROSENBERG, M. (1979). *Conceiving the self*. New York: Basic Books.

SWANN, W. B., JR. (1996). *Self-traps: The elusive quest for higher self-esteem*. New York: W. H. Freeman & Co.

WELLS, G. E., & MARWELL, G. (1976). *Self-esteem: Its conceptualization and measurement*. Beverly Hills, CA: Sage.

WYLIE, R. C. (1979). *The self-concept* (Vol. 2). Lincoln: University of Nebraska Press.

CHAPTER 9

Depression

Wayne McDuffie was a football coach with a solid record of achievement at several Southeastern universities. Football was McDuffie's life; on and off the field, he lived it and breathed it. As long as McDuffie was coaching, McDuffie was happy. But coaching in the world of sports is hardly a secure enterprise, and when McDuffie was fired from his position at the University of Georgia, he slipped into a dark depression. One afternoon, he learned he had been passed over for a coaching job with the Miami Dolphins. Later that day, McDuffie took his life, leaving three children and a wife behind.

Wayne McDuffie's story is extreme, but hardly unique. Approximately 15 percent of the population experiences a depressive episode at one time in their lives (Secunda, Katz, & Friedman, 1973), and most of these arise in response to significant life events (Paykel, 1979). Although these episodes tend to abate in six to nine months, approximately 20 percent of those who become clinically depressed remain depressed for at least two years (Downey & Coyne, 1990). Moreover, those who experience one bout of depression are at risk for future depression, perhaps experiencing as many as five or six depressive episodes in their lives (Amenson & Lewinsohn, 1981). Finally, depression is closely related to suicide. Approximately one in every 200 people with depression attempts suicide, and most people who attempt suicide have experienced a recent bout of depression (Minkoff, Bergman, Beck, & Beck, 1973).

Depression is not only a very prevalent and virulent disorder, it is also a very heterogeneous one. It is influenced by many factors, characterized by a variety of symptoms, and comprised of several subtypes. In this chapter we will focus on understanding the role self-relevant processes play in the onset and maintenance of depression. Our exclusive focus on self-relevant processes means that many other viable approaches to understanding depression, including ones that emphasize genetic, biochemical, and broad-scale environmental factors (e.g., poverty and violence) will not be considered. This inattention does not mean these factors are unimportant, only that they are less relevant to self-psychology.

Our review will focus on three related issues. First, we will examine the onset of depression. What causes depression, and what role do people's thoughts and feelings about themselves play in this matter? The second issue we will consider is the experience of depression itself. Self-referent thoughts and feelings are prominent features of a depressive episode, and people who are depressed process personal information differently than do people who are not depressed. The second part of this chapter will explore these tendencies. Finally, we will look at factors that influence the duration and severity of a depressive episode. Here our concern will be with understanding why some people are able to recover quickly from depression, while others are not.

CONCEPTUAL OVERVIEW

Diathesis-Stress Models of Depression

The model shown in Figure 9.1 will guide our discussion. This model, which is known as a *diathesis-stress* model (Monroe & Simons, 1991), identifies two general factors that influence the onset of depression. One of these factors is a negative life event (or source of stress). These events typically involve the loss of an important source of love, security, identity, or self-worth. The death of a loved one, the breakup of an important romantic relationship, or a significant personal failure are prototypic examples (Arieti & Bemporad, 1978).

The link between events of this nature and depression was revealed in a landmark study by G. Brown and Harris (1978). These investigators interviewed over 400 women (ages 18–65) living in an area of London. Assessments were made regarding the presence or absence of depression in the preceding year and the nature and number of negative life events the women had experienced. Across the entire sample, 30 percent of the women reported experiencing a severe negative event or chronic difficulty in the nine months prior to the interview; among women who had experienced a bout of depression, this percentage jumped to 75 percent.

The data Brown and Harris (1978) gathered document that depression is often preceded by a negative life event. At the same time, the data also showed that only a minority of women who experienced a severe event became depressed. On the basis of these and other findings (Paykel, 1979), researchers now agree that negative life events precipitate depression in some, but not most, people. This fact has led investigators to search for variables that determine who becomes depressed when experiencing stress and who does not.

Formally, these variables are known as *diatheses*. A diathesis is a vulnerability factor that influences how much damage a stressful experience creates. For example, the structural integrity of a building constitutes a diathesis. If an earthquake comes, a poorly made building will suffer greater damage than a well-made building will. In a conceptually similar vein, researchers have sought to identify factors that influence whether people become depressed when faced with a stressful experience. As we will see momentarily, some of these vulnerability factors concern the way people think and feel about themselves.

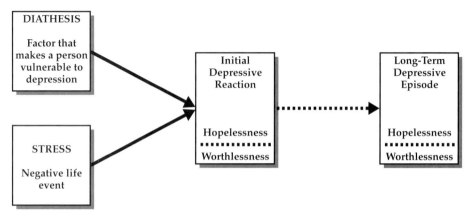

FIGURE 9.1. Schematic representation of a diathesis-stress model of depression. A depressive reaction occurs when a person vulnerable to depression experiences a negative life event. Among other things, this depressive reaction is characterized by feelings of hopelessness and/or worthlessness. Finally, the dashed line indicates that a short-term depressive reaction may resolve quickly or turn into a long-term depressive episode.

Two Self-Relevant Features of Depression: Hopelessness and Worthlessness

In 1917, Sigmund Freud published a book on depression called *Mourning and Melancholia*. Among other things, Freud argued that depression can take two forms. With mourning, depression is a grief reaction to the loss of an actual love object (e.g., the death of a loved one). Mourning is characterized by intense sadness and despair, but not guilt, shame, or self-reproach. With melancholia, depression is a response to a loss of a more psychological nature (e.g., a perceived failure to live up to one's ideals or standards). It is characterized not only by intense sadness but also by self-recrimination and self-deprecation.

Building on these themes, contemporary researchers have distinguished between two self-relevant perceptions commonly seen in depression (see the middle portion of Figure 9.1). People feel *hopeless* when they believe there is nothing they or anyone else can do to bring about a desired outcome or avoid a negative outcome. Hopelessness begets feelings of gloom and resignation, which are important aspects of depression. People feel *worthless* when they think they are weak, depraved, or otherwise globally inadequate or flawed. These perceptions are also prominent features of depression.[1]

In some cases, depression is characterized by only one of these perceptions (e.g., a person can feel hopeless but not worthless regarding the loss of a loved one). Other times, both perceptions are present (when a loved one dies, people may feel hopeless that they will never see the person again and guilty about not having spent more time with the person while he or she was alive).

---

[1]Figure 9.1 highlights only self-relevant features of depression. However, as will be discussed later, depression is characterized by many other symptoms, including somatic disturbances (e.g., trouble sleeping), motivational disturbances (e.g., apathy), and emotional disturbances (e.g., sadness).

Helplessness is also commonly seen in depression. This term refers to the perception that one is powerless to change an undesirable situation. Helplessness is a subset of hopelessness. People can feel helpless without feeling hopeless (e.g., there's nothing I can do but I know someone who can), but by definition, people who feel hopeless also feel helpless. Helplessness also may give rise to worthlessness. For many people, feeling weak, ineffective, and powerless contributes to a sense of worthlessness.

The Course of Depression: Depressive Reactions and Depressive Episodes

Figure 9.1 shows one more point to keep in mind as we survey research on self-relevant processes in depression. Some of the work we will review examines why people experience an immediate depressive reaction to an event; other research is geared toward understanding why a depressive reaction persists into a long-term depressive episode. It's important to make this distinction, because depressed reactions to events of loss and disappointment are fairly common. Most such reactions are self-limiting, however, abating within a period of days or weeks. In a minority of cases, these reactions persist or intensify and result in serious disruptions in normal living.

Unfortunately, this distinction between short-term depressive reactions and clinically significant episodes of depression is not always maintained in depression research. Some studies use the term "depressed participants" to refer to people who are experiencing only mild or transient depressive reactions to an event. These reactions, which are often measured by self-report, are not necessarily the same as more extreme or enduring depressive episodes (for discussions of this issue, see Coyne, 1994; Flett, Vredenburg, & Krause, 1997; Kendall, Hollon, Beck, Hammen, & Ingram, 1987; Vredenburg, Flett, & Krames, 1993). To avoid ambiguity, I will use the term *dysphoria* (rather than depression) when discussing research with participants who have not met a clinical diagnosis of depression.

SELF-ESTEEM MODELS OF DEPRESSION

With this discussion as background, we are ready to consider how self-relevant processes influence the onset and maintenance of depression.

Low Self-Esteem as a Risk Factor in Depression

The first issue we will explore is whether low self-esteem puts people at risk for developing depression. The question here is not simply whether self-reproach and self-recrimination are symptoms of depression (as discussed earlier). The issue here is whether low self-esteem operates as a stable, predisposing vulnerability factor (i.e., a diathesis). In simpler terms: Are low self-esteem people more apt than high self-esteem people to become depressed in the face of negative life events?

Much of the material we reviewed in Chapter 8 is suggestive of such an association. For instance, Keith Dutton and I found that low self-esteem people suffer greater emotional distress when they fail than do high self-esteem people and that this occurs, in part, because failure leads low self-esteem people to feel *bad* about themselves (Brown & Dutton, 1995b; Dutton, 1995; Dutton & Brown, 1997). These findings do not establish that low self-esteem people are at greater risk for developing depression, but they are consistent with this idea.

George Brown and his colleagues (e.g., Brown & Harris, 1978; Brown, Andrews, Harris, Adler, & Bridge, 1986) have offered even more definitive evidence that low self-esteem is a risk factor for depression. Initial support for this conclusion came from the study by Brown and Harris (1978), which we discussed earlier. Recall that Brown and Harris found that many of the women who were depressed had previously experienced a stressful life event, but not all women who had experienced a stressful life event became depressed. Additional data analyses revealed that certain social characteristics increased a person's risk for developing depression. These included the early loss of one's mother in childhood and the lack of an intimate, confiding relationship in adulthood. Brown and Harris speculated that these factors put people at risk for developing depression by lowering self-esteem. In this model, then, prior social experiences involving the loss of a loved one or a lack of intimacy give rise to low self-esteem, and low self-esteem, in conjunction with a subsequent negative life event, increases the risk of depression (Brown, Bifulco, Veiel, & Andrews, 1990). Figure 9.2 shows the model.

G. Brown et al. (1986) conducted a longitudinal study to test this model. In accordance with predictions, low self-esteem (as indexed by the number of negative self-referent statements a participant made during an interview) functioned as a vulnerability factor when accompanied by a stressful life event. The effect was such that women with low self-esteem were nearly twice as likely as women with high self-esteem to develop depression when faced with a negative life event. Additional investigations have found similar support for G. Brown's model (Andrews & Brown, 1993; Brown, Bifulco, & Andrews, 1990; Miller, Kreitman, Ingham, & Sashidharan, 1989; Roberts, Gotlib, & Kassel, 1996), suggesting that low self-esteem puts people at risk for developing depression when negative life events occur.

Self-Worth Contingency Models of Depression

Self-worth contingency models provide another perspective on the role of self-esteem in depression. These models begin by assuming that people strive to feel good about themselves (i.e., to satisfy their self-enhancement needs). People prone to depression have highly conditional feelings of self-worth. They feel good about themselves when certain conditions are met (e.g., they are in a romantic relationship; they are succeeding at their work or schooling) but bad about themselves when these conditions are not being met. Depression arises, according to these models, when experiences threaten these "conditions of self-worth" and people perceive they won't be able to meet their self-enhancement needs in the future (see Figure 9.3).

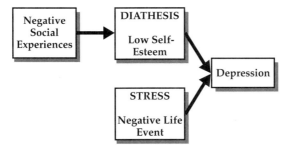

FIGURE 9.2. George Brown's model of self-esteem and depression. Negative social experiences (particularly the loss of one's mother in childhood and the lack of an intimate, confiding relationship in adulthood) give rise to low self-esteem. Low self-esteem then acts as a diathesis for depression when a negative event occurs.
(Adapted from Brown & Harris, 1978, *Social origins of depression: A study of psychiatric disorder in women.* London: Tavistock. Copyright 1978. Reprinted by permission of Tavistock Publications.)

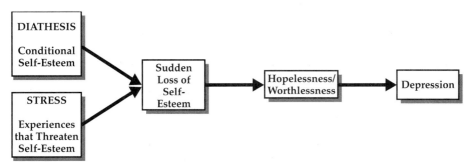

FIGURE 9.3. Self-worth contingency models of depression. Highly conditional self-esteem is a diathesis. Depression arises when negative events threaten these "conditions of self-worth" and people perceive they will be unable to meet these needs in the future.

Psychoanalytic Models

Self-worth contingency models of depression were first developed by theorists working within the psychoanalytic tradition. Rado (1928) and Fenichel (1945) argued that people prone to depression have excessively high interpersonal dependency needs. They desperately seek approval and reassurance from others, and depression arises when they fail to receive it. The situation is much like that of a young child who hungers for the constant and undivided attention and affection of others.

> [People with high interpersonal dependency needs are] never able to get enough care and attention. . . . When these needs are frustrated, as they are bound to be, the already low level of self-esteem, which is without significant other resources to shore it up, is further lowered, and clinical depression results. (Hirschfeld, Klerman, Chodoff, Korchin, & Barrett, 1976, p. 384)

Bibring (1953) subsequently expanded this analysis to include other sources of self-worth. On the basis of his clinical experience, Bibring distinguished three types of self-ideals commonly held by depression-prone individuals: (1) a heightened need to be loved, appreciated, admired, and respected; (2) an ex-aggerated need to be strong, capable, successful, and independent; and (3) an inordinate need to be good, loving, moral, and virtuous (see also, Strauman, 1989; Strauman & Higgins, 1987). According to Bibring, people holding these lofty ideals become depressed when they believe that they are presently fail-ing to meet these standards and will be unable to meet them in the future. Es-sentially, they give up hope, concluding that they are inadequate to realize their aspirations. Note, then, how this model combines elements of both worthlessness (inadequacy) and hopelessness (the belief that one will never be able to live up to one's ideals).

Social Identity Model of Depression

Oatley and Bolton (1985) have offered a conceptually similar analysis with a strong interpersonal emphasis. Their model assumes (1) that people often de-rive their feelings of self-worth from their social roles, and (2) that other people are needed to enact these roles. Depression arises, according to the model, when the loss of another person jeopardizes a highly valued social role and the person has few alternative sources of self-worth available. From this perspec-tive, people vulnerable to loss are those who base their feelings of self-worth on a limited number of social roles (see also, Linville, 1987; Thoits, 1983).

The empty-nest syndrome provides a paradigmatic example. A woman who derives her primary identity from her role as a mother is vulnerable to depression when her children leave home because she is no longer able to ef-fectively enact that role. Depression is especially apt to occur when the woman has few (if any) other sources of self-worth available. A similar sense of de-spair afflicts some workers when they retire from life-long occupations and have no alternative sources of fulfillment.

Congruency Models of Depression

Congruency models of depression (e.g., Arieti & Bemporad, 1978; Beck, 1983; Blatt, Quinlan, Chevron, MacDonald, & Zuroff, 1982; Bowlby, 1973) inte-grate the various self-worth models we've been discussing. These models as-sume that there are two personality types prone to depression. One of these is highly dependent on social sources of approval; the other is highly dependent on achievement outcomes. Table 9.1 presents a description of each type.

People with a conditional interpersonal orientation have inordinately high interpersonal dependency needs. They require the acceptance and love of oth-ers in order to feel good about themselves. They like themselves when they perceive that these needs are being met but dislike themselves when they per-ceive that these needs are not being met. Of course, everyone feels better about themselves when they believe they are liked and respected by others. But for people with high interpersonal dependency needs, the need for approval and affection is constant and virtually insatiable.

People with a conditional achievement orientation base their feelings of self-worth on their ability to succeed and exercise control over the environment.

TABLE 9.1. Congruency Models of Depression

Depression-Prone Personality Type	Bases of Self-Worth	Events that Threaten Self-Worth	Themes Expressed During a Depressive Episode
Conditional interpersonal orientation	Interpersonal relationships; excessive need for acceptance, support, and approval	Social exclusion, rejection, or disapproval	Loneliness, loss, abandonment, rejection
Conditional achievement orientation	Achievement outcomes; meeting internalized standards and goals; excessive need for success and the exertion of power and control	Failure to achieve goals or attain standards	Inadequacy, personal failure, guilt, self-recrimination

They feel good about themselves when they succeed but bad about themselves when they fail. Meeting these standards is no simple matter, however. Individuals with a conditional achievement orientation tend to be perfectionistic. They hold extremely high standards and are rarely satisfied with their level of accomplishment, even though these achievements are often considerable (Blatt, 1995).

In tests of this *congruency* model, researchers have looked at whether depression is most apt to arise when a negative life event is congruent with, or matches, a person's personality type (e.g., Hammen, Ellicott, Gitlin, & Jamison, 1989; Hammen et al., 1985; Robins, 1990; Robins, Block, & Peselow, 1989; Segal, Shaw, Vella, & Katz, 1992). The prediction is that negative interpersonal events (e.g., the break-up of a marriage) are more apt to precipitate depression in people with a conditional interpersonal orientation than in people with a conditional achievement orientation, but that negative achievement-related events (e.g., a significant personal failure) are more likely to precipitate depression in people with a conditional achievement orientation than in people with a conditional interpersonal orientation. So far, tests of this congruency hypothesis have produced mixed support for the model (Coyne & Whiffen, 1995). Although people with a conditional interpersonal orientation appear to be particularly vulnerable to the effects of negative interpersonal events, people with a conditional achievement orientation do not appear to be more vulnerable to negative achievement-related events (for an exception, see Hewitt & Flett, 1993).

Labile Self-Esteem as a Risk Factor in Depression

Because people with conditional self-esteem base their feelings of self-worth on their current outcomes, their self-esteem seems to fluctuate over time. Recognizing this fact, investigators have used fluctuations in self-esteem (termed labile or unstable self-esteem) to predict the onset of depression (Butler,

Hokanson, & Flynn, 1994; Kernis, Granneman, & Mathis, 1991; Roberts, Kassel, & Gotlib, 1995; Roberts & Monroe, 1992, 1994).

An investigation by Butler et al. (1994) illustrates this approach. These investigators measured self-esteem over the course of 30 days in a sample of college students. This allowed them to calculate an index of (1) average self-esteem level (high or low) and (2) self-esteem lability (how much self-esteem varied from one day to the next in response to daily events). Among other things, Butler et al. found that *low self-esteem* was not a risk factor for dysphoria but that students with *labile self-esteem* were more apt to become dysphoric in the face of negative life events than were students with stable self-esteem. These results are consistent with the claim that labile or reactive self-esteem is a better predictor of depression than is a constant level of low self-esteem (but see Roberts et al., 1995).

It is somewhat difficult to interpret these findings, however. In Chapter 8, we likened self-esteem to the love most parents feel for their children. Whether conditional love can be considered true love is debatable. In my opinion, a parent who loves his child on some days but not on others doesn't really love his child at all. In a similar vein, a person who only feels good about himself when things are going well doesn't have true high self-esteem. For this reason, I think of labile self-esteem as a form of low self-esteem, one in which feelings of self-worth are highly conditional and, therefore, volatile.

BECK'S COGNITIVE THEORY OF DEPRESSION

Self-esteem theories of depression emphasize that people's feelings toward themselves are a risk factor for depression. Other theories focus on the role cognitive processes play in depression. These theories assume that depression is maintained (and perhaps caused) by the manner in which people think about themselves and process personal information.

Aaron Beck was one of the first theorists to advocate this position (Beck, 1967, 1976; Beck, Rush, Shaw, & Emery, 1979). As a therapist with an active clinical practice, Beck sought to understand the nature of depression in order to devise effective treatment strategies. Beck began by developing a precise description of the disorder, with special attention given to distinguishing primary symptoms from more secondary ones (on the assumption that if he *cured* the primary symptoms, the secondary ones would resolve as well) (Beck et al., 1979). As his work has evolved, Beck has added causal elements to his descriptive account of depression. Figure 9.4 presents a schematic representation of his theory, based on some of his most recent work (Beck, 1991; see also Haaga, Dyck, & Ernst, 1991).

Theoretical Model

The Negative Cognitive Triad is the Primary Feature of Depression

Beck's most central assumption is that depression is principally a cognitive disorder characterized by three negative, self-relevant beliefs: (1) a negative

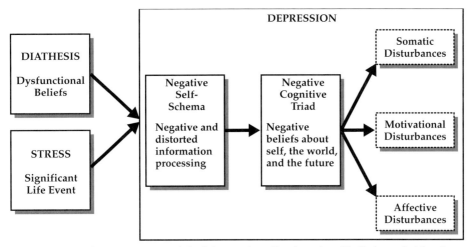

FIGURE 9.4. Beck's cognitive model of depression. Dysfunctional beliefs are held to be a vulnerability factor (a diathesis). When activated by appropriate environmental events (stress), these dysfunctional beliefs lead a person prone to depression to interpret experiences in negative and distorted ways. These negative interpretations, in turn, lead to negative views of oneself, one's world, and one's future. These beliefs, which Beck refers to as the negative cognitive triad, are viewed as the primary symptom of depression, giving rise to other features of the disorder, including somatic (sleeplessness), motivational (passivity), and affective (sadness) disturbances.
(Adapted from Beck, 1991, *American Psychologist, 46,* 368–375. Copyright 1991. Adapted by permission of The American Psychological Association.)

view of the self (when depressed, people believe they are defective, deficient, and worthless); (2) a negative view of the world (when depressed, people are dissatisfied with their current life situation and believe the world is making unreasonable demands upon them); and (3) a negative view of the future (when depressed, people are pessimistic about their ability to attain desired outcomes). Beck refers to these beliefs (which encompass feelings of hopelessness and worthlessness) as the *negative cognitive triad* and assumes that they are the central feature of all types of depression. This means that other aspects of depression, such as somatic disturbances (e.g., trouble sleeping), motivational disturbances (e.g., passivity and withdrawal), and affective disturbances (e.g., intense sadness), arise in response to these beliefs (Beck et al., 1979, p. 11).

Beck also believes that these thoughts have an automatic, reflexive quality. They seem to appear "out of nowhere," without provocation or conscious awareness. As depression worsens, they become increasingly repetitive and intrusive. In extreme cases, they may virtually dominate thinking, making it difficult for the depressed person to concentrate and engage in normal activities. A large part of the therapy Beck developed to treat depression involves monitoring these thoughts, noting when they occur and under what circumstances. By doing so, Beck argues, one can gain control over these thoughts and eliminate them (Beck et al., 1979).

Negative Self-Schemas in the Maintenance of Depression

Figure 9.4 also shows that negatively biased information processing supports and maintains these negative beliefs. Beck discusses these information-processing tendencies in terms of a negative self-schema. As noted in Chapter 5, schemas are hypothetical cognitive structures that guide the processing of information. According to Beck, people who are depressed possess a negative self-schema that leads them to process personal information in a negatively biased and distorted fashion. They dwell on the negative aspects of their life and interpret events in self-defeating ways. These tendencies, in turn, fuel and sustain the negative cognitive triad. A negative self-schema thus explains "why a depressed patient maintains his pain-inducing and self-defeating attitudes despite objective evidence of positive factors in his life" (Beck et al., 1979, p. 12).

Beck believes that these interpretations are often distorted and illogical and that they result from faulty information-processing tendencies (see also, Ellis, 1962). These tendencies include (1) *selective abstraction* (focusing on a detail out of context), (2) *arbitrary inference* (drawing conclusions in the absence of supporting evidence), (3) *overgeneralization* (applying conclusions too broadly), and (4) *absolutistic* or *dichotomous thinking* (the tendency to think in categorical—black or white—terms). To illustrate, imagine that a friend forgets to return your phone call. A depressed person will interpret this oversight as a sign of disrespect and an indication that he or she is entirely unlovable. These interpretations persist, Beck argued, even in the face of evidence that more benign interpretations are plausible (e.g., the friend simply forgot or never got the message).

> In milder depressions the patient is generally able to view his negative thoughts with some objectivity. As the depression worsens, his thinking becomes increasingly dominated by negative ideas, although there may be no logical connection between actual situations and his negative interpretations. As the prepotent idiosyncratic schemas lead to distortions of reality and consequently to systematic errors in the depressed person's thinking, he is less able to entertain the notion that his negative interpretations are erroneous. (Beck et al., 1979, p. 13)

Beck contrasts the biased and illogical information processing found during depression with that found in nondepressed individuals. According to Beck, nondepressed individuals process personal information in a logical and unbiased manner, generally reaching accurate and rational conclusions. We will have more to say about this aspect of Beck's theory in Chapter 10.

Dysfunctional Beliefs as a Vulnerability Factor in Depression

Dysfunctional beliefs form the third component of Beck's cognitive theory (see top left-hand side of Figure 9.4). Dysfunctional beliefs are excessively rigid beliefs about oneself and the world. They develop early in childhood and involve unrealistic and perfectionistic standards by which people judge themselves. For example, a person prone to depression is apt to endorse the following statements: "If I do not perform as well as others, it means that I am an inferior human being," or "My value as a person depends greatly on what others think of me" (Beck et al., 1979).

According to Beck, these absolutistic, contractual beliefs (which parallel the conditions of worth we discussed earlier) make a person vulnerable to depression when a matching life event occurs. By way of illustration, imagine that a person experiences the unwanted dissolution of an important interpersonal relationship. If the person possesses a matching dysfunctional attitude ("I am nothing if a person I love doesn't love me"), the person begins to view the situation in unrealistically negative terms. The person may assume excessive responsibility for the event, selectively recall other failed romantic involvements, and so forth. These information processing biases lead to the negative cognitive triad (a negative view of oneself, one's life, and one's future), which triggers other aspects of depression.

Summary

To summarize, Beck's model assumes that a depressive episode begins when a significant life event (e.g., the death of a loved one; losing one's job) makes contact with one or more dysfunctional beliefs. The confluence of these factors activates a negative self-schema, characterized by negative attentional and interpretational biases. These biases, in turn, give rise to the negative cognitive triad and other symptoms of depression.

Empirical Research

Beck's work has inspired scores of studies (for reviews, see Barnett & Gotlib, 1988; Coyne & Gotlib, 1983; Haaga et al., 1991; Ruehlman, West, & Pasahow, 1985). This research can be divided into three areas: (1) Do depressed people exhibit the negative cognitive triad? (2) Do depressed people process information in a negatively biased and distorted fashion? and (3) Are dysfunctional beliefs a vulnerability factor in the development of depression?

Negative Thinking during a Depressed Episode

There is ample evidence to support Beck's claim that negative thinking is an important aspect of depression. Numerous studies have found that people who are currently depressed regard themselves, their current life situation, and their future in more negative terms than do nondepressed people (for reviews, see Haaga et al., 1991; Ruehlman et al., 1985). These tendencies generally occur only for self-relevant judgments, as depressives are usually not more negative than nondepressives when making judgments about people "in general" (Garber & Hollon, 1980; Haaga et al., 1991; Hoehn-Hyde, Schlottmann, & Rush, 1982; Schlenker & Britt, 1996).

Although these findings support Beck's model, other evidence suggests some qualifications. Depressed people consistently display *relative* negativity (i.e., they describe themselves more negatively than do nondepressed people), but they do not always display *absolute* negativity (i.e., they do not always describe themselves in strongly negative terms). Instead of exhibiting self-abasement and self-deprecation, they often evince modesty or slight self-glorification (Pelham, 1991b). In fact, one survey found that feelings of worth-lessness and inadequacy (which Beck assumes are central features of all types of depression) are present in only two-thirds of clinically diagnosable cases of depression (Buchwald & Rudick-Davis, 1993). This means that a sizable pro-portion of depressed people do not show strong evidence of negative thinking.

Information Processing during Depression

The manner in which depressed people process personal information is a second area of research relevant to Beck's theory. Derry and Kuiper (1981) ex-amined this issue in the context of an experiment on memory for self-relevant material. Using a modified version of the self-reference task developed by Rogers, Kuiper, and Kirker (1977, see Chapter 5), Derry and Kuiper had de-pressed and nondepressed participants rate a series of adjectives for their self-descriptiveness (Does the word describe you?). Half of the adjectives were negative in tone and centered around depression-relevant themes (e.g., help-less, gloomy); the other half were positive in tone and were unrelated to de-pression (e.g., capable, loyal). Later, the participants were unexpectedly asked to recall as many of the words as they could remember.

Figure 9.5 presents some of the results from this investigation. The left-hand panel shows the results for the trait endorsement measure. The nonde-pressed participants rated positive attributes as far more self-descriptive than negative attributes, but the depressed participants rated positive and negative attributes as equally self-descriptive. In terms of content, then, this finding pro-vides evidence that although depressives are more negative in their self-descriptions than are nondepressives, they are not negative in an *absolute* sense.

The right-hand panel of Figure 9.5 shows the results for the recall mea-sure. Depressed participants recalled a greater proportion of negative than positive self-descriptive attributes, but nondepressed participants recalled a greater proportion of positive than negative self-descriptive attributes. These findings support Beck's assertion that depressed people exhibit superior pro-cessing for negative personal information.

An investigation by Bargh and Tota (1988) provides additional support for this conclusion. Modifying Derry and Kuiper's (1981) procedure, Bargh and Tota had nondepressed and dysphoric participants indicate whether a series of positive and negative trait adjectives described themselves or the av-erage person. Participants in the control condition made these judgments under normal conditions, whereas participants in the experimental (memory load) condition were asked to remember a six-digit number while making these judgments.

The critical dependent variable was the speed with which participants made their decisions. The memory-load manipulation requires conscious atten-tion and therefore competes with (and impairs) the conscious processing of other information. It has little effect, however, on the automatic processing of information, as such processing, by definition, does not require conscious at-

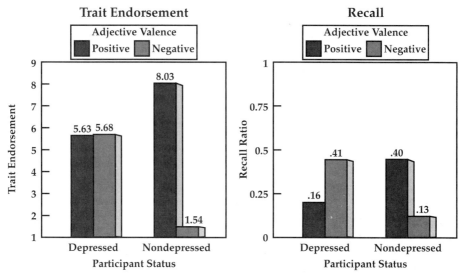

FIGURE 9.5. Self-schema functioning in depressed and nondepressed participants. The left-hand panel shows that depressed participants rated positive and negative adjectives as equally self-descriptive, but nondepressed participants rated positive adjectives as more self-descriptive than negative adjectives. The right-hand panel shows that depressed participants recalled a greater proportion of negative than positive adjectives, whereas nondepressed participants did the opposite.
(Adapted from Derry & Kuiper, 1981, *Journal of Abnormal Psychology, 90,* 286–297. Copyright 1981. Adapted by permission of The American Psychological Association.)

tention. If depressed people process negative (but not positive) personal information in a rather effortless, automatic fashion, the memory-load manipulation should have little effect on the speed with which dysphoric participants judge the self-descriptiveness of negative traits, but it should slow down the speed with which they judge the self-descriptiveness of positive traits. Just the opposite pattern should occur for nondepressives, who presumably process positive (but not negative) personal information in an effortless, automatic fashion.

The data shown in Figure 9.6 provide considerable support for these predictions. The left-hand panel presents the data for self-relevant judgments. The data show that the memory-load manipulation had little effect on the speed with which dysphoric participants judged the self-descriptiveness of *negative* attributes, but it significantly slowed down the speed with which they judged the self-descriptiveness of *positive* attributes. This pattern is reversed among the nondepressed participants.

The right-hand panel shows the results for judgments of other people. There is no effect of participant status here. Among both dysphoric and nondepressed participants, the memory-load manipulation significantly slowed down the time it took to make negative judgments of others, but it had little impact on positive judgments of others. Taken together, these findings are in accordance with the claim that depressed people process negative personal

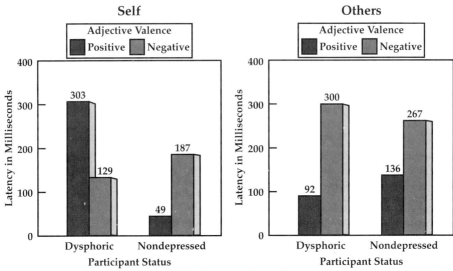

FIGURE 9.6. The speed with which dysphoric and nondepressed participants made judgments about self and others as a function of memory load. The left-hand panel shows
that the memory load manipulation had little effect on the speed with which dysphoric
participants rated the self-descriptiveness of *negative* attributes, but it did slow down the
speed with which they rated the self-descriptiveness of *positive* adjectives. The opposite
occurred among nondepressed participants. The data in the right-hand panel show that
these differences did not extend to judgments of other people, as here the memory-load
manipulation had a similar effect on dysphoric and nondepressed participants. Together, these results are consistent with the claim that depressed people process *negative
personal* information in a rather automatic fashion.
(Adapted from Bargh & Tota, 1988, *Journal of Personality and Social Psychology, 54,* 925–939.
Copyright 1988. Adapted by permission of The American Psychological Association.)

information in an automatic, unintentional fashion (see also Gotlib & Cane,
1987; Gotlib & McCann, 1984).

Dysfunctional Beliefs as a Diathesis for Depression

To this point, we have seen that people who are currently depressed view
themselves in (relatively) negative terms and show superior processing for
negative personal information. These findings are generally consistent with
Beck's model. The third aspect of Beck's theory—whether dysfunctional beliefs constitute a vulnerability factor for depression—has received less support
(Barnett & Gotlib, 1988; Coyne & Gotlib, 1983; Haaga et al., 1991).

Dysfunctional beliefs are presumed to be stable, cognitive structures. When
activated by appropriate environmental events, they lead people to process information in negative ways and to become depressed. The most straightforward (and definitive) way to test this aspect of Beck's theory is to conduct a
longitudinal study in which researchers (1) first measure dysfunctional beliefs
in nondepressed people and (2) then follow these people over time to see
whether those who hold dysfunctional beliefs *and* experience relevant life

events during the course of the study develop depression in the manner specified by the theory. Barnett and Gotlib (1990) performed such a study, but they
did not find support for Beck's model.

Another strategy is to see whether people who used to be depressed hold
more dysfunctional beliefs than do people who have never been depressed
(Lewinsohn, Steinmetz, Larson, & Franklin, 1981). If, as Beck has claimed,
these beliefs predispose a person to become depressed, they should be evident
even after a depressive episode remits. There is little evidence that this occurs.
Although *currently depressed* individuals endorse more dysfunctional beliefs
than do nondepressed individuals, these beliefs generally return to normal
levels once depression lifts (e.g., Dohr, Rush, & Bernstein, 1989; Hamilton &
Abramson, 1983; Segal et al., 1992).

These results indicate that dysfunctional beliefs accompany depression
but do not predict the onset of depression or persist after depression has
abated. In consideration of these findings, several theorists (e.g., Barnett &
Gotlib, 1988; Coyne & Gotlib, 1983) have concluded that dysfunctional beliefs
are symptoms or concomitants of depression rather than predisposing, causal
factors. Like the other negative cognitions Beck describes, they characterize a
depressive episode, but they do not cause the disorder.

Understanding the Link between Negative Cognitions and Depression

Associative network models of memory can explain why negative
thoughts accompany depression. Among other things, these models assume
that moods are encoded in memory and are linked to mood-congruent cognitions. Happiness is linked to positively valenced cognitions (e.g., blue skies,
ice cream, and positive self-attitudes) and sadness is linked to negatively valenced cognitions (e.g., rainy days, famine, and negative self-attitudes). When
a mood is experienced, activation spreads to associated concepts, making
them more accessible to conscious awareness. From this perspective, a depressed mood primes or activates negative self-relevant cognitions, account-
ing for the observed association between negative mood and negative self-
relevant thinking (for a more thorough discussion of this approach, see
Blaney, 1986; Bower, 1981; Ingram, 1984; Isen, 1984; Teasdale, 1983).

In tests of this model, researchers have experimentally induced positive or
negative moods in people and then examined the accessibility of positive and
negative self-relevant thoughts. Across several studies, negative self-relevant
thoughts have been shown to be more accessible when people are in a negative
mood state than when people are in a positive mood state (e.g., Brown & Taylor,
1986; Teasdale & Fogarty, 1979; Teasdale, Taylor, & Fogarty, 1980). These findings
support the claim that depressed moods activate negative self-referent thinking.

An investigation by Clark and Teasdale (1982) provides even more powerful support for this conclusion. These researchers examined the accessibility of
positive and negative personal memories in depressed patients with diurnal
mood variation. Such patients feel considerably more depressed at one time of
day (e.g., early in the morning) than at other times of day (e.g., before going to
bed). To measure the accessibility of negative thinking during each of the two

states, Clark and Teasdale asked the depressed patients to retrieve memories of real-life experiences in response to a neutral cue word. Consistent with the notion that sad moods activate negatively toned material, unhappy experiences were more apt to be recalled during the time of day when patients were more depressed.

The Accessibility of Negative Cognitions and the Persistence of Depression

At the outset of this chapter, we made a distinction between short-term depressive reactions to negative life events and clinically significant episodes of depression. We also noted that depressive reactions to negative life events are common. Most people grieve when a loved one dies and become distraught when they lose their job. Given this, it becomes important to understand why depressive reactions are transient and short-lived in some people but are prolonged and chronic in others.

Teasdale (1988) has suggested that the accessibility of negative cognitions during the early stages of depression is relevant to this issue. Teasdale assumes that people differ in the degree to which negative moods activate negative thinking and that this link influences the length and severity of a depressive episode. For depression-prone people, negative moods are highly apt to trigger negative self-relevant thoughts and lead to negative interpretations of one's present situation and the future. From this perspective, the particular cognitive factors leading to depression are less important than are the cognitive processes that serve to delimit or prolong this reaction.

Tests of this *differential activation* hypothesis have generally been supportive. Negative moods are especially apt to activate negative thinking in formerly depressed people (Miranda & Persons, 1988; Miranda, Persons, & Byers, 1990) and in people who are at risk for depression, such as those with low self-esteem (Brown & Mankowski, 1993). The accessibility of negative thinking has also been shown to predict the duration and depth of a depressive episode. People who show high levels of negative thinking during depression take longer to recover from depression and are at greater risk for relapse than are individuals who are depressed but show low levels of negative thinking (e.g., Dent & Teasdale, 1988; Krantz & Hammen, 1979; Lewinsohn et al., 1981). This pattern suggests that the nature and accessibility of negative thinking *during* depression influences whether depression is mild and transient or severe and recurrent (Teasdale, 1983, 1988).

The differential activation hypothesis may also explain why research has failed to find that negative thinking predicts the *onset* of depression. Beck's claim that dysfunctional beliefs are latent, cognitive structures implies that they need to be activated by particular experiences in order to be observed (Riskind & Rholes, 1984). Negative moods may be one type of activating (or priming) experience. If so, measuring the accessibility of negative thinking during a depressed mood may identify people at risk for depression (Segal & Dobson, 1992).

Summary

Table 9.2 summarizes the issues we have covered in this section. The *concomitant* hypothesis is clearly supported. There is considerable evidence that

TABLE 9.2. Possible Associations between Negative Thinking and Depression

Hypothesis	Explanation	Prediction	Support
Concomitant	Negative thinking accompanies depression.	People who are currently depressed show more evidence of negative thinking than do people who are not currently depressed.	Strongly supported. There is considerable evidence that negative thinking accompanies a depressive episode.
Causal	Negative thinking causes depression.	People who exhibit high levels of negative thinking are at risk for developing depression.	Not supported. There is little evidence that negative thinking predicts who becomes depressed or who has been depressed in the past.
Differential activation	The link between negative moods and negative thinking is stronger in some people than in others.	Depression is more apt to occur among people who show a strong link between negative moods and negative thinking.	Supported. Negative moods are more closely associated with negative thinking among people who have been depressed than among people who have never been depressed, and among people who are at risk for depression than among those who are not at risk for depression.
Duration	Negative thinking predicts the duration of a depressive episode.	Among people who are depressed, those who show strong signs of negative thinking are more likely to remain depressed than are those who do not show strong signs of negative thinking.	Supported. Among people who are depressed, the strength of negative thinking predicts the duration of a depressive episode.

negative thinking accompanies depression and that depressed people process information in a rather negative manner. There is, however, little evidence that dysfunctional beliefs cause depression, although this *causal* hypothesis cannot be completely dismissed. Finally, there is evidence that negative moods are especially apt to activate negative thinking among people prone to depression (*differential activation* hypothesis) and that the accessibility of negative thinking predicts the severity and duration of a depressive episode (*duration* hypothesis).

In light of these findings, what can we conclude about Beck's model? On the one hand, it seems fair to say that Beck's model provides a very useful descriptive account of depression and clarifies how depression is maintained. In this sense, the model gives important insights into how depression can be ameliorated (Beck et al., 1979). On the other hand, the model has proven to be less successful in identifying risk factors for depression and, therefore, in proving useful for purposes of prediction and prevention.

ATTRIBUTIONAL MODELS OF DEPRESSION

Beck's theory is not the only theory to emphasize the role of cognitive processes in depression. Attributional models of depression do so as well. These models assert that the attributions people make for important life events (i.e., Why is this event happening? What is the cause of this event?) influence the onset, magnitude, and duration of depression. In this section, we will trace the historical roots of the model and consider relevant empirical evidence.

Theoretical Development

Attributional models of depression grew out of research in experimental psychology, where it was observed that laboratory dogs first exposed to *inescapable* electrical shocks later displayed motivational deficits when exposed to *escapable* electrical shocks (Overmier & Seligman, 1967). Instead of taking instrumental action (such as crossing over to the other side of the room), the dogs seemed to passively accept their fate, *choosing* to endure the shock rather than try and escape it. Maier, Seligman, and Solomon (1969) interpreted these deficits in cognitive terms, arguing that the animals had learned that nothing they could do could alleviate their distress. They termed this (erroneous) perception, *learned helplessness.*

Learned Helplessness Models of Depression

Seligman (1975) applied these ideas to the study of depression in humans. Seligman speculated that depression arises when people perceive that important life events are beyond their control. Abramson, Seligman, and Teasdale (1978) subsequently modified the theory to include the attributions people make for these events. According to this *reformulated learned helplessness model,* depression results when people (1) perceive that important life events are beyond their control, and (2) attribute these events to causes that are internal (it's something about me rather than something about the situation), stable (it will last forever rather than be temporary), and global (it will affect all areas of my life rather than just this one area). Attributions to internal factors were tied to feelings of worthlessness, while attributions to stable and global factors were linked to feelings of hopelessness and despair (see also, Miller & Norman, 1979; Weiner & Litman-Adizes, 1980).

By way of illustration, consider again a person who is experiencing the break-up of an important interpersonal relationship. Depression is apt to result, Abramson et al. (1978) argued, to the extent that the person attributes this negative event to an enduring and general personal cause (e.g., an inability to get along with other people). Janoff-Bulman (1979, 1982) referred to this type of attribution as a form of characterological self-blame.

Abramson et al. (1978) went on to speculate that some people possess a negative attributional style, defined as a tendency to make internal, stable, and global attributions for negative events. The negative attributional style is thus a diathesis that puts people at risk for developing depression when a negative event occurs (see also, Peterson & Seligman, 1984).

Hopelessness Theory of Depression

Abramson, Metalsky, and Alloy (1988, 1989) presented a further revision of the model that integrates aspects of Beck's (1976) theory with the reformulated learned helplessness model. The revised theory, called the *hopelessness theory of depression*, is shown in Figure 9.7. Like Beck's model, hopelessness theory represents a diathesis-stress model of depression. The model begins with the occurrence of a negative life event. People who possess a matching negative attributional style tend to interpret the event in negative terms. They attribute the event to stable, global causes and perceive the event as having broad and important negative implications for their life. This perception, in turn, leads to hopelessness. Hopelessness is defined as the expectation that one is incapable of changing the negative event or altering its adverse implications for well-being. This perception gives rise to a subtype of depression, called hopelessness depression. Finally, if the negative event is also attributed to an internal cause, depression is accompanied by low self-esteem.[2]

Empirical Research

Tests of the attributional model generally take two forms. Some studies examine whether people who are currently depressed exhibit a negative attributional style; other studies examine whether a negative attributional style combines with stressful life events to predict the development of depression.

---

[2]There is one key difference between Beck's (1967) theory and the hopelessness theory of depression. Beck argued that negative self-relevant cognitions are a defining feature of *all* types of depression; Abramson et al. contend that negative self-relevant cognitions are present in only some types of depression, most notably in the type they call hopelessness depression. A more complete discussion of this and other issues can be found in Abramson et al. (1988, 1989) and Dykman and Abramson (1990).

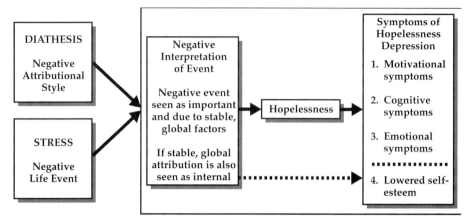

FIGURE 9.7. A hopelessness theory of depression. A depressive episode begins when people with a negative attributional style interpret a negative life event in negative terms. These interpretations, in turn, give rise to hopelessness, which is the immediate cause of hopelessness depression.
(Adapted from Abramson, Metalsky, & Alloy, 1989, *Psychological Review, 96,* 358–372. Copyright 1989. Adapted by permission of The American Psychological Association.)

Attributional Style in Depression

With respect to the first issue, there is abundant evidence that depressed people are more apt to make internal, stable, and global attributions for negative outcomes than are nondepressed people (for reviews, see Brewin, 1985; Coyne & Gotlib, 1983; Peterson & Seligman, 1984; Sweeney, Anderson, & Bailey, 1986). This evidence comes from (1) laboratory studies, in which participants make attributions for experimentally induced failure (Kuiper, 1978; Rizley, 1978); (2) field studies, in which people make attributions for naturally occurring negative life events (e.g., Gong-Guy & Hammen, 1980; Zautra, Guenther, & Chartier, 1985); (3) archival data, in which attributions for negative events are culled from diaries or other written or spoken material (Peterson, Luborsky, & Seligman, 1983); and (4) questionnaire studies, in which a more general attributional style is assessed (see Peterson & Seligman, 1984).

The majority of the questionnaire studies use the Attributional Style Questionnaire developed by Seligman, Abramson, Semmel, and von Baeyer (1979; see also Peterson, Semmel, von Baeyer, Abramson, Metalsky, & Seligman, 1982). Portions of the questionnaire are shown in Table 9.3.

The complete Attributional Style Questionnaire consists of six positive hypothetical events and six negative hypothetical events. Researchers then sum across these events and compare the responses of nondepressed and depressed participants. Figure 9.8 presents the findings from one investigation that adopted this approach (Seligman et al., 1988). The data show that nondepressed participants made more internal, stable, and global attributions for positive events than did depressed participants but that the reverse was true for negative events. Another way of looking at these data is to note that nondepressed participants made more internal, stable, and global attributions for

TABLE 9.3. Attributional Style Questionnaire

Please try to vividly imagine yourself in the situations that follow. If such a situation happened to you, what do you feel would have caused it? While events may have many causes, we want you to pick only one—the *major* cause if this event happened to *you*. Please write this cause in the blank provided after the event. Next we want you to answer some questions about the *cause*.

Sample Item 1: You've been looking for a job unsuccessfully for some time.

1. Write down the *one* major cause _____

2. Is the cause of your unsuccessful job search due to something about you or something about other people or circumstances?

	1	2	3	4	5	6	7

Totally due to other
people or circumstances
                                                              Totally due
                                                              to me

3. In the future when looking for a job, will this cause again be present?

	1	2	3	4	5	6	7

Will never again
be present
                                                              Will always
                                                              be present

4. Is the cause something that just influences looking for a job, or does it also influence other areas of your life?

	1	2	3	4	5	6	7

Influences just this
particular situation
                                                              Influences all
                                                              situations in my life

Sample Item 2: You meet a friend who compliments you on your appearance.

1. Write down the *one* major cause _____

2. Is the cause of the compliment something about you or something about other people or circumstances?

	1	2	3	4	5	6	7

Totally due to other
people or circumstances
                                                              Totally due
                                                              to me

3. In the future when you see your friend, will this cause again be present?

	1	2	3	4	5	6	7

Will never again
be present
                                                              Will always
                                                              be present

4. Is the cause something that just influences this one aspect of your life, or does it also influence other areas of your life?

	1	2	3	4	5	6	7

Influences just this
particular situation
                                                              Influences all
                                                              situations in my life

Source: Adapted from Seligman, Abramson, Semmel, & von Baeyer, 1979, *Journal of Abnormal Psychology, 88,* 242–247. Copyright 1979. Adapted by permission of The American Psychological Association.

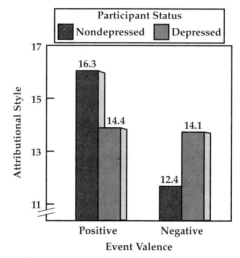

FIGURE 9.8. Attributional style for positive and negative hypothetical events by depressed and nondepressed participants. (Scores represent a composite index found by summing ratings of internal, stable, and global attributions.) The data show that non-depressed participants made more internal, stable, and global attributions for positive events than did depressed participants but that depressed participants made more internal, stable, and global attributions for negative events than did nondepressed participants. These findings are consistent with the claim that depressed people exhibit a negative attributional style.
(Adapted from Seligman et al., 1988, *Journal of Abnormal Psychology, 97,* 13–18. Copyright 1988. Adapted by permission of The American Psychological Association.)

positive events than for negative events but that the attributions of depressed participants were balanced and even-handed.

Attributional Style as a Risk Factor for Depression

To see whether a negative attributional style makes a person vulnerable to depression when faced with a negative life event, Metalsky, Halberstadt, and Abramson (1987) examined how college students with different attributional styles for achievement-related events responded to a poor performance on a midterm exam. Immediately after receiving their grades, students' emotional reactions depended only on the exam grades they received (students who did well felt good; students who did poorly felt bad). Two days later, however, students who had done poorly on the test were more likely to remain in a depressed mood if they also possessed a negative attributional style. Subsequent research with both college students and younger children has replicated these findings and provided additional evidence that thoughts of hopelessness drive these emotional reactions (Hilsman & Garber, 1995; Metalsky & Joiner, 1992; Metalsky, Joiner, Hardin, & Abramson, 1993). Because these studies only examined the duration of depressed mood, not the development of clinically significant cases of depression, the results must be interpreted cautiously. That being said, the findings are certainly consistent with the claim that a negative attributional style functions as a diathesis for depression when negative life events occur.

ATTENTIONAL PROCESSES IN DEPRESSION

Several times in this chapter we have noted that depressive reactions to negative life events are not uncommon and that an important issue to consider is why these reactions are short-lived and self-limiting in some cases but not in others. Teasdale (1988), you may recall, argued that the accessibility of negative thinking during depression is one factor to consider. Depression is more apt to endure and worsen, Teasdale argued, when negative moods automatically activate negative thinking.

Attentional processes also influence the severity and length of a depressive episode. In this section, we will review three lines of research that have examined this issue.

Self-Awareness and Depression

One line of research begins with the observation that depressed people tend to be introspective and self-absorbed. They brood about themselves a lot and spend a good deal of time questioning their motives, mulling over their feelings, and examining their personality traits. Consistent with this observation, research with community and clinical samples has found a positive association between depression and private self-consciousness (Ingram, Lumry, Cruet, & Sieber, 1987; Ingram & Smith, 1984; Smith & Greenberg, 1981; Smith, Ingram, & Roth, 1985). Although these effects are not always strong or unique to depression (see Ingram, 1990), there is little doubt that depressed individuals spend more time thinking about themselves than do nondepressed individuals.[3]

The tendency to focus one's attention inward may influence other aspects of depression. Self-consciousness increases the intensity of emotional states (Scheier & Carver, 1977), particularly negative emotional states (Brockner, Hjelle, & Plant, 1985; Gibbons, Smith, Ingram, Pearce, Brehm, & Schroeder, 1980; Scheier & Carver, 1977). Self-consciousness also can activate a negative self-image, as people who think about themselves a lot often become aware that they are falling short of their ideals and aspirations (Duval & Wicklund, 1972). These parallels suggest that (1) self-consciousness is a central symptom of depression, and (2) that people who are especially susceptible to self-consciousness during

---

[3]Self-awareness and depressed mood appear to be related in a reciprocal fashion. Wood, Saltzberg, and Goldsamt (1990) had participants listen to either sad music or affectively neutral music and then write down "anything that comes to mind" for two minutes afterward. Participants who listened to sad music referred to themselves more often in these essays than did control participants, supporting the claim that negative moods induce self-awareness.

depression may experience more intense and longer-lasting depressive reactions to events than people who are less self-absorbed.

Certain situations may make depressed people particularly self-aware. Pyszczynski and Greenberg (1987b) proposed that depressed people are especially apt to become introspective and self-aware following failure or some other negative, self-relevant experience. To test their ideas, Greenberg and Pyszczynski (1986) led nondepressed and dysphoric participants to succeed or fail at a task that allegedly measured their verbal intelligence. Afterward, participants were instructed to write down whatever thoughts came to mind.

Immediately after failure, both nondepressed and dysphoric participants showed signs of heightened self-awareness (as indexed by the proportion of self-referent statements). Two minutes later, however, nondepressed participants had returned to a nonself-focused state, while dysphoric participants continued to remain highly focused on themselves. These findings are consistent with the claim that depression is characterized by a tendency to stay in a prolonged state of self-awareness following negative outcomes.

This tendency may actually reflect a preference for self-awareness after failure. In another investigation, Pyszczynski and Greenberg (1986) again led nondepressed and dysphoric participants to succeed or fail at an alleged test of verbal ability. Afterward, they gave the participants three minutes to work on each of two puzzles. One of the puzzles was positioned on a table in front of a mirror, so that participants who worked on this puzzle were confronted with their own image; the other puzzle was positioned on a table without a mirror. Nondepressed participants avoided self-focused attention after failure, choosing not to work on the puzzle with the mirror. Dysphoric participants tended to do the reverse, choosing the puzzle with the mirror more after they had failed than after they had succeeded. These findings indicate that nondepressed people avoid self-focusing stimuli after failure but that dysphoric people do not.

Conway, Giannopoulos, Csank, and Mendelson (1993) have offered an explanation for why depressed people seek out self-awareness after failure. They have argued that depressed people think about themselves a lot in an attempt to better understand themselves. They are trying to end their suffering and believe that introspection and intensive self-scrutiny will serve this goal.

Ruminative Coping Style

Unfortunately, excessive introspection and self-preoccupation are rarely effective mood-management strategies. Susan Nolen-Hoeksema and her colleagues have studied this aspect of depression. Their research begins by noting that people differ in the degree to which they ruminate when they are sad. Some people think a lot about how sad they are and why they feel that way; other people attempt to distract themselves and take their mind off their troubles and worries.

Table 9.4 presents portions of a scale that is used to measure these individual differences. People who score high on this scale are said to have a ruminative coping style. When they are depressed, they think a lot about their symptoms and the possible consequences of these symptoms (Nolen-Hoeksema, 1991a, 1993). It's important to note that rumination does not involve a focus on

TABLE 9.4. An Abridged Version of the Responses to Depression Questionnaire

People think and do many different things when they feel depressed. Please read each of the items below and indicate whether you never, sometimes, often, or always think or do each one when you feel down, sad, or depressed. Please indicate what you *generally* do, not what you think you should do.

	1 Almost Never	2 Sometimes	3 Often	4 Almost Always
1. Think about how sad you feel.	____	____	____	____
2. Think "I won't be able to do my job/work because I feel so badly."	____	____	____	____
3. Think about how hard it is to concentrate.	____	____	____	____
4. Try to understand yourself by focusing on your depressed feelings.	____	____	____	____
5. Write down what you are thinking about and analyze it.	____	____	____	____
6. Think about all your shortcomings, failings, faults, and mistakes.	____	____	____	____
7. Go away by yourself and think about why you feel this way.	____	____	____	____
8. Think about how alone you feel.	____	____	____	____
9. Think "There must be something wrong with me or I wouldn't feel this way."	____	____	____	____
10. Think about how passive and unmotivated you feel.	____	____	____	____

Note: To determine your score, add up your responses to all 10 items. Higher numbers indicate a more ruminative coping style.
Source: Nolen-Hoeksema, 1991b, *Coding Guide for Responses to Depression Questionnaire.* Unpublished manuscript. Stanford University, Palo Alto, CA.

the causes of one's depression. It represents a preoccupation with being depressed (e.g., "What's wrong with me?" and "How will being depressed affect my life?"), rather than an active, problem-focused attempt to solve one's problems.

Several investigations have shown that individual differences in rumination are related to the duration and intensity of depression (for reviews, see Nolen-Hoeksema, 1991a, 1993). A study by Nolen-Hoeksema, Parker, and Larson (1994) provides a particularly compelling demonstration of this effect. These researchers studied 253 bereaved adults who had recently lost a member of their family to illness. One month after the family member had passed away, participants completed a modified version of the questionnaire shown in Table 9.4 and a measure of depression. Depression was reassessed six months later. Family members who scored high on the rumination scale had higher depression scores six months later than did those who scored low on the rumination scale. Nolen-Hoeksema and Morrow (1991) found a similar effect when they looked at how people coped with a natural disaster—the 1989 San Francisco Bay area earthquake. These studies establish that people who dwell on their sadness experience unusually long and severe depressive reactions to events.

Nolen-Hoeksema (1987) has applied these ideas to understanding sex differences in depression. Women are nearly twice as likely to be diagnosed with depression as are men. Women also tend to stay depressed longer than do men. Biological, social, and cultural mechanisms may all be involved in these differences. Ruminative coping style may be another relevant factor. At least in Western cultures, women are socialized to attend to their feelings and to express and display their emotions more than men. This is particularly true when these emotions are negative. These differences may make women more susceptible to rumination when depressed. In support of this hypothesis, women are more likely to show a ruminative coping style than are men, and once these differences are controlled, sex differences in the duration of a depressed mood disappear (Nolen-Hoeksema, Morrow, & Fredrickson, 1993).

Unwanted Thinking in Depression

Nolen-Hoeksema's research treats rumination as a conscious mood-management strategy. Rather than distracting themselves with more pleasant thoughts, people with a ruminative coping style ill advisedly choose to dwell on their negative mood state (Lyubomirsky & Nolen-Hoeksema, 1993). A related possibility is that some people have difficulty suppressing negative thoughts. Try as they might, they can't quit thinking of their problems and of how bad they feel.

Of course, everyone has had the feeling of having a negative thought just pop into their head. "There's always something there to remind me" and "I see her face everywhere I go" are familiar themes expressed in popular love songs to capture the degree to which a lost love object seems to automatically come to mind. But like everything else, some people are better at putting such thoughts out of their minds than are others. Early in this century, Freud (1915/1957) argued that the ability to exclude unwanted negative thoughts from conscious awareness is a hallmark of mental health. This is accomplished unconsciously (through repression) and consciously (through suppression).

A study by Wenzlaff, Wegner, and Roper (1988) shows how hard it is for depressed people to keep negative material from coming to mind. These investigators had nondepressed and dysphoric participants imagine themselves as a protagonist in a story. The story ended when the participant accidentally killed an infant in a car crash. Afterward, participants were asked to write down any thoughts that came into their minds during a nine-minute period. Half of the participants were in the control condition and were given no spe-

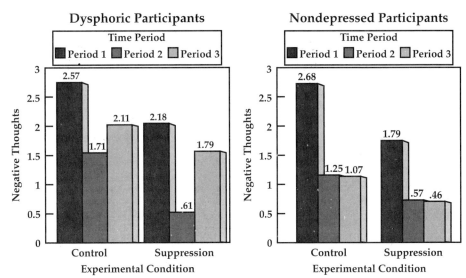

FIGURE 9.9. Suppression of negative thoughts in dysphoric and nondepressed participants. The data show that dysphoric participants in the suppression condition were initially able to suppress negative thoughts but that negative thoughts returned after only a
few minutes. This pattern of resurgence did not occur among nondepressed participants.
(Adapted from Wenzlaff, Wegner, & Roper, 1988, *Journal of Personality and Social Psychology, 55,* 882–892. Copyright 1988. Adapted by permission of The American Psychological Association.)

cial instructions regarding this task; the other half were in the suppression
condition and were explicitly told to try *not* to think about the story they had
just read. The experimenters then noted the number of times participants mentioned the story in each of three, three-minute time periods.

Figure 9.9 presents the results from this investigation. The right-hand panel
shows the results for the nondepressed participants. Notice that in both conditions, negative thinking declined rapidly between Periods 1 and 2 and remained
at a low level during Period 3. Now look at the left-hand panel, which shows the
data for the dysphoric participants. Two things are noteworthy here. First, in the
control condition, negative thinking remained high throughout the nine-minute
period. Second, although the suppression manipulation succeeded in reducing
negative thinking between Periods 1 and 2, the dysphoric participants showed a
rebound effect during Period 3. In fact, negative thinking during Period 3 was
nearly as high for the dysphoric participants in the suppression condition as for
the dysphoric participants in the control condition. These findings suggest that
depressed people are able to keep negative thoughts at bay only for a limited
period of time (see also, Hartlage, Alloy, Vásquez, & Dykman, 1993).

Learning to replace negative thoughts with more positive ones is a key element in recovery from depression. While this is a principal goal of virtually all
therapeutic approaches to the treatment of depression, gaining control of negative thoughts plays a particularly prominent role in Beck's cognitive therapy of

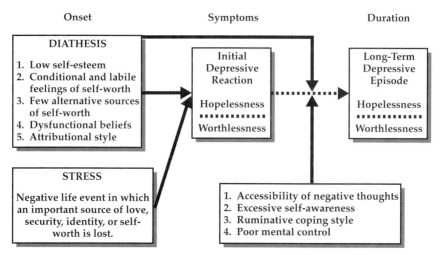

Onset	Symptoms	Duration

DIATHESIS

1. Low self-esteem
2. Conditional and labile feelings of self-worth
3. Few alternative sources of self-worth
4. Dysfunctional beliefs
5. Attributional style

Initial Depressive Reaction

Hopelessness
••••••••••••
Worthlessness

Long-Term Depressive Episode

Hopelessness
••••••••••••
Worthlessness

STRESS

Negative life event in which an important source of love, security, identity, or self-worth is lost.

1. Accessibility of negative thoughts
2. Excessive self-awareness
3. Ruminative coping style
4. Poor mental control

FIGURE 9.10. Schematic representation of a model of depression, with particular emphasis given to self-relevant processes. A depressive reaction occurs when an *object* of value is lost. The value of the object derives from its role as a primary source of love, security, identity, or self-worth. Several self-relevant variables (e.g., low self-esteem, conditional feelings of self-worth) are thought to make people particularly vulnerable to events of this nature. Among other things, a depressive reaction is characterized by feelings of hopelessness and/or worthlessness. Finally, several self-relevant processes, including the accessibility of negative thoughts, and self-awareness influence whether a short-term depressive reaction resolves quickly or turns into a long-term depressive episode.

depression (Beck et al., 1979). Beck, you will recall, assumes that negative thinking is the primary symptom of depression. If it can be eliminated, the other symptoms of depression (e.g., intense sadness, sleep disturbances, and loss of interest in activities) will abate as well. For this reason, "the most critical stage of [Beck's] cognitive therapy involves training the patient to observe and record his cognitions" (Beck et al., 1979, p. 146). According to Beck, by carefully noting the conditions under which these cognitions occur, the patient begins to gain control over these negative automatic thoughts and eliminate them.

CHAPTER SUMMARY

In this chapter, we have explored factors that influence the onset and maintenance of depression. A good deal of material has been covered, from a variety of theoretical perspectives. Despite this diversity, there is general agreement on several important matters regarding the role of self-relevant processes in depression (see Figure 9.10).

First, self-relevant processes play an important role in the onset of depression. Depression can arise when an important source of love, security, identity, or self-worth is lost and there are few alternative sources of love, security, identity, or self-worth to replace it. Low self-esteem and conditional feelings of self-worth are thought to make a person particularly susceptible to events of this nature. Dysfunctional beliefs and attributional style have also been linked to the onset of depression.

Self-relevant processes also figure prominently as symptoms of depression. Depression is characterized by a negative view of oneself and one's future (i.e., by feelings of worthlessness and hopelessness) and a propensity to selectively notice and remember negative personal information. Negative biases in the interpretation of self-relevant events also emerge during a depressive episode. These effects seem to be unique to the processing of self-relevant information rather than affecting information processing in general.

Finally, self-relevant processes influence the severity and duration of a depressive episode. Depression is more extreme and more apt to linger among people who are highly self-aware and ruminate a lot about their moods. The ability to keep unwanted negative self-relevant thoughts outside of conscious awareness may also play a key role in recovery from depression.

- Depression is a common psychological disorder. Approximately one in eight people will experience a depressive episode in their lives. Most of these episodes remit in six to nine months, but in some cases depression can linger for years. Relapse rates are also high, as people who experience one bout of depression are at increased risk for experiencing subsequent bouts of depression.
- Most depressions arise in response to particular life events. These events involve losses in sources of love, security, identity, or self-worth. The death of a loved one, the break-up of an important romantic relationship, or a significant personal failure are common examples.
- Not everyone who experiences a negative life event becomes depressed, however. Certain factors make people particularly vulnerable to depression when a negative event occurs. These factors are called diatheses.
- Self-esteem theories of depression assert that low self-esteem is a vulnerability factor for depression. In support of this assertion, several studies with community samples have found that low self-esteem people are more apt than high self-esteem people to become depressed in the face of negative life events.
- Self-worth contingency models of depression argue that people with conditional feelings of self-worth are particularly vulnerable to depression. People with a conditional *interpersonal* orientation are susceptible to depression when they experience negative interpersonal events (e.g., break-up of an important relationship); people with a conditional *achievement* orientation are susceptible to depression when they experience negative achievement-related events (e.g., loss of a job).
- Beck's cognitive model of depression holds that depression is fundamentally a cognitive disorder, in which negative self-relevant thinking plays a primary role. When depressed, people view themselves, their world, and their future in highly negative terms, and selectively process and focus on negative personal information. These tendencies, in turn, account for other symptoms of depression, such as sleep disturbances, loss of interest in everyday activities, and depressed affect.
- Attributional models of depression assume that the explanations people give for the negative events in their lives are linked to depression. Depressed people are more apt to make internal, stable, and global attributions for negative life events than are nondepressed people. These tendencies may also put people at risk for developing depression.
- Depression is more severe and long-lasting when negative moods activate negative self-relevant thoughts. Depression is also more apt to endure among people who

are self-aware and ruminate about their moods. Finally, the ability to keep unwanted negative thoughts outside of conscious awareness contributes to recovery from depression.

For Further Reading

ALLOY, L. B. (1988). (Ed.). *Cognitive processes in depression.* New York: The Guilford Press.

BARNETT, P. A., & GOTLIB, I. H. (1988). Psychosocial functioning and depression: Distinguishing among antecedents, concomitants, and consequences. *Psychological Bulletin, 104,* 97–126.

BECK, A. T., RUSH, A. J., SHAW, B. F., & EMERY, G. (1979). *Cognitive therapy of depression.* New York: The Guilford Press.

CHAPTER 10

Illusion and Well-Being

An impartial and objective attitude toward oneself . . . is a primary virtue, basic to the development of all others.

—ALLPORT (1937, p. 422)

Life is the art of being well-deceived; and in order that the deception may succeed it must be habitual and uninterrupted.

—HAZLITT (1817)

Allport and Hazlitt offer very different ideas about the value of accurate self-knowledge. Allport extols the merits of accurate self-knowledge. He urges people to "get in touch with themselves," to "know themselves," and "to be true to themselves." In short, Allport counsels us to embrace the truth about ourselves without bias or distortion. Hazlitt presents a different point of view. Hazlitt champions the benefits of self-deception. He argues that "ignorance is bliss" and that people are better served by not knowing what they are really like.

In Chapter 10, we will examine these arguments as they apply to self-knowledge of an evaluative nature. We will begin by considering the relation between self-knowledge and psychological well-being. The key issue here is whether psychological health is characterized by accurate, unbiased self-views. We will then look at research that has examined the benefits of positive thinking. Here we will see that positive beliefs about oneself, one's ability to control important outcomes in life, and an optimistic view of the future are common and are commonly linked to superior psychological functioning. Finally, we will explore some potential limitations of highly positive self-views, especially as they relate to social functioning and risk perception.

SELF-KNOWLEDGE AND PSYCHOLOGICAL HEALTH

Theoretical Perspectives: Accurate Self-Knowledge Is Necessary for Psychological Health

Many theorists have pondered the relation between self-knowledge and psychological well-being. Most have concluded that accurate self-knowledge is a hallmark of mental health. For example, Jahoda (1958) described the mentally healthy person as one who is capable of perceiving oneself as one actually is, without distorting one's perceptions to fit one's wishes. Similarly, Maslow (1950) wrote that healthy individuals are able to accept themselves and their own nature, with all of its discrepancies from their ideal image. Fromm (1955), Haan (1977), Menninger (1963), Rogers (1951), and others have concurred that accurate self-knowledge is a principal component of psychological well-being. Many of the therapies these scholars developed assume that psychological health can be achieved only when individuals come to see themselves as they really are.

In sum, though not the only view of mental health (see, for example, Becker, 1973; Rank, 1936), many prominent theorists have asserted that accurate self-knowledge is an essential element of mental health. In one sense, this assertion is unquestionably true. People who have delusions of grandeur or believe their actions are determined by aliens are not paragons of mental health. Grossly inaccurate self-views are clearly detrimental to psychological well-being. But is accuracy necessary? Must people know what they are really like to be healthy?

Empirical Evidence: Do Most People Possess Accurate Self-Knowledge?

One way to approach this issue is to first ask whether most people possess accurate self-knowledge. This question is relevant because conceptions of mental health are partly based on a normative model: What's normative, is considered normal. To illustrate, people who score near the fiftieth percentile on an anxiety scale are said to have normal anxiety levels; those who score at the upper end of the distribution are said to be abnormally anxious. In a similar vein, we can gain insight into whether accuracy is associated with normal functioning by looking at whether most people possess accurate self-views.

We will use Beck's (1967, 1976) theory of depression as a framework for examining this issue. As discussed in Chapter 9, Beck argued that depressed people possess negatively biased views of themselves, their world, and their future (i.e., the negative cognitive triad). In contrast, nondepressed (normal) people were thought to hold accurate views of themselves in these three areas. In the following sections, we will examine the evidence for these assertions.

Accuracy and Bias in Self-Evaluations

Evidence relevant to the first of these issues has been reviewed throughout this text (see especially, Chapters 3 and 8). When it comes to self-knowledge of an evaluative nature (e.g., people's ideas about how attractive, intelligent, socially skilled, and loyal they are), many people do not possess entirely accurate self-views. Instead, many (perhaps most) people think they are *better* than they really are.

Evidence supporting this conclusion abounds. In Chapter 3, we noted that a 1976 College Board survey of over 1 million high school students found that 70 percent of the students rated themselves above the median in leadership ability, 60 percent rated themselves above the median in athletic ability, and

85 percent rated themselves above the median in their ability to get along well with others (cited in Dunning, Meyerowitz, & Holzberg, 1989). Although it's not possible from such data to know which of the million students were mistaken, if we accept that these students comprise a random sample of high school students, all values over 50 percent represent inaccuracy. At a minimum, then, it would seem that 20 percent of the students possess unrealistically positive beliefs about their leadership ability; 10 percent of the students entertain unrealistically positive beliefs about their athletic ability; and 35 percent of the 1 million students hold mistaken beliefs about their ability to get along with others. It is difficult to explain these rather large percentages within a normative model that assumes that accurate self-knowledge is a necessary condition of mental health.

Another way to assess the accuracy of self-views is to compare people's self-evaluations with the evaluations of neutral observers. A study by Lewinsohn, Mischel, Chaplin, and Barton (1980) adopted this approach. These investigators had nondepressed and depressed participants engage in a series of 20-minute group discussions. After each session, the participants rated their social competence on a 17-item scale (e.g., they indicated how friendly, warm, and confident they thought they were). Trained research assistants, watching the interactions from behind one-way mirrors, made similar ratings of each participant. This allowed Lewinsohn and his colleagues to examine the correspondence between participants' self-views and the way they were regarded by neutral observers.

Figure 10.1 presents some of the results of this investigation. The data show that both groups tended to view themselves in more positive terms than they were viewed by others, and that this tendency was especially pronounced among nondepressed participants. In fact, the depressed participants tended to be fairly accurate in their judgments, generally seeing themselves as they were seen by others.

The general pattern shown in Figure 10.1 has been replicated by others (e.g., Campbell & Fehr, 1990). When self-ratings are compared with the judgments of uninvolved, neutral observers, nondepressed people show a distinct positivity bias, whereas depressed people tend to be relatively accurate.[1] This doesn't mean, however, that nondepressed people wildly exaggerate their virtues or fail to acknowledge that they possess some limitations. In most cases, the degree of bias is modest, and many people are accurate in their judgments. The most appropriate conclusion to be drawn from these and other findings, then, is simply that many people tend to overestimate their positive qualities, and this is particularly true of people who feel good about themselves (Alloy & Abramson, 1988; Greenwald, 1980; Taylor & Brown, 1988, 1994). This fact

---

[1]The pattern is a bit different when self-ratings are compared against the judgments of acquaintances, family members, or other people who are part of our extended self. In this case, nondepressed individuals show greater accuracy than do depressed people, because their highly positive self-evaluations are matched by the highly positive ratings of those with whom they share a close association (Campbell & Fehr, 1990).

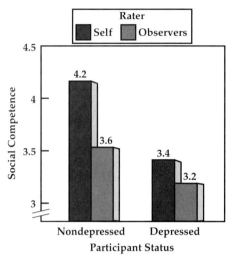

FIGURE 10.1. Self-ratings and observer ratings of social competence as a function of depression status. The data show that both participant groups regarded themselves more positively than they were regarded by neutral observers, and that this self-positivity bias was more apparent among nondepressed participants than among depressed participants.
(Adapted from Lewinsohn, Mischel, Chaplin, & Barton, 1980, *Journal of Abnormal Psychology, 89,* 203–212. Copyright 1980. Adapted by permission of The American Psychological Association.)

argues against the claim that accurate self-knowledge is a *necessary* component of psychological health.

Judgments of Control

The ability to accurately judge our control over environmental events is thought to be another necessary component of mental health. In order to function effectively in the world, it is thought, we need to know when our actions produce particular outcomes and when these outcomes are determined by factors beyond our control. As before, in one sense this is obviously the case. People who believe their thoughts control the moon and stars are not models of mental health. But just because wildly distorted self-views are detrimental to well-being, does not mean that accurate perceptions of control are necessary for psychological health. In fact, the widespread prevalence of superstitious behaviors (which, by definition, involve inaccurate perceptions of control) suggests that many people exaggerate their ability to bring about desired outcomes.

Jenkins and Ward (1965) were one of the first investigators to examine this issue in an experimental setting. In the studies they conducted, participants were given a series of problems and were asked to detect the relation between their actions (e.g., pressing or not pressing a button) and an environmental outcome (e.g., whether or not a light came on). In some conditions, participants' responses exerted control over the onset of the light; in other conditions, the light appeared independent of whether participants pressed the button or not. Across these variations, there was a general tendency for participants to overestimate their control over the onset of the light. The general tendency for people to exaggerate their ability to produce desired outcomes has been dubbed the *illusion of control* (Langer, 1975).

The experimental situation Jenkins and Ward (1965) constructed is admittedly artificial and unfamiliar. People may be better at judging their control under more mundane and familiar conditions. Langer (1975) addressed this issue in the context of gambling events that are entirely determined by chance. Langer had participants cut cards against a competitor, with the one choosing the higher card being the winner. In one condition, the competitor was poorly dressed and nervous; in the other condition, the competitor was dapper and composed. Objectively, these variations shouldn't affect the amount of money participants wagered. But they did. Participants wagered more money when competing against the nervous competitor than when competing against the composed competitor. Related research has found that people are less willing to sell a lottery ticket they have chosen than one given to them, presumably because they believe the act of choosing the number increases their odds of winning. These findings provide further evidence that people misjudge their ability to bring about desired outcomes.

An investigation by Alloy and Abramson (1979) extended these findings to matters of psychological well-being. These investigators were interested in testing aspects of Seligman's (1975) model of learned helplessness. As reviewed in Chapter 9, Seligman argued that depression can arise when people erroneously believe they have no control over environmental events. Building on this framework, Alloy and Abramson predicted that depressed individuals would *underestimate* their control over environmental outcomes.

To test their ideas, Alloy and Abramson (1979, Experiment 3) modified Jenkins and Ward's (1965) procedure. Nondepressed and dysphoric participants were given 40 trials at a task in which the onset of a green light was wholly unrelated to whether the participant pressed the button or not. In the *win* condition, participants received 25¢ when the light appeared; in the *lose* condition, participants lost 25¢ every time they failed to make the light appear. Afterward, participants rated the degree to which their actions (pressing or not pressing the button) influenced the onset of the light.

Figure 10.2 shows some of the results from this investigation. Two findings are of interest. First, all four groups of participants showed an illusion of control (i.e., they all believed they had at least some control over the onset of the light, despite the fact that they had no real control at all). Second, the illusion of control was particularly strong among nondepressed participants in the win condition, when the onset of the light was a highly desired outcome.

This basic result has been replicated numerous times in subsequent research (see Alloy & Abramson, 1988 for a review). Nondepressed individuals overestimate their ability to bring about a desired outcome; dysphoric individuals do so as well, but to a lesser degree. The fact that so many people misjudge their control is inconsistent with the claim that accurate self-knowledge is

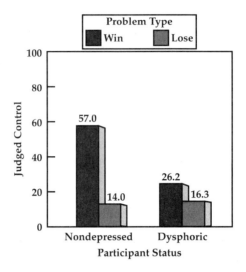

FIGURE 10.2. Judgments of control as a function of problem type among nondepressed and dysphoric participants. The data show that all four groups of participants overestimated their control over an objectively uncontrollable event and that this *illusion of control* was especially pronounced among nondepressed participants in the win condition. (Adapted from Alloy & Abramson, 1979 (Experiment 3), *Journal of Experimental Psychology, 108,* 441–485. Copyright 1979. Adapted by permission of Academic Press, Inc.)

commonly found in the general population; the fact that nondepressed individuals are less accurate than dysphoric individuals is inconsistent with the claim that accurate self-knowledge is the *sine qua non* of psychological well-being.

Optimism

Judgments of the future provide another realm in which to test the accuracy of people's beliefs. The first thing to note here is that most people are very optimistic (Tiger, 1979). They believe they are likely to experience many positive events (e.g., live a long and happy life; have a happy and fulfilling marriage) and few, if any, negative ones (e.g., be victimized by crime; have a serious and debilitating accident). Whether this optimism is warranted is difficult to say. No one can foretell the future. Current divorce rates notwithstanding, the vast majority of couples may enjoy a happy marriage.

One way to address this issue is to have people compare their futures with other peoples' futures. If people consistently claim that their futures will be brighter than the futures of their peers, there is evidence for unrealistic optimism. After all, most people can't have happier marriages than most other people.

Research adopting this approach has found consistent evidence for unrealistic optimism (see Weinstein & Klein, 1995 for a review). Most people believe they are more likely than their peers to experience a wide variety of pleasant events, such as having a gifted child, owning their own home, or living past the age of 80 (Weinstein, 1980). Conversely, most people believe they

TABLE 10.1. Comparative Judgments for Experiencing Future Life Events for Self, a Close Friend, and a Casual Acquaintance

Event	Self	Friend	Acquaintance
Positive Events			
Have a long, happy marriage	1.44	.70	.89
Graduate in top half of class	1.19	.52	.19
Have an intellectually gifted child	1.15	.44	.07
Live past 80	1.00	.48	.43
Achievement recognized in newspaper	.74	.70	.04
Mean	1.30	.57	.32
Negative Events			
Have a drinking problem	−1.96	−1.00	−1.19
Be fired from a job	−1.93	−1.15	−.56
Have a heart attack by age 40	−1.30	−1.19	−.04
Victim of a violent crime	−.63	−.37	−.04
Injured in an automobile accident	−.52	.19	.63
Mean	−1.27	−.70	−.24
Total Optimism (Positive − Negative)			
Mean	2.57	1.27	.56

Note: Scale values could range from −4 (chance of experiencing event is extremely below average) to +4 (chance of experiencing event is extremely above average).
Source: Adapted from Regan, Snyder, & Kassin, 1995, *Personality and Social Psychology Bulletin, 21,* 1073–1082. Copyright 1995, Sage Publications, Inc. Reprinted by permission of Sage Publications, Inc.

are less likely than their peers to experience a wide variety of negative events, such as being involved in an automobile accident (Robertson, 1977), being a crime victim (Perloff & Fetzer, 1986), or becoming ill (Weinstein, 1982, 1984). Since not everyone's future can be rosier than their peers', the optimism people exhibit seems illusory.

This does not mean, however, that people's judgments of the future are unaffected by reality (Gerrard, Gibbons, & Bushman, 1996; van der Velde, van der Pligt, & Hooykaas, 1992). To illustrate, people who smoke generally acknowledge that they are at greater risk for lung disease than are people who don't smoke. At the same time, people consistently underestimate their comparative risk (e.g., people who smoke think they are less likely to get cancer than are most other smokers). It is in this sense, then, that people are overly optimistic.

Several factors influence the extent to which people are optimistic, including the perceived controllability of the event, and its severity (Weinstein, 1984). Self-relevance is another factor. Regan, Snyder, and Kassin (1995) had college students rate how likely it is that they, a very close friend, or a casual acquaintance would experience a number of positive and negative life events in the future. As shown in Table 10.1, people were very optimistic about their own future and the future of a close friend, but they were far less optimistic

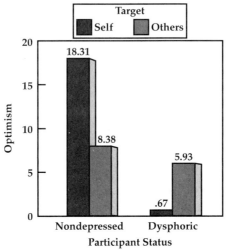

FIGURE 10.3. Optimism as a function of target (self versus others) among nondepressed and dysphoric participants. The data show that only nondepressed participants were optimistically biased.
(Adapted from Pyszczynski, Holt, & Greenberg, 1987, *Journal of Personality and Social Psychology, 52*, 994–1001. Copyright 1987. Adapted by permission of The American Psychological Association.)

about the future of an acquaintance. These findings establish that the more a person is part of our extended self, the more optimistically biased we are regarding the person's future.

The relation between optimism and psychological well-being has also been a topic of inquiry. Pyszczynski, Holt, and Greenberg (1987) had nondepressed and dysphoric students indicate how likely they and the typical undergraduate at their university were to experience a variety of positive and negative events. Figure 10.3 presents some of the results from this investigation. The figure shows that nondepressed participants believed their own future would be *brighter* than the average person's, but that dysphoric participants did not. Once again, then, the data indicate that nondepressed individuals are more positively biased in their self-relevant judgments than are dysphoric individuals (see also, Alloy & Ahrens, 1987).

Summary

Traditional models of mental health assert that well-adjusted individuals possess accurate perceptions of themselves, their capacity to control important events in their lives, and their future. The empirical research we have reviewed thus far challenges this claim. When it comes to self-knowledge of an evaluative nature, most people are not entirely accurate. They possess unrealistically positive views of themselves, an exaggerated belief in their ability to bring about desired outcomes, and a view of their future that is rosier than base-rate data can justify.

Do People Really Believe They're So Wonderful?

Before attempting to reconcile these empirical findings with traditional models of mental health, let's be certain that most people do, in fact, possess overly positive self-views. Several issues deserve attention here.

Sample Limitations

The vast majority of the evidence we've been discussing comes from college-student samples. According to Colvin and Block (1994), college students are warranted in believing they are better than are most other people when it comes to attributes associated with college, such as intelligence, and young people are warranted in believing they are better than are most other people when it comes to attributes associated with age, such as athleticism and attractiveness. These arguments ignore the fact that college students (1) regard themselves as *better* than most other college students and (2) also believe they are *better* than most other people in domains that are completely unrelated to being smart or young (e.g., How kind, loyal, and generous are you?).

A related argument assumes that college students possess overly positive self-views but that adults do not. There is also little evidence to support this claim. As noted in Chapter 3, many adults also view themselves in overly positive terms. For example, 90 percent of business managers rate their performance as superior to other managers, and 86 percent rate themselves as more ethical than their peers (cited in Myers, 1993). Another study found that 94 percent of college professors believe they do above average work (Cross, 1977). Moreover, individuals facing acute health threats believe they are coping better with their condition than are other patients facing the same threat (Buunk, Collins, Taylor, vanYperen, & Dakof, 1990; Helgeson & Taylor, 1993; Taylor, Kemeny, Reed, & Aspinwall, 1991). In short, there is little reason to believe that overly positive self-views are restricted to the young or well educated.

Cultural Limitations

Another possibility is that only people from Western cultures think of themselves in overly positive terms. As noted in Chapter 3, Western cultures are very competitive and individualistic, and people are encouraged to think of themselves in ways that distinguish them from others. In contrast, many Eastern cultures and some Latin American cultures are more collectivistic. People in these cultures are urged to think of themselves in ways that emphasize their commonality with others, rather than their uniqueness or superiority. These cultural differences suggest that self-enhancement biases might characterize people from Western cultures but not people from Eastern cultures. Heine and Lehman (1995) tested this hypothesis and found that Japanese students did, in fact, show less unrealistic optimism than did Canadian students (see also, Chang, 1996; Lee & Seligman, 1997). People from Eastern cultures are also less prone to the illusion of control (Weisz, Rothbaum, & Blackburn, 1984) and are less apt to view themselves in positive terms (Brockner & Chen, 1996; Markus & Kitayama, 1991) than are people from Western cultures.

The degree to which these cultural variations limit the generalizability of the findings we've been discussing is somewhat unclear, however. Although people from Eastern cultures are *less* apt to exhibit self-enhancement biases than are people from Western cultures, they are not necessarily more accurate, just more modest. Moreover, it is not the case that they show no bias at all. When asked to directly compare themselves with their peers, the Japanese students in Heine and Lehman's (1995) study reported that they were less likely than their peers to experience a variety of negative events, such as becoming an alcoholic, developing skin cancer, or having a nervous breakdown. Similarly, Falbo, Poston, Triscari, and Zhang (1997) found that Chinese schoolchildren evaluated themselves more positively than they evaluated a classmate, and they evaluated themselves more positively than they were evaluated by their classmates and teachers. The larger point, then, is that even though self-enhancement biases are more pronounced in Western cultures, they are often found in Eastern cultures as well.

The nature of the extended self is another point to consider. People in Western cultures do not exaggerate their superiority over their family members and close friends (Brown, 1986; Murray, Holmes, & Griffin, 1996a). When people from Eastern cultures fail to exhibit comparative self-enhancement biases, it may simply be because they have a more inclusive extended self. They treat their neighbors and fellow citizens as part of their extended self and, therefore, do not regard themselves as superior to them (Heine & Lehman, 1996). Outgroup biases (e.g., a tendency for Japanese citizens to regard themselves more positively than they regard Korean or Chinese citizens) may reveal strong evidence of self-enhancement in these cultures.

Finally, even if it were the case that people from Eastern cultures never exhibit self-enhancing biases, it would still be the case that people from Western cultures do. Unless we assume that people from Western cultures are less psychologically healthy than are people from Eastern cultures, we must conclude that accurate self-knowledge is not *essential* for psychological health.

To summarize, cultures influence the way people evaluate themselves, and people from Western cultures are particularly apt to evaluate themselves in overly positive terms. But there is scant evidence that people from Eastern cultures possess accurate self-knowledge or that people from Western cultures suffer diminished psychological health because they don't possess accurate self-knowledge.

Self-Evaluations Are *Tainted*

Another issue to consider is whether people are being truthful when they describe themselves in overly positive terms. For example, do people who claim to be smarter, more attractive, and more likable than others really believe what they say?

At least two sources of bias could contaminate these reports. First, overly positive self-evaluations could represent a form of self-presentation. According to this account, people *publicly* claim to possess positive qualities in an attempt to impress or deceive others, but privately, they do not believe these claims. We have already considered evidence relevant to this possibility in Chapter 7. There we noted that positive self-evaluations are not simply self-presentational ploys. People do not claim to possess many positive qualities merely to convince others that this is so. Not only are positive self-evaluations found under conditions of complete anonymity, but private self-evaluations are oftentimes more self-aggrandizing than are public ones. This occurs when people temper their public claims to appear modest rather than conceited. In general, then, although there is no doubt that people modify their self-descriptions when they present them publicly, there is little reason to believe that positive self-evaluations are offered only for public consumption (Greenwald & Breckler, 1985; Schlenker, 1986; Tesser & Moore, 1986).

Another possibility is that overly positive self-evaluations represent a form of self-deception. This account assumes that people who claim to possess many wonderful qualities are deceiving themselves. This is a harder issue to dismiss. Since its very inception, the field of psychology has had difficulty understanding the nature of self-deception. The term implies a fundamental contradiction: To be self-deceived, a person must know something and not know it at the same time. Here's how the French philosopher Jean-Paul Sartre framed the issue:

> [In self-deception] the one to whom the lie is told and the one who lies are one and the same person, which means that I must know in my capacity as deceiver the truth which is hidden from me in my capacity as the one deceived. Better yet I must know the truth very exactly in *order* to conceal it more carefully—and this not at two different moments, which at a pinch would allow us to reestablish the semblance of a duality—but in the unitary structure of a single project. How then can the lie subsist if the duality which conditions it is suppressed? (Sartre, 1958, p. 49)

In an empirical demonstration of self-deception, Gur and Sackeim (1979) had participants listen to a number of recorded voices and indicate when the voice was their own or someone else's. During the procedure, the participant's galvanic skin response (a measure of psychophysiological reactivity) was continuously monitored. The results showed that the participant's galvanic skin response increased to the sound of their own voice, even when they failed to recognize that the voice they heard was their own. Gur and Sackeim argued that this pattern represents a form of self-deception, insofar as people who consciously failed to recognize a voice was their own unconsciously *knew* it was so.

Of course, self-deception involves more than a failure to recognize the sound of one's own voice; it more commonly refers to a motivated attempt to avoid confronting undesirable aspects of oneself. Gur and Sackeim (1979) conducted a follow-up study to address this issue. In this investigation, participants first succeeded or failed at an alleged test of their intellectual ability before participating in the voice-recognition task. The experimenters then noted how long it took participants to recognize their own voice. The thinking here is that participants who had just failed a test would find self-awareness aversive (Duval & Wicklund, 1972) and that this desire to avoid self-confrontation would lead them to require more time to recognize the sound of their own voice. The results supported this prediction. Participants in the failure group were slower to recognize the sound of their own voice than were participants in the success condition, but the two groups did not differ in the time it took to recognize the voices of other people. Failure participants also failed to recognize their own voice more often, and rated the sound of their own voice as less pleasant, than did those in the success condition. These findings suggest that failure fueled the need for self-deception.

Self-Deception and Psychological Well-Being

To this point, we have seen that self-deception can occur and may be motivated by a desire to avoid self-confrontation. We have yet to consider the relation between self-deception and psychological well-being. Researchers who have addressed this issue begin by distinguishing between two forms of self-deception. Self-deception *enhancement* occurs when individuals unrealistically attribute positive characteristics to themselves; self-deception *denial* occurs when individuals unrealistically deny possessing negative characteristics.

Paulhus (1994; Paulhus & Reid, 1991) has devised a scale to measure these two forms of self-deception. People who score high in self-deception enhancement describe themselves in terms that seem too good to be true (e.g., "I always know why I like the things I do" and "I am fully in control of my fate"). People who score high in self-deception denial disavow possessing common negative qualities or traits ("I never get jealous over the good fortunes of others" and "I have never done anything that I am ashamed of").

Scores on the two scales are only modestly correlated, indicating that the tendency to attribute positive characteristics to oneself is somewhat independent of the tendency to deny that negative attributes characterize oneself. The two forms of self-deception also exhibit different correlations with psychological adjustment. Scores on the self-deception denial scale tend to be uncorrelated with psychological adjustment, whereas scores on the deception enhancement scale are positively related to psychological well-being (Paulhus & Reid, 1991; Roth, Snyder, & Pace, 1986).

Figure 10.4 illustrates the nature of these effects. The data come from a study I conducted at the University of Washington. In this study, participants completed the self-deception enhancement subscale of the measure Paulhus (1994) developed and a common, self-report measure of depression (Radloff, 1977). I then plotted self-deception scores as a function of depression scores.

The data show several interesting effects. First, note that all participant groups showed some evidence of self-deception enhancement. Note also, however, that in all cases, this deception is rather mild (i.e., all of the means are far below the highest possible score of 20). Finally, note that scores on the two scales are negatively related in a near linear fashion. The higher participants scored on the self-deception questionnaire, the lower they scored on the depression scale. This finding is consistent with the claim that self-deception enhancement is a component of psychological well-being (Paulhus & Reid, 1991; Roth & Ingram, 1985; Roth et al., 1986).

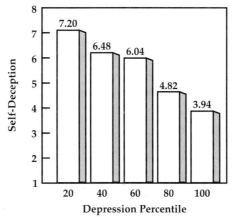

FIGURE 10.4. Self-deception enhancement scores as a function of depression scores. The data show that self-deception enhancement scores and depression scores are negatively correlated. This finding is consistent with the claim that self-deception enhancement is a feature of psychological well-being. (Scores could range from 1 to 20.)

Depressive Realism

Throughout this chapter, we have seen that depressed individuals are less positively biased than are nondepressed individuals; we have also seen that they are less prone to self-deception than are nondepressed individuals. One explanation for this finding is that depression involves a breakdown in self-enhancing illusions (Bibring, 1953). From this perspective, it is not so much that depressives are negatively biased, as Beck (1967) claimed, but that they lack self-protective positive biases.

The relative lack of self-enhancement biases during depression also suggests that depressed individuals may possess accurate self-knowledge. Mischel (1979) coined the term *depressive realism* to refer to this possibility, although it was discussed many years earlier by Sigmund Freud (1917/1957):

> [The melancholic may have] a keener eye for the truth than other people who are not melancholic. When in his heightened self-criticism he describes himself as petty, egoistic, dishonest, lacking in independence, one whose sole aim has been to hide the weaknesses of his own nature, it may be, so far as we know, that he has come pretty near to understanding himself; we only wonder why a man has to be ill before he can be accessible to a truth of this kind. (Freud, 1917/1957, p. 246)

Whether depressed individuals are actually more accurate and realistic than nondepressives is difficult to say, however. First, although mildly depressed or dysphoric people view themselves in balanced or even-handed terms, severely depressed individuals view themselves in unrealistically negative terms (Ruehlman, West, & Pasahow, 1985). Moreover, even moderately depressed individuals sometimes display less accuracy than do nondepressed people (e.g., Campbell & Fehr, 1990; Dunning & Story, 1991). Finally, the accuracy depressives show may sometimes be adventitious. On average, people who describe themselves as being of average intelligence or attractiveness are apt to be more accurate than are people who describe themselves in overly positive (or overly negative) terms. By being modest, then, depressed individuals may appear to be more accurate without possessing any special insight or awareness into what they are like (Brown & Dutton, 1995a). Given this possibility, it is probably best to conclude that depressed individuals are less positively biased, but they are not necessarily more accurate than nondepressed individuals.

POSITIVE ILLUSIONS AND PSYCHOLOGICAL HEALTH

So far we have seen that many psychologically healthy people do not possess accurate self-knowledge. This evidence has inspired a new view on the nature of psychological well-being. Instead of assuming that psychological health is characterized by accurate self-knowledge, several theorists have speculated that well-being is associated with overly (though not excessively) positive self-knowledge (Alloy & Abramson, 1988; Greenwald, 1980; Lazarus, 1983; Sackeim, 1983; Taylor, 1983; Taylor & Brown, 1988). Shelley Taylor and I (Taylor & Brown, 1988) referred to these beliefs as *positive illusions* to emphasize that these beliefs are more positive than can realistically be justified.

In essence, Taylor and I made two related arguments regarding the relation between self-knowledge and psychological health. First, we argued that most *normal* people do not possess accurate self-views; they possess overly positive self-views.[2] This claim is important because it contradicts the notion that psychological health demands accuracy. We also argued that positive illusions are conducive to well-being. We contended that not only do most people possess positive self-views, but that it is generally good that they do, because these views promote other aspects of mental health and enable people to function more effectively in the world.

The link Taylor and Brown (1988) proposed between positive illusions and psychological well-being has attracted a great deal of attention and sparked a good deal of controversy (Colvin & Block, 1994; Taylor & Brown, 1994). Before turning to some of the evidence relevant to this thesis, let's clarify what Taylor and I did (and did not) claim. First, we did not claim that illusory self-perceptions are never destructive. It is absolutely clear that some illusions or distortions (e.g., delusions of grandeur, hallucinations, gross misperceptions of physical reality) are detrimental to mental health. The only illusions we have linked to mental health are mildly positive ones.

Nor did we claim that positive illusions are a necessary component of mental health or that people are never accurate. As noted earlier, not all healthy people show the positive biases we have documented in this chapter, and there are certainly times in life when people seek accurate self-relevant in-

---

[2]I am using the word *normal* here primarily in a statistical sense (i.e., what the average person does) and also to refer to the absence of psychopathology.

formation (Gollwitzer & Kinney, 1989; Taylor & Gollwitzer, 1995). In this sense, we did not claim that psychological health demands positively biased self-views; we claimed that psychological health does not demand entirely accurate self-views.

That being said, Taylor and I did conclude that positive illusions are often beneficial. To understand this claim, we must first identify established criteria of psychological health. Although there is not total agreement on the matter, many theorists have concluded that psychological health includes the following components: (1) a subjective state of happiness or well-being; (2) the capacity to form and maintain satisfying interpersonal relationships; (3) the ability to engage in productive and meaningful work; and (4) the capacity to grow and mature by successfully coping with life's challenges (Jahoda, 1958; Jourard & Landsman, 1980; Ryff, 1989, 1995).

Positive Illusions, Happiness, and Love

Research has linked positive illusions to each of these criteria. Consider happiness. Many of the things people commonly assume bring happiness (e.g., money, beauty, youth) turn out to be largely unrelated to how happy people are (Myers & Diener, 1995). Happiness is, however, strongly related to how people think and feel about themselves. Happy people (1) hold positive views of themselves, (2) have high feelings of personal control, and (3) are generally optimistic about their future (Myers & Diener, 1995). In short, happy people exhibit the positive illusions we have documented in this chapter. The strength of this association varies somewhat across cultures, but the general pattern seems to hold for people everywhere (Diener & Diener, 1995).

Positive illusions have also been linked to satisfying interpersonal relationships. Murray, Holmes, and Griffin (1996a, 1996b) had 82 couples (many of whom were married) evaluate themselves and their partner along a number of evaluative dimensions (e.g., How kind, affectionate, accepting, and intelligent are you/is your partner?). Couples who viewed their partners in more positive terms than their partners viewed themselves were happier and more satisfied in their relationship than were couples whose appraisals of one another were more accurate. These findings suggest that idealistic, rather than realistic, perceptions of one's partner are linked to satisfying interpersonal relationships.

Positive Illusions and Work

Positive illusions have also been linked to creative and productive work. As first noted in Chapter 6, people who believe they have high ability and hold high expectations of success work harder, persist longer, and often perform better on intellectual and manual tasks than do those whose beliefs in these areas are more negative or modest (e.g., Bandura, 1989; Dweck & Leggett, 1988; Mortimer & Lorence, 1979; Schaufeli, 1988). These effects remain even after actual ability levels are taken into account. This means that a positive belief in one's ability, even if somewhat illusory, can promote achievement. Here's how one prominent theorist summarized the findings in this area:

> It is widely believed that misjudgment produces dysfunction. Certainly, gross miscalculation can create problems. However, optimistic self-appraisals of capability that are not unduly disparate from what is possible can be advantageous, whereas veridical judgments can be self-limiting. When people err in their self-appraisals, they tend to overestimate their capabilities. This is a benefit rather than a cognitive failing to be eradicated. If self-efficacy beliefs always reflected only what people could do routinely, they would rarely fail but they would not mount the extra effort needed to surpass their ordinary performances. (Bandura, 1989, p. 1177)

Positive illusions may be particularly prevalent and beneficial in childhood. Young children are very self-enhancing. They hold very positive beliefs about their ability to accomplish a variety of tasks (e.g., many expect to become famous scientists, rock stars, or fire fighters). These positive beliefs decline when children enter elementary school, but they are still evident (Stipek, 1984). Many adults treat these positive beliefs as amusing and ephemeral chimera of youth, but they may very well serve a more serious function. Bjorklund and Green (1992) have argued that optimistic assessments of ability facilitate children's acquisition of language and the development of problem-solving and motor skills (see also, Phillips & Zimmerman, 1990; Stipek, 1984).

> Unrealistic optimism about their own abilities and . . . ignorance of their limitations [allow] children to try more diverse and complex behaviors they would not otherwise try if they had more realistic conceptions of their abilities. . . . This allows them to practice skills to a greater degree and may foster long-term . . . benefits. (Bjorklund & Green 1992, p. 47)

Positive Illusions, Stress, and Coping

The ability to successfully meet life's challenges is another component of mental health. Before reading about the effects of positive illusions in this area, stop and ask yourself what you think it would be like to suffer a debilitating personal injury or develop a life-threatening illness. For example, how would you cope if you developed cancer, had a serious heart attack, or became paralyzed in an automobile accident?

You might be surprised to know that most people cope quite well with personal tragedies of this sort. In fact, although they are initially distressed and depressed, within two years most people who experience such traumas report being at least as happy and satisfied with their lives as those who have never experienced such events (Brickman, Coates, & Janoff-Bulman, 1978; Diener, 1994; Schulz & Decker, 1985; Taylor, 1983). Some even report that their lives have changed for the better. Naturally, not everyone copes well with tragedy, and some people require counseling or other forms of treatment to help them adjust. But the majority of people who suffer serious illnesses and injuries return to a level of psychological functioning that is at least as positive as the one they enjoyed before experiencing the traumatic event.

Although the means by which people achieve recovery differ, certain commonalities emerge. In an analysis of how women cope with breast cancer, Taylor (1983) noted that readjustment often involves (1) restoring a positive sense of self-worth, (2) reasserting control over one's life, and (3) finding meaning in the experience. To this we can add (4) reclaiming an optimistic view of the future. Thus, recovery from traumatic events often involves restoring the positive illusions that were in place prior to the experience.

It is somewhat paradoxical, but illusions play a role in the restoration process itself. People regain a favorable self-image, recapture perceived control, and reclaim optimism by construing events in overly positive ways. For example, people believe that they are coping better than the average person with their illness or condition. They also believe they have more control over the course of their disease than is objectively so, and they construct a view of the future that is unrealistically optimistic given their condition. As before, these illusions are typically subtle and involve mild (rather than gross) distortions of reality. But they are unrealistic nonetheless.

> The cognitions upon which meaning, mastery, and self-enhancement depend are in a large part founded on illusions. Causes for cancer are manufactured despite the fact that the true causes of cancer remain substantially unknown. Belief in control over one's cancer persists despite little evidence that such faith is well-placed. Self-enhancing social comparisons are drawn, and when no disadvantaged person exists against whom one can compare oneself, [one] is made up. . . . these illusions are beneficial in bringing about psychological adaptation. (Taylor, 1983, p. 1167)

Of the three illusions we have considered, perceived control and optimism have received the most attention as coping mechanisms. In the following sections, we will examine how each of these perceptions helps people cope with stressful life events.

Perceived Control and Coping

Perceived control—the perception that one can bring about desired outcomes—is regarded as a fundamental human need and a central component of psychological health (deCharms, 1968; Erikson, 1963; White, 1959). Developmentally, these feelings of mastery and efficacy emerge during the earliest years of life (Erikson, 1963), and many of the negative consequences of aging have been traced to declines in feelings of control (Rodin, 1986). Finally, people react negatively to a loss of perceived control, responding with either anger and active attempts to restore control (Wortman & Brehm, 1975) or with depression and passivity (Seligman, 1975).

The benefits of perceived control are diverse (for reviews, see Cohen, 1980; Shapiro, Schwartz, & Astin, 1996; Skinner, 1996; Taylor & Clark, 1986; Thompson, 1981; Thompson & Spacapan, 1991). People who believe they have control over events in their lives feel better about themselves, cope better with adversity, and perform better on a variety of cognitive and manual tasks than do those who believe they lack control. There is also evidence that perceptions of control influence physical well-being and longevity. In one study, nursing-home patients given control over aspects of their daily functioning lived longer than those who had little control (Langer & Rodin, 1976; see also, Janoff-Bulman & Marshall, 1982).

One of the most interesting aspects of this research area is that the *perception* of control is at least as important as actual control itself. To illustrate, laboratory studies have exposed participants to a noxious stimulus, such as electric shock or intense noise. Participants in the high-control condition are told they can terminate the noxious stimulus whenever they want (e.g., they can press a button to terminate the shock); participants in the low-control condition are not told they can terminate the noxious stimulus. In general, participants in the high-control condition are less anxious and distressed prior to the procedure and are able to withstand more painful levels of the stimulus than are participants in the low-control condition (Averill, 1973; Glass & Singer, 1972; Thompson, 1981). This is so despite the fact that participants in the high-control condition never actually exercise their controlling option. Thus, the mere perception of control—the belief that one can do something to terminate or reduce a noxious event—reduces anxiety and increases tolerance for the experience.

In addition to helping people cope with mild, short-lived stressors, perceptions of control also help people cope with naturally occurring stressful life events (for a review, see Thompson & Spacapan, 1991). An investigation by Alloy and Clements (1992) makes this point. These researchers first had college students perform the judgment of control task developed by Alloy and Abramson (1979). The students were then asked to keep track of the number of stressful life events they experienced in the following month, and their emotional reactions to these events. Students who overestimated their control over the onset of the light (i.e., those who showed an illusion of control) became less discouraged and depressed when faced with stressful life events than did those who underestimated their control. Alloy and Clements concluded that the belief that one can control desired events (even if somewhat illusory) reduces the negative effects of life stress.

An investigation by Taylor, Lichtman, and Wood (1984) provides even more dramatic support for this claim. These investigators interviewed 78 breast cancer patients in the Los Angeles area. Among other things, the women were asked how much control they believed they had over their disease. Perceptions of control were generally high and were positively related to psychological health: Most of the women thought they had at least some control over the course of the disease, and those who did so enjoyed higher levels of psychological well-being than those who did not.

Because there is little scientific evidence that people can alter the course of their cancer, the control these women believed they had over their illness is somewhat illusory. Nevertheless, perceived control was psychologically beneficial. In fact, perceptions of control may be particularly advantageous when actual control is the most minimal. Thompson, Sobolew-Shubin, Galbraith, Schwankovsky, and Cruzen (1993) found that perceived control was most strongly related to psychological well-being among cancer patients with poor physical functioning. They concluded that perceived control is especially beneficial when objective health outcomes are the most grim.

Optimism and Coping

Like perceived control, optimism has been linked to effective coping. Scheier, Carver, and their associates (Carver et al., 1993; Scheier & Carver, 1985, 1987; Scheier et al., 1989) have conducted much of the research in this area. Table 10.2 presents a scale these investigators use to measure the extent to which people are optimistic. People who score high on this scale cope more effectively with a variety of stressors than do those who score low on this scale.

A study of men undergoing coronary artery bypass surgery makes this point (Scheier et al., 1989). On the day before their surgery, the men completed a version of the questionnaire shown in Table 10.2. High scores on this scale were linked to a faster rate of physical recovery from surgery and to a faster rate of return to normal life activities in the months after surgery. These and other findings (e.g., Carver et al., 1993) suggest that an optimistic outlook plays a key role in how people cope with life-threatening events.

Scheier and Carver have also examined why optimists cope better with stress than do pessimists. Their analysis begins by noting that people deal with life stress in two ways. One way, termed *problem-focused coping* by Lazarus and his colleagues (Lazarus & Folkman, 1984; Lazarus & Launier,

TABLE 10.2. The Life Orientation Test

Indicate your level of agreement with each of the following statements by circling one number on the rating scale beside each item. Use the following scale as your guide.

0 = strongly disagree
1 = disagree
2 = neutral
3 = agree
4 = strongly agree

1. In uncertain times, I usually expect the best.	0	1	2	3	4
2. If something can go wrong for me, it will.	0	1	2	3	4
3. I always look on the bright side of things.	0	1	2	3	4
4. I'm always optimistic about my future.	0	1	2	3	4
5. I hardly ever expect things to go my way.	0	1	2	3	4
6. Things never work out the way I want them to.	0	1	2	3	4
7. I'm a believer in the idea that "every cloud has a silver lining."	0	1	2	3	4
8. I rarely count on good things happening to me.	0	1	2	3	4

Note: To determine your optimism score, first reverse the scoring for items 2, 5, 6, and 8 (0 = 4; 1 = 3; 2 = 2; 3 = 1; 4 = 0), then add you scores for all eight items. Higher scores indicate greater optimism.
Source: Scheier & Carver, 1985, *Health Psychology, 4,* 219–247. Copyright 1985. Reprinted by permission of Lawrence Erlbaum Associates, Inc.

1978), involves taking active steps to deal with the source of stress. For example, a person who is laid off from work may immediately start looking for another job. This is problem-focused coping, because the person's efforts are directed at resolving the source of stress. A second coping strategy, termed *emotion-focused coping,* occurs when individuals attempt to eliminate or reduce the emotional distress a stressful event brings about. Sometimes emotion-focused coping is constructive (under stressful circumstances, a person may exercise to alleviate anxiety); other times it is destructive (a person under stress can abuse alcohol or drugs in an effort to reduce anxiety).

Which of these strategies do optimists typically use? Numerous studies have found that optimists are more inclined than pessimists to use problem-focused coping strategies (Aspinwall & Brunhart, 1996; Carver et al., 1993; Scheier et al., 1989; Scheier, Weintraub, & Carver, 1986). When faced with a stressful situation, optimists seek out relevant information and actively attempt to solve their problems, either by directly attacking the source of distress or by looking at the situation in ways that cast things in the most positive light (e.g., believing they have learned a lot from the experience and are a better person for having gone through it).

Optimism, like perceived control, appears to be beneficial even when it's illusory. Taylor, Kemeny, Aspinwall, Schneider, Rodriguez, and Herbert (1992) studied 550 gay men who had tested for the presence of the AIDS virus (HIV). About half of the men were HIV positive; the other half were HIV negative. After receiving their test results, the men were asked to indicate their agreement with a number of statements (e.g., "I feel safe from AIDS because I've developed an immunity" and "I think my immune system would be (is) more capable of fighting the AIDS virus than that of other gay men"). These items were combined to create an index of how optimistic the men were that they would not develop AIDS.

Realistically, people who are HIV positive are much more likely to develop AIDS than are people who are HIV negative. Nevertheless, men who knew they were HIV positive were significantly *more optimistic* about not developing AIDS than were men who knew they were HIV negative. Moreover, this optimism appeared to confer a number of benefits. Optimists reported lower levels of psychological distress and reported engaging in more health-promoting behaviors (e.g., healthy diet, exercise, getting enough sleep) than did pessimists.

To summarize, the picture that emerges from the research we have been discussing is not one of an optimistic person who blithely assumes that everything will be fine and then does nothing to bring this state of affairs about. Instead, optimists adopt constructive, problem-focused coping strategies. They set goals and then take active aims to achieve their goals. They look at their situation in the most positive terms and attempt to construe benefit from tragedy. In short, they actively strive to "make lemonade out of lemons."

They are able to do this, in part, because the three positive illusions we have considered are related to one another (Scheier, Carver, & Bridges, 1994). People who think they have many fine qualities also believe they can use these qualities to bring about desired outcomes; people who believe they can bring about desired outcomes are optimistic about their future. In this sense, positive illusions support and fortify one another.

Positive Illusions and Coping with Existential Terror

. . . to see the world as it really is is devastating and terrifying
(Becker, 1973, p. 60).

In his award-winning book *The Denial of Death*, the anthropologist Ernest Becker (1973) outlined another benefit of positive illusions. As noted in Chapter 8, Becker argued that the capacity to contemplate one's own death creates existential terror in people and that a great deal of psychological life is devoted to managing this terror (see also, Rank, 1936). The positive illusions we have discussed in this chapter are among the vehicles Becker believes serve to partially mollify terror. According to Becker, exaggerated beliefs about one's virtue, power, and value imbue life with meaning and offer the reward of immortality. Without these beliefs, the individual sinks into a state of abject terror and paralyzing anxiety, immobilized by the awareness of his ultimate demise. Indeed, for Becker, "life is possible only with illusions" (Becker, 1973, p. 189).

Greenberg, Solomon, and Pyszczynski (1997) report numerous investigations inspired by Becker's ideas. In one investigation (Greenberg et al., 1992), participants were first given either positive personality feedback (e.g., your personality is fundamentally strong) or neutral personality feedback (e.g., some of your aspirations may be a bit unrealistic). Later, all participants viewed one of two videotapes. In the *mortality-salient* condition, the videotape depicted scenes of death and destruction, including an autopsy and electrocution of an inmate on death row. In the control condition, the videotape did not contain any death-related images or scenes. Finally, after viewing the videotapes, participants completed a measure of anxiety.

Recall Becker's (1973) claim that positive illusions serve to mitigate anxiety in response to an awareness of one's death. Based on this idea, Greenberg et al. (1992) predicted that participants who had been given positive personality feedback would experience less anxiety in response to the death-relevant videotape than would participants given neutral personality feedback. As can be seen in Figure 10.5, this proved to be the case. Participants given neutral personality feedback were very anxious after viewing death-relevant images, but participants given positive personality feedback were not. Although there are alternative explanations for this finding, one possibility is that positive self-relevant beliefs help people cope with existential terror.

LIMITATIONS AND POTENTIAL COSTS OF POSITIVE ILLUSIONS

So far, we have considered only the benefits of positive illusions. Although these benefits are considerable, there are also some important limitations and

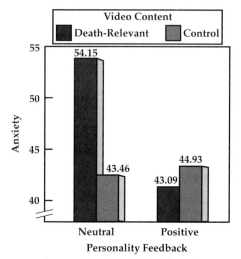

FIGURE 10.5. Anxiety scores in response to death-relevant or neutral videotapes. The data show that the death-relevant videotape increased anxiety in the neutral personality feedback condition but not in the positive personality feedback condition. These findings are consistent with the claim that positive self-relevant beliefs help people cope with existential terror.
(Adapted from Greenberg et al., 1992, *Journal of Personality and Social Psychology*, *63*, 913–922. Copyright 1992. Adapted by permission of The American Psychological Association.)

costs to consider. Perhaps the most important point to be made is that there is little evidence that positive illusions can cure people of actual physical disease. The effects we've been discussing focus on *psychological* adjustment—with how people feel about their illness or injury. I have not argued that positive thinking can prevent or cure serious illnesses.

It is also the case that not everyone who deals well with stressful circumstances exhibits positive illusions. In fact, some people who cope well with stress prefer to relinquish control to others (Burger, McWard, & LaTorre, 1989; Rothbaum, Weisz, & Snyder, 1982) or are somewhat pessimistic (Norem & Cantor, 1986).

Beyond these limitations, each of the three illusions we have considered can bring serious costs when they become excessive. In the following section, we will discuss some of the most important problems that can arise.

Potential Costs of Overly Positive Self-Views

The first illusion we discussed was the tendency for people to view themselves in overly positive terms. We noted that most people show this effect and that the effect is related to psychological adjustment. But this does not mean that the more positively biased one is, the better.

TABLE 10.3. Sample Items from the Narcissistic Personality Inventory

Name _____ Date _____

Sex _____ Age _____ Occupation _____

Instructions: In each of the following pairs of attitudes, choose the one that you MOST AGREE with. Mark your answer by writing EITHER A or B in the space provided. Only mark ONE ANSWER for each attitude pair, and please DO NOT skip any items.

_____ 1. A I have a natural talent for influencing people.
       B I am not good at influencing people.
_____ 2. A Modesty doesn't become me.
       B I am essentially a modest person.
_____ 3. A I would do almost anything on a dare.
       B I tend to be a fairly cautious person.
_____ 4. A When people compliment me I sometimes get embarrassed.
       B I know that I am good because everybody keeps telling me so.
_____ 5. A The thought of ruling the world frightens the hell out of me.
       B If I ruled the world it would be a better place.

_____ 6. A I can usually talk my way out of anything.
       B I try to accept the consequences of my behavior.
_____ 7. A I prefer to blend in with the crowd.
       B I like to be the center of attention.
_____ 8. A I will be a success.
       B I am not too concerned about success.
_____ 9. A I am no better or no worse than most people.
       B I think I am a special person.
_____ 10. A I am not sure if I would make a good leader.
        B I see myself as a good leader.

Note: Answer key: a, a, a, b, b, a, b, a, b, b. Score one point for each correct answer. High scores indicate higher narcissism.

Source: Raskin & Hall, 1979, *Psychological Reports, 46,* 55–60. Copyright 1979. Reprinted by permission of R. Raskin.

Narcissism

People who are overly conceited or excessively self-involved may possess a narcissistic personality disorder. According to established clinical guidelines (DSM-IV), narcissists tend to be *grandiose* (they have an exaggerated sense of self-importance and uniqueness), are *exhibitionistic* (they require near constant attention and admiration from others), possess an exaggerated *sense of entitlement* (they expect that their wishes should automatically be met and that others should grant them special favors without reciprocity), and are *interpersonally exploitative* (they use others as objects of selfish gains).

Table 10.3 presents some items from a questionnaire that has been used to measure narcissistic tendencies in the general population (Raskin & Hall, 1979). A moderate degree of narcissism is considered to be a component of a healthy personality (Bibring, 1953; Kernberg, 1975; Kohut, 1971; Raskin, Novacek, & Hogan, 1991; Westen, 1990b), but excessive narcissism is not. In keeping with this idea, people with extreme scores on the narcissism scale are judged rather negatively by others (Raskin & Terry, 1988; see also, Colvin, Block, & Funder, 1995; John & Robins, 1994). These effects establish that overly positive self-views can bring social costs. People who are extremely self-aggrandizing or exceedingly self-involved are not warmly embraced by others.

Interpersonal Violence

Overly positive self-views may also beget aggression. Baumeister, Smart, and Boden (1996) reviewed a great deal of evidence on the predictors of interpersonal violence. They found that people who have highly inflated, unstable, or uncertain self-views are prone to violence when circumstances threaten these positive self-appraisals (see also, Kernis, Grannemann, & Barclay, 1989; Waschull & Kernis, 1996). For example, a man who believes he is a fantastic lover and provider may turn violent if his wife leaves him. In his subsequent work, Baumeister (1997) has even argued that much of the evil in this world is carried out by people who hold excessively positive views of themselves.

Repressive Coping Style

Overly positive self-views may also have important health-related costs. Weinberger and Schwartz (Weinberger, 1990; Weinberger, Schwartz, & David-son, 1979) have identified people with a *repressive coping style*. Under stress, people with this coping style show a strong dissociation between self-reports of anxiety and physiological indicators of anxiety (i.e., they say they feel fine and relaxed but show an elevated heart rate and high skin conductance levels) (but see also, Tomaka, Blascovich, & Kelsey, 1992). A failure to acknowledge and attend to physiological arousal may contribute to the development of physical illness, including ulcers, cancer, and heart disease (Jensen, 1987; Pen-nebaker, 1989, 1993; Schwartz, 1977; Shedler, Mayman, & Manis, 1993).

Potential Costs of Exaggerated Perceptions of Control

A tendency to exaggerate one's ability to bring about desired outcomes also carries some potential costs.

Unproductive and Prolonged Persistence

One possibility is that people who exaggerate their ability to bring about desired outcomes may display maladaptive persistence. Persistence is nor-mally a good thing. Many important tasks in life require working long and hard to overcome obstacles. But it's also important in life to know when to quit. As the singer Kenny Rogers noted, "You got to know when to hold them, know when to fold them."

People who exaggerate their ability to control events may be prone to mal-adaptive persistence. They may continue to pursue goals that are beyond their reach. Currently, the evidence on this point is mixed: Some studies find that people with high self-perceptions of ability do not quit when they should (Baumeister & Tice, 1985; McFarlin, Baumeister, & Blascovich, 1984); other studies find that this is not the case (Janoff-Bulman & Brickman, 1982; McFar-lin, 1985; Sandelands, Brockner, & Glynn, 1988). After reviewing this research, Aspinwall and Taylor (1997) concluded that people who possess a strong be-lief in their ability to bring about success are very sensitive to when persis-tence pays off and when it does not (see also, Sandelands et al., 1988). This re-search suggests that positive illusions are not a liability in this domain.

Self-Regulatory Failure

People who exaggerate their abilities may set their sights too high, "biting off more than they can chew." Baumeister, Heatherton, and Tice (1993) ex-plored this issue. These investigators had participants perform a manual dexterity task. Afterward, participants were given the opportunity to set goals for themselves on an upcoming test, with the understanding that if they matched their goal they would win money but if they fell short of their goal they would lose money. Some participants (those in the ego-threat condition) were told that they might want to set low goals for themselves if they thought they were the kind of person who choked under pressure; other participants (those in the control condition) were not *threatened* in this way.

High self-esteem participants (who have strong beliefs of personal control) earned less money than did low self-esteem participants in the ego-threat condition, in part because they set their sights too high, believing they could perform better than was actually the case. Baumeister et al. (1993) concluded that positive self-views can be a liability when individuals commit themselves to goals that are beyond their reach, and that this is most likely to occur when ego-involvement is high.

Potential Costs of Excessive Optimism

Excessive optimism may also have attendant costs. Earlier, we noted that people believe they are less likely than are others to experience a wide range of negative events. This optimism may lead people to ignore safety considerations or fail to take appropriate precautionary behaviors (Weinstein, 1988). For example, people who underestimate their risk of being injured in an automobile accident may decide not to wear seat belts.

The evidence on this point is currently mixed. Some studies find that optimism is negatively correlated with precautionary behaviors (e.g., Burger & Burns, 1988), some studies find that optimism is positively correlated with precautionary behaviors (Aspinwall & Brunhart, 1996; Whitley & Hern, 1991), and some studies find little effect either way (see Gerrard et al., 1996). One explanation for this inconsistency is that people are often overly optimistic precisely *because* they engage in precautionary behaviors. As an example, people who always wear their seat belts are engaging in appropriate precautionary behaviors, but they still might overestimate the degree to which wearing seat belts reduces their risk of personal injury from an automobile accident. In such cases, exaggerated perceptions of control (the belief that one's behavior can bring about a desired outcome) may underlie unrealistic optimism.

Positive Illusions and Career Decisions

A final issue to consider is whether people need to know the truth about themselves in order to maximize their outcomes in life. A classic example would be an individual who is contemplating a career as a dancer. Before deciding whether or not to pursue this profession, shouldn't this person know whether or not he truly has the talent to succeed?

This argument seems compelling, but it is not without flaws. It assumes that the sole (or at least primary) issue people face when making such decisions is probability of success. This is questionable. Individuals pursue careers in the arts for many reasons, not the least of which may be because they truly enjoy doing what they are doing. A dancer may choose this career not simply because he has plans of one day "making it big" but also because he loves to dance. One can certainly love to dance without knowing precisely how much innate dancing ability one possesses, so it is arguable whether people need to know the truth about themselves in these situations. In fact, there is reason to believe that the less concerned people are with external indicators of success, the happier and healthier they are (Kasser & Ryan, 1993).

The point here is not that people are unconcerned with whether they succeed or fail; nor am I suggesting that those who fail are not emotionally distraught. What I am suggesting is (1) that the *journey* is often as important to people as the final *destination,* and (2) that although people who fail may be temporarily distressed, they rarely regret having tried to fulfill their dreams. If anything, the opposite seems to be the case: Regret is greater among people who failed to try than among those who tried and failed (Gilovich & Medvec, 1994; Kinnier & Metha, 1989). In light of these considerations, it is unclear whether people should know just how much ability they possess in a given domain before making career choices.

But even if one assumes that future outcomes are the sole consideration (which I do not), it is an open question as to whether accurate knowledge of one's ability is needed or desirable. Ability level is only one factor that determines performance outcomes. Effort, perseverance, and the effective application of one's talents are also important. As noted earlier, high self-perceptions of ability, even if somewhat illusory, appear to promote these factors. Consequently, a positive view of one's ability may be more facilitative of success than a purely accurate assessment.

CHAPTER SUMMARY

In this chapter we have examined the relation between self-knowledge and psychological well-being. We began by noting that accurate self-knowledge has traditionally been thought to be a necessary component of mental health; that is, in order to be healthy, people need to see themselves as they really are. We then reviewed evidence that challenges this claim. Many people who enjoy psychological health do not view themselves in entirely accurate terms. Instead, they view themselves in terms that are a bit more favorable than realistic. They believe they possess more positive (and fewer negative) qualities than is actually the case, they exaggerate their ability to bring about desired outcomes, and they are unduly optimistic about their future. These perceptions (which we called positive illusions) are not wildly divergent from what is true, but neither are they entirely accurate.

The next issue we considered is whether positive illusions promote psychological adjustment. We noted that positive illusions have been associated with greater happiness, more satisfying interpersonal relationships, and more productive and creative work. The benefits of positive illusions are particularly apparent when people face life-threatening illnesses or other traumatic events. People who exhibit positive illusions under such circumstances cope better than those who do not.

Finally, we looked at some potential costs of positive illusions. Although illusions seem to be beneficial when they are modest, they can be costly when they are excessive. These costs include negative interpersonal relationships, maladaptive persistence and poor self-regulation, and threats to physical well-being.

These potential risks highlight that illusions must be modest in order to be effective. A fitting analogy can be drawn between positive illusions and the new magnetic levitation vehicles currently being developed in Japan, France, and Germany. These passenger trains are capable of achieving speeds of up to 300 miles per hour by riding an electromagnetic current that raises them slightly above the rails. The trick is in keeping the train just the right distance off the ground: Rising too high causes the train to gyrate and crash; riding too close to the ground causes the train to grind to a halt.

In a similar vein, self-enhancing illusions are most effective when they are only slightly more positive than can realistically be justified (Baumeister, 1989; Brown, 1991; Taylor & Brown, 1988, 1994). Being too grandiose in one's thinking can have serious consequences, as the destructive delusions of grandeur that accompany a manic episode illustrate. But being too modest in one's self-appraisals can also be debilitating, as research on *depressive realism* attests. Thus, much like the new passenger trains under development, individual's self-appraisals may be most effective when they rise just slightly above the ground.

- Some theories of mental health assert that accurate self-knowledge is a necessary component of psychological well-being. Other theories hold that although wildly distorted self-views are clearly dysfunctional, people do not need to know precisely what they are really like in order to function effectively.
- Many healthy people do not possess entirely accurate self-views. Instead, they view themselves, their ability to bring about desired outcomes, and their future in overly positive terms. These biases (or positive illusions) are not extreme, but they are commonly observed.
- Positive illusions have been linked to several criteria of psychological health, including happiness, satisfying and fulfilling interpersonal relationships, and the ability to do creative and productive work.
- Positive illusions may be particularly beneficial when people confront stressful life events. People who exaggerate their control and remain optimistic when faced with such circumstances tend to cope better than do those who fail to exhibit these illusions.
- If excessive, positive illusions can carry serious costs. These include negative interpersonal outcomes (including interpersonal violence), maladaptive persistence and poor self-regulation, and serious risks to health. These potential costs underscore that in order to be effective, positive illusions must be modest.

For Further Reading

ALLOY, L. B., & ABRAMSON, L. Y. (1988). Depressive realism: Four theoretical perspectives. In L. B. Alloy (Ed.), *Cognitive processes in depression* (pp. 223–265). New York: Guilford.

LOCKARD, J. S., & PAULHUS, D. L. (1988) (Eds.). *Self-deception: An adaptive mechanism?* Englewood Cliffs, NJ: Prentice Hall.

MYERS, D. G. (1993). *The pursuit of happiness.* New York: Avon Books.

TAYLOR, S. E., & BROWN, J. D. (1988). Illusion and well-being: A social psychological perspective on mental health. *Psychological Bulletin, 103,* 193–210.

References

ABELSON, R. P. (1986). Beliefs are like possessions. *Journal for the Theory of Social Behaviour, 16,* 222–250.

ABRAMSON, L. Y., METALSKY, G. I., & ALLOY, L. B. (1988). The hopelessness theory of depression: Does the research test the theory? In L. Y. Abramson (Ed.), *Social cognition and clinical psychology: A synthesis* (pp. 33–65). New York: Guilford Press.

ABRAMSON, L. Y., METALSKY, G. I., & ALLOY, L. B. (1989). Hopelessness depression: A theory-based subtype of depression. *Psychological Review, 96,* 358–372.

ABRAMSON, L. Y., SELIGMAN, M. E. P., & TEASDALE, J. D. (1978). Learned helplessness in humans: Critique and reformulation. *Journal of Abnormal Psychology, 87,* 49–74.

ADAMS, G. R., ABRAHAM, K. G., & MARKSTROM, C. A. (1987). The relations among identity development, self-consciousness, and self-focusing during middle and late adolescence. *Developmental Psychology, 23,* 292–297.

AFFLECK, G., & TENNEN, H. (1991). Social comparison and coping with major medical problems. In J. Suls & T. A. Wills (Eds.), *Social comparison: Contemporary theory and research* (pp. 369–393). Hillsdale, NJ: Lawrence Erlbaum Associates.

AINSWORTH, M. D. S., BLEHAR, M. C., WATERS, E., & WALL, S. (1978). *Patterns of attachment: A psychological study of the strange situation.* Hillsdale, NJ: Lawrence Erlbaum Associates.

ALBRIGHT, L., KENNY, D. A., & MALLOY, T. E. (1988). Consensus in personality judgments at zero acquaintance. *Journal of Personality and Social Psychology, 55,* 387–395.

ALEXANDER, N. C., & KNIGHT, G. W. (1971). Situated identities and social psychological experimentation. *Sociometry, 34,* 65–82.

ALICKE, M. D. (1985). Global self-evaluation as determined by the desirability and controllability of trait adjectives. *Journal of Personality and Social Psychology, 49,* 1621–1630.

ALLOY, L. B., & ABRAMSON, L. Y. (1979). Judgments of contingency in depressed and nondepressed students: Sadder but wiser? *Journal of Experimental Psychology: General, 108,* 441–485.

ALLOY, L. B., & ABRAMSON, L. Y. (1988). Depressive realism: Four theoretical perspectives. In L. B. Alloy (Ed.), *Cognitive processes in depression* (pp. 223–265). New York: Guilford.

ALLOY, L. B., & AHRENS, A. H. (1987). Depression and pessimism for the future: Biased use of statistically relevant information in predictions for self versus others. *Journal of Personality and Social Psychology, 52,* 366–378.

ALLOY, L. B., & CLEMENTS, C. M. (1992). Illusion of control: Invulnerability to negative affect and depressive symptoms after laboratory and natural stressors. *Journal of Abnormal Psychology, 101,* 234–245.

ALLOY, L. B., & LIPMAN, A. J. (1992). Depression and selection of positive and negative social feedback: Motivated preference or cognitive balance? *Journal of Abnormal Psychology, 101,* 310–313.

ALLPORT, G. W. (1937). *Personality: A psychological interpretation.* New York: Holt, Rinehart, & Winston.

ALLPORT, G. W. (1943). The ego in contemporary psychology. *Psychological Review, 50,* 451–478.

AMABILE, T. M. (1983). *The social psychology of creativity.* New York: Springer-Verlag.

AMABILE, T. M. (1985). Motivation and creativity: Effects of motivational orientation on creative writers. *Journal of Personality and Social Psychology, 48,* 393–399.

AMABILE, T. M., HILL, K. G., HENNESSEY, B. A., & TIGHE, E. M. (1994). The work preference inventory: Assessing intrinsic and extrinsic motivational orientations. *Journal of Personality and Social Psychology, 66,* 950–967.

AMENSON, C. S., & LEWINSOHN, P. M. (1981). An investigation into the observed sex difference in prevalence of unipolar depression. *Journal of Abnormal Psychology, 90,* 1–13.

AMES, C., & AMES, R. (1984). Systems of student and teacher motivation: Toward a qualitative definition. *Journal of Educational Psychology, 76,* 535–566.

ANDERSEN, S. M. (1984). Self-knowledge and social inference: II. The diagnosticity of cognitive/affective and behavioral data. *Journal of Personality and Social Psychology, 46,* 294–307.

ANDERSEN, S. M., & BAUM, A. (1994). Transference in interpersonal relations: Inferences and affect based on significant-other representations. *Journal of Personality, 62,* 459–497.

ANDERSEN, S. M., & ROSS, L. (1984). Self-knowledge and social inference: I. The impact of cognitive/affective and behavioral data. *Journal of Personality and Social Psychology, 46,* 280–293.

ANDERSON, C. A., & SLUSHER, M. P. (1986). Relocating motivational effects: A synthesis of cognitive and motivational effects on attributions for success and failure. *Social Cognition, 4,* 270–292.

ANDERSON, J. R. (1983). *The architecture of cognition.* Cambridge, MA: Harvard University Press.

ANDREWS, B., & BROWN, G. W. (1993). Self-esteem and vulnerability to depression: The concurrent validity of interview and questionnaire measures. *Journal of Abnormal Psychology, 102,* 565–572.

ARIETI, S., & BEMPORAD, J. R. (1978). *Severe and mild depression: The therapeutic approach.* New York: Basic Books.

ARKIN, R. M. (1981). Self-presentation styles. In J. T. Tedeschi (Ed.), *Impression management theory and social psychological research* (pp. 311–333). San Diego, CA: Academic Press.

ARKIN, R. M. (1987). Shyness and self-presentation. In K. Yardley & T. Honess (Eds.), *Self and identity: Psychosocial perspectives* (pp. 187–195). New York: John Wiley & Sons.

ARKIN, R. M., & BAUMGARDNER, A. H. (1985). Self-handicapping. In J. H. Harvey & G. Weary (Eds.), *Basis issues in attribution theory and research* (pp. 169–202). New York: Academic Press.

ARON, A., ARON, E. N., TUDOR, M., & NELSON, G. (1991). Close relationships as including other in the self. *Journal of Personality and Social Psychology, 60,* 241–253.

ARONSON, E. (1968). Dissonance theory: Progress and problems. In R. P. Abelson, E. Aronson, W. J. McGuire, T. M. Newcomb, M. J. Rosenberg, & P. H. Tannenbaum (Eds.), *Theories of cognitive consistency: A sourcebook* (pp. 5–27). Skokie, IL: Rand McNally.

ARONSON, E. (1992). The return of the repressed: Dissonance theory makes a comeback. *Psychological Inquiry, 3,* 303–311.

ARONSON, E., & MILLS, J. (1959). The effect of severity of initiation on liking for a group. *Journal of Abnormal and Social Psychology, 59,* 177–181.

ASCH, S. (1952). *Social psychology.* Englewood Cliffs, NJ: Prentice Hall.

ASPINWALL, L. G., & BRUNHART, S. M. (1996). Distinguishing optimism from denial: Optimistic beliefs predict attention to health threats. *Personality and Social Psychology Bulletin, 22,* 993–1003.

ASPINWALL, L. G., & TAYLOR, S. E. (1993). Effects of social comparison direction, threat, and self-esteem on affect, self-evaluation, and expected success. *Journal of Personality and Social Psychology, 64,* 708–722.

ASPINWALL, L. G., & TAYLOR, S. E. (1997). A stitch in time: Self-regulation and proactive coping. *Psychological Bulletin.*

ATKINSON, J. W. (1964). *An introduction to motivation.* Princeton, NJ: Van Nostrand.

AVERILL, J. R. (1973). Personal control over aversive stimuli and its relationship to stress. *Psychological Bulletin, 80,* 286–303.

AXSOM, D. (1989). Cognitive dissonance and behavior change in psychotherapy. *Journal of Experimental Social Psychology, 25,* 234–252.

AXSOM, D., & COOPER, J. (1985). Cognitive dissonance and psychotherapy: The role of effort justification in inducing weight loss. *Journal of Experimental Social Psychology, 21,* 149–160.

BACHMAN, J. G., & O'MALLEY, P. M. (1986). Self-concepts, self-esteem, and educational experiences: The frog pond revisited (again). *Journal of Personality and Social Psychology, 50,* 33–46.

BACKMAN, C. W., & SECORD, P. F. (1968). The self and role selection. In C. Gordon & K. J. Gergen (Eds), *The self in social interaction* (pp. 289–296). New York: Wiley.

BALDWIN, J. M. (1897). *Social and ethical interpretations in mental development.* New York: Macmillan.

BALDWIN, M. W. (1994). Primed relational schemas as a source of self-evaluative reactions. *Journal of Social and Clinical Psychology, 13,* 380–403.

BALDWIN, M. W., CARRELL, S. E., & LOPEZ, D. F. (1990). Priming relationship schemas: My advisor and the Pope are watching me from the back of my mind. *Journal of Experimental Social Psychology, 26,* 435–454.

BALDWIN, M. W., & SINCLAIR, L. (1996). Self-esteem and "If . . . then" contingencies of interpersonal acceptance. *Journal of Personality and Social Psychology, 71,* 1130–1141.

BANAJI, M. R., & STEELE, C. M. (1989). Alcohol and self-evaluation: Is a social cognitive approach beneficial? *Social Cognition, 7,* 139–153.

BANDURA, A. (1986). *Social foundations of thought and action.* Englewood Cliffs, NJ: Prentice Hall.

BANDURA, A. (1989). Human agency in social cognitive theory. *American Psychologist, 44,* 1175–1184.

BANDURA, A., & WOOD, R. E. (1989). Effect of perceived controllability and performance standards on self-regulation of complex decision-making. *Journal of Personality and Social Psychology, 56,* 805–814.

BARGH, J. A. (1982). Attention and automaticity in the processing of self-relevant information. *Journal of Personality and Social Psychology, 43,* 425–436.

BARGH, J. A., & TOTA, M. E. (1988). Context-dependent automatic processing in depression: Accessibility of negative constructs with regard to self but not others. *Journal of Personality and Social Psychology, 54,* 925–939.

BARNETT, P. A., & GOTLIB, I. H. (1988). Psychosocial functioning and depression: Distinguishing among antecedents, concomitants, and consequences. *Psychological Bulletin, 104,* 97–126.

BARNETT, P. A., & GOTLIB, I. H. (1990). Cognitive vulnerability to depressive symptoms among men and women. *Cognitive Therapy and Research, 14,* 47–61.

BARRETT, K. C. (1995). A functionalist approach to shame and guilt. In J. P. Tangney & K. W. Fischer (Eds.), *Self-conscious emotions: The psychology of shame, guilt, pride, and embarrassment* (pp. 25–63). New York: Guilford Press.

BARTHOLOMEW, K., & HOROWITZ, L. M. (1991). Attachment styles among young adults: A test of a four-category model. *Journal of Personality and Social Psychology, 61,* 226–244.

BARTLETT, F. C. (1932). *Remembering: A study in experimental and social psychology.* London: Cambridge University Press.

BAUMEISTER, R. F. (1982a). Self-esteem, self-presentation, and future interaction: A dilemma of reputation. *Journal of Personality, 50,* 29–45.

BAUMEISTER, R. F. (1982b). A self-presentational view of social phenomena. *Psychological Bulletin, 91,* 3–26.

BAUMEISTER, R. F. (1984). Choking under pressure: Self-consciousness and paradoxical effects of incentives on skillful performance. *Journal of Personality and Social Psychology, 46,* 610–620.

BAUMEISTER, R. F. (1986). *Identity: Cultural change and the struggle for self.* New York: Oxford University Press.

BAUMEISTER, R. F. (1989). The optimal margin of illusion. *Journal of Social and Clinical Psychology, 8,* 176–189.

BAUMEISTER, R. F. (1990). Suicide as escape from self. *Psychological Review, 97,* 90–113.

BAUMEISTER, R. F. (1993). (Ed.). *Self-esteem: The puzzle of low self-regard.* New York: Plenum Press.

BAUMEISTER, R. F. (1997). *Evil: Inside human violence and cruelty.* New York: W. H. Freeman.

BAUMEISTER, R. F., HAMILTON, J. C., & TICE, D. M. (1985). Public versus private expectancy of success: Confidence booster or performance pressure? *Journal of Personality and Social Psychology, 48,* 1447–1457.

BAUMEISTER, R. F., & HEATHERTON, T. F. (1996). Self-regulation failure: An overview. *Psychological Inquiry, 7,* 1–15.

BAUMEISTER, R. F., HEATHERTON, T. F., & TICE, D. M. (1993). When ego threats lead to self-regulation failure: Negative consequences of high self-esteem. *Journal of Personality and Social Psychology, 64,* 141–156.

BAUMEISTER, R. F., HEATHERTON, T. F., & TICE, D. M. (1994). *Losing control: How and why people fail at self-regulation.* San Diego, CA: Academic Press.

BAUMEISTER, R. F., & JONES, E. E. (1978). When self-presentation is constrained by the target's knowledge: Consistency and compensation. *Journal of Personality and Social Psychology, 36,* 608–618.

BAUMEISTER, R. F., & LEARY, M. R. (1995). The need to belong: Desire for interpersonal attachments as a fundamental human motivation. *Psychological Bulletin, 117,* 497–529.

BAUMEISTER, R. F., & SCHER, S. J. (1988). Self-defeating behavior patterns among normal individuals: Review and analysis of common self-destructive tendencies. *Psychological Bulletin, 104,* 3–22.

BAUMEISTER, R. F., SMART, L., & BODEN, J. M. (1996). Relation of threatened egotism to violence and aggression: The dark side of high self-esteem. *Psychological Review, 103,* 5–33.

BAUMEISTER, R. F., & STEINHILBER, A. (1984). Paradoxical effects of supportive audiences on performance under pressure: The home field disadvantage in sports championships. *Journal of Personality and Social Psychology, 47,* 85–93.

BAUMEISTER, R. F., & TICE, D. M. (1985). Self-esteem and responses to success and failure: Subsequent performance and intrinsic motivation. *Journal of Personality, 53,* 450–467.

BAUMEISTER, R. F., & TICE, D. M. (1986). How adolescence became the struggle for self: A historical transformation of psychological development. In J. Suls & A. G. Greenwald (Eds.), *Psychological perspectives on the self* (Vol. 3, pp. 183–201). Hillsdale, NJ: Erlbaum.

BAUMEISTER, R. F., TICE, D. M., & HUTTON, D. G. (1989). Self-presentational motivations and personality differences in self-esteem. *Journal of Personality, 57,* 547–579.

BAUMGARDNER, A. H. (1990). To know oneself is to like oneself: Self-certainty and self-affect. *Journal of Personality and Social Psychology, 58,* 1062–1072.

BAUMGARDNER, A. H., & BROWNLEE, E. A. (1987). Strategic failure in social interaction: Evidence for expectancy disconfirmation processes. *Journal of Personality and Social Psychology, 52,* 525–535.

BAUMGARDNER, A. H., LAKE, E. A., & ARKIN, R. M. (1985). Claiming mood as a self-handicap: The influence of spoiled and unspoiled social identities. *Personality and Social Psychology Bulletin, 11,* 349–358.

BEACH, S. R. H., & TESSER, A. (1995). Self-esteem and the extended self-evaluation maintenance model. In M. H. Kernis (Ed.), *Efficacy, agency, and self-esteem* (pp. 145–170). New York: Plenum Press.

BEAMAN, A. L., KLENTZ, B., DIENER, E., & SVANUM, S. (1979). Self-awareness and transgression in children: Two field studies. *Journal of Personality and Social Psychology, 37,* 1835–1846.

BECK, A. T. (1967). *Depression: Clinical, experimental, and theoretical aspects.* New York: Harper & Row.

BECK, A. T. (1976). *Cognitive therapy and the emotional disorders.* New York: International Universities Press.

BECK, A. T. (1983). Cognitive therapy of depression: New perspectives. In P. J. Clayton & J. E. Barrett (Eds.), *Treatment of depression: Old controversies and new approaches* (pp. 265–290). New York: Raven Press.

BECK, A. T. (1991). Cognitive therapy: A 30-year retrospective. *American Psychologist, 46,* 368–375.

BECK, A. T., RUSH, A. J., SHAW, B. F., & EMERY, G. (1979). *Cognitive therapy of depression.* New York: Guilford Press.

BECKER, E. (1968). *The structure of evil.* New York: George Braziller.

BECKER, E. (1973). *The denial of death.* New York: The Free Press.

BEDNAR, R. L., WELLS, M. G., & PETERSON, S. R. (1989). *Self-esteem: Paradoxes and innovations in clinical theory and practice.* Washington, D.C.: American Psychological Association.

BEGGAN, J. K. (1992). On the social nature of nonsocial perception: The mere ownership effect. *Journal of Personality and Social Psychology, 62,* 229–237.

BELK, R. W. (1988). Possessions and the extended self. *Journal of Consumer Research, 15,* 139–168.

BEM, D. J. (1972). Self-perception theory. In L. Berkowitz (Ed.), *Advances in experimental social psychology* (Vol. 6, pp. 1–63). New York: Academic Press.

BEM, D. J., & ALLEN, A. (1974). On predicting some of the people some of the time: The search for cross-situational consistencies in behavior. *Psychological Review, 81,* 506–520.

BERGLAS, S., & JONES, E. E. (1978). Drug choice as a self-handicapping strategy in response to noncontingent success. *Journal of Personality and Social Psychology, 36,* 405–417.

BEYER, S. (1990). Gender differences in the accuracy of self-evaluations of performance. *Journal of Personality and Social Psychology, 59,* 960–970.

BIBRING, E. (1953). The mechanism of depression. In P. Greenacre (Ed.), *Affective disorders: Psychoanalytic contributions to their study* (pp. 13–48). New York: International Universities Press.

BJORKLUND, D. F., & GREEN, B. L. (1992). The adaptive nature of cognitive immaturity. *American Psychologist, 47,* 46–54.

BLAINE, B., & CROCKER, J. (1993). Self-esteem and self-serving biases in reactions to positive and negative events: An integrative review. In R. F. Baumeister (Ed.), *Self-esteem: The puzzle of low self-regard* (pp. 55–85). New York: Plenum Press.

BLANEY, P. H. (1986). Affect and memory: A review. *Psychological Bulletin, 99,* 229–246.

BLASCOVICH, J., & TOMAKA, J. (1990). Measures of self-esteem. In J. P. Robinson, P. R. Shaver, & L. M. Wrightsman (Eds.), *Measures of social psychological attitudes* (3rd ed.). Orlando, FL: Academic Press.

BLATT, S. J. (1985). The destructiveness of perfectionism. *American Psychologist, 50,* 1003–1020.

BLATT, S. J., QUINLAN, D. M., CHEVRON, E. S., McDONALD, C., & ZUROFF, D. C. (1982). Dependence and self-criticism: Psychological dimensions of depression. *Journal of Counseling and Clinical Psychology, 50,* 113–124.

BLOCH, M., FAHY, M., FOX, S., & HAYDEN, M. R. (1989). Predictive testing for Huntington's disease: II. Demographic characteristics, life-style patterns, attitudes, and psychosocial assessments of the first fifty-one test candidates. *American Journal of Medical Genetics, 32,* 217–224.

BLUMBERG, H. H. (1972). Communication of interpersonal evaluations. *Journal of Personality and Social Psychology, 23,* 157–162.

BOGGIANO, A. K., & MAIN, D. S. (1986). Enhancing children's interest in activities used as rewards: The bonus effect. *Journal of Personality and Social Psychology, 51,* 1116–1126.

BOHRNSTEDT, G. W., & FELSON, R. B. (1983). Explaining the relations among children's actual and perceived performances and self-esteem: A comparison of several causal models. *Journal of Personality and Social Psychology, 45,* 43–56.

BORING, E. G. (1951). *A history of experimental psychology.* New York: Appleton, Century, Crofts.

BORKENAU, P., & LIEBLER, A. (1992). Trait inferences: Sources of validity at zero acquaintance. *Journal of Personality and Social Psychology, 62,* 645–657.

BORKENAU, P., & LIEBLER, A. (1993). Convergence of stranger ratings of personality and intelligence with self-ratings, partner ratings, and measured intelligence. *Journal of Personality and Social Psychology, 65,* 546–553.

BOWER, G. H. (1981). Mood and memory. *American Psychologist, 36,* 129–148.

BOWER, G. H., & GILLIGAN, S. G. (1979). Remembering information related to one's self. *Journal of Research in Personality, 13,* 420–432.

BOWERMAN, W. R. (1978). Subjective competence: The structure, process, and function of self-referent causal attributions. *Journal of the Theory of Social Behaviour, 8,* 45–75.

BOWLBY, J. (1969). *Attachment and loss: Vol. 1. Attachment.* New York: Basic Books.

BOWLBY, J. (1973). *Attachment and loss: Vol. 2. Separation: Anxiety and anger.* New York: Basic Books.

BOWLBY, J. (1979). *The making and breaking of affectional bonds.* London: Tavistock.

BOWLBY, J. (1988). Developmental psychiatry comes of age. *The American Journal of Psychiatry, 145,* 1–10.

BRADLEY, G. W. (1978). Self-serving biases in the attribution process: A reexamination of the fact or fiction question. *Journal of Personality and Social Psychology, 36,* 56–71.

BRANDEN, N. (1994). *The six pillars of self-esteem.* New York: Bantam Books.

BRANDTSTÄDTER, J., & GREVE, W. (1994). The aging self: Stabilizing and protective processes. *Developmental Review, 14,* 52–80.

BRENNAN, K. A., & MORRIS, K. A. (1997). Attachment styles, self-esteem, and patterns of seeking feedback from romantic partners. *Personality and Social Psychology Bulletin, 23,* 23–31.

BRETHERTON, I. (1984). Representing the social world in symbolic play: Reality and fantasy. In I. Bretherton (Ed.), *Symbolic play* (pp. 3–41). New York: Academic Press.

BREWER, M. B. (1991). The social self: On being the same and different at the same time. *Personality and Social Psychology Bulletin, 17,* 475–482.

BREWER, M. B., & GARDNER, W. (1996). Who is this "we"? Levels of collective identity and self-representations. *Journal of Personality and Social Psychology, 71,* 83–93.

BREWER, M. B., MANZI, J. M., & SHAW, J. S. (1993). In-group identification as a function of depersonalization, distinctiveness, and status. *Psychological Science, 4,* 88–92.

BREWER, M. B., & WEBER, J. G. (1994). Self-evaluation effects of interpersonal versus intergroup social comparison. *Journal of Personality and Social Psychology, 66,* 268–275.

BREWIN, C. R. (1985). Depression and causal attributions: What is their relation? *Psychological Bulletin, 98,* 297–309.

BRICKMAN, P., COATES, D., & JANOFF-BULMAN, R. J. (1978). Lottery winners and accident victims: Is happiness relative? *Journal of Personality and Social Psychology, 36,* 916–927.

BRICKMAN, P., & BULMAN, R. J. (1977). Pleasure and pain in social comparison. In J. Suls & R. Miller (Eds.), *Social comparison processes: Theoretical and empirical perspectives* (pp. 149–186). Washington, DC: Hemisphere.

BRIGGS, S. R., CHEEK, J. M., & BUSS, A. H. (1980). An analysis of the self-monitoring scale. *Journal of Personality and Social Psychology, 38,* 679–686.

BRISSETT, D. (1972). Toward a clarification of self-esteem. *Psychiatry, 35,* 255–263.

BROCKNER, J. (1979). The effects of self-esteem, success-failure, and self-consciousness on task performance. *Journal of Personality and Social Psychology, 37,* 1732–1741.

BROCKNER, J. (1984). Low self-esteem and behavioral plasticity: Some implications for personality and social psychology. In L. Wheeler (Ed.), *Review of personality and social psychology* (Vol. 4, pp. 237–271). Beverly Hills: Sage.

BROCKNER, J., & CHEN, Y-R. (1996). The moderating role of self-esteem and self-construal in reaction to a threat to the self: Evidence from the People's Republic of China and the United States. *Journal of Personality and Social Psychology, 71,* 603–615.

BROCKNER, J., GARDNER, M., BIERMAN, J., MAHAN, T., THOMAS, B., WEISS, W., WINTERS, L., & MITCHELL, A. (1983). The roles of self-esteem and self-consciousness in the Wortman-Brehm model of reactance and learned helplessness. *Journal of Personality and Social Psychology, 45,* 199–209.

BROCKNER, J., & GUARE, J. (1983). Improving the performance of low self-esteem individuals: An attributional approach. *Academy of Management Journal, 26,* 642–656.

BROCKNER, J., HJELLE, L., & PLANT, R. (1985). Self-focused attention, self-esteem, and the experience of state depression. *Journal of Personality, 53,* 425–434.

BROCKNER, J., & HULTON, A. J. B. (1978). How to reverse the vicious cycle of low self-esteem: The importance of attentional focus. *Journal of Experimental Social Psychology, 14,* 564–578.

BROCKNER, J., WIESENFELD, B. M., & RASKAS, D. F. (1993). Self-esteem and expectancy-value discrepancy: The effects of believing that you can (or can't) get what you want. In R. F. Baumeister (Ed.), *Self-esteem: The puzzle of low self-regard* (pp. 219–240). New York: Plenum Press.

BROWN, G. W., ANDREWS, B., HARRIS, T. O., ADLER, Z., & BRIDGE, L. (1986). Social support, self-esteem, and depression. *Psychological Medicine, 16,* 813–831.

BROWN, G. W., BIFULCO, A., & ANDREWS, B. (1990). Self-esteem and depression: III. Aetiological issues. *Social Psychiatry and Psychiatric Epidemiology, 25,* 235–243.

BROWN, G. W., BIFULCO, A., VEIEL, H. O. F., & ANDREWS, B. (1990). Self-esteem and depression: II. Social correlates of self-esteem. *Social Psychiatry and Psychiatric Epidemiology, 25,* 225–234.

BROWN, G. W., & HARRIS, T. O. (1978). *Social origins of depression: A study of psychiatric disorder in women.* London: Tavistock.

BROWN, J. D. (1986). Evaluations of self and others: Self-enhancement biases in social judgments. *Social Cognition, 4,* 353–376.

BROWN, J. D. (1990). Evaluating one's abilities: Shortcuts and stumbling blocks on the road to self-knowledge. *Journal of Experimental Social Psychology, 26,* 149–167.

BROWN, J. D. (1991). Accuracy and bias in self-knowledge. In C. R. Snyder & D. F. Forsyth (Eds.), *Handbook of social and clinical psychology: The health perspective* (pp. 158–178). New York: Pergamon Press.

BROWN, J. D. (1993). Self-esteem and self-evaluation: Feeling is believing. In J. Suls (Ed.), *Psychological perspectives on the self* (Vol. 4, pp. 27–58). Hillsdale, NJ: Lawrence Erlbaum Associates.

BROWN, J. D., COLLINS, R. L., & SCHMIDT, G. W. (1988). Self-esteem and direct versus indirect forms of self-enhancement. *Journal of Personality and Social Psychology, 55,* 445–453.

BROWN, J. D., & DUTTON K. A. (1991). *The many faces of self-love: Self-esteem and its correlates.* Unpublished manuscript. University of Washington, Seattle.

BROWN, J. D., & DUTTON, K. A. (1995a). Truth and consequences: The costs and benefits of accurate self-knowledge. *Personality and Social Psychology Bulletin, 21,* 1288–1296.

BROWN, J. D., & DUTTON, K. A. (1995b). The thrill of victory, the complexity of defeat: Self-esteem and people's emotional reactions to success and failure. *Journal of Personality and Social Psychology, 68,* 712–722.

BROWN, J. D., DUTTON, K. A., & COOK, K. E. (1997). *From the top down: Self-esteem and self-evaluation.* Manuscript submitted for publication.

BROWN, J. D., & GALLAGHER, F. M. (1992). Coming to terms with failure: Private self-enhancement and public self-effacement. *Journal of Experimental Social Psychology, 28,* 3–22.

BROWN, J. D., & MANKOWSKI, T. A. (1993). Self-esteem, mood, and self-evaluation: Changes in mood and the way you see you. *Journal of Personality and Social Psychology, 64,* 421–430.

BROWN, J. D., & MCGILL, K. L. (1989). The cost of good fortune: When positive life events produce negative health consequences. *Journal of Personality and Social Psychology, 57*, 1103–1110.

BROWN, J. D., NOVICK, N. J., LORD, K. A., & RICHARDS, J. M. (1992). When Gulliver travels: Social context, psychological closeness, and self-appraisals. *Journal of Personality and Social Psychology, 60*, 717–727.

BROWN, J. D., & ROGERS, R. J. (1991). Self-serving attributions: The role of physiological arousal. *Personality and Social Psychology Bulletin, 17*, 501–506.

BROWN, J. D., & SMART, S. A. (1991). The self and social conduct: Linking self-representations to prosocial behavior. *Journal of Personality and Social Psychology, 60*, 368–375.

BROWN, J. D., & TAYLOR, S. E. (1986). Affect and the processing of personal information: Evidence for mood-activated self-schemata. *Journal of Experimental Social Psychology, 22*, 436–452.

BRUNER, J. S. (1957). On perceptual readiness. *Psychological Review, 64*, 123–152.

BRUNSTEIN, J. C. (1993). Personal goals and subjective well-being: A longitudinal study. *Journal of Personality and Social Psychology, 65*, 1061–1070.

BUCHANAN, C. M., ECCLES, J. S., & BECKER, J. B. (1992). Are adolescents the victims of raging hormones: Evidence for activational effects of hormones on moods and behavior at adolescence. *Psychological Bulletin, 111*, 62–107.

BUCHWALD, A. M., & RUDICK-DAVIS, D. (1993). The symptoms of major depression. *Journal of Abnormal Psychology, 102*, 197–295.

BURGER, J. M., & BURNS, L. (1988). The illusion of unique invulnerability and the use of effective contraception. *Personality and Social Psychology Bulletin, 14*, 264–270.

BURGER, J. M., MCWARD, J., & LATORRE, D. (1989). Boundaries of self-control: Relinquishing control over aversive events. *Journal of Social and Clinical Psychology, 8*, 209–221.

BURKE, P. A., KRAUT, R. E., & DWORKIN, R. H. (1984). Traits, consistency, and self-schemata: What do our methods measure? *Journal of Personality and Social Psychology, 47*, 568–579.

BURNS, R. B. (1979). *The self-concept: Theory, measurement, development, and behaviour.* London: Longman.

BUSS, A. H. (1980). *Self-consciousness and social anxiety.* San Francisco: W. H. Freeman.

BUSS, A. H., & BRIGGS, S. R. (1984). Drama and the self in social interaction. *Journal of Personality and Social Psychology, 47*, 1310–1324.

BUTLER, A. C., HOKANSON, J. E., & FLYNN, H. A. (1994). A comparison of self-esteem lability and low self-esteem as vulnerability factors for depression. *Journal of Personality and Social Psychology, 66*, 166–177.

BUTTERWORTH, G. (1992). Origins of self-perception in infancy. *Psychological Inquiry, 3*, 103–111.

BUUNK, B. P., COLLINS, R. L., TAYLOR, S. E., VANYPEREN, N. W., & DAKOF, G. A. (1990). The affective consequences of social comparison: Either ways has its ups and down. *Journal of Personality and Social Psychology, 59*, 1238–1249.

BUUNK, B. P., & VAN DER EIJNDEN, R. J. J. M. (1997). Perceived prevalence, perceived superiority, relationship satisfaction: Most relationships are good, but ours is the best. *Personality and Social Psychology Bulletin, 23*, 219–228.

BYRNE, B. M., & SHAVELSON, R. J. (1996). On the structure of social self-concept for pre-, early, and late adolescents: A test of the Shavelson, Hubner, and Stanton (1976) model. *Journal of Personality and Social Psychology, 70*, 599–613.

CAMPBELL, J. D. (1990). Self-esteem and clarity of the self-concept. *Journal of Personality and Social Psychology, 59,* 538–549.

CAMPBELL, J. D., & FAIREY, P. J. (1985). Effects of self-esteem, hypothetical explanations, and verbalization of expectancies on future performance. *Journal of Personality and Social Psychology, 48,* 1097–1111.

CAMPBELL, J. D., & FEHR, B. (1990). Self-esteem and perceptions of conveyed impressions: Is negative affectivity associated with greater realism? *Journal of Personality and Social Psychology, 58,* 122–133.

CAMPBELL, J. D., & LAVALLEE, L. F. (1993). Who am I? The role of self-concept confusion in understanding the behavior of people with low self-esteem. In R. F. Baumeister (Ed.), *Self-esteem: The puzzle of low self-regard* (pp. 3–20). New York: Plenum Press.

CANTOR, N., & NOREM, J. K. (1989). Defensive pessimism and stress and coping. *Social Cognition, 7,* 92–112.

CARNEGIE, D. (1936). *How to win friends and influence people.* New York: Simon & Schuster.

CARSTENSEN, L. L., & FREUND, A. M. (1994). The resilience of the aging self. *Developmental Review, 14,* 81–92.

CARVER, C. S., BLANEY, P. H., & SCHEIER, M. F. (1979). Reassertion and giving up: The interactive role of self-directed attention and outcome expectancy. *Journal of Personality and Social Psychology, 37,* 1859–1870.

CARVER, C. S., & GANELLEN, R. J. (1983). Depression and components of self-punitiveness: High standards, self-criticism, and overgeneralization. *Journal of Abnormal Psychology, 92,* 330–337.

CARVER, C. S., GANELLEN, R. J., & BEHAR-MITRANI, V. (1985). Depression and cognitive style: Comparisons between measures. *Journal of Personality and Social Psychology, 49,* 722–728.

CARVER, C. S., POZO, C., HARRIS, S. D., NORIEGA, V., SCHEIER, M. F., ROBINSON, D. S., KETCHAM, A. S., MOFFAT, F. L., JR., & CLARK, K. C. (1993). How coping mediates the effects of optimism on distress: A study of women with early stage breast cancer. *Journal of Personality and Social Psychology, 65,* 375–390.

CARVER, C. S., & SCHEIER, M. F. (1981). *Attention and self-regulation: A control-theory approach to human behavior.* New York: Springer-Verlag.

CARVER, C. S., & SCHEIER, M. F. (1982a). Control theory: A useful framework for personality-social, clinical, and health psychology. *Psychological Bulletin, 92,* 111–135.

CARVER, C. S., & SCHEIER, M. F. (1982b). Outcome expectancy, locus of attribution for expectancy, and self-directed attention as determinants of evaluations and performance. *Journal of Experimental Social Psychology, 18,* 184–200.

CARVER, C. S., & SCHEIER, M. F. (1985). Aspects of self, and the control of behavior. In B. R. Schlenker (Ed.), *The self and social life* (pp. 146–174). New York: McGraw-Hill.

CARVER, C. S., & SCHEIER, M. F. (1990). Origins and functions of positive and negative affect: A control-process view. *Psychological Review, 97,* 19–35.

CASSIDY, J. (1990). Theoretical and methodological considerations in the study of attachment and the self in young children. In M. T. Greenberg, D. Cicchetti, & E. M. Cummings (Eds.), *Attachment in the preschool years: Theory, research, and intervention* (pp. 87–119). Chicago: The University of Chicago Press.

CAUCE, A. M. (1987). School and peer competence in early adolescence: A test of domain-specific self-perceived competence. *Developmental Psychology, 23,* 287–291.

CHANG, E. C. (1996). Cultural differences in optimism, pessimism, and coping: Predictors of subsequent adjustment in Asian American and Caucasian American college students. *Journal of Counseling Psychology, 43,* 113–123.

CHEEK, J. M. (1989). Identity-orientations and self-interpretation. In D. Buss & N. Cantor (Eds.), *Personality psychology: Recent trends and emerging directions* (pp. 275–285). New York: Springer-Verlag.

CHEEK, J. M., TROPP, L. R., CHEN, L. C., & UNDERWOOD, M. K. (1994). *Identity orientations: Personal, social, and collective.* Paper presented at the 102nd Annual Convention of the American Psychological Association, Los Angeles.

CIALDINI, R. B., BORDEN, R. J., THORNE, A., WALKER, M. R., FREEMAN, S., & SLOAN, L. R. (1976). Basking in reflected glory: Three (football) field studies. *Journal of Personality and Social Psychology, 34,* 366–375.

CIALDINI, R. B., & DE NICHOLAS, M. E. (1989). Self-presentation by association. *Journal of Personality and Social Psychology, 57,* 626–631.

CIALDINI, R. B., & RICHARDSON, K. D. (1980). Two indirect tactics of image management: Basking and blasting. *Journal of Personality and Social Psychology, 39,* 406–415.

CLARK, D. M., & TEASDALE, J. D. (1982). Diurnal variation in clinical depression and accessibility of memories of positive and negative experiences. *Journal of Abnormal Psychology, 91,* 87–95.

COHEN, S. (1980). Aftereffects of stress on human performance and social behavior: A review of research and theory. *Psychological Bulletin, 88,* 82–108.

COHLER, B. J. (1982). Personal narrative and life course. In P. B. Baltes & O. G. Brim, Jr. (Eds.), *Life span development and behavior* (Vol. 4, pp. 205–241). New York: Academic Press.

COLLINS, N. L., & READ, S. J. (1990). Adult attachment, working models, and relationship quality in dating couples. *Journal of Personality and Social Psychology, 58,* 644–663.

COLLINS, R. L. (1996). For better or worse: The impact of upward social comparisons on self-evaluations. *Psychological Bulletin, 119,* 51–69.

COLVIN, C. R., & BLOCK, J. (1994). Do positive illusions foster mental health? An examination of the Taylor and Brown formulation. *Psychological Bulletin, 116,* 3–20.

COLVIN, C. R., BLOCK, J., & FUNDER, D. C. (1995). Overly positive self-evaluations and personality: Negative implications for mental health. *Journal of Personality and Social Psychology, 68,* 1152–1162.

CONWAY, M., GIANNOPOULOS, C., CSANK, P., & MENDELSON, M. (1993). Dysphoria and specificity in self-focused attention. *Personality and Social Psychology Bulletin, 19,* 265–268.

CONWAY, M., & ROSS, M. (1984). Getting what you want by revising what you had. *Journal of Personality and Social Psychology, 47,* 738–748.

COOLEY, C. H. (1902). *Human nature and the social order.* New York: Charles Scribner's Sons.

COOPER, J., & FAZIO, R. H. (1984). A new look at dissonance theory. In L. Berkowitz (Ed.), *Advances in experimental social psychology* (Vol. 17, pp. 229–266). Orlando, FL: Academic Press.

COOPERSMITH, S. (1967). *The antecedents of self-esteem.* San Francisco: W. H. Freeman.

COSTA, P. T., JR., & MCCRAE, R. R. (1988). Personality in adulthood: A six-year longitudinal study of self-reports and spouse ratings on the NEO Personality Inventory. *Journal of Personality and Social Psychology, 54,* 853–863.

COUSINS, S. D. (1989). Culture and self-perception in Japan and the United States. *Journal of Personality and Social Psychology, 56,* 124–131.

COVINGTON, M. V., & BEERY, R. (1976). *Self-worth and school learning.* New York: Holt, Rinehart, & Winston.

COYNE, J. C. (1994). Self-reported distress: Analog or ersatz depression. *Psychological Bulletin, 116,* 29–45.

COYNE, J. C., & GOTLIB, I. H. (1983). The role of cognition in depression: A critical appraisal. *Psychological Bulletin, 94*, 472–505.

COYNE, J. C., & WHIFFEN, V. E. (1995). Issues in personality as diathesis for depression: The case of sociotropy-dependence and autonomy self-criticism. *Psychological Bulletin, 118*, 358–378.

CRAIK, F. I. M., & TULVING, E. (1975). Depth of processing and the retention of words in episodic memory. *Journal of Experimental Psychology: General, 11*, 268–294.

CROCKER, J. LUHTANEN, R., BLAINE, B., & BROADNAX, S. (1994). Collective self-esteem and psychological well-being among White, Black, and Asian college students. *Personality and Social Psychology Bulletin, 20*, 503–513.

CROCKER, J., & MAJOR, B. (1989). Social stigma and self-esteem: The self-protective properties of stigmas. *Psychological Review, 96*, 608–630.

CROCKER, J., THOMPSON, L. L., McGRAW, K. M., & INGERMAN, C. (1987). Downward comparison, prejudice and evaluations of others: Effects of self-esteem and threat. *Journal of Personality and Social Psychology, 52*, 907–916.

CROCKER, J., VOELKL, K., TESTA, M., & MAJOR, B. (1991). Social stigma: The affective consequences of attributional ambiguity. *Journal of Personality and Social Psychology, 60*, 218–228.

CRONBACH, L. J. (1955). Processes affecting scores on "understanding of others" and "assumed similarity." *Psychological Bulletin, 52*, 177–193.

CROSS, P. (1977). Not can but will college teaching be improved. *New Directions for Higher Education, 17*, 1–15.

CROSS, S., & MARKUS, H. (1991). Possible selves across the life span. *Human Development, 34*, 230–255.

CROWNE, D. P., & MARLOWE, D. (1964). *The approval motive: Studies in evaluative dependence.* New York: Wiley.

CROYLE, R. T., SUN, Y-C., & LOUIE, D. H. (1993). Psychological minimization of cholesterol test results: Moderators of appraisal in college students and community residents. *Health Psychology, 12*, 503–507.

CSIKSZENTMIHALYI, M. (1975). *Beyond boredom and anxiety.* San Francisco: Jossey-Bass.

CUSHMAN, P. (1990). Why the self is empty: Toward a historically situated psychology. *American Psychologist, 45*, 599–611.

DAMON, W., & HART, D. (1988). *Self-understanding in childhood and adolescence.* New York: Cambridge University Press.

DARLEY, J. M., & GOETHALS, G. R. (1980). People's analyses of the causes of ability-linked performances. In L. Berkowitz (Ed.), *Advances in experimental social psychology* (Vol. 13, pp. 1–37). San Diego, CA: Academic Press.

DARWIN, C. (1872). *The expression of the emotions in man and animals.* London: John Murray.

DAVIS, J. A. (1966). The campus as a frog pond: An application of the theory of relative deprivation to career decisions of college men. *American Journal of Sociology, 72*, 17–31.

DAVIS, M. H., CONKLIN, L., Smith, A., & LUCE, C. (1996). Effect of perspective taking on the cognitive representation of persons: A merging of self and other. *Journal of Personality and Social Psychology, 70*, 713–726.

DAWES, R. M. (1976). Shallow psychology. In J. S. Carroll & J. W. Payne (Eds.), *Cognition and social behavior* (pp. 3–11). Hillsdale, NJ: Lawrence Erlbaum Associates.

DE LA RONDE, C., & SWANN, W. B., JR. (1993). Caught in the crossfire: Positivity and self-verification strivings among people with low self-esteem. In R. F. Baumeister (Ed.), *Self-esteem: The puzzle of low self-regard* (pp. 147–165). New York: Plenum Press.

DEAUX, K., REID, A., MIZRAHI, K., & ETHIER, K. A. (1995). Parameters of social identity. *Journal of Personality and Social Psychology, 68,* 280–291.

DECHARMS, R. (1968). *Personal causation: The internal-affective determinants of behavior.* New York: Academic Press.

DECI, E. L. (1971). Effects of externally mediated rewards on intrinsic motivation. *Journal of Personality and Social Psychology, 18,* 105–115.

DECI, E. L. (1975). *Intrinsic motivation.* New York: Plenum Press.

DECI, E. L., & RYAN, R. M. (1995). Human autonomy: The basis for true self-esteem. In M. H. Kernis (Ed.), *Efficacy, agency, and self-esteem* (pp. 31–49). New York: Plenum Press.

DECI, E. L., VALLERAND, R. J., PELLETIER, L. G., & RYAN, R. M. (1991). Motivation and education: The self-determination perspective. *Educational Psychologist, 26,* 325–346.

DEMO, D. H. (1985). The measurement of self-esteem: Refining our methods. *Journal of Personality and Social Psychology, 48,* 1490–1502.

DEMO, D. H. (1992). The self-concept over time: Research issues and directions. *Annual Review of Sociology, 18,* 303–326.

DENT, J., & TEASDALE, J. D. (1988). Negative cognition and the persistence of depression. *Journal of Abnormal Psychology, 97,* 29–34.

DEPAULO, B. M., KASHY, D. A., KIRKENDOL, S. E., WYER, M. M., & EPSTEIN, J. A. (1996). Lying in everyday life. *Journal of Personality and Social Psychology, 70,* 979–995.

DERRY, P. A., & KUIPER, N. A. (1981). Schematic processing and self-reference in clinical depression. *Journal of Abnormal Psychology, 90,* 286–297.

DEUTSCH, F. M., RUBLE, D. N., FLEMING, A., BROOKS-GUNN, J., & STANGOR, C. (1988). Information-seeking and maternal self-definition during the transition to motherhood. *Journal of Personality and Social Psychology, 55,* 420–431.

DIENER, E. (1994). Assessing subjective well-being: Progress and opportunities. *Social Indicators Research, 31,* 103–157.

DIENER, E., & DIENER, M. (1995). Cross-cultural correlates of life satisfaction and self-esteem. *Journal of Personality & Social Psychology, 68,* 653–663.

DIENER, E., & WALLBOM, M. (1976). Effects of self-awareness on antinormative behavior. *Journal of Research in Personality, 10,* 413–423.

DITTES, J. (1959). Attractiveness of a group as a function of self-esteem and acceptance by group. *Journal of Abnormal and Social Psychology, 59,* 77–82.

DITTO, P. H., & LOPEZ, D. F. (1992). Motivated skepticism: Use of differential decision criteria for preferred and nonpreferred conclusions. *Journal of Personality and Social Psychology, 63,* 568–584.

DIXON, T. M., & BAUMEISTER, R. F. (1991). Escaping the self: The moderating effect of self-complexity. *Personality and Social Psychology Bulletin, 17,* 363–368.

DOHR, K. B., RUSH, A. J., & BERNSTEIN, I. H. (1989). Cognitive biases and depression. *Journal of Abnormal Psychology, 98,* 263–267.

DOLLINGER, S. J., & CLANCY, S. M. (1993). Identity, self, and personality: II. Glimpses through the autophotographic eye. *Journal of Personality and Social Psychology, 64,* 1064–1071.

DOLLINGER, S. J., PRESTON, L. A., O'BRIEN, S. P., & DILALLA, D. L. (1996). Individuality and relatedness of the self: An autophotographic study. *Journal of Personality and Social Psychology, 71,* 1268–1278.

DONAHUE, E. M., ROBINS, R. W., ROBERTS, B. W., & JOHN, O. P. (1993). The divided self: Concurrent and longitudinal effects of psychological adjustment and social roles on self-concept differentiation. *Journal of Personality and Social Psychology, 64,* 834–846.

DOWNEY, G., & COYNE, J. C. (1990). Children of depressed parents: An integrative review. *Psychological Bulletin, 108,* 50–76.

DUNNING, D. (1993). Words to live by: The self and definitions of social concepts and categories. In J. Suls (Ed.), *Psychological perspectives on the self* (Vol. 4, pp. 99–126). Hillsdale, NJ: Lawrence Erlbaum Associates.

DUNNING, D. (1995). Trait importance and modifiability as factors influencing self-assessment and self-enhancement motives. *Personality and Social Psychology Bulletin, 21,* 1297–1306.

DUNNING, D., & HAYES, A. F. (1996). Evidence for egocentric comparison in social judgment. *Journal of Personality and Social Psychology, 71,* 213–229.

DUNNING, D., LEUENBERGER, A., & SHERMAN, D. A. (1995). A new look at motivated inference: Are self-serving theories of success a product of motivational forces. *Journal of Personality and Social Psychology, 69,* 58–68.

DUNNING, D., MEYEROWITZ, J. A., & HOLZBERG, A. D. (1989). Ambiguity and self-evaluation: The role of idiosyncratic trait definitions in self-serving assessments of ability. *Journal of Personality and Social Psychology, 57,* 1082–1090.

DUNNING, D., PERIE, M., & STORY, A. L. (1991). Self-serving prototypes of social categories. *Journal of Personality and Social Psychology, 61,* 957–968.

DUNNING, D., & STORY, A. L. (1991). Depression, realism, and the overconfidence effect: Are the sadder wiser when predicting future actions and events? *Journal of Personality and Social Psychology, 61,* 521–532.

DUTTON, K. A. (1995). *Self-esteem and cognitive reactions to failure.* Unpublished raw data, University of Washington, Seattle.

DUTTON, K. A., & BROWN, J. D. (1997). Global self-esteem and specific self-views as determinants of people's reactions to success and failure. *Journal of Personality and Social Psychology.*

DUVAL, S. & WICKLUND, R. A. (1972). *A theory of objective self-awareness.* New York: Academic Press.

DWECK, C. S. (1991). Self-theories and goals: Their role in motivation, personality, and development. In R. Dienstbar (Ed.), *Nebraska symposium on motivation* (Vol. 38, pp. 199–235). Lincoln: University of Nebraska Press.

DWECK, C. S., & LEGGETT, E. L. (1988). A social-cognitive approach to motivation and personality. *Psychological Review, 95,* 256–273.

DYKMAN, B. M., & ABRAMSON, L. Y. (1990). Contributions of basic research to the cognitive theories of depression. *Personality and Social Psychology Bulletin, 16,* 42–57.

ECCLES, J. S., WIGFIELD, A., HAROLD, R. D., & BLUMENFELD, P. (1993). Age and gender differences in children's self- and task perceptions during elementary school. *Child Development, 64,* 830–847.

EDWARDS, A. L. (1957). *The social desirability variable in personality assessment and research.* New York: Wiley.

EKMAN, P. (1993). Facial expression and emotion. *American Psychologist, 48,* 384–392.

ELKIND, D. (1967). Egocentrism in adolescence. *Child Development, 38,* 1025–1034.

ELLIOTT, E. S., & DWECK, C. S. (1988). Goals: An approach to motivation and achievement. *Journal of Personality and Social Psychology, 54,* 5–12.

ELLIS, A. (1962). *Reason and emotion in psychotherapy.* Secaucus, NJ: Citadel Press.

EMMONS, R. A. (1986). Personal strivings: An approach to personality and subjective well-being. *Journal of Personality and Social Psychology, 51,* 1058–1068.

EPSTEIN, S. (1973). The self-concept revisited: Or a theory of a theory. *American Psychologist, 28,* 404–416.

EPSTEIN, S. (1980). The self-concept: A review and the proposal of an integrated theory of personality. In E. Staub (Ed.), *Personality: Basic issues and current research* (pp. 82–132). Englewood Cliffs, NJ: Prentice-Hall.

EPSTEIN, S. (1990). Cognitive-experiential self-theory. In L. A. Pervin (Ed.), *Handbook of personality: Theory and research* (pp. 165–192). New York: Guilford Press.

EPSTEIN, S. (1992). Coping ability, negative self-evaluation, and overgeneralization: Experiment and theory. *Journal of Personality and Social Psychology, 62,* 826–836.

EPSTEIN, S., & FEIST, G. J. (1988). Relation between self- and other-acceptance and its moderation by identification. *Journal of Personality and Social Psychology, 54,* 309–315.

ERDELYI, M. H. (1974). A new look at the new look: Perceptual defense and vigilance. *Psychological Review, 81,* 1–25.

ERIKSON, E. (1956). The problem of ego identity. *Journal of the American Psychiatric Association, 4,* 56–121.

ERIKSON, E. H. (1963). *Childhood and society* (2nd ed.). New York: W. W. Norton.

ERIKSON, E. H. (1968). *Identity youth and crisis.* New York: W. W. Norton.

ETHIER, K. A., DEAUX, K. (1994). Negotiating social identity when contexts change: Maintaining identification and responding to threat. *Journal of Personality and Social Psychology, 67,* 243–251.

FALBO, T. POSTON, D. L., JR., TRISCARI, R. S., & ZHANG, X. (1997). Positive evaluations of the self and others among Chinese schoolchildren. *Journal of Cross Cultural Psychology, 28,* 172–191.

FAUNCE, W. A. (1984). School achievement, social status, and self-esteem. *Social Psychology Quarterly, 47,* 3–14.

FAZIO, R. H., EFFREIN, E. A., & FALENDER, V. J. (1981). Self-perception following social interaction. *Journal of Personality and Social Psychology, 41,* 232–242.

FEATHER, N. T. (1969). Attribution of responsibility and valence of success and failure in relation to initial confidence and task performance. *Journal of Personality and Social Psychology, 13,* 129–144.

FEENEY, J. A., & NOLLER, P. (1990). Attachment style as a predictor of adult romantic relationships. *Journal of Personality and Social Psychology, 58,* 281–291.

FEINGOLD, A. (1992). Good-looking people are not what we think. *Psychological Bulletin, 111,* 304–341.

FEINGOLD, A. (1994). Gender differences in personality: A meta analysis. *Psychological Bulletin, 116,* 429–456.

FELSON, R. B. (1981). Ambiguity and bias in the self-concept. *Social Psychology Quarterly, 44,* 64–69.

FELSON, R. B. (1984). The effect of self-appraisals of ability on academic performance. *Journal of Personality and Social Psychology, 47,* 944–952.

FELSON, R. B. (1993). The (somewhat) social self: How others affect self-appraisals. In J. Suls (Ed.), *Psychological perspectives on the self* (Vol. 4, pp. 1–27). Hillsdale, NJ: Lawrence Erlbaum Associates.

FELTZ, D. L., & LANDERS, D. M. (1983). The effects of mental practice on motor skill learning and performance: A meta analysis. *Journal of Sport Psychology, 5,* 25–57.

FENICHEL, O. (1945). *The psychoanalytic theory of neurosis.* New York: W. W. Norton.

FENIGSTEIN, A., SCHEIER, M. F., & BUSS, A. H. (1975). Public and private self-consciousness: Assessment and theory. *Journal of Consulting and Clinical Psychology, 43,* 522–528.

FESTINGER, L. (1954). A theory of social comparison processes. *Human Relations, 7,* 117–140.

FESTINGER, L. (1957). *A theory of cognitive dissonance.* Evanston, IL: Row Peterson.

FILIPP, S-H., & KLAUER, T. (1986). Conceptions of self over the life span: Reflections on the dialectics of change. In. M. M. Baltes & P. B. Baltes (Eds.), *The psychology of control and aging* (pp. 167–205). Hillsdale, NJ: Lawrence Erlbaum Associates.

FINCH, J. F., & CIALDINI, R. B. (1989). Another indirect tactic of (self-) image management: Boosting. *Personality and Social Psychology Bulletin, 15,* 222–232.

FISKE, S. T., & TAYLOR, S. E. (1991). *Social cognition* (2nd ed.). New York: McGraw-Hill.

FLETT, G.L., VREDENBURG, K., & KRAMES, L. (1997). The continuity of depression in clinical and nonclinical samples. *Psychological Bulletin, 121,* 395–416.

FOLKMAN, S. (1984). Personal control and stress and coping processes: A theoretical analysis. *Journal of Personality and Social Psychology, 46,* 839–852.

FONG, G. T., & MARKUS, H. (1982). Self-schemas and judgments about others. *Social Cognition, 3,* 191–204.

FRANKS, D. D., & MAROLLA, J. (1976). Efficacious action and social approval as interacting dimensions of self-esteem: A tentative formulation through construct validation. *Social Psychology Quarterly, 39,* 324–341.

FREUD, S. (1957). Mourning and melancholia. In J. Strachey (Ed. and Trans.), *The standard edition of the complete psychological works of Sigmund Freud* (Vol. 14, pp. 243–258). London: Hogarth Press. Original work published 1917.

FREUD, S. (1957). Repression. In J. Strachey (Ed. and Trans.), *The standard edition of the complete psychological works of Sigmund Freud* (Vol. 14, pp. 143–158). London: Hogarth Press. Original work published 1915.

FREY, D. (1978). Reactions to success and failure in public and private conditions. *Journal of Experimental Social Psychology, 14,* 172–179.

FROMM, E. (1955). *The sane society.* New York: Rinehart.

FROMM, E. (1963). *The art of loving.* New York: Bantam.

FUNDER, D. C. (1987). Errors and mistakes: Evaluating the accuracy of social judgment. *Psychological Bulletin, 101,* 75–90.

FUNDER, D. C. (1995). On the accuracy of personality judgment: A realistic approach. *Psychological Review, 102,* 652–670.

FUNDER, D. C., & COLVIN, C. R. (1988). Friends and strangers: Acquaintanceship, agreement, and the accuracy of personality judgment. *Journal of Personality and Social Psychology, 55,* 149–158.

FUNDER, D. C., & DOBROTH, K. M. (1987). Differences between traits: Properties associated with interjudge agreement. *Journal of Personality and Social Psychology, 52,* 409–418.

GALLUP, G. S. (1977). Self-recognition in primates: A comparative approach in bidirectional properties of consciousness. *American Psychologist, 32,* 329–338.

GANGESTAD, S., & SNYDER, M. (1985). "To carve nature at its joints": On the existence of discrete classes in personality. *Psychological Review, 92,* 317–349.

GARBER, J., & HOLLON, S. D. (1980). Universal versus personal helplessness in depression: Belief in uncontrollability or incompetence? *Journal of Abnormal Psychology, 89,* 56–66.

GARLAND, A. F., & ZIGLER, E. (1993). Adolescent suicide prevention: Current research and social policy implications. *American Psychologist, 48,* 169–182.

GECAS, V., & SCHWALBE, M. L. (1983). Beyond the looking-glass self: Social structure and efficacy-based self-esteem. *Social Psychology Quarterly, 46,* 77–88.

GERGEN, K. J. (1971). *The concept of self.* New York: Holt, Rinehart, & Winston.

GERGEN, K. J. (1982). From self to science: What is there to know? In J. Suls (Ed.), *Psychological perspectives on the self* (Vol. 1, pp. 129–149). Hillsdale, NJ: Lawrence Erlbaum Associates.

GERGEN, K. J. (1985). The social constructionist movement in modern psychology. *American Psychologist, 40*, 266–275.

GERGEN, K. J., & GERGEN, M. (1983). Narrative of the self. In T. Sarbin & K. Scheibe (Eds.), *Studies in social identity* (pp. 254–273). New York: Praeger.

GERRARD, M., GIBBONS, F. X., & BUSHMAN, B. J. (1996). Relation between perceived vulnerability to HIV and precautionary sexual behavior. *Psychological Bulletin, 119*, 390–409.

GIBBONS, F. X., & GERRARD, M. (1989). Effects of upward and downward social comparison on mood states. *Journal of Social and Clinical Psychology, 8*, 14–31.

GIBBONS, F. X., & GERRARD, M. (1991). Downward comparison and coping with threat. In J. Suls & T. A. Wills (Eds.), *Social comparison: Contemporary theory and research* (pp. 317–345). Hillsdale, NJ: Lawrence Erlbaum Associates.

GIBBONS, F. X., SMITH, T. W., INGRAM, R. E., PEARCE, K., BREHM, S. S., & SCHROEDER, D. J. (1985). Self-awareness and self-confrontation: Effects of self-focused attention on members of a clinical population. *Journal of Personality and Social Psychology, 48*, 662–675.

GILBERT, D. T., & MALONE, P. S. (1995). The correspondence bias. *Psychological Bulletin, 117*, 21–38.

GILOVICH, T. (1991). *How we know what isn't so: The fallibility of human reason in everyday life.* New York: The Free Press.

GILOVICH, T., & MEDVEC, V. H. (1994). The temporal pattern to the experience of regret. *Journal of Personality and Social Psychology, 67*, 357–365.

GLASS, D. C., & SINGER, J. E. (1972). *Urban stress.* New York: Academic Press.

GOETHALS, G. R., & DARLEY, J. (1977). Social comparison theory: An attributional approach. In J. Suls & R. L. Miller (Eds.), *Social comparison processes: Theoretical and empirical perspectives* (pp. 259–278). Washington, DC: Hemisphere.

GOFFMAN, E. (1959). *The presentation of self in everyday life.* New York: Doubleday.

GOLDSTEIN, K. (1940). *Human nature in the light of psychopathology.* Cambridge, MA: Harvard University Press.

GOLLWITZER, P. M. (1986). Striving for specific identities: The social reality of self-symbolizing. In R. F. Baumeister (Ed.), *Public self and private life* (pp. 143–159). New York: Springer-Verlag.

GOLLWITZER, P. M., EARLE, W. B., & STEPHAN, W. G. (1982). Affect as a determinant of egotism: Residual excitation and performance attributions. *Journal of Personality and Social Psychology, 43*, 702–709.

GOLLWITZER, P. M., & KINNEY, R. F. (1989). Effects of deliberative and implemental mind-sets on illusion of control. *Journal of Personality and Social Psychology, 56*, 531–542.

GONG-GUY, E., & HAMMEN, C. (1980). Causal perceptions of stressful events in depressed and nondepressed outpatients. *Journal of Abnormal Psychology, 89*, 662–669.

GONZALES, R., & GRIFFIN, D. (1995). The statistics of interdependence: Treating dyadic data with respect. In S. W. Duck (Ed.), *Handbook of personal relationships: Theory, research, and interventions* (2nd ed., pp. 1–22). Chichester, England: Wiley.

GORDON, C. (1968). Self-conceptions: Configurations of content. In C. Gordon & K. J. Gergen (Eds.), *The self in social interaction* (pp. 115–136). New York: Wiley.

GOTLIB, I. B., & CANE, D. B. (1987). Construct accessibility and clinical depression: A longitudinal investigation. *Journal of Abnormal Psychology, 96*, 199–204.

GOTLIB, I. B., & McCANN, C. D. (1984). Construct accessibility and depression: An examination of cognitive and affective factors. *Journal of Personality and Social Psychology, 47*, 427–439.

GOVE, W. R., HUGHES, M., & GEERKEN, M. R. (1980). Playing dumb: A form of impression management with undesirable side effects. *Social Psychology Quarterly, 43*, 89–102.

GREENBERG, J., & PYSZCZYNSKI, T. (1985). Compensatory self-inflation: A response to the threat to self-regard of public failure. *Journal of Personality and Social Psychology, 49*, 273–280.

GREENBERG, J., & PYSZCZYNSKI, T. (1986). Persistent high self-focus after failure and low self-focus after success: The depressive self-focusing style. *Journal of Personality and Social Psychology, 50*, 1039–1044.

GREENBERG, J., PYSZCZYNSKI, T., & SOLOMON, S. (1982). The self-serving attributional bias: Beyond self-presentation. *Journal of Experimental Social Psychology, 18*, 56–67.

GREENBERG, J., SOLOMON, S., & PYSZCZYNSKI, T. (1997). Terror management theory of self-esteem and cultural worldviews: Empirical assessments and cultural refinements. In M. P. Zanna (Ed.), *Advances in experimental social psychology* (Vol. 29). Orlando: Academic Press.

GREENBERG, J., SOLOMON, S., PYSZCZYNSKI, T., ROSENBLATT, A., BURLING, J., LYON, D., SIMON, L., & PINEL, E. (1992). Why do people need self-esteem? Converging evidence that self-esteem serves an anxiety-buffering function. *Journal of Personality and Social Psychology, 63*, 913–922.

GREENWALD, A. G. (1980). The totalitarian ego: Fabrication and revision of personal history. *American Psychologist, 35*, 603–618.

GREENWALD, A. G. (1981). Self and memory. *The Psychology of Learning and Motivation, 15*, 201–236.

GREENWALD, A. G. (1988). Self-knowledge and self-deception. In J. S. Lockard & D. L. Paulhus (Eds.), *Self-deception: An adaptive mechanism?* (pp. 113–131). Englewood Cliffs, NJ: Prentice Hall.

GREENWALD, A. G., & BANAJI, M. R. (1989). The self as a memory system: Powerful but ordinary. *Journal of Personality and Social Psychology, 57*, 41–54.

GREENWALD, A. G., & BANAJI, M. R. (1991). Implicit social cognition: Attitudes, self-esteem, and stereotypes. *Psychological Review, 102*, 4–27.

GREENWALD, A. G., & BRECKLER, S. J. (1985). To whom is the self presented? In B. R. Schlenker (Ed.), *The self and social life* (pp. 126–145). New York: McGraw-Hill.

GREENWALD, A. G., CARNOT, C. G., BEACH, R., & YOUNG, B. (1987). Increasing voting behavior by asking people if they expect to vote. *Journal of Applied Psychology, 72*, 315–318.

GREENWALD, A. G., & PRATKANIS, A. R. (1984). The self. In R. S. Wyer & T. K. Srull (Eds.), *Handbook of social cognition* (Vol. 3, pp. 3–26). Hillsdale, NJ: Lawrence Erlbaum Associates.

GRIFFIN, D., & BARTHOLOMEW, K. (1994). Models of the self and other: Fundamental dimensions underlying measures of adult attachment. *Journal of Personality and Social Psychology, 67*, 430–445.

GUMP, B. B., & KULIK, J. A. (1995). The effect of a model's HIV status on self-perceptions: A self-protective similarity bias. *Personality and Social Psychology Bulletin, 21*, 827–833.

GUR, R. C, & SACKEIM, H. A. (1979). Self-deception: A concept in search of a phenomenon. *Journal of Personality and Social Psychology, 37*, 147–169.

HAAGA, D. A. F., DYCK, M. J., & ERNST, D. (1991). Empirical status of cognitive theory of depression. *Psychological Bulletin, 110*, 215–236.

HAAN, N. (1977). *Coping and defending: Processes of self-environment organization.* New York: Academic Press.

HAMILTON, E. W., & ABRAMSON, L. Y. (1983). Cognitive patterns and major depressive disorder: A longitudinal study in a hospital setting. *Journal of Abnormal Psychology, 92,* 173–184.

HAMMEN, C., ELLICOTT, A., GITLIN, M., & JAMISON, K. R. (1989). Sociotropy/autonomy and vulnerability to specific life events in patients with unipolar depression and bipolar depressives. *Journal of Abnormal Psychology, 98,* 154–160.

HAMMEN, C., MARKS, T., deMAYO, R., & MAYOL, A. (1985). Self-schemas and risk for depression: A prospective study. *Journal of Personality and Social Psychology, 49,* 1147–1159.

HANSFORD, B. C., & HATTIE, J. A. (1982). The relationship between self and achievement/performance measures. *Review of Educational Research, 52,* 123–142.

HARACKIEWICZ, J. M., & ELLIOT, A. J. (1988). Achievement goals and intrinsic motivation. *Journal of Personality and Social Psychology, 65,* 904–915.

HARDIN, C., & HIGGINS, E. T. (1996). Shared reality: How social verification makes the subjective objective. In R. M. Sorrentino & E. T. Higgins (Eds.), *Handbook of motivation and cognition: The interpersonal context* (Vol. 3, pp. 28–84). New York: Guilford.

HARTER, S. (1983). Developmental perspectives on the self-system. In M. Hetherington (Ed.), *Handbook of child psychology: Social and personality development* (Vol. 4, pp. 275–385). New York: Wiley.

HARTER, S. (1986). Processes underlying the construction, maintenance, and enhancement of the self-concept in children. In J. Suls & A. G. Greenwald (Eds.), *Psychological perspectives on the self* (Vol. 3, pp. 137–181). Hillsdale, NJ: Lawrence Erlbaum Associates.

HARTER, S. (1993). Causes and consequences of low self-esteem in children and adolescents. In R. F. Baumeister (Ed.), *Self-esteem: The puzzle of low self-regard* (pp. 87–116). New York: Plenum Press.

HARTLAGE, S., ALLOY, L. B., VÁSQUEZ, C., & DYKMAN, B. (1993). Automatic and effortful processing in depression. *Psychological Bulletin, 113,* 247–278.

HATFIELD, E. (1965). The effect of self-esteem on romantic liking. *Journal of Experimental Social Psychology, 1,* 184–197.

HAWKINS, J. D., CATALANO, R. F., & MILLER, J. Y. (1992). Risk and protective factors for alcohol and other drug problems in adolescence and early adulthood: Implications for substance abuse programs. *Psychological Bulletin, 112,* 64–105.

HAYES, A. F., & DUNNING, D. (1997). Construal processes and trait ambiguity: Implications for self-peer agreement in personality judgment. *Journal of Personality and Social Psychology, 72,* 664–677.

HEATHERTON, T. F., & POLIVY, J. (1991). Development and validation of a scale for measuring state self-esteem. *Journal of Personality and Social Psychology, 60,* 895–910.

HEIDER, F. (1958). *The psychology of interpersonal relationships.* New York: Wiley.

HEINE, S. J., & LEHMAN, D. R. (1995). Cultural variation in unrealistic optimism: Does the West feel more invulnerable than the East? *Journal of Personality and Social Psychology, 68,* 595–607.

HEINE, S. J., & LEHMAN, D. R. (1996). *Culture and group-serving biases.* Manuscript submitted for publication.

HELGESON, V. S., & MICKELSON, K. D. (1995). Motives for social comparison. *Personality and Social Psychology Bulletin, 21,* 1200–1209.

HELGESON, V. S., & TAYLOR, S. E. (1993). Social comparisons and adjustment among cardiac patients. *Journal of Applied Social Psychology, 23,* 1171–1195.

KOHUT, H. K. (1971). *The analysis of the self.* Madison, WI: International University Press.

KOLDITZ, T. A., & ARKIN, R. M. (1982). An impression management interpretation of the self-handicapping strategy. *Journal of Personality and Social Psychology, 43,* 492–502.

KRAMER, P. D. (1993). *Listening to Prozac.* New York: Penguin Books.

KRANTZ, S., & HAMMEN, C. (1979). Assessment of cognitive bias in depression. *Journal of Abnormal Psychology, 88,* 611–619.

KRUGLANSKI, A. W. (1989). The psychology of being "right": The problem of accuracy in social perception and cognition. *Psychological Bulletin, 106,* 395–409.

KRUGLANSKI, A. W. (1990). Lay epistemic theory in social-cognitive psychology. *Psychological Inquiry, 1,* 181–197.

KUHL, J. (1985). Volitional mediators of cognition-behavior consistency: Self-regulatory processes and action versus state orientation. In J. Kuhl & L. Beckman (Eds.), *Action control: From cognition to behavior.* New York: Springer-Verlag.

KUHN, M. H., & MCPARTLAND, T. S. (1954). An empirical investigation of self-attitudes. *American Sociological Review, 19,* 68–76.

KUIPER, N. A. (1978). Depressed and causal attributions for success and failure. *Journal of Personality and Social Psychology, 36,* 236–246.

KUIPER, N. A., & DERRY, P. A. (1982). Depressed and nondepressed content self-reference in mild depression. *Journal of Personality, 50,* 67–79.

KUNDA, Z. (1987). Motivated inference: Self-serving generation and evaluation of causal theories. *Journal of Personality and Social Psychology, 53,* 636–647.

KUNDA, Z. (1990). The case for motivated reasoning. *Psychological Bulletin, 108,* 480–498.

KUNDA, Z., FONG, G. T., SANITIOSO, R., & REBER, E. (1993). Directional questions direct self-conceptions. *Journal of Experimental Social Psychology, 29,* 63–86.

KUNDA, Z., & SANITIOSO, R. (1989). Motivated changes in the self-concept. *Journal of Experimental Social Psychology, 25,* 272–285.

KURMAN, J., & SRIRAM, N. (1995). *Self-enhancement, generality of self-evaluation, and affectivity in Israel and Singapore.* Manuscript submitted for publication.

LAIRD, J. D. (1974). Self-attribution of emotion: The effects of expressive behavior on the quality of emotional experience. *Journal of Personality and Social Psychology, 29,* 475–486.

LANGER, E. J. (1975). The illusion of control. *Journal of Personality and Social Psychology, 32,* 311–328.

LANGER, E., & RODIN, J. (1976). The effects of choice and enhanced personal responsibility for the aged: A field experiment in an institutional setting. *Journal of Personality and Social Psychology, 34,* 191–198.

LARRICK, R. P. (1993). Motivational factors in decision theories: The role of self-protection. *Psychological Bulletin, 113,* 440–450.

LAVALLEE, L. F., & CAMPBELL, J. D. (1995). Impact of personal goals on self-regulation processes elicited by daily negative events. *Journal of Personality and Social Psychology, 69,* 341–352.

LAZARUS, R. S. (1983). The costs and benefits of denial. In S. Breznitz (Ed.), *Denial of stress* (pp. 1–30). New York: International Universities Press.

LAZARUS, R. S. (1991). *Emotion and adaptation.* New York: Oxford University Press.

LAZARUS, R. S., & FOLKMAN, S. (1984). *Stress, adaptation, and coping.* New York: Springer.

LAZARUS, R. S., & LAUNIER, R. (1978). Stress-related transactions between person and environment. In L. A. Pervin & M. Lewis (Eds.), *Perspectives in interactional psychology* (pp. 287–327). New York: Plenum.

LEARY, M. R. (1993). The interplay of private self-processes and interpersonal factors in self-presentation. In J. Suls (Ed.), *Psychological perspectives on the self* (Vol. 4, pp. 127–155). Hillsdale, NJ: Lawrence Erlbaum Associates.

LEARY, M. R., & KOWALSKI, R. M. (1990). Impression management: A literature review and two-component model. *Psychological Bulletin, 107,* 34–47.

LEARY, M. R., & MILLER, R. S. (1986). *Social psychology and dysfunctional behavior.* New York: Springer-Verlag.

LEARY, M. R., NEZLEK, J. B., DOWNS, D., RADFORD-DAVENPORT, J., MARTIN, J., & McMULLEN, A. (1994). Self-presentation in everyday interactions: Effects of target familiarity and gender composition. *Journal of Personality and Social Psychology, 67,* 664–673.

LEARY, M. R., TAMBOR, E. S., TERDAL, S. K., & DOWNS, D. L. (1995). Self-esteem as an interpersonal social monitor: The sociometer hypothesis. *Journal of Personality and Social Psychology, 68,* 518–530.

LEARY, M. R., TCHIVIDJIAN, L. R., & KRAXBERGER, B. E. (1994). Self-presentation can be hazardous to your health: Impression management and health risk. *Health Psychology, 13,* 461–470.

LECKY, P. (1945). *Self-consistency: A theory of personality.* New York: Island Press.

LEE, Y-T., & SELIGMAN, M. E. P. (1997). Are Americans more optimistic than the Chinese? *Personality and Social Psychology Bulletin, 23,* 32–40.

LEFCOURT, H. M. (1973). The function of the illusions of control and freedom. *American Psychologist, 28,* 417–425.

LEMYRE, L., & SMITH, P. M. (1985). Intergroup discrimination and self-esteem in the minimal group paradigm. *Journal of Personality and Social Psychology, 49,* 660–670.

LEPPER, M. R., GREENE, D., & NISBETT, R. E. (1973). Undermining of children's intrinsic interest with extrinsic rewards: A test of the "overjustification" hypothesis. *Journal of Personality and Social Psychology, 28,* 129–137.

LEWICKI, P. (1983). Self-image bias in person perception. *Journal of Personality and Social Psychology, 45,* 384–393.

LEWICKI, P. (1984). Self-schema and social information processing. *Journal of Personality and Social Psychology, 47,* 1177–1190.

LEWIN, K. (1948). *Resolving social conflicts.* New York: Harper.

LEWIN, K. (1951). *Field theory in social science.* New York: Harper & Brothers.

LEWIN, K., DEMBO, T., FESTINGER, L., & SEARS, P. S. (1944). Level of aspiration. In J. M. Hunt (Ed.), *Personality and the behavioral disorders* (pp. 333–378). New York: Holt.

LEWINSOHN, P. M., MISCHEL, W., CHAPLIN, W., & BARTON, R. (1980). Social competence and depression: The role of illusory self-perceptions. *Journal of Abnormal Psychology, 89,* 203–212.

LEWINSOHN, P. M., STEINMETZ, J. L. LARSON, D. W., & FRANKLIN, J. (1981). Depression-related cognitions: Antecedent or consequence? *Journal of Abnormal Psychology, 90,* 213–219.

LEWIS, H. B. (1971). *Shame and guilt in neurosis.* New York: International Universities Press.

LEWIS, M., & BROOKS-GUNN, J. (1979). *Social cognition and the acquisition of self.* New York: Plenum Press.

LIBERMAN, A., & CHAIKEN, S. (1992). Defensive processing of personally relevant health messages. *Personality and Social Psychology Bulletin, 18,* 669–679.

LINVILLE, P. W. (1985). Self-complexity and affective extremity: Don't put all of your eggs in one cognitive basket. *Social Cognition, 3,* 94–120.

LINVILLE, P. W. (1987). Self-complexity as a cognitive buffer against stress-related illness and depression. *Journal of Personality and Social Psychology, 52,* 663–676.

LINVILLE, P. W., & CARLSTON, D. (1994). Social cognition of the self. In P. G. Devine, D. L. Hamilton, & T. M. Ostrom (Eds.), *Social cognition: Its impact on social psychology* (pp. 143–193). New York: Academic Press.

LITTLE, B. R. (1981). Personal projects analysis: Trivial pursuits, magnificent obsessions, and the search for coherence. In N. Cantor & J. F. Kihlstrom (Eds.), *Personality, cognition, and social interaction* (pp. 15–31). Hillsdale, NJ: Lawrence Erlbaum Associates.

LOCKE, E. A., & LATHAM, G. P. (1990). *A theory of goal setting and task performance.* Englewood Cliffs, NJ: Prentice Hall.

LOCKE, J. (1979). *An essay concerning human understanding.* New York: Oxford University Press. (Original work published in 1690).

LOFTUS, E. (1980). *Memory.* Reading, MA: Addison-Wesley.

LORD, C. G. (1980). Schemas and images as memory aids: Two modes of processing social information. *Journal of Personality and Social Psychology, 38,* 257–269.

LUGINBUHL, J., & PALMER, R. (1991). Impression management aspects of self-handicapping: Positive and negative effects. *Personality and Social Psychology Bulletin, 17,* 655–662.

LUHTANEN, R., & CROCKER, J. (1992). A collective self-esteem scale: Self-evaluation of one's social identity. *Personality and Social Psychology Bulletin, 18,* 302–318.

LYON, A. J. (1988). Problems of personal identity. In G. Parkinson (Ed.), *An Encyclopedia of Philosophy* (pp. 441–462). London: Rutledge.

LYONS, W. (1986). *The disappearance of introspection.* Cambridge, MA: MIT Press.

LYUBOMIRSKY, S., & NOLEN-HOEKSEMA, S. (1993). Self-perpetuating properties of dysphoric rumination. *Journal of Personality and Social Psychology, 65,* 339–349.

MAASS, A., CECCARELLI, R., & RUDIN, S. (1996). Linguistic intergroup bias: Evidence for in-group protective motivation. *Journal of Personality and Social Psychology, 71,* 512–526.

MACCOBY, E. E., & JACKLIN, C. N. (1974). *The psychology of sex differences.* Stanford, CA: Stanford University Press.

MACDONALD, T. K., ZANNA, M. P., & FONG, G. T. (1996). Why common sense goes out the window: Effects of alcohol on intentions to use condoms. *Personality and Social Psychology Bulletin, 22,* 763–775.

MACFARLAND, C., & ROSS, M. (1982). The impact of causal attributions on affective reactions to success and failure. *Journal of Personality and Social Psychology, 43,* 937–946.

MAHLER, M. S., PINE, F., & BERGMAN, A. (1975). *The psychological birth of the human infant.* New York: Basic Books.

MAIER, S. F., SELIGMAN, M. E. P., & SOLOMON, R. S. (1969). Pavlovian fear conditioning and learned helplessness. In B. A. Campbell, & R. A. Church (Eds.), *Punishment and aversive behavior* (pp. 229–243). New York: Appleton-Century Crofts.

MAJOR, B., TESTA, M., & BYLSMA, W. H. (1991). Responses to upward and downward social comparison: The impact of esteem-relevance and perceived control. In J. Suls & T. A. Wills (Eds.), *Social comparison: Contemporary theory and research* (pp. 237–257). Hillsdale, NJ: Lawrence Erlbaum Associates.

MALLOY, T. E., YARLAS, A., MONTVILO, R. K., & SUGARMAN, D. B. (1996). Agreement and accuracy in children's interpersonal perceptions: A social relations analysis. *Journal of Personality and Social Psychology, 71,* 692–702.

MANDLER, J. M. (1990). A new perspective on cognitive development in infancy. *American Scientist, 78,* 236–243.

MARCIA, J. E. (1966). Development and validation of ego-identity status. *Journal of Personality and Social Psychology, 5,* 551–558.

MARECEK, J., & METTEE, D. R. (1972). Avoidance of continued success as a function of self-esteem, level of esteem certainty, and responsibility for success. *Journal of Personality and Social Psychology, 22,* 98–107.

MARKUS, H. (1977). Self-schemata and processing information about the self. *Journal of Personality and Social Psychology, 35,* 63–78.

MARKUS, H. (1983). Self-knowledge: An expanded view. *Journal of Personality, 51,* 543–565.

MARKUS, H., CROSS, S., & WURF, E. (1990). The role of the self-system in competence. In R. Sternberg & J. Kolligan (Eds.), *Competence considered* (pp. 205–225). New Haven, CT: Yale University Press.

MARKUS, H. R., & KITAYAMA, S. (1991). Culture and the self: Implications for cognition, emotion, and motivation. *Psychological Review, 98,* 224–253.   BFI PSI

MARKUS, H., & KUNDA, Z. (1986). Stability and malleability of the self-concept. *Journal of Personality and Social Psychology, 51,* 858–866.   BFI J64

MARKUS, H., & NURIUS, P. (1986). Possible selves. *American Psychologist, 41,* 954–969.

MARKUS, H., & OYSERMAN, D. (1989). Gender and thought: The role of the self-concept. In M. Crawford & M. Gentry (Eds.), *Gender and thought: Psychological perspectives* (pp. 100–127). New York: Springer-Verlag.

MARKUS, H., & RUVOLO, A. (1989). Possible selves: Personalized representations of goals. In L. A. Pervin (Ed.), *Goal concepts in personality and social psychology* (pp. 211–242). Hillsdale, NJ: Lawrence Erlbaum Associates.

MARKUS, H., & SMITH, J. (1981). The influence of self-schemata on the perception of others. In N. Cantor & J. F. Kihlstrom (Eds.), *Personality, cognition, and social interaction* (pp. 232–262). Hillsdale, NJ: Lawrence Erlbaum Associates.

MARKUS, H., & WURF, E. (1987). The dynamic self-concept: A social psychological perspective. *Annual Review of Psychology, 38,* 299–337.

MARSH, H. W. (1986). Global self-esteem: Its relation to specific facets of self concept and their importance. *Journal of Personality and Social Psychology, 51,* 1224–1236.

MARSH, H. W. (1989). Age and sex effects in multiple dimensions of self-concept: Preadolescence to adulthood. *Journal of Educational Psychology, 81,* 417–430.

MARSH, H. W. (1990). A multidimensional, hierarchical model of self-concept: Theoretical and empirical justification. *Educational Psychology Review, 2,* 77–172.

MARSH, H. W. (1993a). Academic self-concept: Theory, measurement, and research. In J. Suls (Ed.), *Psychological perspectives on the self* (Vol. 4, pp. 59–98). Hillsdale, NJ: Lawrence Erlbaum Associates.

MARSH, H. W. (1993b). Relations between global and specific domains of self: The importance of individual importance, certainty, and ideals. *Journal of Personality and Social Psychology, 65,* 975–992.

MARSH, H. W. (1995). A Jamesian model of self-investment and self-esteem: Comment on Pelham (1995). *Journal of Personality and Social Psychology, 69,* 1151–1160.

MARSH, H. W., & PARKER, J. W. (1984). Determinants of student self-concept: Is it better to be a relatively large fish in a small pond even if you don't learn to swim as well? *Journal of Personality and Social Psychology, 47,* 213–231.

MASLOW, A. H. (1950). Self-actualizing people: A study of psychological health. *Personality,* Symposium No. 1, 11–34.

MASLOW, A. H. (1970). *Motivation and personality* (rev. ed.). New York: Harper & Row.

McADAMS, D. P. (1996). Personality, modernity, and the storied self: A contemporary framework for studying persons. *Psychological Inquiry, 7,* 295–321.

McARTHUR, L. Z., & BARON, R. M. (1983). Toward an ecological theory of social perception. *Psychological Review, 90,* 215–238.

McCall, G. J., & Simmons, J. L. (1966). *Identities and interactions*. New York: The Free Press.

McCrae, R. R. (1982). Consensual validation of personality traits: Evidence from self-reports and ratings. *Journal of Personality and Social Psychology, 43,* 293–303.

McCrae, R. R., & Costa, P. T., Jr. (1988). Age, personality, and the spontaneous self-concept. *Journal of Gerontology, 43,* S177–S185.

McCrae, R. R., & Costa, P. T., Jr. (1994). The stability of personality: Observations and evaluations. *Current Directions in Psychological Science, 3,* 173–175.

McCune-Nicolich, L. (1981). Toward symbolic functioning: Structure of early pretend games and potential parallels with language. *Child Development, 52,* 785–797.

McDougall, W. (1923). *Outline of psychology*. New York: Scribner.

McFarland, C., & Buehler, R. (1995). Collective self-esteem as a moderator of the frog-pond effect in reactions to performance feedback. *Journal of Personality and Social Psychology, 68,* 1055–1070.

McFarlin, D. B. (1985). Persistence in the face of failure: The impact of self-esteem and contingency information. *Personality and Social Psychology Bulletin, 11,* 153–163.

McFarlin, D. B., Baumeister, R. F., & Blascovich, J. (1984). On knowing when to quit: Task failure, self-esteem, advice, and nonproductive assistance. *Journal of Personality, 52,* 138–155.

McGuire, W. J., & McGuire, C. V. (1981). The spontaneous self-concept as affected by personal distinctiveness. In M. D. Lynch, A. A. Norem-Hebeisen, & K. J. Gergen (Eds.), *Self-concept: Advances in theory and research* (pp. 147–171). Cambridge, MA: Balinger.

McGuire, W. J., & McGuire, C. V. (1988). Content and process in the experience of self. In L. Berkowitz (Ed.), *Advances in experimental social psychology* (Vol. 21, pp. 97–144). New York: Academic Press.

McGuire, W. J., & McGuire, C. V. (1996). Enhancing self-esteem by directed-thinking tasks: Cognitive and affective positivity asymmetries. *Journal of Personality and Social Psychology, 70,* 1117–1125.

McLeod, B. (1984). In the wake of disaster. *Psychology Today, 18,* 54–57.

McNulty, S. E., & Swann, W. B., Jr. (1994). Identity negotiation in roommate relationships: The self as architect and consequence of social reality. *Journal of Personality and Social Psychology, 67,* 1012–1023.

Mead, G. H. (1934). *Mind, self, and society*. Chicago: The University of Chicago Press.

Mecca, A. M., Smelser, N. J., & Vasconcellos, J. (1989). (Eds.) *The social importance of self-esteem*. Berkeley: University of California Press.

Meddin, J. (1979). Chimpanzees, symbols, and the reflective self. *Social Psychology Quarterly, 42,* 99–109.

Medvec, V. H., Madey, S. F., & Gilovich, T. (1995). When less is more: Counterfactual thinking and satisfaction among Olympic medalists. *Journal of Personality and Social Psychology, 69,* 603–610.

Meltzer, B. N., Petras, J. W., & Reynolds, L. T. (1975). *Symbolic interactionism: Genesis, varieties, and criticism*. London: Routledge & Kegan Paul.

Meltzoff, A. N. (1990). Foundations for developing a concept of self: The role of imitation in relating self to other and the value of social mirroring, social modeling, and self practice in infancy. In D. Cicchetti & M. Beeghly (Eds.), *The self in transition: Infancy to childhood* (pp. 139–164). Chicago: The University of Chicago Press.

Meltzoff, A. N., & Moore, M. K. (1977). Imitation of facial and manual gestures by human neonates. *Science, 198,* 75–78.

MELTZOFF, A. N., & MOORE, M. K. (1993). Newborn infants imitate adult facial gestures. *Child Development, 54,* 265–301.

MELTZOFF, A. N., & MOORE, M. K. (1994). Imitation, memory, and the representation of persons. *Infant Behavior and Development, 17,* 83–99.

MENNINGER, K. A. (1963). *The vital balance.* New York: Viking.

MESSICK, D. M., BLOOM, S., BOLDIZAR, J. P., & SAMUELSON, C. D. (1985). Why we are fairer than others. *Journal of Experiment Social Psychology, 21,* 480–500.

METALSKY, G. I., HALBERSTADT, L. J., & ABRAMSON, L. Y. (1987). Vulnerability to depressive mood reactions: Toward a more powerful test of the diathesis-stress and causal mediation components of the reformulated theory of depression. *Journal of Personality and Social Psychology, 52,* 386–393.

METALSKY, G. I., & JOINER, T. E., JR. (1992). Vulnerability to depressive symptomatology: A prospective test of the diathesis-stress and causal mediation components of the hopelessness theory of depression. *Journal of Personality and Social Psychology, 63,* 667–675.

METALSKY, G. I., JOINER, T. E., JR., HARDIN, T. S., & ABRAMSON, L. Y. (1993). Depressive reactions to failure in a naturalistic setting: A test of the hopelessness and self-esteem theories of depression. *Journal of Abnormal Psychology, 102,* 101–109.

MILLAR, M. G., & TESSER, A. (1992). The role of beliefs and feelings in guiding behavior: The mismatch model. In L. L. Martin & A. Tesser (Eds.), *The construction of social judgments* (pp. 277–300). Hillsdale, NJ: Lawrence Erlbaum Associates.

MILLER, D. T. (1976). Ego involvement and attributions for success and failure. *Journal of Personality and Social Psychology, 34,* 901–906.

MILLER, D. T., & ROSS, M. (1975). Self-serving biases in the attribution of causality: Fact or fiction? *Psychological Bulletin, 82,* 213–235.

MILLER, I. W., III, & NORMAN, W. H. (1979). Learned helplessness in humans: A review and attribution-theory model. *Psychological Bulletin, 86,* 93–118.

MILLER, P. M., KREITMAN, N. B., INGHAM, J. G., & SASHIDHARAN, S. P. (1989). Self-esteem, life stress, and psychiatric disorder. *Journal of Affective Disorders, 17,* 65–75.

MINKOFF, K., BERGMAN, E., BECK, A. T., & BECK, R. (1973). Hopelessness, depression, and attempted suicide. *American Journal of Psychiatry, 130,* 455–459.

MIRANDA, J., & PERSONS, J. B. (1988). Dysfunctional attitudes are mood-state dependent. *Journal of Abnormal Psychology, 97,* 76–79.

MIRANDA, J., PERSONS, J. B., & BYERS, C. N. (1990). Endorsement of dysfunctional beliefs depends on current mood state. *Journal of Abnormal Psychology, 99,* 237–241.

MISCHEL, W. (1968). *Personality and assessment.* New York: Wiley.

MISCHEL, W. (1979). On the interface of cognition and personality: Beyond the person-situation debate. *American Psychologist, 34,* 740–754.

MISCHEL, W., SHODA, Y., & PEAKE, P. K. (1988). The nature of adolescent competencies predicted by preschool delay of gratification. *Journal of Personality and Social Psychology, 54,* 687–696.

MONROE, S. M., & SIMONS, A. D. (1991). Diathesis-stress theories in the context of life stress research: Implications for the depressive disorders. *Psychological Bulletin, 110,* 406–425.

MORELAND, R. L., & SWEENEY, P. D. (1984). Self-expectancies and reactions to evaluations of personal performance. *Journal of Personality, 52,* 156–176.

MORSE, S., & GERGEN, K. J. (1970). Social comparison, self-consistency, and the concept of the self. *Journal of Personality and Social Psychology, 16,* 148–156.

MORTIMER, J. T., FINCH, M. D., & KUMKA, D. (1982). Persistence and change in development: The multidimensional self-concept. In P. B. Baltes & O. G. Brim, Jr.

(Eds.), *Life span development and behavior* (Vol. 4, pp. 263–313). New York: Academic Press.

MORTIMER, J. T., & LORENCE, J. (1979). Occupational experience and the self-concept: A longitudinal study. *Social Psychology Quarterly, 42,* 307–323.

MRUK, C. (1995). *Self-esteem: Research, theory, and practice.* New York: Springer.

MULLEN, B. (1986). Atrocity as a function of lynch mob composition: A self-attention perspective. *Personality and Social Psychology Bulletin, 12,* 187–197.

MURRAY, S. L., HOLMES, J. G., & GRIFFIN, D. W. (1996a). The benefits of positive illusions: Idealization and the construction of satisfaction in close relationships. *Journal of Personality and Social Psychology, 70,* 79–98.

MURRAY, S. L., HOLMES, J. G., & GRIFFIN, D. W. (1996b). The self-fulfilling nature of positive illusions in romantic relationships: Love is not blind but perscient. *Journal of Personality and Social Psychology, 71,* 1155–1180.

MYERS, D. G. (1993). *Social psychology* (4th ed.). New York: McGraw-Hill.

MYERS, D. G., & DIENER, E. (1995). Who is happy? *Psychological Science, 6,* 10–19.

MYERS, T., ORR, K. W., LOCKER, D., & JACKSON, E. A. (1993). Factors affecting gay and bisexual men's decisions and intentions to seek HIV testing. *American Journal of Public Health, 83,* 701–704.

NEISSER, U. (1988). Five kinds of self-knowledge. *Philosophical Psychology, 1,* 35–59.

NELSON, L. J., & MILLER, D. T. (1995). The distinctiveness effect in social categorization: You are what makes you unusual. *Psychological Science, 6,* 246–249.

NICHOLLS, J. G. (1984). Achievement motivation: Conceptions of ability, subjective experience, task choice, and performance. *Psychological Review, 91,* 328–346.

NIEDENTHAL, P. M., CANTOR, N., & KIHLSTROM, J. F. (1985). Prototype matching: A strategy for social decision making. *Journal of Personality and Social Psychology, 48,* 575–584.

NIEDENTHAL, P. M., SETTERLUND, M. B., & WHERRY, M. B. (1992). Possible self-complexity and affective reactions to goal-relevant evaluation. *Journal of Personality and Social Psychology, 63,* 5–16.

NIEDENTHAL, P. M., TANGNEY, J. P., & GAVANSKI, I. (1994). "If only I weren't" versus "If only I hadn't": Distinguishing shame and guilt in counterfactual thinking. *Journal of Personality and Social Psychology, 67,* 585–595.

NISBETT, R. E., & ROSS, L. (1980). *Human inference: Strategies and shortcomings of social judgment.* Englewood Cliffs, NJ: Prentice Hall.

NISBETT, R. E., & WILSON, T. D. (1977). Telling more than we can know: Verbal reports on mental processes. *Psychological Review, 84,* 231–259.

NOLEN-HOEKSEMA, S. (1987). Sex differences in unipolar depression: Evidence and theory. *Psychological Bulletin, 101,* 259–282.

NOLEN-HOEKSEMA, S. (1991a). Responses to depression and their effects on the duration of depressive episodes. *Journal of Abnormal Psychology, 100,* 569–582.

NOLEN-HOEKSEMA, S. (1991b). *Coding guide for Responses to Depression Questionnaire.* Unpublished manuscript, Stanford University, Palo Alto, CA.

NOLEN-HOEKSEMA, S. (1993). Sex differences in control of depression. In D. M. Wegner & J. W. Pennebaker (Eds.), *Handbook of mental control* (pp. 306–324). Englewood Cliffs, NJ: Prentice Hall.

NOLEN-HOEKSEMA, S., & GIRGUS, J. S. (1994). The emergence of gender differences in depression during adolescence. *Psychological Bulletin, 115,* 424–443.

NOLEN-HOEKSEMA, S., & MORROW, J. (1991). A prospective study of depression and posttraumatic stress symptoms after a natural disaster: The 1989 Loma Prieta earthquake. *Journal of Personality and Social Psychology, 61,* 115–121.

Nolen-Hoeksema, S., Morrow, J., & Fredrickson, B. L. (1993). Response styles and the duration of depressed mood. *Journal of Abnormal Psychology, 102,* 20–28.

Nolen-Hoeksema, S., Parker, L. E., & Larson, J. (1994). Ruminative coping with depressed mood following loss. *Journal of Personality and Social Psychology, 67,* 92–104.

Norem, J. K., & Cantor, N. (1986). Anticipatory and post hoc cushioning strategies: Optimism and defensive pessimism in "risky" situations. *Cognitive Therapy and Research, 10,* 347–362.

Nozick, R. (1981). *Philosophical explanations.* Cambridge, MA: Harvard University Press.

Nuttin, J. M. (1985). Narcissism beyond Gestalt and awareness: The name letter effect. *European Journal of Social Psychology, 15,* 353–361.

Nuttin, J. M. (1987). Affective consequences of mere ownership: The name letter effect in twelve European languages. *European Journal of Social Psychology, 17,* 381–402.

Oakes, P. J., & Turner, J. C. (1980). Social categorization and intergroup behavior: Does minimal intergroup discrimination make social identity more positive? *European Journal of Social Psychology, 10,* 295–301.

Oakley, A. (1980). *Women confined: Towards a sociology of childbirth.* New York: Schocken Books.

Oatley, K., & Bolton, W. (1985). A social-cognitive theory of depression in reaction to life events. *Psychological Review, 92,* 372–388.

Ogilvie, D. M. (1987). The undesired self: A neglected variable in personality research. *Journal of Personality and Social Psychology, 52,* 379–385.

Olson, J. M., & Hafer, C. L. (1990). Self-inference processes: Looking back and ahead. In J. M. Olson & M. P. Zanna (Eds.), *Self-inference processes: The Ontario symposium* (Vol. 6, pp. 293–320). Hillsdale, NJ: Lawrence Erlbaum Associates.

Orwell, G. (1949). *1984.* New York: Harcourt, Brace.

Osberg, T. M., & Shrauger, J. S. (1986). Self-prediction: Exploring the parameters of accuracy. *Journal of Personality and Social Psychology, 51,* 1044–1057.

Overmier, J. B., & Seligman, M. E. P. (1967). Effects of inescapable shock upon subsequent escape and avoidance learning. *Journal of Comparative and Physiological Psychology, 89,* 358–367.

Oyserman, D., & Markus, H. R. (1990). Possible selves and delinquency. *Journal of Personality and Social Psychology, 59,* 112–125.

Park, B., & Judd, C. M. (1989). Agreement on initial impressions: Differences due to perceivers, trait dimensions, and target behaviors. *Journal of Personality and Social Psychology, 56,* 493–505.

Park, R. E. (1927). Human nature and collective behavior. *American Journal of Sociology, 32,* 733–741.

Paulhus, D. L. (1984). Two-component model of socially desirable responding. *Journal of Personality and Social Psychology, 46,* 598–609.

Paulhus, D. L. (1994). *Reference manual for The Balanced Inventory of Desirable Responding—Version 6.* University of British Columbia, Vancouver. Unpublished manuscript.

Paulhus, D. L., & Bruce, M. N. (1992). The effect of acquaintanceship on the validity of personality impressions: A longitudinal study. *Journal of Personality and Social Psychology, 63,* 816–824.

Paulhus, D. L., & Reid, D. B. (1991). Enhancement and denial in socially desirable responding. *Journal of Personality and Social Psychology, 60,* 307–317.

Paunonen, S. V. (1989). Consensus in personality judgments: Moderating effect of target-rater acquaintanceship and behavior observability. *Journal of Personality and Social Psychology, 56,* 823–833.

PAYKEL, E. S. (1979). Recent life events in the development of the depressive disorder. In R. A. Depue (Ed.), *The psychobiology of the depressive disorders: Implications for the effects of stress* (pp. 245–262). New York: Academic Press.

PELHAM, B. W. (1991a). On confidence and consequence: The certainty and importance of self-knowledge. *Journal of Personality and Social Psychology, 60,* 518–530.

PELHAM, B. W. (1991b). On the benefits of misery: Self-serving biases in the depressive self-concept. *Journal of Personality and Social Psychology, 61,* 670–681.

PELHAM, B. W. (1995). Self-investment and self-esteem: Evidence for a Jamesian model of self-worth. *Journal of Personality and Social Psychology, 69,* 1141–1150.

PELHAM, B. W., & SWANN, W. B., JR. (1989). From self-conceptions to self-worth: On the sources and structure of global self-esteem. *Journal of Personality and Social Psychology, 57,* 672–680.

PELHAM, B. W., & WACHSMUTH, J. O. (1995). The waxing and waning of the social self: Assimilation and contrast in social comparison. *Journal of Personality and Social Psychology, 69,* 825–838.

PENNEBAKER, J. W. (1989). Confession, inhibition, and disease. In L. Berkowitz (Ed.), *Advances in experimental social psychology* (Vol. 22, pp. 211–244). New York: Academic Press.

PENNEBAKER, J. W. (1993). Putting stress into words: Health, linguistic, and therapeutic implications. *Behaviour Research and Therapy, 31,* 539–548.

PERLOFF, L. S., & FETZER, B. K. (1986). Self-other judgments and perceived vulnerability of victimization. *Journal of Personality and Social Psychology, 50,* 502–510.

PETERSEN, A. C., COMPAS, B. E., BROOKS-GUNN, J., STEMMLER, M., EY, S., & GRANT, K. E. (1993). Depression in adolescence. *American Psychologist, 48,* 155–164.

PETERSON, C., LUBORSKY, L., & SELIGMAN, M. E. P. (1983). Attributions and depressive mood shifts: A case study using the symptom-context method. *Journal of Abnormal Psychology, 92,* 96–103.

PETERSON, C., & SELIGMAN, M. E. P. (1984). Causal explanations as a risk factor for depression: Theory and evidence. *Psychological Review, 91,* 347–374.

PETERSON, C., SEMMEL, A., VON BAEYER, C., ABRAMSON, L. Y., METALSKY, G. I., & SELIGMAN, M. E. P. (1982). The Attributional Style Questionnaire. *Cognitive Therapy and Research, 6,* 287–300.

PETTIGREW, T. F. (1967). Social evaluation theory: Convergences and applications. In D. Levine (Ed.), *Nebraska symposium on motivation* (Vol. 15, pp. 241–311). Lincoln: University of Nebraska Press.

PETTIGREW, T. F. (1979). The ultimate attribution error: Extending Allport's cognitive analysis of prejudice. *Personality and Social Psychology Bulletin, 5,* 461–476.

PHILLIPS, D. A., & ZIMMERMAN, M. (1990). The developmental course of perceived competence and incompetence among competent children. In R. J. Sternberg & J. Kolligan (Eds.), *Competence considered* (pp. 41–67). New Haven, CT: Yale University Press.

PHINNEY, J. S. (1990). Ethnic identity in adolescents and adults: Review of research. *Psychological Bulletin, 108,* 499–514.

PIAGET, J. (1952). *The origins of intelligence in children.* New York: International Universities Press.

PLINER, P., CHAIKEN, S., & FLETT, G. L. (1990). Gender differences in concern with body weight and physical appearance over the life span. *Personality and Social Psychology Bulletin, 16,* 263–273.

POVINELLI, D. J., RULF, A. B., LANDAU, K. R., & BIERSCHWALE, D. T. (1993). Self-recognition in chimpanzees (*Pan troglodytes*): Distribution, ontogeny, and patterns of emergence. *Journal of Comparative Psychology, 107,* 347–372.

POWERS, W. T. (1973). *Behavior: The control of perception.* Chicago: Aldine.

PRATKANIS, A. R., ESKENAZI, J., & GREENWALD, A. G. (1994). What you expect is what you believe (but not necessarily what you get): A test of the effectiveness of subliminal self-help audiotapes. *Basic & Applied Social Psychology, 15,* 251–276.

PRENTICE, D. A. (1990). Familiarity and differences in self- and other-representations. *Journal of Personality and Social Psychology, 59,* 369–383.

PRENTICE, D. A., MILLER, D. T., & LIGHTDALE, J. R. (1994). Asymmetries in attachments to groups and to their members: Distinguishing between common-identity and common-bond groups. *Personality and Social Psychology Bulletin, 20,* 484–493.

PYSZCZYNSKI, T., & GREENBERG, J. (1986). Evidence for a depressive self-focusing style. *Journal of Research in Personality, 20,* 95–106.

PYSZCZYNSKI, T., & GREENBERG, J. (1987a). Toward an integration of cognitive and motivational perspectives on social inference: A biased hypothesis-testing model. In L. Berkowitz (Ed.), *Advances in experimental social psychology* (Vol. 20, pp. 297–340). New York: Academic Press.

PYSZCZYNSKI, T., & GREENBERG, J. (1987b). Self-regulatory perseveration and the depressive self-focusing style: A self-awareness theory of reactive depression. *Psychological Bulletin, 102,* 122–138.

PYSZCZYNSKI, T., GREENBERG, J., & LAPRELLE, J. (1985). Social comparison after success and failure: Biased search for information consistent with a self-serving conclusion. *Journal of Experimental Social Psychology, 21,* 195–211.

PYSZCZYNSKI, T., HOLT, K., & GREENBERG, J. (1987). Depression, self-focused attention, and expectancies for positive and negative future life events for self and others. *Journal of Personality and Social Psychology, 52,* 994–1001.

QUADREL, M. J., FISCHHOFF, B., & DAVIS, W. (1993). Adolescent (In)vulnerability. *American Psychologist, 48,* 102–116.

QUATRRONE, G. A., & TVERSKY, A. (1984). Causal versus diagnostic contingencies: On self-deception and on the voter's illusion. *Journal of Personality and Social Psychology, 46,* 237–248.

RADLOFF, L. S. (1977). The CES-D scale: A self-report depression scale for research in the general population. *Applied Psychological Measurement, 1,* 385–401.

RADO, S. (1928). The problem of melancholia. *International Journal of Psychoanalysis, 9,* 420–438.

RANK, O. (1936). *Will therapy and truth and reality.* New York: Knopf.

RASKIN, R., & HALL, C. S. (1979). A narcissistic personality inventory. *Psychological Reports, 46,* 55–60.

RASKIN, R., & TERRY, H. (1988). A principal-components analysis of the Narcissistic Personality Inventory and further evidence of its construct validity. *Journal of Personality and Social Psychology, 54,* 890–902.

RASKIN, R., NOVACEK, J., & HOGAN, R. (1991). Narcissism, self-esteem, and defensive self-enhancement. *Journal of Personality, 59,* 19–37.

REGAN, P. C., SNYDER, M., & KASSIN, S. M. (1995). Unrealistic optimism: Self-enhancement or person positivity. *Personality and Social Psychology Bulletin, 21,* 1073–1082.

REISS, M., ROSENFELD, P., MELBURG, V., & TEDESCHI, J. T. (1981). Self-serving attributions: Biased private perceptions and distorted public descriptions. *Journal of Personality and Social Psychology, 41,* 224–251.

RHODES, N., & WOOD, W. (1992). Self-esteem and intelligence affect influenceability: The mediating role of message reception. *Psychological Bulletin, 111,* 156–171.

RHODEWALT, F., & AGUSTSDOTTIR, S. (1986). Effects of self-presentation on the phenomenal self. *Journal of Personality and Social Psychology, 50,* 47–55.

RHODEWALT, F., MORF, C., HAZLETT, S., & FAIRFIELD, M. (1991). Self-handicapping: The role of discounting and augmentation in the preservation of self-esteem. *Journal of Personality and Social Psychology, 61,* 122–131.

RHODEWALT, F., SANBONMATSU, D. M., TSCHANZ, B., FEICK, D. L., & WALLER, A. (1995). Self-handicapping and interpersonal trade-offs: The effects of claimed self-handicaps on observers' performance evaluations and feedback. *Personality and Social Psychology Bulletin, 10,* 1042–1050.

RIESS, M., ROSENFELD, P., MELBURG, V., & TEDESCHI, J. T. (1981). Self-serving attributions: Biased private perceptions and distorted public descriptions. *Journal of Personality and Social Psychology, 41,* 224–231.

RINGER, R. J. (1973). *Winning through intimidation.* Los Angeles: Los Angeles Publishing.

RISKIND, J. H., & RHOLES, W. S. (1984). Cognitive accessibility and the capacity of cognitions to predict future depression: A theoretical note. *Cognitive Therapy and Research, 8,* 1–12.

RIZLEY, R. (1978). Depression and distortion in the attribution of causality. *Journal of Abnormal Psychology, 87,* 32–48.

ROBERTS, B. W., & DONAHUE, E. M. (1994). One personality, multiple selves: Integrating personality and social roles. *Journal of Personality, 62,* 199–218.

ROBERTS, J. E., GOTLIB, I. H., & KASSEL, J. D. (1996). Adult attachment security and symptoms of depression: The mediating role of dysfunctional attitudes and low self-esteem. *Journal of Personality and Social Psychology, 70,* 310–320.

ROBERTS, J. E., KASSEL, J. D., & GOTLIB, I. H. (1995). Level and stability of self-esteem as predictors of depressive symptoms. *Personality and Individual Differences, 19,* 217–224.

ROBERTS, J. E., & MONROE, S. M. (1992). Vulnerable self-esteem and depressive symptoms: Prospective findings comparing three alternative conceptualizations. *Journal of Personality and Social Psychology, 62,* 804–812.

ROBERTS, J. E., & MONROE, S. M. (1994). A multidimensional model of self-esteem in depression. *Clinical Psychology Review, 14,* 161–182.

ROBERTSON, L. S. (1977). Car crashes: Perceived vulnerability and willingness to pay for crash protection. *Journal of Community Health, 3,* 136–141.

ROBINS, C. J. (1990). Congruence of personality and life events in depression. *Journal of Abnormal Psychology, 99,* 393–397.

ROBINS, C. J., BLOCK, P., & PESELOW, E. D. (1989). Relations of sociotropic and autonomous personality characteristics to specific symptoms in depressed patients. *Journal of Abnormal Psychology, 98,* 86–88.

ROBINS, R. W., & JOHN, O. P. (1997). The quest for self-insight: Theory and research on accuracy and bias in self-perception. In R. Hogan, J. Johnson, & S. Briggs (Eds.), *Handbook of personality psychology* (pp. 649–679). New York: Academic Press.

ROBSON, P. J. (1988). Self-esteem: A psychiatric view. *British Journal of Psychology, 153,* 6–15.

RODIN, J. (1986). Aging and health: Effects of the sense of control. *Science, 233,* 1271–1276.

ROGERS, C. R. (1951). *Client-centered therapy.* Boston: Houghton Mifflin.

ROGERS, C. R., & DYMOND, R. (1954). (Eds.). *Psychotherapy and personality change.* Chicago: The University of Chicago Press.

ROGERS, T. B., KUIPER, N. A., & KIRKER, W. S. (1977). Self-reference and the encoding of personal information. *Journal of Personality and Social Psychology, 35*, 677–688.

ROSEMAN, I. J., WIEST, C., & SWARTZ, T. S. (1994). Phenomenology, behaviors, and goals differentiate discrete emotions. *Journal of Personality and Social Psychology, 67*, 206–221.

ROSENBERG, M. (1965). *Society and the adolescent self-image.* Princeton, NJ: Princeton University Press.

ROSENBERG, M. (1979). *Conceiving the self.* New York: Basic Books.

ROSENBERG, M., SCHOOLER, C., SCHOENBACH, C., & ROSENBERG, F. (1995). Global self-esteem and specific self-esteem: Different concepts, different outcomes. *American Sociological Review, 60*, 141–156.

ROSENBERG, S., & GARA, M. A. (1985). The multiplicity of personal identity. *Review of Personality and Social Psychology, 6*, 87–113.

ROSS, L. (1977a). The intuitive scientist and his shortcomings: Distortions in the attribution process. In L. Berkowitz (Ed.), *Advances in experimental social psychology* (Vol. 10, pp. 174–221). New York: Academic Press.

ROSS, L. (1977b). Problems in the interpretation of "self-serving" asymmetries in causal attribution: Comments on the Stephan et al. paper. *Sociometry, 40*, 112–114.

ROSS, M. (1989). Relation of implicit theories to the construction of personal histories. *Psychological Review, 96*, 341–357.

ROSS, M., & SICOLY, P. (1979). Egocentric biases in availability and attribution. *Journal of Personality and Social Psychology, 37*, 322–336.

ROTH, D. L., & INGRAM, R. E. (1985). Factors in the Self-Deception Questionnaire: Associations with depression. *Journal of Personality and Social Psychology, 48*, 243–251.

ROTH, D. L., SNYDER, C. R., & PACE, L. M. (1986). Dimensions of favorable self-presentation. *Journal of Personality and Social Psychology, 51*, 867–874.

ROTHBAUM, F., WEISZ, J. R., & SNYDER, S. S. (1982). Changing the world and changing the self: A two-process model of perceived control. *Journal of Personality and Social Psychology, 42*, 5–37.

ROTTER, J. B. (1954). *Social learning and clinical psychology.* Englewood Cliffs, NJ: Prentice Hall.

RUBIN, J. Z., PROVENZANO, F. J., & LURIA, Z. (1974). The eye of the beholder: Parents' views on sex of newborns. *American Journal of Orthopsychiatry, 44*, 512–519.

RUBLE, D. (1983). The development of social comparison processes and their role in achievement-related self-socialization, In E. T. Higgins, D. N. Ruble, & W. W. Hartup (Eds.), *Social cognition and social development: A socio-cultural perspective* (pp. 134–157). New York: Cambridge University Press.

RUBLE, D. N., EISENBERG, R., & HIGGINS, E. T. (1994). Developmental changes in achievement evaluation: Motivational implications of self-other differences. *Child Development, 65*, 1095–1110.

RUGGIERO, K. M., & TAYLOR, D. M. (1997). Why minority group members perceive or do not perceive the discrimination that confronts them: The role of self-esteem and perceived control. *Journal of Personality and Social Psychology, 72*, 373–389.

RUEHLMAN, L. S., WEST, S. G., & PASAHOW, R. J. (1985). Depression and evaluative schemata. *Journal of Personality, 53*, 46–92.

RYAN, R. M., & KUCZKOWSKI, R. (1994). The imaginary audience, self-consciousness, and public individuation in adolescence. *Journal of Personality, 62*, 219–238.

RYAN, R. M., MIMS, V., & KOESTNER, R. (1983). Relation of reward contingency and interpersonal context to intrinsic motivation: A review and test using cognitive evaluation theory. *Journal of Personality and Social Psychology, 45,* 736–770.

RYFF, C. D. (1989). Happiness is everything, or is it? Explorations on the meaning of psychological well-being. *Journal of Personality and Social Psychology, 57,* 1069–1081.

RYFF, C. D. (1995). Psychological well-being in adult life. *Current Directions in Psychological Science, 4,* 99–104.

SACHS, P. R. (1982). Avoidance of diagnostic information in self-evaluation of ability. *Personality and Social Psychology Bulletin, 8,* 242–246.

SACKEIM, H. A. (1983). Self-deception, self-esteem, and depression: The adaptive value of lying to oneself. In J. Masling (Ed.), *Empirical studies of psychoanalytical theories* (Vol. 1, pp. 101–157). Hillsdale, NJ: Analytic Press.

SACKEIM, H. A., & GUR, R. C. (1979). Self-deception, other-deception, and self-reported psychopathology. *Journal of Consulting and Clinical Psychology, 47,* 213–215.

SALANCIK, G. R., & CONWAY, M. (1975). Attitude inference from salient and relevant cognitive content about behavior. *Journal of Personality and Social Psychology, 32,* 829–840.

SAMPSON, E. E. (1985). The decentralization of identity: Towards a revised concept of personal and social order. *American Psychologist, 40,* 1203–1211.

SANBONMATSU, D. M., HARPSTER, L. L., AKIMOTO, S. A., & MOULIN, J. B. (1994). Selectivity in generalizations about self and others from performance. *Personality and Social Psychology Bulletin, 20,* 358–366.

SANDE, G. N., GOETHALS, G. R., & RADLOFF, C. E. (1988). Perceiving one's own traits and others': The multifaceted self. *Journal of Personality and Social Psychology, 54,* 13–20.

SANDELANDS, L. E., BROCKNER, J., & GLYNN, M. A. (1988). If at first you don't succeed, try, try again: Effects of persistence-performance contingencies, ego-involvement, and self-esteem in task persistence. *Journal of Applied Psychology, 73,* 208–216.

SANITIOSO, R., KUNDA, Z., & FONG, G. T. (1990). Motivated recruitment of autobiographical memories. *Journal of Personality and Social Psychology, 59,* 229–241.

SARBIN, T. R. (1952). A preface to a psychological analysis of the self. *Psychological Review, 59,* 11–22.

SARBIN, T. R., & ALLEN, V. L. (1968). Role theory. In G. Lindzey & E. Aronson (Eds.), *The handbook of social psychology* (2nd ed., Vol. 1, pp. 488–567). Reading, MA: Addison-Wesley.

SARTRE, J-P. (1958). *Being and nothingness: An essay on phenomenological ontology.* (H. Barnes, Trans.). London: Methuen.

SCHACHTER, S., & SINGER, J. (1962). Cognitive, social, and physiological determinants of the emotional state. *Psychological Review, 69,* 379–399.

SCHAUFELI, W. B. (1988). Perceiving the causes of unemployment: An evaluation of the causal dimension scale in a real-life situation. *Journal of Personality and Social Psychology, 54,* 347–356.

SCHEIBE, K. E. (1985). Historical perspectives on the presented self. In B. R. Schlenker (Ed.), *The self and social life* (pp. 33–64). New York: McGraw-Hill.

SCHEIER, M. F., & CARVER, C. S. (1977). Self-focused attention and the experience of emotion: Attraction, repulsion, elation, and depression. *Journal of Personality and Social Psychology, 35,* 625–636.

SCHEIER, M. F., & CARVER, C. S. (1982a). Self-consciousness, outcome expectancy, and persistence. *Journal of Experimental Social Psychology, 16,* 409–418.

SCHEIER, M. F., & CARVER, C. S. (1982b). Two sides of the self: One for you and one for me. In J. Suls & A. G. Greenwald (Eds.), *Psychological perspectives on the self* (Vol. 2, pp. 123–157). Hillsdale, NJ: Lawrence Erlbaum Associates.

SCHEIER, M. F., & CARVER, C. S. (1983). Self-directed attention and the comparison of self with standards. *Journal of Experimental Social Psychology, 19,* 205–222.

SCHEIER, M. F., & CARVER, C. S. (1985). Optimism, coping, and health: Assessment and implications of generalized outcome expectancies. *Health Psychology, 4,* 219–247.

SCHEIER, M. F., & CARVER, C. S. (1987). Dispositional optimism and physical well-being: The influence of generalized outcome expectancies on health. *Journal of Personality, 55,* 169–210.

SCHEIER, M. F., CARVER, C. S., & Bridges, M. W. (1994). Distinguishing optimism from neuroticism (and trait anxiety, self-mastery, and self-esteem): A reevaluation of the life orientation test. *Journal of Personality and Social Psychology, 67,* 1063–1078.

SCHEIER, M. F., MATHEWS, K. A., OWENS, J. F., MAGOVERN, G. J., SR., LEFEBVRE, R. C., ABBOTT, R. A., & CARVER, C. S. (1989). Dispositional optimism and recovery from coronary artery bypass surgery: The beneficial effects on physical and psychological well-being. *Journal of Personality, 57,* 1024–1040.

SCHEIER, M. F., WEINTRAUB, J. K., & CARVER, C. S. (1986). Coping with stress: Divergent strategies of optimists and pessimists. *Journal of Personality and Social Psychology, 51,* 1257–1264.

SCHLENKER, B. R. (1975). Self-presentation: Managing the impression of consistency when reality interferes with self-enhancement. *Journal of Personality and Social Psychology, 32,* 1030–1037.

SCHLENKER, B. R. (1980). *Impression management: The self-concept, social identity, and interpersonal relationships.* Monterey, CA: Brooks/Cole.

SCHLENKER, B. R. (1982). Translating actions into attitudes: An identity-analytic approach to the explanation of social conduct. In L. Berkowitz (Ed.), *Advances in experimental social psychology* (Vol. 15, pp. 193–247). New York: Academic Press.

SCHLENKER, B. R. (1985). Identity and self-identification. In B. R. Schlenker (Ed.), *The self and social life* (pp. 65–99). New York: McGraw-Hill.

SCHLENKER, B. R. (1986). Self-identification: Toward an integration of the private and public self. In R. F. Baumeister (Ed.), *Public self and private life* (pp. 21–62). New York: Springer-Verlag.

SCHLENKER, B. R., & BRITT, T. W. (1996). Depression and the explanation of events that happen to self, close others, and strangers. *Journal of Personality and Social Psychology, 71,* 180–192.

SCHLENKER, B. R., DLUGOLECKI, D. W., & DOHERTY, K. (1994). The impact of self-presentations on self-appraisals and behavior: The power of public commitment. *Personality and Social Psychology Bulletin, 20,* 20–33.

SCHLENKER, B. R., & LEARY, M. R. (1982a). Social anxiety and self-presentation: A conceptualization and model. *Psychological Bulletin, 92,* 641–669.

SCHLENKER, B. R., & LEARY, M. R. (1982b). Audiences' reactions to self-enhancing, self-denigrating, and accurate self-presentations. *Journal of Experimental Social Psychology, 18,* 89–104.

SCHLENKER, B. R., PHILLIPS, S. T., BONIECKI, K. A., & SCHLENKER, D. R. (1995). Championship pressures: Choking or triumphing in one's own territory? *Journal of Personality and Social Psychology, 68,* 632–643.

SCHLENKER, B. R., & TRUDEAU, J. V. (1990). The impact of self-presentations on private self beliefs: Effects of prior self-beliefs and misattribution. *Journal of Personality and Social Psychology, 58,* 22–32.

Schlenker, B. R., & Weigold, M. F. (1989). Goals and the self-identification process: Constructing desired identities. In L. A. Pervin (Ed.), *Goal concepts in personality and social psychology* (pp. 243–290). Hillsdale, NJ: Erlbaum.

Schlenker, B. R., & Weigold, M. F. (1990). Self-consciousness and self-presentation: Being autonomous versus appearing autonomous. *Journal of Personality and Social Psychology, 59,* 820–828.

Schlenker, B. R., & Weigold, M. F. (1992). Interpersonal processes involving impression regulation and management. *Annual Review of Psychology, 43,* 133–168.

Schlenker, B. R., Weigold, M. F., & Doherty, K. (1991). Coping with accountability: Self-identification and evaluative reckonings. In C. R. Snyder & D. F. Forsyth (Eds.), *Handbook of social and clinical psychology: The health perspective* (pp. 96–115). Elmsford, NY: Pergamon Press.

Schlenker, B. R., Weigold, M. F., & Hallam, J. R. (1990). Self-serving attributions in social context: Effects of self-esteem and social pressure. *Journal of Personality and Social Psychology, 58,* 855–863.

Schneider, M. E., Major, B., Luhtanen, R., & Crocker, J. (1996). Social stigma and the potential costs of assumptive help. *Personality and Social Psychology Bulletin, 22,* 201–209.

Schulz, R., & Decker, S. (1985). Long-term adjustment to physical disability: The role of social support, perceived control, and self-blame. *Journal of Personality and Social Psychology, 48,* 1162–1172.

Schutz, A. (1972). *The phenomenology of the social world.* London: Heinemann.

Schwartz, G. E. (1977). Psychosomatic disorders and biofeedback: A psychobiological model of disregulation. In J. A. Maser & M. E. P. Seligman (Eds.), *Psychopathology: Experimental models* (pp. 271–307). San Francisco: W. H. Freeman.

Scott, M. B., & Lyman, S. M. (1960). Accounts. *American Sociological Review, 33,* 46–62.

Sears, D. O. (1986). College sophomores in the laboratory: Influences of a narrow data base on social psychology's view of human nature. *Journal of Personality and Social Psychology, 51,* 515–530.

Secord, P. F., & Backman, C. W. (1965). An interactional approach to personality. In B. A. Maher (Ed.), *Progress in experimental personality research* (pp. 91–125). New York: Academic Press.

Secunda, S., Katz, M. M., & Friedman, R. (1973). The depressive disorders in 1973. National Institute of Mental Health. Washington, DC: U.S. Government Printing Office.

Sedikides, C. (1993). Assessment, enhancement, and verification determinants of the self-evaluation process. *Journal of Personality and Social Psychology, 65,* 317–338.

Sedikides, C. (1995). Central and peripheral self-conceptions are differentially influenced by mood: Tests of the different sensitivity hypothesis. *Journal of Personality and Social Psychology, 69,* 759–777.

Sedikides, C., & Strube, M. J. (in press). Motivated self-evaluation: To thine own self be good, to thine own self be sure, and to thine own self by true. In M. P. Zanna (Ed.), *Advances in experimental social psychology.* San Diego: Academic Press.

Segal, Z. V., & Dobson, K. S. (1992). Cognitive models of depression: Report from a consensus development conference. *Psychological Inquiry, 3,* 219–224.

Segal, Z. V., Shaw, B. F., Vella, D. D., & Katz, R. (1992). Cognitive and life stress predictors of relapse in remitted unipolar depressed patients: Test of the congruency hypothesis. *Journal of Abnormal Psychology, 101,* 26–36.

Seligman, M. E. P. (1975). *Helplessness: On depression, development, and death.* San Francisco: W. H. Freeman.

Seligman, M. E. P. (1991). *Learned optimism.* New York: Knopf.

SELIGMAN, M. E. P., ABRAMSON, L. Y., SEMMEL, A., & VON BAEYER, C. (1979). Depressive attributional style. *Journal of Abnormal Psychology, 88,* 242–247.

SELIGMAN, M. E. P., CASTELLON, C., CACCIOLA, J., SCHULMAN, P., LUBORSKY, L., OLLOVE, M., & DOWNING, R. (1988). Explanatory style change during cognitive therapy for unipolar depression. *Journal of Abnormal Psychology, 97,* 13–18.

SENNETT, R. (1978). *The fall of public man: On the social psychology of capitalism.* New York: Vintage.

SETTERLUND, M. B., & NIEDENTHAL, P. M. (1993). "Who am I? Why am I here?" Self-esteem, self-clarity, and prototype matching. *Journal of Personality and Social Psychology, 65,* 769–780.

SHAPIRO, D. H., SCHWARTZ, C. E., & ASTIN, J. A. (1996). Controlling ourselves, controlling our world: Psychology's role in understanding positive and negative consequences of seeking and gaining control. *American Psychologist, 51,* 1213–1230.

SHARP, M. J., & GETZ, J. G. (1996). Substance use as impression management. *Personality and Social Psychology Bulletin, 22,* 60–67.

SHAVELSON, R. J., HUBNER, J. J., & STANTON, G. C. (1976). Self-concept: Validation of construct interpretations. *Review of Educational Research, 46,* 407–441.

SHEDLER, J., MAYMAN, M., & MANIS, M. (1993). The *illusion* of mental health. *American Psychologist, 48,* 1117–1131.

SHEPPERD, J. A. (1993). Student derogation of the scholastic aptitude test: Biases in perceptions and presentations of college board scores. *Basic and Applied Social Psychology, 14,* 455–473.

SHERMAN, S. J., SKOV, R. B., HERVITZ, E. F., & STOCK, C. B. (1981). The effects of explaining hypothetical future events: From possibility to probability to actuality and beyond. *Journal of Experimental Social Psychology, 17,* 142–158.

SHRAUGER, J. S. (1972). Self-esteem and reactions to being observed by others. *Journal of Personality and Social Psychology, 23,* 192–200.

SHRAUGER, J. S. (1975). Responses to evaluation as a function of initial self-perceptions. *Psychological Bulletin, 82,* 581–596.

SHRAUGER, J. S. (1982). Selection and processing of self-evaluative information: Experimental evidence and clinical implications. In G. Weary & H. L. Mirels (Eds.), *Integrations of clinical and social psychology* (pp. 128–153). New York: Oxford University Press.

SHRAUGER, J. S., & LUND, A. K. (1975). Self-evaluation and reactions to evaluations from others. *Journal of Personality, 43,* 94–108.

SHRAUGER, J. S., & PATTERSON, M. B. (1974). Self-evaluation and the selection of dimensions for evaluating others. *Journal of Personality, 42,* 569–585.

SHRAUGER, J. S., & ROSENBERG, S. E. (1970). Self-esteem and the effects of success and failure feedback on performance. *Journal of Personality, 38,* 404–417.

SHRAUGER, J. S., & SCHOENEMAN, T. J. (1979). Symbolic interactionist view of self-concept: Through the looking glass darkly. *Psychological Bulletin, 86,* 549–573.

SHRAUGER, J. S., & SORMAN, P. B. (1977). Self-evaluations, initial success and failure, and improvement as determinants of persistence. *Journal of Consulting and Clinical Psychology, 45,* 784–795.

SIMMONS, R. G., BLYTH, D. A., VAN CLEAVE, E. F., & BUSH, D. M. (1979). Entry into early adolescence: The impact of school structure, puberty, and early dating on self-esteem. *American Sociological Review, 44,* 948–967.

SIMON, B., & HAMILTON, D. L. (1994). Self-stereotyping and social context: The effects of relative in-group size and in-group status. *Journal of Personality and Social Psychology, 66,* 699–711.

SIMON, B., PANTALEO, G., & MUMMENDEY, A. (1995). Unique individual or interchangeable group member: Accentuation of intragroup differences versus similarities as an indicator of the individual self versus the collective self. *Journal of Personality and Social Psychology, 69,* 106–119.

SKINNER, B. F. (1990). Can psychology be a science of mind? *American Psychologist, 45,* 1206–1210.

SKINNER, E. A. (1996). A guide to constructs of control. *Journal of Personality and Social Psychology, 71,* 549–570.

SMITH, E. R., & HENRY, S. (1996). An in-group becomes part of the self: Response time evidence. *Personality and Social Psychology Bulletin, 22,* 635–642.

SMITH, R. E., & SMOLL, F. L. (1990). Self-esteem and children's reactions to youth sport coaching behaviors: A field study of self-enhancement processes. *Developmental Psychology, 26,* 987–993.

SMITH, S. H., & WHITEHEAD, G. I., III (1988). The public and private use of consensus-raising excuses. *Journal of Personality, 56,* 355–371.

SMITH, S. M., & PETTY, R. E. (1995). Personality moderators of mood congruency effects on cognition: The role of self-esteem and negative mood regulation. *Journal of Personality and Social Psychology, 68,* 1092–1107.

SMITH, T. W., & GREENBERG, J. (1981). Depression and self-focused attention. *Motivation and Emotion, 5,* 323–331.

SMITH T. W., INGRAM, R. E., & ROTH, D. L. (1985). Self-focused attention and depression: Self-evaluation, affect, and life stress. *Motivation and Emotion, 9,* 381–389.

SMITH, T. W., SNYDER, C. R., & HANDELSMAN, M. M. (1982). On the self-serving function of an academic wooden leg: Test anxiety as a self-handicapping strategy. *Journal of Personality and Social Psychology, 42,* 314–321.

SMITH, T. W., SNYDER, C. R., & PERKINS, S. C. (1983). The self-serving function of hypochondriacal complaints: Physical symptoms as self-handicapping strategies. *Journal of Personality and Social Psychology, 44,* 787–797.

SNYDER, C. R. (1985). Collaborative companions: The relationship of self-deception and excuse making. In M. W. Martin (Ed.), *Self-deception and self-understanding: New essays in philosophy and psychology* (pp. 35–51). Lawrence: University of Kansas Press.

SNYDER, C. R., & HIGGINS, R. L. (1988). Excuses: Their effective role in the negotiation of reality. *Psychological Bulletin, 104,* 23–35.

SNYDER, C. R., & SMITH, T. W. (1982). Symptoms as self-handicapping strategies: The virtues of old wine in a new bottle. In G. Weary & H. R. Mirels (Eds.), *Integration of clinical and social psychology* (pp. 104–127). New York: Oxford University Press.

SNYDER, C. R., SMITH, T. W., AUGELLI, R. W., & INGRAM, R. E. (1985). On the self-serving function of social anxiety: Shyness as a self-handicapping strategy. *Journal of Personality and Social Psychology, 48,* 970–980.

SNYDER, M. (1974). Self-monitoring of expressive behavior. *Journal of Personality and Social Psychology, 30,* 526–537.

SNYDER, M. (1979). Self-monitoring processes. In L. Berkowitz (Ed.), *Advances in experimental social psychology* (Vol. 12, pp. 85–128). New York: Academic Press.

SNYDER, M. (1987). *Public appearances/private realities: The psychology of self-monitoring.* New York: W. H. Freeman.

SNYDER, M. L., & WICKLUND, R. A. (1981). Attribute ambiguity. In J. Harvey, W. Ickes, & R. F. Kidd (Eds.), *New directions in attribution research* (Vol. 3, pp. 197–221). Hillsdale, NJ: Lawrence Erlbaum Associates.

SNYGG, D, & COMBS, A. W. (1949). *Individual behavior.* New York: Harper & Row.

SOLOMON, S., GREENBERG, J., & PYSZCZYNSKI, T. (1991). A terror management theory of social behavior: The psychological function of self-esteem and cultural worldviews. In M. P. Zanna (Ed.), *Advances in experimental social psychology* (Vol. 24, pp. 93–159). San Diego, CA: Academic Press.

SOROKIN, P. A. (1947). *Society, culture, and personality: Their structure and dynamics.* New York: Harper.

SPENCER, S. J., JOSEPHS, R. A., & STEELE, C. M. (1993). Low self-esteem: The uphill struggle for self-integrity. In R. F. Baumeister (Ed.), *Self-esteem: The puzzle of low self-regard* (pp. 21–36). New York: Plenum Press.

SPENCER, S. M., & NOREM, J. K. (1996). Reflection and distraction: Defensive pessimism, strategic optimism, and performance. *Personality and Social Psychology Bulletin, 22,* 354–365.

SROUFE, L. A. (1983). Infant-caregiver attachment and patterns of adaptation in preschool: The roots of maladaptation and competence. *Minnesota Symposium on Child Psychology, 16,* 41–85.

SROUFE, L. A., CARLSON, E., & SHULMAN, S. (1993). Individuals in relationships: Development from infancy through adolescence. In D. F. Funder, R. D. Parke, C. Tomlinson-Keasey, & K. Widaman (Eds.), *Studying lives through time: Personality and development* (pp. 315–342). Washington, DC: American Psychological Association.

STEELE, C. M. (1988). The psychology of self-affirmation: Sustaining the integrity of the self. In L. Berkowitz (Ed.), *Advances in experimental social psychology* (Vol. 21, 261–302). New York: Academic Press.

STEELE, C. M. (1992). Race and the schooling of Black Americans. *The Atlantic Monthly* (April), 68–80.

STEELE, C. M., & ARONSON, J. (1995). Stereotype threat and the intellectual test performance of African Americans. *Journal of Personality and Social Psychology, 69,* 797–811.

STEELE, C. M., & JOSEPHS, R. A. (1990). Alcohol myopia: Its prized and dangerous effects. *American Psychologist, 45,* 921–933.

STEELE, C. M., & LUI, T. J. (1983). Dissonance processes as self-affirmation. *Journal of Personality and Social Psychology, 45,* 5–19.

STEELE, C. M., SOUTHWICK, L., & CRITCHLOW, B. (1981). Dissonance and alcohol: Drinking your troubles away. *Journal of Personality and Social Psychology, 41,* 831–846.

STEELE, C. M., & SPENCER, S. J. (1992). The primacy of self-integrity. *Psychological Inquiry, 3,* 345–346.

STEELE, C. M., SPENCER, S. J., & LYNCH, M. (1993). Self-image resilience and dissonance: The role of affirmational resources. *Journal of Personality and Social Psychology, 64,* 885–896.

STEPHAN, W. G., BERNSTEIN, W. M., STEPHAN, C., & DAVIS, M. H. (1979). Attributions for achievement: Egotism vs. expectancy confirmation. *Social Psychology Quarterly, 42,* 5–17.

STEPHAN, W. G., & GOLLWITZER, P. M. (1981). Affect as a determinant of attributional egotism. *Journal of Experimental Social Psychology, 17,* 443–458.

STEVENS, L., & JONES, E. E. (1976). Defensive attribution and the Kelley Cube. *Journal of Personality and Social Psychology, 34,* 809–820.

STIPEK, D. (1984). Young children's performance expectations: Logical analysis or wishful thinking? In J. G. Nicholls (Ed.), *Advances in motivation and achievement: Vol. 3. The development of achievement motivation* (pp. 33–56). Greenwich, CT: JAI Press.

STIPEK, D., RECCHIA, S., & McCLINTIC, S. (1992). Self-evaluation in young children. *Monographs of the Society for Research in Child Development,* Serial No. 226, Volume 57.

STOUFFER, S. A., SUCHMAN, E. A., DEVINNEY, L. C., STARR, S. A., & WILLIAMS, R. M. (1949). *The American soldier: Adjustment during Army life* (Vol. 1). Princeton, NJ: Princeton University Press.

STRACK, F., MARTIN, L. L., & STEPPER, S. (1988). Inhibiting and facilitating conditions of the human smile: A nonobtrusive test of the facial feedback hypothesis. *Journal of Personality and Social Psychology, 54,* 768–777.

STRAUMAN, T. J. (1989). Self-discrepancies in clinical depression and social phobia: Cognitive structures that underlie emotional disorders? *Journal of Abnormal Psychology, 98,* 14–22.

STRAUMAN, T. J., & HIGGINS, E. T. (1987). Automatic activation of self-discrepancies and emotional syndromes: When cognitive structures influence affect. *Journal of Personality and Social Psychology, 53,* 1004–1014.

STRUBE, M. J., LOTT, C. L., LE-XUAN-HY, G. M., OXENBERG, J., & DEICHMANN, A. K. (1986). Self-evaluation of abilities: Accurate self-assessment versus biased self-enhancement. *Journal of Personality and Social Psychology, 51,* 16–25.

STRYKER, S. (1980). *Symbolic interactionism.* Menlo Park, CA: Benjamin Cummings.

STRYKER, S., & STATHAM, A. (1985). Symbolic interaction and role theory. In G. Lindzey & E. Aronson (Eds.), *The handbook of social psychology* (3rd ed., Vol. 1, pp. 311–378). New York: Random House.

SULLIVAN, H. S. (1953). *The interpersonal theory of psychiatry.* New York: W. W. Norton.

SVENSON, O. (1981). Are we all less risky and more skillful than our fellow drivers? *Acta Psychologica, 47,* 143–148.

SWANN, W. B., JR. (1984). Quest for accuracy in person perception. A matter of pragmatics. *Psychological Review, 91,* 457–477.

SWANN, W. B., JR. (1990). To be adored or to be known? The interplay of self-enhancement and self-verification. In R. M. Sorrentino & E. T. Higgins (Eds.), *Motivation and cognition* (Vol. 2, pp. 408–448). New York: Guilford Press.

SWANN, W. B., JR. (1996). *Self-traps: The elusive quest for higher self-esteem.* New York: W. H. Freeman.

SWANN, W. B., JR., DE LA RONDE, C., & HIXON, J. G. (1994). Authenticity and positivity strivings in marriage and courtship. *Journal of Personality and Social Psychology, 66,* 857–869.

SWANN, W. B., JR., & ELY, R. J. (1984). A battle of wills: Self-verification versus behavioral confirmation. *Journal of Personality and Social Psychology, 46,* 1287–1302.

SWANN, W. B., JR., GRIFFIN, J. J., PREDMORE, S. C., & GAINES, B. (1987). The cognitive-affective crossfire: When self-consistency confronts self-enhancement. *Journal of Personality and Social Psychology, 52,* 881–889.

SWANN, W. B., JR., & HILL, C. A. (1982). When our identities are mistaken: Reaffirming self-conceptions through social interaction. *Journal of Personality and Social Psychology, 43,* 59–66.

SWANN, W. B., JR., PELHAM, B. W., & KRULL, D. S. (1989). Agreeable fancy or disagreeable truth? Reconciling self-enhancement and self-verification. *Journal of Personality and Social Psychology, 57,* 782–791.

SWANN, W. B., JR., STEIN-SEROUSSI, A., & GIESLER, R. B. (1992). Why people self-verify. *Journal of Personality and Social Psychology, 62,* 392–401.

SWANN, W. B., JR., WENZLAFF, R. M., KRULL, D. S., & PELHAM, B. W. (1992). Allure of negative feedback: Self-verification strivings among depressed persons. *Journal of Abnormal Psychology, 101,* 293–306.

SWEENEY, P. D., ANDERSON, K., & BAILEY, S. (1986). Attributional style in depression: A meta-analytic review. *Journal of Personality and Social Psychology, 50,* 974–991.

SYMONS, C. S., & JOHNSON, B. T. (1997). The self-reference effect in memory: A meta-analysis. *Psychological Bulletin, 121,* 371–394.

TAFARODI, R. W., & SWANN, W. B., JR. (1995). Self-liking and self-competence as dimensions of global self-esteem: Initial validation of a measure. *Journal of Personality Assessment, 65,* 322–342.

TAJFEL, H., & TURNER, J. C. (1986). The social identity theory of intergroup behavior. In S. Worchel & W. Austin (Eds.), *Psychology of intergroup relations* (pp. 7–24). Chicago: Nelson-Hall.

TANGNEY, J. P., & FISCHER, K. W. (Eds.) (1995). *Self-conscious emotions: The psychology of shame, guilt, pride, and embarrassment.* New York: Guilford Press.

TAYLOR, S. E. (1983). Adjustment to threatening events: A theory of cognitive adaptation. *American Psychologist, 38,* 1161–1173.

TAYLOR, S. E. (1989). *Positive illusions: Creative self-deception and the healthy mind.* New York: Basic Books.

TAYLOR, S. E. (1991). Asymmetrical effects of positive and negative events: The mobilization-minimization hypothesis. *Psychological Bulletin, 110,* 67–85.

TAYLOR, S. E., & BROWN, J. D. (1988). Illusion and well-being: A social psychological perspective on mental health. *Psychological Bulletin, 103,* 193–210.

TAYLOR, S. E., & BROWN, J. D. (1994). Positive illusions and well-being revisited: Separating fact from fiction. *Psychological Bulletin, 116,* 21–27.

TAYLOR, S. E., & CLARK, L. F. (1986). Does information improve adjustment to noxious medical procedures? In M. J. Saks & L. Saxe (Eds.), *Advances in applied social psychology* (Vol. 3, pp. 1–28). Hillsdale, NJ: Lawrence Erlbaum Associates.

TAYLOR, S. E., & GOLLWITZER, P. M. (195). Effects of mindset on positive illusions. *Journal of Personality and Social Psychology, 69,* 213–226.

TAYLOR, S. E., KEMENY, M. E., ASPINWALL, L. G., SCHNEIDER, S. G., RODRIGUEZ, R., & HERBERT, M. (1992). Optimism, coping, psychological distress, and high-risk sexual behavior among men at risk for AIDS. *Journal of Personality and Social Psychology, 63,* 460–473.

TAYLOR, S. E., KEMENY, M. E., REED, G. M., & ASPINWALL, L. G. (1991). Assault on the self: Positive illusions and adjustment to threatening events. In G. A. Goethals & J. A. Strauss (Eds.), *The self: An interdisciplinary perspective* (pp. 239–254). New York: Springer-Verlag.

TAYLOR, S. E., LICHTMAN, R. R., & WOOD, J. V. (1984). Attributions, beliefs about control, and adjustment to breast cancer. *Journal of Personality and Social Psychology, 46,* 489–502.

TAYLOR, S. E., & LOBEL, M. (1989). Social comparison activity under threat: Downward evaluation and upward contacts. *Psychological Review, 96,* 569–575.

TEASDALE, J. D. (1983). Negative thinking in depression: Cause, effect, or reciprocal relationship? *Advances in Behaviour Research and Therapy, 5,* 3–25.

TEASDALE, J. D. (1988). Cognitive vulnerability to persistent depression. *Cognition and Emotion, 2,* 247–274.

TEASDALE, J. D., & FOGARTY, S. J. (1979). Differential effects of induced mood on retrieval of pleasant and unpleasant events from episodic memory. *Journal of Abnormal Psychology, 88,* 248–257.

TEASDALE, J. D., TAYLOR, R., & FOGARTY, S. J. (1980). Effects of induced elation-depression on the accessibility of memories of happy and unhappy experiences. *Behaviour Research and Therapy, 18,* 339–346.

TEDESCHI, J. T. (1986). Private and public experiences and the self. In R. F. Baumeister (Ed.), *Public self and private life* (pp. 1–20). New York: Springer-Verlag.

TEDESCHI, J. T., & NORMAN, N. (1985). Social power, self-presentation, and the self. In
    B. R. Schlenker (Ed.), *The self and social life* (pp. 293–322). New York: McGraw-Hill.

TEDESCHI, J. T., SCHLENKER, B. R., & BONOMA, T. V. (1971). Cognitive dissonance: Private
    ratiocination or public spectacle? *American Psychologist, 26,* 685–695.

TENNEN, H., & AFFLECK, G. (1987). The costs and benefits of optimistic explanations and
    dispositional optimism. *Journal of Personality, 55,* 378–393.

TESSER, A. (1988). Toward a self-evaluation maintenance model of social behavior. In L.
    Berkowitz (Ed.), *Advances in experimental social psychology* (Vol. 21, pp. 181–227).
    New York: Academic Press.

TESSER, A. (1991). Emotion in social comparison and reflection processes. In J. Suls &
    T. A. Wills (Eds.), *Social comparison: Contemporary theory and research* (pp. 115–145).
    Hillsdale, NJ: Lawrence Erlbaum Associates.

TESSER, A., CAMPBELL, J., & SMITH, M. (1984). Friendship choice and performance: Self-
    evaluation maintenance in children. *Journal of Personality and Social Psychology, 46,*
    561–574.

TESSER, A., & CORNELL, D. P. (1991). On the confluence of self processes. *Journal of
    Experimental Social Psychology, 27,* 501–526.

TESSER, A., & MOORE, J. (1986). On the convergence of public and private aspects of self.
    In R. F. Baumeister (Ed.), *Public self and private life* (pp. 99–116). New York:
    Springer-Verlag.

TESSER, A., & ROSEN, S. (1975). The reluctance to transmit bad news. In L. Berkowitz
    (Ed.), *Advances in experimental social psychology* (Vol. 8, pp. 193–232). New York:
    Academic Press.

TETLOCK, P. E., & LEVI, A. (1982). Attribution bias: On the inconclusiveness of the
    cognition-motivation debate. *Journal of Experimental Social Psychology, 18,* 68–88.

TETLOCK, P. E., & MANSTEAD, A. S. R. (1985). Impression management versus
    intrapsychic explanations in social psychology. *Psychological Review, 92,* 59–77.

THOITS, P. (1983). Multiple identities and psychological well-being. *American Sociological
    Review, 48,* 174–187.

THOMPSON, S. C. (1981). Will it hurt less if I can control it? A complex answer to a simple
    question. *Psychological Bulletin, 90,* 89–101.

THOMPSON, S. C., SOBOLEW-SHUBIN, A., GALBRAITH, M. E., SCHWANKOVSKY, L., & CRUZEN, D.
    (1993). Maintaining perceptions of control: Finding perceived control in low-
    control circumstances. *Journal of Personality and Social Psychology, 64,* 293–304.

THOMPSON, S. C., & SPACAPAN, S. (1991). Perceptions of control in vulnerable
    populations. *Journal of Social Issues, 47,* 1–21.

THORNDIKE, E. L. (1911). *Animal intelligence.* New York: Macmillan.

TICE, D. M. (1991). Esteem protection or enhancement? Self-handicapping motives and
    attributions differ by trait self-esteem. *Journal of Personality and Social Psychology,
    60,* 711–725.

TICE, D. M. (1992). Self-concept change and self-presentation: The looking glass self is
    also a magnifying glass. *Journal of Personality and Social Psychology, 63,* 435–451.

TICE, D. M. (1993). The social motivations of people with low self-esteem. In R. F.
    Baumeister (Ed.), *Self-esteem: The puzzle of low self-regard* (pp. 37–53). New York:
    Plenum Press.

TICE, D. M., BUTLER, J. L., MURAVEN, M. B., & STILLWELL, A. M. (1995). When modesty
    prevails: Differential favorability of self-presentation to friends and strangers.
    Journal of Personality and Social Psychology, 69, 1120–1138.

TIGER, L. (1979). *Optimism: The biology of hope.* New York: Simon & Schuster.

TOLMAN, E. C. (1948). Cognitive maps in rats and men. *Psychological Review, 55,* 189–208.

TOMAKA, J., BLASCOVICH, J., & KELSEY, R. M. (1992). Effects of self-deception, social desirability, and repressive coping on psychophysiological reactivity to stress. *Personality and Social Psychology Bulletin, 18,* 616–624.

TOMARELLI, M. M., & SHAFFER, D. R. (1985). What aspects of self do self-monitors monitor? *Bulletin of the Psychonomic Society, 23,* 135–138.

TRAFIMOW, D., TRIANDIS, H. C., & GOTO, S. G. (1991). Some tests of the distinction between the private and the collective self. *Journal of Personality and Social Psychology, 60,* 649–655.

TRIANDIS, H. C. (1989). The self and social behavior in differing cultural contexts. *Psychological Review, 96,* 506–520.

TRILLING, L. (1971). *Sincerity and authenticity.* Cambridge, MA: Harvard University Press.

TROPE, Y. (1975). Seeking information about one's ability as a determinant of choice among tasks. *Journal of Personality and Social Psychology, 32,* 1004–1013.

TROPE, Y. (1979). Uncertainty-reducing properties of achievement tasks. *Journal of Personality and Social Psychology, 37,* 1505–1518.

TROPE, Y. (1986). Self-enhancement, self-assessment, and achievement behavior. In R. M. Sorrentino & E. T. Higgins (Eds.), *Handbook of motivation and cognition* (pp. 350–378). New York: Guilford Press.

TURNER, J. C., HOGG, M. A., OAKES, P. J., REICHER, S. D., & WETHERELL, M. S. (1987). *Rediscovering the social group: A self-categorization theory.* Oxford, England: Basil Blackwell.

TVERSKY, A., & KAHNEMAN, D. (1981). The framing of decisions and the psychology of choice. *Science, 211,* 453–458.

UNRUH, D. R. (1983). Death and personal history: Strategies of identity preservation. *Social Problems, 30,* 340–351.

VALLACHER, R. R., & WEGNER, D. M. (1987). What do people think they're doing? Action identification and human behavior. *Psychological Review, 94,* 3–15.

VALLONE, R. P., GRIFFIN, D. W., LIN, S., & ROSS, L. (1990). Overconfident prediction of future actions and outcomes by self and others. *Journal of Personality and Social Psychology, 58,* 582–592.

VAN DER VELDE, F. W., VAN DER PLIGT, J., & HOOYKAAS, C. (1994). Perceiving AIDS-related risk: Accuracy as a function of differences in actual risk. *Health Psychology, 13,* 25–33.

VAN LANGE, P. A. M., & RUSBULT, C. E. (1995). My relationship is better than—and not as bad as—yours is: The perception of superiority in close relationships. *Personality and Social Psychology Bulletin, 21,* 32–44.

VREDENBURG, K., FLETT, G. L., & KRAMES, L. (1993). Analogue versus clinical depression: A clinical reappraisal. *Psychological Bulletin, 113,* 327–344.

WASCHULL, S. B., & KERNIS, M. H. (1996). Level and stability of self-esteem as predictors of children's intrinsic motivation and reasons for anger. *Personality and Social Psychology Bulletin, 22,* 4–13.

WATERMAN, A. S. (1982). Identity development from adolescence to adulthood: An extension of theory and a review of research. *Developmental Psychology, 18,* 341–358.

WATSON, D. (1989). Strangers' ratings of the five robust personality factors: Evidence of a surprising convergence with self-report. *Journal of Personality and Social Psychology, 57,* 120–128.

WATSON, D., & CLARK, L. A. (1984). Negative affectivity: The disposition to experience aversive emotional states. *Psychological Bulletin, 96,* 465–490.

WATSON, J. B. (1913). Psychology as the behaviorist views it. *Psychological Review, 20,* 158–177.

WATZLAWICK, P. (1976). *How real is real?* New York: Random House.

WEARY BRADLEY, G. (1978). Self-serving biases in the attribution process: A reexamination of the fact or fiction question. *Journal of Personality and Social Psychology, 36*, 56–71.

WEARY, G., HARVEY, J. H., SCHWIEGER, P., OLSON, C. T., PERLOFF, R., & PRITCHARD, S. (1982). Self-presentation and the moderation of self-serving attributional biases. *Social Cognition, 2*, 140–159.

WEBER, J. G. (1994). The nature of ethnocentric attribution bias: Ingroup protection or enhancement? *Journal of Experimental Social Psychology, 30*, 482–504.

WEINBERGER, D. A. (1990). The construct validity of the repressive coping style. In J. L. Singer (Ed.), *Repression and dissociation* (pp. 337–386). Chicago: University of Chicago Press.

WEINBERGER, D. A., SCHWARTZ, G. E., & DAVIDSON, R. J. (1979). Low-anxious, high-anxious, and repressive coping styles: Psychometric patterns and behavioral and physiological responses to stress. *Journal of Abnormal Psychology, 88*, 369–380.

WEINER, B. (1980). *Human motivation.* New York: Holt, Rinehart, & Winston.

WEINER, B. (1985). An attributional theory of achievement motivation and emotion. *Psychological Review, 92*, 548–573.

WEINER, B. (1993). On sin versus sickness: A theory of perceived responsibility and social motivation. *American Psychologist, 48*, 957–965.

WEINER, B., AMIRKHAN, J., FOLKES, V. S., & VERETTE, J. A. (1987). An attributional analysis of excuse giving: Studies of a naïve theory of emotion. *Journal of Personality and Social Psychology, 52*, 316–324.

WEINER, B., & LITMAN-ADIZES, T. (1980). An attributional, expectancy-value analysis of learned helplessness and depression. In J. Garber & M. E. P. Seligman (Eds.), *Human helplessness: Theory and applications* (pp. 35–58). New York: Academic Press.

WEINSTEIN, N. D. (1980). Unrealistic optimism about future life events. *Journal of Personality and Social Psychology, 39*, 806–820.

WEINSTEIN, N. D. (1982). Unrealistic optimism about susceptibility to health problems. *Journal of Behavioral Medicine, 5*, 441–460.

WEINSTEIN, N. D. (1984). Why it won't happen to me: Perceptions of risk factors and susceptibility. *Health Psychology, 3*, 431–457.

WEINSTEIN, N. D., & KLEIN, W. M. (1995). Resistance of personal risk perceptions to debiasing interventions. *Health Psychology, 14*, 132–140.

WEISZ, J. R., ROTHBAUM, F. M., & BLACKBURN, T. C. (1984). Standing out and standing in: The psychology of control in American and Japan. *American Psychologist, 39*, 955–969.

WELLS, G. E., & MARWELL, G. (1976). *Self-esteem: Its conceptualization and measurement.* Beverly Hills, CA: Sage.

WENZLAFF, R. M., & GROZIER, S. A. (1988). Depression and the magnification of failure. *Journal of Abnormal Psychology, 97*, 90–93.

WENZLAFF, R. M., WEGNER, D. M., & ROPER, D. W. (1988). Depression and mental control: The resurgence of unwanted negative thoughts. *Journal of Personality and Social Psychology, 55*, 882–892.

WERTHEIMER, M. (1912). Über das Denken des Naturvolker. *Zeitschrift Psychologie, 60*, 321–378.

WESTEN, D. (1990a). Psychoanalytic approaches to personality. In L. A. Pervin (Ed.), *Handbook of personality: Theory and research* (pp. 21–276). New York: Guilford Press.

WESTEN, D. (1990b). The relations among narcissism, egocentrism, self-concept, and self-esteem: Experimental, clinical, and theoretical considerations. *Psychoanalysis and Contemporary Thought, 13*, 183–239.

WHEELER, L., & MIYAKE, K. (1992). Social comparison in everyday life. *Journal of Personality and Social Psychology, 62,* 760–773.

WHITE, J. (1982). *Rejection.* Reading, MA: Addison-Wesley.

WHITE, R. W. (1959). Motivation reconsidered: The concept of competence. *Psychological Review, 66,* 297–335.

WHITLEY, B. E., & HERN, A. L. (1991). Perceptions of vulnerability to pregnancy and the use of effective contraception. *Personality and Social Psychology Bulletin, 17,* 104–110.

WICKER, A. W. (1969). Attitudes vs. actions: The relationship of verbal and overt behavioral responses to attitude objects. *Journal of Social Issues, 41,* 41–78.

WICKLUND, R. A., & GOLLWITZER, P. M. (1982). *Symbolic self-completion.* Hillsdale, NJ: Erlbaum.

WICKLUND, R. A., & GOLLWITZER, P. M. (1987). The fallacy of the private-public self-focus distinction. *Journal of Personality, 55,* 491–523.

WIENER, N. (1948). *Cybernetics: Control and communication in the animal and the machine.* Cambridge, MA: MIT Press.

WILLS, T. A. (1981). Downward comparison principles in social psychology. *Psychological Bulletin, 90,* 245–271.

WILSON, T. D., & HODGES, S. D. (1992). Attitudes as temporary constructions. In L. L. Martin & A. Tesser (Eds.), *The construction of social judgments* (pp. 37–65). Hillsdale, NJ: Lawrence Erlbaum Associates.

WILSON, T. D., & LAFLEUR, S. J. (1995). Knowing what you'll do: Effects of analyzing reasons on self-prediction. *Journal of Personality and Social Psychology, 68,* 21–35.

WILSON, T. D., LISLE, D., SCHOOLER, J., HODGES, S. D., KLAAREN, K. J., & LAFLEUR, S. J. (1993). Introspecting about reasons can reduce post-choice satisfaction. *Personality and Social Psychology Bulletin, 19,* 331–339.

WOOD, J. V. (1989). Theory and research concerning social comparisons of personal attributes. *Psychological Bulletin, 106,* 231–248.

WOOD, J. V., GIORDANO-BEECH, M., TAYLOR, K. L., MICHELA, J. L., & GAUS, V. (1994). Strategies of social comparison among people with low self-esteem: Self-protection and self-enhancement. *Journal of Personality and Social Psychology, 67,* 713–731.

WOOD, J. V., SALTZBERG, J. A., & GOLDSAMT, L. A. (1990). Does affect induce self-focused attention? *Journal of Personality and Social Psychology, 58,* 899–908.

WOOD, J. V., TAYLOR, S. E., & LICHTMAN, R. R. (1985). Social comparison and adjustment to breast cancer. *Journal of Personality and Social Psychology, 49,* 1169–1183.

WOODWORTH, R. S. (1948). *Contemporary schools of psychology* (2nd ed.). New York: Ronald Press.

WOOLFOLK, R. L., NOVALANY, J., GARA, M. A., ALLEN, L. A., & POLINO, M. (1995). Self-complexity, self-evaluation, and depression: An examination of forma and content within the self-schema. *Journal of Personality and Social Psychology, 68,* 1108–1120.

WORTMAN, C. B., & BREHM, J. C. (1975). Responses to uncontrollable outcomes: An integration of reactance theory and the learned helplessness model. In L. Berkowitz (Ed.), *Advances in experimental social psychology* (Vol. 8, pp. 278–336). San Diego, CA: Academic Press.

WYLIE, R. C. (1979). *The self-concept* (Vol. 2). Lincoln: University of Nebraska Press.

ZAUTRA, A. J., GUENTHER, R. T., & CHARTIER, G. M. (1985). Attributions for real and hypothetical events: Their relation to self-esteem and depression. *Journal of Abnormal Psychology, 94,* 530–540.

ZIRKEL, S., & CANTOR, N. (1990). Personal construal of life tasks: Those who struggle for independence. *Journal of Personality and Social Psychology, 58,* 172–185.

ZUCKERMAN, M. (1979). Attribution of success and failure revisited, or: The motivational bias is alive and well in attribution theory. *Journal of Personality, 47,* 245–287.

Author Index

Pittman, T. S., 170
Plant, R., 253
Pliner, P., 207, 224
Polino, M., 110
Polivy, J., 193
Poston, D. L., Jr., 69, 270
Povinelli, D. J., 92
Powers, W. T., 133
Pratkanis, A. R., 108, 125, 131
Predmore, S. C., 79, 221
Prentice, D., 38, 112
Preston, L. A., 31
Pritchard, S., 185
Provenzano, F. J., 50
Pyszczynski, T., 76, 120, 128–129, 145, 185, 187, 191, 254, 268, 281

Quadrel, M. J., 101
Quattrone, G. A., 72
Quinlan, D. M., 236

Radford-Davenport, J., 164
Radloff, C. E., 64
Rado, S., 235
Rank, O., 262, 281
Rapkin, B. D., 101
Raskin, R., 283
Read, S. J., 199
Reber, E., 122
Recchia, S., 198
Reed, G. M., 64, 269
Regan, P. C., 267
Reicher, S. D., 116
Reid, A., 24
Reid, D. B., 196, 272
Reiss, M., 128
Reynolds, L. T., 83
Rhodes, N., 190
Rhodewalt, F., 178, 180, 182, 216
Rholes, W. S., 246
Richards, J. M., 75, 118–119
Richardson, K. D., 178
Richters, J. E., 79
Riess, M., 186
Ringer, R. J., 162
Riskind, J. H., 246
Rizley, R., 250
Roberts, B. W., 24, 110, 115
Roberts, J. E., 234, 238
Robertson, L. S., 267
Robins, C. J., 237
Robins, R. W., 65, 67–69, 110, 283

Robson, P. J., 191
Rodin, J., 277–278
Rodriguez, R., 280
Rogers, C. R., 12, 197, 202, 203, 227, 262
Rogers, Kenny, 284
Rogers, R. J., 77, 128
Rogers, T. B., 14, 106, 111, 123–124, 242
Roper, D. W., 256–257
Roseman, I. J., 36
Rosen, S., 74
Rosenberg, F., 222
Rosenberg, M., 3, 21, 26, 36, 51–52, 100, 111, 194, 196, 202–203, 206–207, 210, 222, 229
Rosenberg, S., 108
Rosenberg, S. E., 217
Rosenfeld, P., 128, 186
Ross, L., 58, 68, 77, 128
Ross, M., 76, 77, 123, 125–126, 128, 209
Roth, D. L., 253, 272
Rothbaum, F., 269, 282
Rotter, J. B., 133
Rubin, J. Z., 50
Ruble, D. N., 50, 96, 98
Rudick-Davis, D., 242
Rudin, S., 38
Ruehlman, L. S., 241, 273
Ruggiero, K. M., 207
Rulf, A. B., 92
Rusbult, C. E., 64
Rush, A. J., 238, 241, 245, 260
Ruvolo, A., 15, 36, 136
Ryan, R. M., 100, 151, 153, 197, 286
Ryff, C. D., 275

Sachs, P. R., 71
Sackeim, H. A., 196, 271, 274
Salancik, G. R., 121
Salovey, P., 145
Saltzberg, J. A., 253
Sampson, E., 16
Samuelson, C. D., 64
Sanbonmatsu, D. M., 178, 214
Sande, G. N., 64
Sandelands, L. E., 217, 284
Sanitioso, R., 70, 76, 114–115, 122
Sarbin, T. R., 106, 179
Sartre, J. P., 23, 271
Sashidharan, S. P., 234
Schachter, S., 60
Schaufeli, W. B., 275
Scheibe, K. E., 21
Scheier, M. F., 135, 137, 142–147, 159, 164, 253, 279, 280

Subject Index